SUFISM IN EUROPE

Advances in the Study of Islam

Series Editors: Abbas Aghdassi and Aaron W. Hughes

Advances in the Study of Islam publishes cutting-edge research that reflects the long history and geographic breadth of Islam. It seeks to rethink traditional literary canons while simultaneously offering innovative and alternative approaches to push beyond traditional understandings of Islam. The series provides a platform for creative studies spanning:

- Disciplines including religious studies, legal studies, archaeology and anthropology
- Theoretical questions including historical, philological, ethnographic, comparative and redescriptive
- Time periods from late antiquity to the present
- Geographical regions including the so-called Arab World, South Asia, Africa, Iran and the Persian World, Europe and North America

The series highlights both disciplinary and inter-disciplinary approaches to Islamic studies and challenges existing paradigms and norms by providing alternatives for the study of Islam. By doing this it pushes the study of Islam to the forefront of larger conversations in the Humanities and Social Sciences

Available Titles

New Methods in the Study of Islam
Abbas Aghdassi and Adam Hughes

Traces of the Prophets: Relics and Sacred Spaces in Early Islam
Adam Bursi

Sufism in Europe: Islam, Esotericism and the New Age
Francesco Piraino

edinburghuniversitypress.com/series/asi

SUFISM IN EUROPE

Islam, Esotericism and the New Age

Francesco Piraino

EDINBURGH
University Press

Edinburgh University Press is one of the leading university presses in the UK. We publish academic books and journals in our selected subject areas across the humanities and social sciences, combining cutting-edge scholarship with high editorial and production values to produce academic works of lasting importance. For more information visit our website: edinburghuniversitypress.com

© Francesco Piraino, 2024, 2025
English translation © Anna Fitzgerald, 2024, 2025

Originally published in French in 2023 by Karthala under the title
Le soufisme en Europe: Islam, ésotérisme et New Age

Edinburgh University Press Ltd
13 Infirmary Street
Edinburgh EH1 1LT

First published in hardback by Edinburgh University Press 2024

Typeset in 11/15 EB Garamond by
IDSUK (DataConnection) Ltd

A CIP record for this book is available from the British Library

ISBN 978 1 3995 3609 7 (hardback)
ISBN 978 1 3995 3610 3 (paperback)
ISBN 978 1 3995 3611 0 (webready PDF)
ISBN 978 1 3995 3612 7 (epub)

The right of Francesco Piraino to be identified as author of this work has been asserted in accordance with the Copyright, Designs and Patents Act 1988 and the Copyright and Related Rights Regulations 2003 (SI No. 2498).

CONTENTS

Acknowledgements vi
Glossary viii
Foreword by Mark Sedgwick xi

Introduction 1
1 Sufism as Mysticism – *Scientia Experimentalis* and as Discursive Tradition – *Sacra Doctrina* 15
2 Sufi Pioneers in Europe 49
3 Qādiriyya Būdshīshiyya 94
4 ʿAlāwiyya Darqāwiyya Shādhiliyya 153
5 Naqshbandiyya Ḥaqqāniyya 216
6 Aḥmadiyya Idrīsiyya Shādhiliyya 282
Conclusions 323

Bibliography 342
Index 368

ACKNOWLEDGEMENTS

Scholars who began their doctorate in the 2010s found themselves in an academic world undergoing a major transformation. We faced a systematic lack of research funds, increasingly stifling competition, and often the need to change countries to work. Most of us live in precarious conditions, while others have had to give up this career, even though they had the skill and energy to pursue it. This book is dedicated to all colleagues who are dedicated to their research work despite difficult situations.

The time of young postdocs is devoured by continuous writing around research projects or by poorly paid teaching positions. This is required to make up for a weak university system. In this context, the first book for a young researcher often becomes an insurmountable burden: an obligation impossible to carry out due to lack of time. This burden was even heavier for me, as I have always enjoyed the writing phase, in my opinion one of the most satisfying aspects of research.

The academic frenzy came to an abrupt halt in March 2020 due to COVID-19. The pandemic has disrupted academic activities, the pace of work and, in general, our lives. However, confinement finally allowed me to focus full-time on this book. I was lucky enough that my parents and friends were healthy, which allowed me the necessary concentration for writing. This book is dedicated to all those who suffered during COVID-19 and to those who worked to heal and care for us.

The ability to transform the systematic and exceptional difficulties that life imposes on us is part of the lessons I learned from my family: I would like to thank my parents Patrizia and Mario and my sister Enrica.

I would also like to thank other researchers, some of whom have become friends, allowing me to grow as a researcher and as a human being. In the geographical order of my university pilgrimage: the 'Padouans' Salvatore La Mendola, Khalid Rhazzali, Giuseppe Giordan, Giorgio Bonaccorso, Vincenzo Pace, Carlo Saccone, Adone Brandalise and Chantal Saint-Blancat; the 'Milanese' Laura Zambelli, Bianca Maria Mennini, Lorenzo Giudici and Diego Coletto; the 'Lundensians' Leif Stenberg, Simon Stjernholm, Stefano Bigliardi, Eric Onglund, Dan-Erik Andersson and Spyros Sofos; the 'Parisians' Waddick Doyle, Jean-Pierre Brach, Danièle Hervieu-Léger, Éric Geoffroy, Naim Jeanbart, Nadège Chabloz and Hajar Masbah; the 'South Africans' Tayob Abudlkader, Andrea Brigaglia and Louis Blond; the 'Venetians' Pasquale Gagliardi and Emilio Quinté; the 'Louvanists' Francesco Cerchiaro, Michele Petrone, Grégory Vandamme, Nadia Fadil, Arjan Post and Dick Houtman; the 'Amsterdammers' Marco Pasi and Liana Saif; and the 'Aixois' Katia Boissevain, Loïc Le Pape, Sophie Bava, Dionigi Albera, Manoël Pénicaud and Guillaume Silhol. I would like to thank Anna Fitzgerald who translated this book from French to English with professionalism and care and Maïmouna Guerresi for the cover image of this book.

I also thank the researchers I met during conferences: Feyza Burak Adli, Fabio Vicini, Armando Salvatore, Samuli Schielke, Aymon Kreil, Shobhana Xavier, Rory Dickson, Besnik Sinani, Laurens De Rooij and Usaama al-Azami. I am especially grateful to Mark Sedgwick for his unwavering support throughout my research. Finally, many thanks to the Sufi disciples and masters who welcomed me into their mosques and homes with kindness.

GLOSSARY

aḥwāl – ecstatic states, singular *ḥāl*

'alīm – theologian, plural *'ulamā'*

baqā' – return to daily life after annihilation in God

baraka – blessing, grace

bāṭin – the hidden dimension

bay'a – initiatory pact or attachment between master and disciple

bid'a – innovation

dhikr – remembrance prayer which implies the rhythmic repetition of God's names

du'ā – invocation, prayer

fanā' – passing away of the ego, annihilation in God

faqīr – male disciple, plural *fuqarā'*

faqīra – female disciple, plural *faqīrāt*

fiqh – Islamic law

fiṭra –state of the natural soul in contact with God, before birth

Futuwwa – Islamic chivalry

ḥaḍra – ecstatic dance, danced *dhikr*

Ḥajj – pilgrimage to Mecca

ḥāl – ecstatic state, plural *aḥwāl*

ḥalāl – lawful

ḥaqīqa – divine reality, truth

ḥarām – forbidden, illicit

idhn – generic authorisation

ijāza – permission to teach

ijtihād – effort to understand and interpret the sharia

ʿimāra – divine presence

jinn – spirits, supernatural creatures

kāfir – infidel, plural *kuffār*

karāmāt – miracles

khalīfa – vicar, responsible, leader, plural *khalīfat*

khalwa – spiritual retreat

khuṭba – imam's speech during Friday prayers

laṭāʾif – subtle centres of the body, both physical and metaphysical places

madhab – legal school, plural *madhāhib*

maʿrifa – inner knowledge, gnostic

mawlānā – 'my master'

Mawlid – celebration of the birth of Prophet Muhammad

mudhakara – speech, teaching of the Sufi master

mujaddid – one who revives religion

muqaddam – literally, the one who introduces, meaning the local leader representing the sheikh

murīd – Sufi disciple

musammiʿūn – singer of Sufi music

quṭb – axis, pole of existence, living saint

ṣalāt – prayer

samāʿ – Sufi music

shahāda – profession of faith

sheikh – Sufi master, plural sheikhs

sīdī – sir

silsila – initiatory chain

tasbīh – Islamic rosary

ṭarīqa – Sufi brotherhood, plural *ṭuruq*

tawḥīd – principle of unity

'Umra – off-season pilgrimage to Mecca

waẓīfa – set of *dhikr*, Qur'an recitations and prayers

ẓāhir – exoteric, manifest dimension

zāwiya – 'the corner', place where Sufi disciples gather, plural *zawāyā*

ziyāra – pious visit

FOREWORD BY MARK SEDGWICK

There is much discussion of the future of Islam in Europe. Some scholars expect a process of secularisation, during which Muslims will become as secular as most Europeans are. Others think this unlikely, given that Europeans in general do not actually seem to have become as secular as was once thought. Religion has not vanished from Europe, but has instead been replaced by so-called 'spirituality', an individualised form of religiosity. Perhaps Islam in Europe will become individualised, especially given that individualisation is a characteristic of modernity.[1] The question of the future of Islam in Europe thus becomes mixed with another major question, that of the future of religion in Europe: will Europe become ever more rationalist and materialist, or will God have his revenge when believers reconquer the world, as Gilles Kepel suggested in 1991?[2]

Beyond the universities, a very different type of speculation is found. Muslims will not assimilate, but rather remain different, it is thought, and the

[1] There is a large body of literature. See, for example, Olivier Roy, *Secularism Confronts Islam* (New York: Columbia University Press, 2009); Frank Peter, 'Individualization and Religious Authority in Western European Islam', *Islam and Christian–Muslim Relations* 17, no. 1 (2006): 105–18; David Voas and Fenella Fleischmann, 'Islam Moves West: Religious Change in the First and Second Generations', *Annual Review of Sociology* 38 (2012): 525–45.

[2] Gilles Kepel, *La Revanche de Dieu. Chrétiens, juifs et musulmans à la reconquête du monde* (Paris: Seuil, 1991).

proportion of Muslims in the European population will continue to grow until they become the majority and take over. The demographic issues behind these expectations are difficult, as calculations depend not just on factors that can be predicted, like future changes in relative fertility rates, but also on factors that cannot be predicted, such as the nature and effectiveness of future migration controls. In any case, none of these calculations make any sense without the assumption that there will continue to be a binary difference between Muslim and non-Muslim Europeans. Such binaries depend on clear markers of ethnic difference, and religion and language are classic markers. Language changes relatively easily, it is thought, and people are often bilingual, so it is not language that will matter. Conversion from one religion to another is unusual, however, and it is not really possible to be bi-religious in the way that it is possible to be bilingual. If Muslim and non-Muslim Europeans remain a binary pair, some think it will be because of religion.

For those interested in such questions, the development of Sufism in Europe is of special importance. It is where Islam and Europe meet most intimately. First-generation immigrants and their European-born children, both brought up Muslim since birth, meet not just European converts to Islam but also European Sufis who do not consider themselves Muslim. European thought meets the sharia, spirituality meets religion, and religion meets secularism. The study of Sufism in Europe can tell us more about the future of religion in general and of Islam in particular than almost any other comparable study. Sufism in Europe is also not only in Europe, of course, but is also part of the transnational and transregional sphere which is so characteristic of the current phase of modernity, and where European Muslims are often more at home than are their less globalised non-Muslim fellow citizens.

When I first started looking at Sufism in Europe in 1996, there was little real scholarship to help. Laurence P. Elwell-Sutton, Professor of Persian at the University of Edinburgh, had published an article on the prolific English Sufi Idries Shah in 1972, entitled 'Sufism and Pseudo-Sufism', condemning Shah as a 'pseudo-Sufi',[3] but this was less an objective study than the continuation of a feud between Elwell-Sutton and Shah that had begun in 1968 with a high-profile dispute over an alleged manuscript of the work of the medieval Persian

[3] Laurence P. Elwell-Sutton, 'Sufism & Pseudo-Sufism', *Encounter* 44, no. 5 (1975): 9–17.

poet 'Umar Khayyām.[4] The sociologist Frank Musgrove published what is probably the first ever objective study of Sufis in Europe, 'Dervishes in Dorsetshire', in 1975,[5] and Daphne Habibis then completed a PhD thesis on Sheikh Nazim's Naqshbandiyya in London and Beirut in 1985.[6] In 1994, Gisela Webb published the first study of Sufism in America, a paper on the Bawa Muhaiyadeen Fellowship of Philadelphia.[7] These three studies of individual Sufi groups were objective and scholarly, but, as studies of individual groups, revealed little about the wider phenomenon of Sufism in Europe and America.

The systematic study of the wider phenomenon began the following year with Webb's entry on 'Sufism in America' in a volume on *America's Alternative Religions*,[8] and continued in 1997 with Marcia Hermansen's article on 'American Sufi Movements: Hybrids and Perennials'[9] and, in the same year, with the sections on Sufis and Sufism in Andrew Rawlinson's encyclopedic *Book of Enlightened Masters: Western Teachers in Eastern Traditions*.[10] Since 1997, the field has grown enormously and encouragingly, but much work has followed the model of Musgrove and Habibis in focusing on individual

4 Mark Sedgwick, *Western Sufism: From the Abbasids to the New Age* (New York: Oxford University Press, 2016), 219–21.

5 Frank Musgrove, 'Dervishes in Dorsetshire: An English Commune', *Youth and Society* 6 (1975): 449–80. There was also Thomas Robbins and Dick Anthony, 'Getting Straight with Meher Baba: A Study of Mysticism, Drug Rehabilitation and Postadolescent Role Conflict', *Journal for the Scientific Study of Religion* 11 (1972): 122–40, but this was not really about Sufism.

6 Daphne Habibis, 'A Comparative Study of the Workings of a Branch of the Naqshbandi Sufi Order in Lebanon and the UK', PhD thesis: London School of Economics and Political Science, 1985.

7 Gisela Webb, 'Tradition and Innovation in Contemporary American Islamic Spirituality: The Bawa Muhaiyaddeen Fellowship', in *Muslim Communities in North America*, edited by Yvonne Haddad and Jane Smith (Albany: State University of New York Press, 1994), 95–108.

8 Gisela Webb, 'Sufism in America', in *America's Alternative Religions*, edited by Timothy Miller (Albany: State University of New York Press, 1995), 249–59.

9 Marcia K. Hermansen, 'In the Garden of American Sufi Movements: Hybrids and Perennials', in *New Trends and Developments in the World of Islam*, edited by Peter Clarke (London: Luzac Oriental Press, 1997), 155–78.

10 Andrew Rawlinson, *The Book of Enlightened Masters: Western Teachers in Eastern Traditions* (Chicago: Open Court, 1997).

groups, and many studies have also continued to ask the question asked about Bawa Muhaiyadeen by Webb in 1994: 'in what way does he perpetuate fundamental Islamic doctrines and practice?'[11] Hemansen asked a similar question in 1997, dividing American Sufi orders between those she termed 'hybrids', which 'identify more closely with an Islamic source and content', and 'perennials', in which 'the specifically Islamic identification and content of the movement have been de-emphasized in favor of a "perennialist" outlook.'[12] This resembled the question that Elwell-Sutton had asked in 1972: was this real, Islamic Sufism or was it 'pseudo-Sufism'?

Francesco Piraino's *Sufism in Europe* takes us far beyond these limitations. Rather than limiting itself to one group, it looks comparatively at four of the most important Sufi groups in Europe: the Būdshīshiyya, the 'Alāwiyya, the Naqshbandiyya Ḥaqqāniyya (first studied by Habibis) and the Aḥmadiyya Idrīsiyya Shādhiliyya (classified by Hermansen as perennial, and first studied by myself).[13] Rather than asking whether or not these groups represent pseudo-Sufism and what their relationship to Islam is, Piraino's starting point is that they are all hybrid, in a somewhat different sense from that in which Hermansen used the word. He therefore examines the consequences of hybridisation, and the different responses of the four groups to much the same issues raised by Europe and modernity. He looks, as his subtitle promises, at the interplay of Islam, esotericism and the New Age, and in doing so tells us not only about Sufism in Europe, but about even bigger questions. He shows a reality that is anything but binary. As a gifted observer, he paints his pictures sensitively, and as a careful sociologist, his analyses have the rigour that is needed.

Piraino's *Sufism in Europe* takes us into the space in which those brought up Muslim since birth meet converts and non-Muslim Sufis, a space in which things are a lot more complicated and nuanced than the standard binary of Muslim and non-Muslim allows. This space is national (in Italy and France) and transregional (in Morocco and Algeria), taking us into places that have until

[11] Webb, 'Tradition and Innovation', 77.

[12] Hermansen, 'In the Garden of American Sufi Movements', 155.

[13] Mark Sedgwick, *Against the Modern World: Traditionalism and the Secret Intellectual History of the Twentieth Century* (New York: Oxford University Press, 2004), 131, 136–42.

now been relatively less visited, as much existing scholarship has continued to focus, as Musgrove and Hermansen did, on the United Kingdom and United States. And in this space Islam mixes with perennialism and the New Age, and Sufism mixes with esotericism and the legacy of Eranos. *Sufism in Europe* not only provides a new and fascinating approach to its subject, but also suggests answers to larger questions about the future of religion in general, and of Islam in particular, in Europe, not just of Sufism.

For Laura and Iris

INTRODUCTION

There are several intellectual challenges to studying and describing Sufism. First of all, Sufism is a protean phenomenon: mysticism, esotericism, spirituality, metaphysics, popular religion, occultism, philosophy, theology, asceticism – we need all these categories to discuss Sufism. Secondly, this phenomenon is not strictly distinct from Islam. A substantial and definitive definition would thus run the risk of being not only futile, but also deceptive.

The protean nature of Sufism is due to its paradoxicality, which consists in mystical knowledge based on a direct experience of God, ineffable and incommunicable, that has nonetheless been communicated, transmitted and constructed as a tradition, through religious movements with their doctrines, practices and organisational structures. Through its charismatic leaders and its adaptable organisational structures, Sufism has been able to disseminate itself throughout the Islamic world, but also beyond it. This dissemination has most often involved the conversion of new disciples to Islam–Sufism and, in rare cases, the creation of syncretic forms: non-Islamic Sufism.

The dual definition of Sufism I will use in this book corresponds to the tension between the Arabic terms *taṣawwuf* and *ṭarīqa*.[1] *Taṣawwuf* expresses

[1] The transliteration system for the romanisation of Arabic is ALA–LC, used in the *Encyclopaedia of Islam Online* (2007).

a dynamic dimension, the 'path of purification of the soul' or the 'knowledge of God'; in fact, according to Ibn 'Arabī , the science of *taṣawwuf* is *al-ʿilm al-ummi*, an 'illiterate' science[2] or a 'sur-literate' science.[3] Inversely, *ṭarīqa* – the way – indicates the religious organisation, the brotherhood, which for several centuries has been the tool of transmission and dissemination of Sufi tradition.[4] Furthermore, I will argue that this tension can be found in the relationship between mysticism or *scientia experimentalis*, on one hand, and tradition or *sacra doctrina*, on the other.

This dual dimension of Sufism, as both religious tradition and mystical knowledge–experience, has led to two different epistemological and methodological approaches.[5] Some researchers (generally philologists and historians) have focused on Sufi doctrines, relegating the practices and daily lives of Sufis to the background, or even considering the social dimensions as a form of decadence of noble ideas. Other researchers (generally sociologists and anthropologists) have reversed this perspective by considering the ideas to be secondary. Both these approaches have advantages and disadvantages. Researchers who focus on discourses and ideas run the risk of idealising or even romanticising Sufism by forgetting the social nature of the phenomenon, while those who reverse the perspective run the risk of accrediting a presentist vision that is unable to situate contemporary Sufism in its historical context and thus considers all phenomena to be the effect of contemporary social influences. In this book, I will seek to maintain a dual perspective by attempting to link these two approaches.

We can imagine the complex relationship between Islam and Sufism as two circles that overlap and change position over the course of history. At times, they perfectly coincide, while in other historical and/or geographical contexts, significant differences arise. We should not imagine these orthodoxies as separate and monolithic, because the primary criticisms of certain Sufi practices and doctrines have come from Sufis themselves.[6] While Sufi and

[2] Gril, 'Les débuts du soufisme', 27.

[3] Expression used by Éric Geoffroy during a seminar in Paris on 8 March 2020, at Forum 104.

[4] Veinstein and Popovic, *Les Voies d'Allah*.

[5] Knysh, *Sufism*.

[6] Take, for example, Aḥmad al-Fārūqī al-Sirhindī (1564–1624) and his critique of Ibn 'Arabī (1165–1240). Cf. Green, *Sufism*.

Islamic orthodoxies have changed over the centuries, influenced by several factors, the subjects leading to controversy have often been identical: the extraordinary role of Sufi masters who, like the saints, are called the 'friends of God'; ecstatic practices; allegorical–esoteric exegesis; practices linked to the graves of saints; the use of spiritual–medical rituals for healing; and a degree of porosity with exogenous languages and practices.

The conceptual separation between Islam and Sufism is a relatively recent invention, promoted first and foremost by Salafism and Wahhabism[7] in a quest for purity and a return to origins. This has led to a veritable war against Sufism, the effects of which can be seen in the recent terrorist attacks in Egypt, Pakistan and Tunisia. The Wahhabis found unexpected allies among some European intellectuals of the nineteenth and twentieth centuries who sought in Sufism the origins of Aryanism in opposition to Semitic Islam;[8] others wanted to demonstrate the Christian origins of Sufism;[9] while still others sought a universal religion.[10] All of them disparaged the Islamity of Sufism. Today, this is no longer debated in academic circles, but the exogenous influences past and present that have contributed to shaping Sufism are nonetheless recognised.

Among the most significant influences in contemporary Sufism is what we might call the 'universalisation of Sufism'.[11] In this book, we will see how theories on a universal religion have been proposed in various academic, esoteric and 'New Age' fields. These theories have profoundly influenced contemporary Sufism. Some of the 'apostles of universalism', such as Carl Gustav Jung, Henry Corbin, Louis Massignon, Gershom Scholem and Mircea Eliade, participated in the Eranos conferences, focused on myths, symbols and universal archetypes.[12] The esotericist René Guénon created, in spite of himself, the Traditionalist current,[13] centred on the concept of 'Primordial Tradition'

[7] This religious–political movement arose in Arabia in the eighteenth century.

[8] Renan, *Averroès et l'averroïsme*; Palmer, *Oriental Mysticism*.

[9] Palacios, *La escatología musulmana en la Divina Comedia*.

[10] Pfleiderer, *Religion and Historic Faiths*.

[11] Process discussed in a seminar organised at École des hautes études en sciences sociales (EHESS) in 2019–20 by Nadège Chabloz, then in 2020–21 by Nadège Chabloz and me.

[12] Wasserstrom, *Religion after Religion*; Hanegraaff, *Esotericism and the Academy*; Hakl, *Eranos*.

[13] Sedgwick, *Against the Modern World*.

and on a critique of modernity. Finally, the esoteric/New Age milieu of the Theosophical Society saw the development of the idea of a universal religion that could encompass all religious forms at once.[14]

Despite some degree of continuity between the various forms of universalism, these currents gave rise to independent movements that were often opposed to each other, having doctrinal, ethical and political differences. The dialectic between the universal and the particular is also part of the history of Sufism and Islam; entirely Islamic universalisms may thus exist, but with doctrinal, ethical and political specificities. It would be an error to assume that there is only one form of universalism, or that all universalisms are 'made in Europe'.

This process of universalisation, and a certain degree of porosity in Sufism, have created several stereotypes among the general public and in the academic world. For example, some consider Sufism to be the 'good Islam', as opposed to Islamism and Salafism. The other side of the coin is to view Sufism as a domesticated Islam, submissive to Western modernity. According to these stereotypes, Sufism is a kind of 'light' Islam, a natural, liberal ally of the West with no ties to sharia.

Nothing could be more false than this dichotomy. There are many examples of Islamist and Salafist Sufis in contemporary societies.[15] Furthermore, we will see in this book that, contrary to what one might think, the Muslims most committed to discourses on sharia are often the most progressive, whereas in Sufi brotherhoods heavily influenced by New Age culture, violently anti-modernist and anti-democratic narratives can be encountered. Finally, some Sufis take advantage of the penchant for the 'good Muslim' in public opinion and the fear of Salafism to advance their vision of Islam, skilfully occupying the Islamic religious field. That is not to say this zealous Sufism is necessarily liberal; on the contrary, I have found it to be surprisingly conservative.

As underscored by Michel de Certeau, mysticism haunts Western epistemology because it is a subterranean subject, at once forgotten by and central to the human sciences.[16] We could say the same thing, *mutatis mutandis*, about

[14] Godwin, 'Blavatsky and the First Generation of Theosophy'.

[15] Howell, 'Indonesia's Salafist Sufis'; Philippon, '"Bons Soufis" et "mauvais Islamistes"'.

[16] Certeau, *La fable mystique*.

Sufism in the history of Islam, as it is both an undeniable discourse and an uncomfortable presence. This tension pushes us to question and rework our heuristic categories, not to build a new totalising theory but rather to think about Islam in its 'coherent contradiction'.[17]

Dissemination of Sufism in Western Europe

There are multiple reasons explaining the dissemination of Sufism in contemporary Western Europe[18] and in the United States. One of them is linked to a strong artistic–aesthetic appeal; the poetry of Jalāl al-Din Rūmī (1207–73), Ḥāfeẓ (1315–90) and Farīd al-Dīn 'Aṭṭār (1145–1221) has been translated into various European languages with an impressive number of copies sold. A case in point is Rūmī, who has become one of the most well-known poets in the United States. His poetry collections have topped best-seller lists, and the pop star Madonna has even sung his verses.[19] Clearly, Sufi literature cannot be consigned to the Middle Ages. A good example in this regard is the Turkish writer Elif Shafak.[20] Her novels, translated into several languages, have familiarised a wide readership with Sufism.

This process of 'artification'[21] of Sufism also affects music, both in terms of the dissemination of 'traditional' music (such as the work of Kudsi Ergüner, the Rābiʿa Ensemble, Abida Parveen, Nusrat Fateh Ali Khan, and so on) and in terms of its modern reworkings influenced by Western music; take, for example, the work of Allah-Rakha Rahman, Youssou N'Dour, Abd Al Malik, Franco Battiato or Radiodervish. Sufi music has also been used in the soundtracks of mainstream films. For instance, the Indian Sufi music known as *qawwālī* was used in *Dead Man Walking* and *The Last Temptation of Christ*.[22] Sufism itself

[17] Ahmed, *What Is Islam?* 405.

[18] Sufism spread in the Balkans starting in the thirteenth century (cf. Popovic, 'Les turuq balkaniques'), and Sufi brotherhoods were present in Andalusia and Sicily in the Middle Ages (cf. Barone, 'Islām in Sicilia'; Arkoun, *Histoire de l'islam et des musulmans*; and Ebstein, *Mysticism and Philosophy in al-Andalus*).

[19] Irwin, 'Global Rumi'; Haviland, 'The Roar of Rumi – 800 Years On', *BBC News*, 30 September 2007. Available at <http://news.bbc.co.uk/2/hi/7016090.stm> (last accessed 27 October 2023).

[20] Shafak, *The Bastard of Istanbul*; Shafak, *Soufi, mon amour*; Shafak, *The Forty Rules of Love*.

[21] Shapiro, 'Artification as Process'.

[22] Hermansen, 'Hybrid Identity Formations in Muslim America'.

has 'starred' in several films; examples include the documentary of Arnaud Desjardins[23] or such fiction films as *Monsieur Ibrahim*, *Rumi Returning: The Triumph of Divine Passion* and *Mimosas*.

Beyond artification, Sufism has also become a tourist phenomenon. Tourists in Istanbul and Konya can watch *samāʿ*, the sacred music–dance of the 'whirling dervishes' of the Mevleviyya brotherhood. Moreover, *samāʿ* has been exported to the major cities of Europe where audiences can attend whirling dervish shows. These new forms of merchandisation, which Éric Geoffroy refers to as 'Sufi business',[24] are flagrant on websites such as Tripadvisor where rituals are evaluated as performances.

The propagation of Sufism in Europe is not limited to its cultural aspects or its new forms, but is mostly due to Muslims of Maghrebi, Pakistani, Turkish or sub-Saharan descent – that is, migrants who have gradually become European citizens. They started out by 'transplanting'[25] their Sufi brotherhoods and eventually gave rise to a hybrid Sufism in Europe. In turn, this Sufism has been influenced by the European social and cultural context and by converts, who have gradually begun to participate in the activities of the brotherhoods. The resultant hybrid, transnational organisations are seeing a rise in their membership as they pass down a millennial tradition and introduce another Islam to Muslims and a new religion to non-Muslims.

Sufism's importance in Europe can be seen not only in European art and culture, but also in its sciences and politics. Hence Sufism is shaping Islam in Europe, and in turn, European Islam is influencing global Islam. The dissemination of Sufism in Europe also leads to questions about the process of hybridisation, which works both ways. Sufism is a vehicle of Islamisation in new geographical areas, in turn absorbing certain local elements. We should thus set aside the question of 'authenticity', instead focusing on the various consequences of the hybridisation process, which always entails the transmission of tradition and its transformation.

[23] A. Desjardins, 1974, 'Documentaire soufis d'Afghanistan: maître et disciple' [video], *Dailymotion*. Available at <https://www.dailymotion.com/video/x5tmob> (last accessed 27 October 2023).

[24] Geoffroy, *Le soufisme voie intérieure de l'Islam*, 307.

[25] Hermansen, 'What's American about American Sufi Movements?'.

My perspective departs from the bias of presentism; this era is 'exceptional' like all others and, as a result, this Sufism is 'ordinary' like all others. The use of categories such as 'New Age', sect and esotericism does not have a pejorative connotation, nor does it indicate a lesser degree of conformity with the traditional–orthodox Sufi–Islamic ideal. On the contrary, I will show that the new forms, such as New Age Sufism, are coterminous with the older forms and are made possible by the significant assonances with historical Sufism.

Field Studies and Methods

The Sufi brotherhoods considered in this book are:

- Qādiriyya Būdshīshiyya, of sheikhs Hamza al-Qādirī al-Būdshīshī and Jamāl al-Qādirī al-Būdshīshī, based in Morocco and studied in France and Italy;
- ʿAlāwiyya Darqāwiyya Shādhiliyya, of Sheikh Khaled Bentounes, based in Algeria and studied in France;
- Naqshbandiyya Ḥaqqāniyya, of sheikhs Nāzim ʿAdil al-Qubrusī and Mehmet ʿAdil al-Ḥaqqāni, based in Cyprus and studied in France and Italy;
- and Aḥmadiyya Idrīsiyya Shādhiliyya, of sheikhs ʿAbd Wāḥid Pallavicini and Yaḥya Pallavicini, based and studied in France and Italy.

The long field study in Paris and Milan, between 2013 and 2014, was spread over a period ranging from six to eight months per brotherhood, according to the availability of the disciples and the number of organised activities. This fieldwork included weekly participation in prayer meetings, participation in religious holidays and spiritual retreats, participation in events that were not strictly religious such as conferences and meetings, and pilgrimages with French and Italian disciples to Morocco, Algeria, Cyprus and Turkey. Shortly before the end of each study, I chose between eight and twelve disciples with whom to conduct interviews and record life histories. Sampling, where possible, was designed to best represent the heterogeneity and took into account the following factors: age, gender, whether the person belonged to Islam (as a convert or someone raised as Muslim) and education level. This fieldwork undertaken during my PhD (Scuola Normale Superiore – EHESS, 2011–16) has been enhanced during my postdoctoral research in Belgium (KU Leuven

2017–19) and in Italy (Venice University 2020–22), where I continued studying Sufi orders between Europe and North Africa.

Rituals play a central role; they structure a belonging to Islam, and they create and recreate ties between the disciples, establishing limits. Above all, they are the active expression of theology.[26] Trying to understand how the rituals change and how they are adapted to the European context is fundamental. However, I did not merely examine the norm of religious rituals. In keeping with both the theories of Goffman[27] and contemporary anthropology,[28] an effort must be made to understand the rituals of daily life: the construction of the master's speech; the greetings between the disciples; and the interactions at play 'behind the scenes', in relation to the visible, external part of the process. The aim is to understand how one becomes a disciple and what the written and non-written rules are. Various details can have significant value in the ethnographic work. An eloquent example involves cigarettes. As a smoker at the time of my fieldwork, I was particularly interested in this detail. How is the act of smoking seen by the disciples? Do they smoke? Where do they smoke? We will see how a marginal detail such as this one can turn out to be illuminating.

Limits of the Research and Book Outline

The choice of these countries, France and Italy, serves to fills a void. Unlike Sufism in the United Kingdom, which has been widely studied,[29] French Sufism, although one of the most significant Sufism in Europe,[30] suffers from a lack of systematic social-anthropological research. Some studies describe specific aspects such as rituals,[31] or focus on a specific brotherhood,[32] or examine a certain form of Sufism, such as the Traditionalist–Guénonian current.[33] However, no overall perspective is available. Concerning Italy, the articles of

[26] Goffman, *The Presentation of Self in Everyday Life*; Collins, *Interaction Ritual Chains*.

[27] Goffman, *The Presentation of Self in Everyday Life*.

[28] Schielke, 'Second Thoughts about the Anthropology of Islam'; McGuire, *Lived Religion*.

[29] A few examples are Geaves, *The Sufis of Britain*; Geaves and Gabriel, *Sufism in Britain*; Stjernholm, 'Sufi Politics in Britain'.

[30] Westerlund, *Sufism in Europe and North America*.

[31] Nabti, 'Des soufis en banlieue parisienne'.

[32] Voix, 'Implantation d'une confrérie marocaine en France'; Cottin, 'La Tijâniyya Lyonnaise'.

[33] Zarcone and Vale, 'Rereadings and Transformations of Sufism in the West'; Bisson, 'Soufisme et tradition'; Le Pape, 'Engagement religieux, engagements politiques'.

Speziale,[34] Guolo,[35] Abenante[36] and Marchi,[37] and the book by Schmidt di Friedberg,[38] represent almost all the Italian academic writing on the subject.

The choice of countries was limited by logistical realities; in-depth analysis using the ethnographic approach is incomparably useful but requires significant resources. Envisaging a broader comparison would have been more difficult. In any case, the significant differences between France and Italy offer us instructive analytical comparisons regarding migration history, integration models, and models of laicity.

Although the field studies were conducted in France and Italy, I use the 'European' label for the following reasons: most of the Sufi brotherhoods considered are also present in other European countries, and the aggregative forms and theological tendencies do not seem very different overall. Structural influences on Sufism, notably New Age influences and esoteric milieus, are similar throughout Europe. During my research, particularly during my travels in the countries of origin, I met Belgian, German, English and Spanish disciples, among others. Though I did not study Sufism in all European countries, I believe it is possible to describe the main tendencies of the European phenomenon based on the French and Italian cases. As we will see, however, the cultural–geographical context has its importance.

This 'European Sufism' label does not purport to describe all the Sufi phenomena in Europe. Each brotherhood has its own particularities; including or excluding a Sufi brotherhood means adding or losing a variant of the phenomenon. My research is focused on the processes of hybridisation in European Sufism. I did not study brotherhoods originating in sub-Saharan Africa or the Indian subcontinent; these are often 'transplanted' brotherhoods comprising exclusively first- and second-generation migrants and characterised by a homogeneous ethnic group. They reproduce the doctrines, rituals and structures of the country of origin and often function as a network and an 'acclimatisation chamber' for newly arrived migrants in Europe.[39]

[34] Speziale, 'Adapting Mystic Identity to Italian Mainstream Islam'.

[35] Guolo, 'L'islam nascosto'.

[36] Abenante, 'Essentializing Difference'; Abenante, 'La Tariqa Burhaniyya'.

[37] Marchi, 'Il Sufismo in Italia'.

[38] Schmidt di Friedberg, *Islam, solidarietà e lavoro*.

[39] Bava, 'Reconversions et nouveaux mondes commerciaux des Mourides à Marseille'; Schmidt di Friedberg, *Islam, solidarietà e lavoro*.

There are other forms of Sufism that will not be covered in this book, such as Sufi movements that define themselves as progressive and use narratives outside the frame of Sufi brotherhoods,[40] Sufi movements specialised in Islamic jurisprudence,[41] and de-Islamised Sufism such as that of Inayat Khan.[42]

This book comprises seven chapters. In the first, I discuss the general framework of Sufism as mystical knowledge and discursive tradition. The second chapter describes the pioneers of Sufism in Europe, who have contributed to building and imagining present-day Sufism. This also makes it possible to clarify the use of categories such as esotericism and New Age. Chapters three to six are each devoted to a different brotherhood. In the concluding chapter, I situate European Sufism in the public sphere and expand on its complex relationship with modernity and politics.

Who Am I? Positioning

My status and the purpose of my research are of ethical and methodological importance; I have always made them clear to the Sufi disciples and masters I have interacted with over the years. I have systematically asked the local leader for authorisation to observe the brotherhood, which has often been accorded in the form of a blessing. My presence has been both invisible and visible, invisible because have I tried not to be noticed, taking no notes during my field studies and rarely taking photos or making audio or video recordings. By contrast, I have been visible because when asked about my research or religious beliefs, I have responded frankly, even if this meant offending those who questioned me. This sincerity has helped me build trust and work heuristically, to the extent that the discussions helped me go beyond certain conventional ideas.

In my field research, I participated in all the Islamic and Sufi rituals, such as prayer, *dhikr* and *ḥaḍra*. I kissed the hand of the Sufi master if etiquette

[40] Bidar, *Self islam*; Bidar, *Un islam Pour Notre Temps*. The website of the association Voix d'un Islam éclairé (VIE) is available at <http://www.voix-islam-eclaire.fr/> (last accessed 27 October 2023).

[41] Tigra, *À la recherche de l'islam perdu*. See also the Syrian sheikh Muḥammad al-Yaʿqūbī, who has several disciples in Europe.

[42] Dickson, *Living Sufism in North America*.

required me to do so – that is, I learned the *adab*, the 'proper conduct' within the brotherhood. Sometimes I was invited to participate in rituals despite my being an outsider, perhaps so I could be converted, but for the most part the disciples were indifferent to my presence. In only one brotherhood did the disciples suggest that it would be inappropriate for me to partake in the rituals without being officially converted.

The religious beliefs of anthropologists and sociologists are often a taboo argument in scientific debates, while at the same time an open secret; everyone talks about them, but rarely are they addressed in the literature. I doubt that belonging to a religious movement, or not belonging to one, can result in a more in-depth analysis or, on the contrary, one that is less effective, because the capacity to employ socio-anthropological language has nothing to do with the researcher's religious practices. That said, I prefer to clarify my position as a matter of intellectual honesty; I am not a Sufi disciple, nor do I belong to any religion.

My interest in Sufism, and mysticism in general, dates back to my first years in college studying philosophy. Then, as now, I found the thinking of Meister Eckhart and Ibn ʿArabī more audacious and compelling than the philosophies of Martin Heidegger and Emanuele Severino, philosophies that dominated most discussions, at least in the philosophy department at the University of Ca' Foscari, Venice. This intellectual attraction led me to become a researcher and dedicate several years of my life to the subject, but it did not result in my adopting a religious practice or specific religious beliefs.

I adhered to this principle in my interactions with the disciples in the fieldwork. When asked about my beliefs, I responded that I 'didn't know', that I was 'a seeker', that I was 'a curious agnostic' or that I felt close to monotheism. In some conservative and traditionalist milieus, my lack of religious affiliation was frowned upon because my interlocutors preferred clear religious boundaries, which the agnostic suspension of judgement does not allow. In other milieus, I was seen as a possible candidate for conversion. All these differences between the brotherhoods helped me better understand different approaches to Sufism, such as the various techniques of proselytism.

Despite a transparent research approach, several Sufi disciples saw spiritual qualities in me and a progressive process of purification. Others interpreted my research as providential; one sheikh even said, 'God has sent us a sociologist'

(Chapter 6). Several disciples considered me a 'brother'. Of course, I could neither accept nor reject this form of inclusion in the esoteric and invisible realm. I thus had to work with this ambivalence between my role as a researcher and my metaphysical representation/perception in the minds of some disciples. This ambivalence is not new in research within religious movements.[43] As William Shaffir asserted, in field research, despite an open and transparent approach, we do not have total control over our representation and there is always a certain form of 'deception'[44] with regard to the participants.

Concerning my ontological approach to religious phenomena, I identify with 'methodological agnosticism',[45] which requires the researcher to suspend the big metaphysical questions and leave the door open to the possibility of a world beyond this one, in contrast to 'methodological atheism',[46] which posits that all religious phenomena are the result of a social construct. Using this possibilistic approach, I was able to take on sensitive subjects such as ecstasy and miracles, without asking questions about the veracity of religious experience, instead focusing on how this experience is embodied, practised, described and transmitted.

While methodological agnosticism has become a dominant way of framing the social sciences, several researchers have questioned its validity in recent years. For example, the anthropologist Joel Kahn[47] has proposed a syncretic epistemology between Gnosticism and the human and social sciences, making it possible to move beyond certain kinds of reductionism in anthropology by bringing together various ontologies. Among the key figures of this new epistemological perspective is René Guénon, an esotericist who converted to Sufism. He is one of the protagonists of this book.

It is my belief that this gnostic anthropology creates more problems than it solves, especially concerning its concrete applications and the clear division it makes between the secular and the religious, an approach I do not share. That said, the epistemological provocation of Kahn helps us ask other pertinent questions in this book. First of all, Kahn proposes making the question

[43] Sutcliffe, *Children of the New Age*.

[44] Shaffir, 'Managing a Convincing Self-presentation', 77.

[45] Porpora, 'Methodological Atheism, Methodological Agnosticism and Religious Experience'.

[46] Berger, *The Sacred Canopy*.

[47] Kahn, *Asia, Modernity and the Pursuit of the Sacred*.

of universals a central one, universals that were abandoned after the 'abuses' of the twentieth century, but are still relevant today, as we will see. Secondly, Kahn implicitly asks us what an anthropologist can learn from religions, and from gnostic religions in particular. I reframe the question to ask: what can an anthropologist learn from Sufis? I have been asked this question several times, in academic circles and by friends and acquaintances.

In my personal experience, the exchanges I have had with several Sufi disciples and brotherhoods over several years of field research does not directly pertain to the field of ontology in the way that Kahn might wish. This does not mean that I learned nothing nor that I remained insensitive to Sufi experience and teaching. But exchange, rather than big metaphysical and epistemological discourses, relates to daily life. With 'my Sufis', I encountered values that I share – hospitality, respect, modesty, compassion, honesty, justice – but that were articulated and experienced in different ways. With the Sufi disciples, I had the opportunity to think about the question of ego and how ego affects our private and professional lives, how it is often sanctified in many career paths, including in academia. These differences and continuities pushed me to question my epistemological, ethical, political and moral assumptions.

This experience of alterity, whether in the banlieues around Paris or Milan or in the Algerian desert, and these personal and scientific questions, have led me in the opposite direction than the one Kahn has taken. Rather than thinking of mysticism as something that cannot be reduced to modern–secular thinking, I have been able to perceive with greater acuity the overlaps between different cultures, religions and systems of thought.

I have also perceived other overlaps, such as a degree of continuity between the gentle melancholy of certain Sufi songs and the blues-jazz-rock I grew up with. Perhaps this resonance is due to the Islamic influence on the first forms of the blues (well established by historians and musicologists),[48] or perhaps I recognised a similar feeling – that is, the nostalgia for the ineffable, for an unknown state: reminiscence, to use Platonic language,[49] or the 'blue melody', to cite the song of Tim Buckley.[50] I have found myself on a liminal path through different

[48] Shibli, 'Islam and the Blues'.

[49] Plato, *Phaedo*.

[50] T. Buckley, 1969, 'Blue Melody', on the album *Blue Afternoon*, Los Angeles, Straight Records.

worlds, as described by Thomas Tweed.[51] In this movement, radical alterity is not a wild animal to be domesticated with our categories, but rather a possibility yet to be realised, or within the meaning of Joel Robbins, a foundation of hope in a present as yet unknown.[52]

[51] Tweed, 'On Moving Across'.
[52] Robbins, 'Anthropology and Theology'.

1

SUFISM AS MYSTICISM – *SCIENTIA EXPERIMENTALIS* AND AS DISCURSIVE TRADITION – *SACRA DOCTRINA*

> Of that passing and contradictory science there has survived a ghost that has continued to haunt Western epistemology . . . This phantom of a passage, repressed during periods secure in their knowledge, reappears in the gaps within scientific certainty, as if ever returning to its birthplace. At such times it evokes something beyond verifiable or falsifiable systems, an 'inner' strangeness that borrows its form from the far away regions of the Orient, Islam, or the Middle Ages.[1]

Using the category of mysticism, in general and especially outside the Christian context, raises the eyebrows of many researchers. Post-colonial intellectuals point out that mysticism has been privatised and separated from religion.[2] Hans Penner describes mysticism as a false category, an 'essentialist illusion',[3] whereas Steven Wasserstrom alludes to 'mystocentrism'[4] to denote the academic obsession of some researchers.

'Mystico-phobia' is justified by the use of mysticism in the Orientalist and 'religionist'[5] frame of the nineteenth and twentieth centuries, when mysticism

[1] Certeau, *The Mystic Fable*, translated by Michael B. Smith, 77–8.

[2] Jantzen, *Power, Gender and Christian Mysticism*; King, *Orientalism and Religion*.

[3] Penner, 'The Mystical Illusion'.

[4] Wasserstrom, *Religion after Religion*.

[5] Religionism was a twentieth-century intellectual current led by researchers in various fields who were seeking universal dimensions in religious, artistic and psychoanalytical phenomena and

represented a universal religion, the common source of all religions and all human beings. This universalisation of mysticism often led to projecting biases on other religions. That being said, at the beginning of the twentieth century, nearly all the analytical terms arose from this essentialist frame, including the categories of religion, ritual, culture, identity, and so on. The essentialist past of a category is thus not reason enough to deny its heuristic value.

The implicit issue raised by using this category is its translatability into various religions. Can a word created in the Christian context be used to describe an Islamic phenomenon? In this chapter and over the course of this book, I will show that the answer is yes, for several reasons. The first is a genealogical reason, in that Christian and Muslim mystics have reciprocally influenced each other throughout history and have been influenced by Neoplatonism and other phenomena. Secondly, for a similar reason,[6] and without formalising archetypal theories, we can grasp some common discourses and practices that extend beyond the various religions. The relevance and effectiveness of a comparative approach is ensured by a 'light touch'; we can recognise and describe common dimensions by highlighting the doctrinal, social and cultural specificities of each phenomenon, without formalising a unifying theory of religions.

Several researchers who study Sufism, such as Karamustafa[7] and Knysh,[8] use this category *cum grano salis*. Nile Green acknowledges the mystical elements of Sufism[9] but prefers to consider it as a discursive tradition for explanatory reasons.

While its conceptualisation as discursive tradition facilitates understanding in the *longue durée*, it has drawbacks for a targeted investigation. In addition, observing the mystical dimensions enables us to take a socio-anthropological approach that is open to theological categories,[10] whereas ignoring the mystical

came together as part of Eranos. Its most famous authors included Mircea Eliade (1907–86), Henry Corbin (1903–78), Carl Gustav Jung (1875–1961), Gershom Scholem (1897–1982) and D. T. Suzuki (1870–1966). Cf. Hakl, *Eranos*; Hanegraaff, *Esotericism and the Academy*.

6 Asprem, 'Beyond the West Towards a New Comparativism in the Study of Esotericism'.

7 Karamustafa, *Sufism, the Formative Period*.

8 Knysh, *Sufism*.

9 Green, *Sufism*, 3–4.

10 Robbins, 'Anthropology and Theology'.

dimensions of Sufism would mean losing its specificity. As I will argue, the most effective solution is to maintain the tension of a double definition, between Sufism as discursive tradition and Sufism as mysticism. In this chapter, I will lay out an archaeology of mysticism, then show how human and social sciences have reworked this category.

This approach is fundamental, not only in the theoretical frame, but especially for grasping the differences between mysticism and other phenomena, such as esotericism, New Age discourse and modern individualism – differences that might, at first glance, be seen as similarities. For example, the pre-eminence of the religious, ecstatic experience of closeness with God, which affects all the body's senses in a holistic relationship between body, soul and intellect, is certainly one of the characteristics of postmodern alternative spiritualities,[11] but it also characterises medieval Christian and Islamic mysticism. As Danièle Hervieu-Léger invites us to do, we must grasp the difference between 'mystical religious individualism' and 'modern individualism'.[12]

The socio-anthropology of mysticism I will propose in this chapter is, in reality, another way of looking at religious phenomena that takes into account the symbiotic relationship between religion and mysticism, as a dialectic between creativity and tradition, innovation and conservatism. This will enable us to consider mystical phenomena not as caused by exogenous influences, be they religious or social, but as integral parts of religious phenomena.

Archaeology of Mysticism

The word 'archaeology' as it is understood in the history of systems of thought is based on Michel Foucault's *Les mots et les choses*.[13] Adopting his approach, I propose an archaeology of mysticism to avoid stripping this category of the meanings stratified over the centuries. The aim is to grasp the various meanings, errors, aporias and contradictions that this category has encompassed over time.

Louis Bouyer[14] asserts that at the beginnings of Christianity, *mustikos* (mysticism) was related to three dimensions: (1) the hermeneutics of the Bible,

[11] Hanegraaff, *New Age Religion and Western Culture*.

[12] Hervieu-Léger, 'Le partage du croire religieux dans des sociétés d'individus'.

[13] Foucault, *Les mots et les choses*.

[14] Bouyer, 'Mysticism'.

based on allegorical interpretation; (2) the liturgy, in the description of the mystery of the Eucharist; and (3) the denotation of contemplative or experiential knowledge of God. The word 'mysticism' also represented a particular theological vision: the apophatic or negative theology of Augustine of Hippo, Dionysius the Areopagite and John Scotus Eriugena – a theology influenced by Neoplatonism but nonetheless Christian.[15]

Until the Middle Ages, mysticism was inseparable from religion, in terms of understanding sacred texts, rituals, experience and theology. Mysticism was, according to Bouyer, synonymous with the sacred and the spiritual, as opposed to the material world; it represented an essential dimension of the Christian religion. A shift began in the sixteenth century, particularly during the process of secularisation which, as Michel de Certeau,[16] King,[17] and Christmann and Searle-Chatterjee[18] have argued, led to marginalising mysticism through the profound transformation of its meaning. Martin Luther excoriated both mystical hermeneutics (the Bible, he believed, should be read and understood by each believer) and mystical theology, which he considered more Platonic than Christian.[19]

In the seventeenth century, mysticism began to lose its hermeneutic role, becoming a literary genre, a manner of speaking.[20] Thus, as de Certeau maintains, over the course of the seventeenth century a mystical tradition emerged that was confined to the hagiographies of the saints, namely their virtues, miracles and extraordinary experiences.[21]

In the eighteenth century, the Enlightenment influence on Christian theology, which called for 'reasonable religion', gave the word 'mysticism' a pejorative connotation. Mysticism, accused of 'syncretism',[22] became for some theologians the 'dark side'[23] of religion. In the psychological sciences,

[15] Turner, *The Darkness of God.*

[16] Certeau, *La fable mystique.*

[17] King, *Orientalism and Religion.*

[18] Christmann and Searle-Chatterjee, 'Reclaiming Mysticism'.

[19] Luther, *On the Babylonian Captivity of the Church.*

[20] King, *Orientalism and Religion.*

[21] Certeau, *La fable mystique.*

[22] Hanegraaff, *Esotericism and the Academy*, 109.

[23] Christmann and Searle-Chatterjee, 'Reclaiming Mysticism', 58.

Théodule-Armand Ribot[24] and Pierre Janet[25] compared mystical alienation and irrationality to expressions of primitive societies, 'a return to an earlier stage of psychic evolution'.[26] Mysticism became 'irrational', 'non-rational'[27] and 'prelogical',[28] symbolised by primitive peoples or the distant Orient.

At the opposite end of the spectrum, a philosophical current developed (Hartley, Law, Fletcher, Okely, Stiles) that saw mysticism as the natural form of religion, or even 'true religion'.[29] Starting in the middle of the nineteenth century, in transcendentalist circles, 'perennial philosophy' took wing; mysticism was redefined as a form of universal spirituality, beyond religious borders.

In the wake of this universal mysticism emerged the psychological and psychoanalytical thought of William James[30] and Carl Gustav Jung.[31] For these authors, mysticism was a timeless and universal religious experience, without specific denomination and strictly related to the realm of subjectivity. For the American psychologist James, mysticism was an ineffable, passive, fleeting and noetic experience – that is, illuminative and a means of attaining supra-rational truths. This change in direction also involved a dimension of secularising mystical experience, comparable to artistic or narcotic experiences, of which the most well-known example is undoubtedly the mystical quest of Aldous Huxley.[32]

The psychologisation of mysticism, according to Richard King's interpretation, had three conceptual consequences. The first was the essentialisation of organised–institutional religion which became a 'second-hand' religion, whereby true religion had to be sought in the subjective and private spheres. Secondly, this true religion was perceived as an object of alienation, in line with the example of James who, in describing 'modified states of consciousness', sequestered mystical experience, making it inaccessible and ineffable.

[24] Ribot, *La logique des sentiments*.

[25] Janet, *De l'angoisse à l'extase*.

[26] Keck, 'Le primitif et le mystique chez Lévy-Bruhl, Bergson et Bataille', 4.

[27] Otto, *Mysticism East and West*.

[28] Lévy-Bruhl, *L'expérience mystique et les symboles*.

[29] Christmann and Searle-Chatterjee, 'Reclaiming Mysticism', 58.

[30] James, *The Varieties of Religious Experience*.

[31] Jung, *Psychology and Alchemy*.

[32] Huxley, *The Doors of Perception*.

Finally, mysticism was 'privatised' and 'domesticated';[33] all social and political aspects were excluded, power relationships were forgotten, and mysticism was confined to an ineffable, private experience, hermetically sealed off from the world's transformations.[34]

The historical development of the word 'mysticism' did not only concern intellectuals; it also impacted those who practised it. As Giordan[35] notes, the Catholic Church used the concepts of mysticism and spirituality less and less frequently. In this regard, the distinction between mysticism and the esotericism of René Guénon,[36] one of this book's protagonists, is illuminating. According to this famous French thinker who converted to Islam–Sufism, mysticism is characterised by experience, passivity and the absence of knowledge transmission. It is interesting to note that these characteristics are related to the definition forged by James, rather than Christian theological sources.

The separation between religion and mysticism can be read as resulting from the decomposition and recomposition of the sacred, secularisation and sacralisation that characterise contemporary societies.[37] While during the pre-modern era, the different spheres of meaning, such as religion, politics, science and mysticism, were intrinsically linked, in the modern era, each sphere became autonomous, fragmenting and multiplying the production of meaning.[38] In sum, mysticism is linked to various aspects of religious life, such as cognitive–hermeneutic and liturgical aspects, and is a form of experiential and contemplative knowledge of God. Modernisation added other dimensions: mysticism became a subjective, bodily and universal experience separate from religion.

Social Sciences and Mysticism

Religious phenomena have often been described in social and human sciences as a dialogue between a formal, dogmatic and ordaining force and a

33 King, *Orientalism and Religion*.

34 Jantzen, *Power, Gender and Christian Mysticism*.

35 Giordan, 'Spirituality'.

36 Guénon, *Aperçus sur l'initiation*.

37 Hervieu-Léger, *La religion pour mémoire*; Hervieu-Léger, *Le pélerin et le converti*; Willaime, *Sociologie des religions*.

38 Fenn, *Liturgies and Trials*; Hervieu-Léger, *La religion pour mémoire*.

creative, spiritual, innovative and mystical force. George Simmel describes the relationship as being between 'religiosity and religion',[39] Émile Durkheim as being between 'religion as institutionalisation of the sacred' and 'collective effervescence',[40] Henri Bergson as being between 'static religion and dynamic religion',[41] Joachim Wach as being between 'expression and experience'[42] and Roger Bastide as being between 'lived religion and religion "kept as preserves"'.[43] Giorgio Colli, reworking Nietzsche,[44] describes this relationship as being between 'the Dionysian and the Apollonian',[45] Enzo Pace as being between 'the virtue of improvisation, or the power of pure speech, and the organised system',[46] Danièle Hervieu-Léger as being between 'ritual religion' and 'religion of interiority',[47] whereas Giorgio Agamben revisits the categories of Francis of Assisi regarding the tensions between the 'form of life' and the 'rule'.[48] We also find this dual relationship, sometimes in a less formalised way, in the works of Max Weber,[49] who situates the religious phenomenon between 'charisma and functional charisma', whereas Ernest Troeltsch[50] situates it between 'church–sect and *spiritualismus*–mystical group'. This dialectic is not new; it appears in the categories of the theologian, philosopher and alchemist Roger Bacon (1214–94),[51] who distinguished between *scientia experimentalis* and *sacra doctrina*. This opposition can also be read at the etymological level, as the word 'religion' derives from '*religare*' – that is, 'unite'; and '*re-ligere*' – that is, 'choose', 'care for'.[52]

[39] Simmel, *Die Religion*.

[40] Durkheim, *Les forms élémentaires de la vie religieuse*.

[41] Bergson, *Les deux sources de la morale et de la religion*.

[42] Wach, *Sociologie de la religion*.

[43] Bastide, *Les amériques noires*.

[44] Nietzsche, *On the Genealogy of Morality*.

[45] Colli, *La sapienza greca*.

[46] Pace, *Raccontare Dio*.

[47] Hervieu-Léger, 'Le partage du croire religieux dans des sociétés d'individus'.

[48] Agamben, *Altissima povertà*.

[49] Weber, *Sociologie des religions*.

[50] Troeltsch, *Die Soziallehren der christlichen Kirchen und Gruppen*.

[51] Sluhovsky, *Believe Not Every Spirit*, 100.

[52] Hoyt, 'The Etymology of Religion'.

Henri Bergson was profoundly influenced by the work of James. He described two sources of religion and morality, the first static (ordaining, regulating, dogmatic and conservative) and the second dynamic (creative, innovative, corresponding to mysticism). For Bergson, 'The most authentic religion is clearly dynamic religion; mysticism puts man into contact with vital energy.'[53]

Compared to Bergson's philosophical discourse centred on the individual, Durkheim's sociological approach instead situates the primeval form of religion, primitive in the genealogical sense, in the collective effervescence and its emotions. Thus, this form is

> a solidary system of beliefs and practices relative to the sacred, which is separated and prohibited – beliefs and practices that unite all those who adhere to the same moral community, called a Church.[54]

From this perspective, religion and the sacred cannot be separated, representing society itself. Collective effervescence marks the birth of a new religion and its society, as well as its revivification through rituals: 'Once individuals are brought together, a kind of electricity emanates from their *rapprochement* that rapidly transports them to an extraordinary degree of exaltation.'[55] Though Durkheim did not directly use the term 'mysticism', the parallels are nonetheless evident. The concept of collective effervescence leads us to consider mysticism as a collective process, not a strictly individual one. Collective mystical experience (effervescence) is also a symbolic site where the religious message is revivified or created. This mystical energy, this collective effervescence also takes on shades of Orientalism, corresponding to Western prejudices concerning primitive peoples, characterised by an 'orgiastic chaos of a sum of individuals no longer subject to any rules'.[56]

While Bergson translated James's intuitions into a philosophical language, Troeltsch did so in the field of sociology. It is difficult to attach any form of religious organisation to the *spiritualismus*–mystical group, as it lacks exterior

[53] Löwy and Dianteill, *Sociologies et religion*, 140.

[54] Durkheim, *Les formes élémentaires de la vie religieuse*, 65.

[55] Durkheim, *Les formes élémentaires de la vie religieuse*, 308.

[56] Löwy and Dianteill, *Sociologies et religion*, 124.

worship, predicators and visible organisation, thereby corresponding to 'a loose group that gives priority to personal connections based on spiritual affinity',[57] hence an unstable group with porous borders. Troeltsch describes mysticism as direct contact with divinity, which exists outside rites and dogmas, but unlike James, he does not equate it with religious subjectivism, since mystical experience is both individual and collective. The mystical form also fosters religious tolerance and relativism: 'Mystical individualism assumes neither an attitude of rejection, nor of acceptance or adaptation, for what is important is the pure union of thought.'[58] Mysticism also lies outside identity, to the extent that it surpasses the borders between 'them' and 'us'. The merit of this ideal type is that it releases sociology of religion from the dichotomy of the Weberian ideal types of 'church' and 'sect', given that mystical expressions cannot, for Troeltsch, be reduced to them.

Maurice Halbwachs[59] identifies the dogmatic dimension of official theology in memory and mysticism as a revivifying form of this memory. According to Halbwachs, 'Contestation comes from mystics reacting to the insufficiencies and dryness of official theological thought.'[60] Mystics are a community of virtuosos, the spiritual avant-garde, their aim being to 'return religion to its principle and its origins, either by trying to reproduce the life of the primitive Christian community, or by claiming to abolish duration and enter into contact with Christ'.[61]

In his cardinal work, *La fable mystique*, Michel de Certeau brings together many of the aspects of mysticism described above. Mysticism maintains an ineffable dimension, an absolute alterity, which does not remain unexpressed; on the contrary, it is sublimated in poetic language, in the body and in erotic tension. Mysticism is also an epistemological renovation, contributing to the modification of language all while expressing a revolutionary–vivifying social dimension: 'One who detaches themselves from the institution becomes a mystic.'[62] Mystics are often outcasts; de Certeau tells of a Christian mysticism strongly linked to a humiliated tradition, the decadent aristocracy, or Marranos (Jewish converts

[57] Hervieu-Léger and Willaime, *Sociologies et religions*, 74.

[58] Marchisio, *Sociologia delle forme religiose*, 50.

[59] Halbwachs, *La mémoire collective*.

[60] Hervieu-Léger and Willaime, *Sociologies et religion*, 218.

[61] Halbwachs, *La mémoire collective*, 217.

[62] Certeau, *La fable mystique*, 116.

to Christianity who were always considered inferior). The social and theological marginality of mystics often translates into claims in the political field: 'They oscillate between ecstasy and Jacquerie.'[63] The figures that dominate the mystical fable are thus the madman, the child and the illiterate.

This dangerous and sometimes revolutionary dimension of mysticism or of spirituality is also noted by Williams[64] and Ozment.[65] Similarly, Antonio Gramsci describes a non-monolithic Catholicism, subject to different currents that construct various representations of spiritual and social reality. Popular religion and certain forms of mysticism thus become a means of opposing the cultural hegemony of the dominant classes.[66]

Moshe Sluhovsky[67] is even more incisive in the description of the revolutionary dimension of mysticism, pointing out that interiorised spirituality raises problematic theological questions, like that of the relationship and hierarchy between doctrine and religious experience. What is more important, learning through the love of God or learning through books? What are the most important rituals, supererogatory rituals or canonical rituals? Who has the authority and capacity to control these interior spiritual experiences?[68] Likewise, Sluhovsky notes that sixteenth-century mystical Quietism subverted gender norms and hierarchies.

The last author who helps us understand these opposed forces in the religious field is the anthropologist Victor Turner.[69] Turner describes religion as both a structure that organises meaning and an anti-structural force that deconstructs it. The anti-structural force takes concrete form in *communitas*, where religious rituals construct new, direct, non-rational relationships that are nonetheless existential and egalitarian and that call social identities into question. This *communitas*, according to Turner, gives rise to innovative communities of prophets, saints, gurus and disciples in search of unity through overcoming the dualism that exists in society. Turner's *communitas* differs from Durkheim's 'collective effervescence' due to the absence of the orgiastic dimension; *communitas* does not imply the

[63] Certeau, *La fable mystique*, 116.

[64] Williams, *The Radical Reformation*.

[65] Ozment, *Mysticism and Dissent*.

[66] Gramsci, *Quaderni del carcere*.

[67] Sluhovsky, *Believe Not Every Spirit*.

[68] Sluhovsky, *Believe Not Every Spirit*, 98.

[69] Turner, *Dramas, Fields, and Metaphors*, 1987; Turner, *The Ritual Process*.

suspension of communitarian rules and links, but rather the foundation and/or refoundation of communitarian and religious links and rules.

> Communitas is not structure with its signs reversed, minuses instead of pluses, but rather the fons et origo of all structures and, at the same time their critique.[70]

The symbiotic relationship between ritual and *communitas*, noted by Turner, paved the way for theologian and anthropologist Giorgio Bonaccorso[71] who, referring to Greek etymology,[72] described mysticism as a continuous ritual, a foundational ritual that is never formalised but is continually constructed and deconstructed. According to this perspective partway between theology and anthropology, mysticism is not a phenomenon that is totally other, separate from daily life or other religious phenomena; rather, it gives profound meaning to reality by sacralising each act and each moment.

For a Socio-anthropology of Mysticism

We have seen that the definition of mysticism in the social sciences oscillates between the conceptualisation of a primitive, irrational, prelogical, orgiastic and anomic energy (Durkheim, Lévy-Bruhl, Otto), and one that portrays a true interior, subjective, tolerant and universal religion (Bergson, Troeltsch). However, these two perspectives converge in the separation between mysticism and institutional religion.

The abstract, essentialist and sometimes Orientalist interpretations were re-examined with the new developments of Halbwachs, de Certeau, Turner, Sluhovsky and Bonaccorso, who noted the social and even political dimensions of mysticism. They stressed that no mystical path exists in a vacuum but instead possesses a code of conduct, a discipline, and is part of a community. While experience appears to be strictly individual and may effectively include periods of isolation, it is always, in reality, a social experience. What is more, mystical experience, described as ineffable, has paradoxically given rise to an abundant production of metaphysical, poetic and artistic discourses and works.

[70] Turner, *Dramas, Fields, and Metaphors*, 1987, 202.

[71] Bonaccorso, *Il tempo come segno*; Bonaccorso, *La liturgia e la fede*.

[72] '*Mystikos*', 'μυστικός', comes from the verb 'μυω' – that is, 'close', 'close one's eyes', which, according to Boyer, is related to 'secret rituals'. Moreover, Bonaccorso suggests that *mystikos* was translated by the Fathers of the Church by *sacramentum* – that is, ritual.

These authors also affirmed that mysticism does not involve an absence of rules. On the contrary, it can be understood as a form of orthopraxy – that is, the space where the formal adherence to religious values is examined, not with the aim of orgiastic anomie, but in a process of becoming, to embody these values/norms. Finally, these interpretations remind us that religion is not only a 'system for regulating life',[73] or an ordaining dimension (communalisation and legitimation of power); it is also a dynamic and creative energy, capable of challenging the same structures it helped create.

The socio-anthropology of mysticism that I propose concerns not only so-called 'mystical' religious movements, but all religious phenomena. It is thus a matter of grasping the dialectic between creativity and tradition that is specific to religious phenomena, by considering mysticism as part of this process and not reduced to exogenous influences, such as Neoplatonism, shamanism or, more recently, New Age discourse.

This entails taking a fresh look at religious phenomena, rather than founding a new branch of study. Mysticism and tradition, *scientia experimentalis* and *sacra doctrina*, each exist by way of the other. Representing abstractions useful for understanding complex phenomena, these two forces belong to a continuum where the religious movements of interest could ideally be situated.

In sum, mysticism or *scientia experimentalis* is an experiential, bodily and intimate knowledge of the sacred that comprises a sense of union with God and the totality of God. This experiential dimension is not irrational; on the contrary, it becomes a special tool for the symbolic exegesis of sacred texts. The resulting knowledge is characterised by a multiplicity and instability of languages and epistemologies. Indeed, *scientia experimentalis* is expressed through poetry, music, philosophy and theology. Mystical language is a 'grammatical transgression'[74] that feeds on oxymorons,[75] leading to a form of 'literary nomadism'.[76] Or, in the words of the poet Petrarch: 'The first theologians were poets.'[77] This knowledge often brings fluidity to the borders between identities, cultures and ethnicities, and to the social boundaries between 'us' and 'them'.

[73] Weber, *Sociologie des religions*, 331.

[74] Baldini, *Il linguaggio dei mistici*, 44.

[75] Certeau, *La fable mystique*.

[76] Bonaccorso, *Il tempo come segno*.

[77] Pétrarque, *Lettres familières*, 280.

This mystical knowledge is embodied by exceptional and charismatic religious authorities capable of attaining intimacy with God and interpreting the symbolic meaning of religious texts. In the hands of mystics, sacred texts expand and become mysterious oceans which, as Umberto Eco maintains, carry 'an inexhaustible profundity'.[78] These exceptional religious authorities, in unison with the semantic and epistemological instability and creativity, imply possible anti-structural consequences, understood not as forms of anomie, but as the creation, revivification and deconstruction of norms, practices and hierarchies.

Symmetrically, *sacra doctrina–doxa* is based on discursive reason, born of the transmission and dissemination of doctrinal, juridical, cultual and political knowledge. Sacred texts are read in light of this traditional vision, the focus being on manifest meaning. *Sacra doctrina* is expressed in a language and an epistemological framework that are homogeneous and codified and that govern the visible borders between 'us' and 'others', thereby dictating the norms to follow to become part of this tradition. The institutionalisation of the act of believing also entails the formalisation of religious authorities who have specific roles as well as functional charisma, to use Weberian language. Their knowledge does not come from personal experience, but is acquired, along with competencies, through training within religious institutions. *Sacra doctrina* represents the structural force, the moral and political order, and continuity in the transmission of knowledge.

Table 1.1 The main elements of *scientia experimentalis* – mysticism and *sacra doctrina* – discursive tradition

Scientia experimentalis – mysticism	*Sacra doctrina* – discursive tradition
Experiential knowledge	Discursive knowledge
Symbolic reading	Exoteric reading
Linguistic and epistemological multiplicity and instability	Linguistic and epistemological homogeneity and stability
Fluid identity borders	Determinate religious borders
Orthopraxy	Legalism
Charismatic authority	Functional authority
Anti-structural force	Structural force

[78] Eco, *The Limits of Interpretation*, 12.

It bears repeating that these *scientia experimentalis* and *sacra doctrina* dimensions are abstractions useful in guiding us but do not represent 'flesh and blood' phenomena. So-called mystical phenomena have been variously positioned along this continuum over the centuries. In the next section, I will show how we can grasp this mystical dimension in the history of Sufism, and then in the next again section, I will focus on Sufism as tradition. It should be noted that *scientia experimentalis* is not 'true religion', nor is *sacra doctrina*, its decadent form. Moreover, these two abstractions are intrinsically linked, and neither can exist without the other.

Scientia Experimentalis in Sufism

Experiential Knowledge

In Sufi literature, there are several ways of describing experiential knowledge of God. Abū Yazīd al-Bisṭāmī, cited by Ibn 'Arabī, speaks of a 'living science': '[You] received your science from a dead man, who in turn received it from a dead man, whereas we have received our science from the Ever-Living who does not die.'[79] Others prefer the expression *'ilm ḥuḍūrī*, science of the (divine) presence, as opposed to the science of representation, *'ilm ḥuṣūlī*. Still others speak of *ma'rifa*, as interior or experiential knowledge.[80] Everyone agrees that this knowledge implies the human being in their totality, not only in the rational dimension, but also in their taste, *dhawq*. It is also commonly accepted that this knowledge is revealed as a form of amorous passion, *'ishq*, a term often used to describe romantic relationships between human beings.[81]

Experience of God implies uniting with all existence since, in the unity of being, *waḥdat al-wujūd*, 'existence belongs solely to God'.[82] Thus, experiential knowledge requires a *rapprochement* with God. In the words of Ibn 'Arabī, 'Take on the characteristics of God', and 'Become perfect in the perfections of God.'[83] This has led some Sufis to confuse the borders between human beings and God, and to proclaim they have abolished their own ego by merging with

[79] Ibn 'Arabī, *Les illuminations de la Mecque Futûhât al-Makkiyya*, 280, chapter 54.

[80] Karamustafa, *Sufism, the Formative Period*, 13.

[81] Karamustafa, *Sufism, the Formative Period*.

[82] Gril, 'Doctrine et croyances', 131.

[83] Chittick, 'Worship', 235.

divinity, as attests the famous phrase of Manṣūr al-Ḥallāj (858–922), *'ānā al-ḥaqq'*: 'I am the truth.'

This knowledge is only possible through a true purification of one's ego, *nafs* in Arabic, denoting the inferior soul, the 'centre of egocentric tendencies'.[84] Among the most important tools in this purification is the practice of *dhikr* (remembrance of God) – that is, the rhythmical repetition of divine names. This central ritual can transform into ecstatic dance, such as *ḥaḍra* or *'imāra* (the presence of God), with outward manifestations such as weeping or yelling.

Symbolic Reading

Though this divine experience disrupts the body and soul of Sufi disciples, it leads to extraordinary knowledge that can still be applied to Qur'anic exegesis. Instead of irrational, this knowledge is supra-rational and surpasses the principle of non-contradiction, as argued by the Sufi master Abū Sa'īd al-Kharrāz (d. 890): 'I have known God in His union of contraries.'[85]

Allegorical and symbolical exegesis draws its legitimacy from several Qur'anic passages that describe the path of the friends of God[86] or allude to hidden symbolic teachings.[87] The symbolical reading of hidden meaning, *bāṭin*, does not take the place of manifest meaning, *ẓāhir*, instead accompanying and completing it. This symbolic reading expands sacred texts and their unpredictable, potentially infinite meanings. All of existence becomes a sacred text; the profane ceases to exist. In fact, all of creation can be read as the totality of signs of the divine *oeuvre*: 'The world is but letters written inwardly and outwardly in the folds of the parchment that is existence,' says Ibn 'Arabī.[88] Ibn Barrajān (d. 1141) describes *ḥikma* as the supreme knowledge of non-visible realities, of both divine speech and creation.[89] This expansion of sacred speech is also found in the correspondences between macrocosm and microcosm, between human being and sacred text.[90]

84 Böwering, 'Régles et rituels soufis', 140.

85 Gril, 'Doctrine et croyances', 132.

86 Qur'an 2: 3–4; 5: 55; 8: 34; 9: 71.

87 We can cite the enigmatic figure of al-Khidr (Q.18) and the ascension of the Prophet Muhammad (Q.17).

88 Ibn 'Arabī, *Le livre des chatons des sagesses*, 1:101.

89 Böwering and Casewit, *A Qur'ān Commentary by Ibn Barrajān of Seville (d. 536/1141).*

90 Chittick, *Divine Love*.

Orthopraxy

Alexander Knysh describes Sufism as an ascetic–mystical form, underscoring the strong self-discipline it requires.[91] Sharia, or Islamic law, must be scrupulously followed in its various juridical formalisations, or *fiqh*. The antinomic attitude of Sufis, by which they supposedly refuse *fiqh*, is a constant figure in the history of Orientalism,[92] but a rarity in the history of Sufism. While there is no opposition between Sufism and religious norms, it remains true that intention, or *niyya*, is accentuated, rather than the literal and formal dimension.[93] But there is still the complicated relationship between canonical and supererogatory practices. Some assert the superiority of *dhikr* over *ṣalāt* (canonical prayer), but most consider them to be inseparable.

Using the category of orthopraxy rather than orthodoxy is a way of contesting the false opposition between the literal meaning and the spiritual meaning of religious norms. In *scientia experimentalis*, the norms only have meaning in the purity of intentions and the quest of love toward the divine. This theme is made palpable by the Sufi poet Rābiʿa al-ʿAdawiyya al-Qaysiyya:

> I will carry fire to Heaven and pour water on Hell. Then Heaven and Hell will disappear, and only the One who is the aim will appear. Then all will consider God without hope or fear, and in this way they will love God. For if there were no longer hope in Heaven nor fear of Hell, would they not show more adoration and obedience towards the Truth?[94]

Linguistic and Epistemological Multiplicity and Instability

The fact that Sufism is an experiential science, never resolved, has been expressed through a plurality of languages and registers: allusive, overwhelming, unpredictable, as is the case in poetry, calligraphy and music. Several famous Sufi poets recounted their mystical quest in verse, such as Farīd al-Dīn ʿAṭṭār (1145–1221), Jalāl al-Dīn Rūmī (1207–73), Ḥāfiẓ (1315–90) and Yunus Emre (1240–1321). Though poetic language has been an instrument of Islamisation and instruction, it has also caused scandal at times; take, for

[91] Knysh, *Sufism*.

[92] Knysh, 'Historiography of Sufi Studies in the West'.

[93] Gaborieau, 'Tarîqa et orthodoxie'.

[94] Rābiʿa al-ʿAdawiyya, *Les chants de la recluse*, 15.

example, poems that use the metaphor of wine for divine ecstasy. Some of the most scandalous images can be found in the poetry of Rūzbihān al-Baqlī (1128–1209), who tells how he met the Prophet Muhammad and drank with him in a dream,[95] and in the poetry of Ibn al-Fāriḍ (1181–1235), who extols spiritual drunkenness.

Linguistic multiplicity and instability can be seen in the theological treatises of Ibn ʿArabī, who often uses symbolic and allusive language to allow several interpretive readings. This multiplicity and instability also appear in dream interpretations, hallucinations, and experiences with *jinns* (spirits), given that the imagination, or *khayal*, plays a fundamental role in the mystical quest.[96]

The multiplicity also concerns Islamic epistemology, always in the process of becoming, never resolved: 'My knowledge about God is my perplexity about God,' says Ibn ʿArabī,[97] affirming that God remains ever a mystery. On this subject, Alexander Knysh, elaborating on Eco's category, speaks of 'hermeneutic drift',[98] capable of up-ending classical interpretations. This also applies to Aaron's adoration of the golden calf, which is described by Ibn ʿArabī not as a form of idolatry, but as an adoration of God, because every prayer, even idolatry, is necessarily a prayer to God.[99]

Fluid Identity Borders

The linguistic and epistemological multiplicity and the charisma of Sufi saints have sometimes led to blurred religious borders. If truth is everywhere, what religion should be practised? Is there a universal religion? Is it possible to experience religion *hic et nunc*? Does universality mean the relativisation of religious teachings, practices and norms? Is it possible to be Sufi without being Muslim? Are other religions valid? Sufis have given very different answers to these questions over the centuries and depending on the context. Most have asserted the supremacy of Islam relative to other religions; some have chosen to focus on the common points between religions.

[95] Green, *Sufism*, 76.

[96] Corbin, *L'imagination créatrice dans le soufisme d'Ibn Arabi*; Ewing, *Arguing Sainthood*.

[97] Ibn ʿArabī, *Les illuminations de la Mecque Futûhât al-Makkiyya*, 4: 140.

[98] Knysh, *Sufism*, 147.

[99] Ibn ʿArabī, *Le livre des chatons des sagesses*.

Sufism is a vector of Islamisation as one of the 'doors' for converting new disciples to Islam.[100] Saintliness tears down boundaries and attracts people of all origins, first and foremost Muslims, among whom Sufi masters have won over as many Sunnis as Shiites.[101] In the Bektāchīyya, an expression aptly sums up this point: 'A saint is for everybody.'[102] This is exemplified by some Christians in the Balkans who have taken an interest in Sufism and in certain Islamo-Christian forms of syncretism.

The fluidity between religious borders can also be read as pedagogical, without adverse effects on religious practices or norms. The expression, 'God loves the infidel',[103] of Aḥmed al-Tijānī (1735–1815), serves to jostle the egos of disciples who have grown complacent in believing their path to be the true one.

The description of a universal and supra-confessional religious truth, which can be found in the various forms of Sufi poetry, does not imply inventing a new religion, nor abandoning Islamic norms and practices. Manṣūr al-Ḥallāj describes a 'single principle with numerous ramifications',[104] but the most famous formulation is undoubtedly that of Ibn ʿArabī:

> My heart can take on any form:
> A meadow for gazelles, a cloister for monks,
> An abode of idols, the Kaʿba of the pilgrim,
> The tables of the Torah, the book of the Qur'an.
> My religion is love – wherever its caravan turns
> Love is my belief, my faith.[105]

The complex, subtle relationship between the universal and the particular, between a 'religion of love' and quotidian Islam, has taken on various forms over the centuries and, as we will see in this book, remains fundamental in the European Sufism of today. Those who describe a universal Sufism detached

[100] Salvatore, 'Sufi Articulations of Civility, Globality, and Sovereignty'.

[101] Werbner, *Pilgrims of Love*.

[102] Geoffroy, *Le soufisme voie intérieure de l'Islam*, 59.

[103] Geoffroy, *Le soufisme voie intérieure de l'Islam*, 283.

[104] Hussein Mansur al-Hallaj, *Dîwân*, 108.

[105] Ibn ʿArabī, *L'interprète des désirs*, 147.

from Islam, and those who deny any universal dimension, fail to grasp this complexity inherent to Sufism.

Mystical Authority: Charisma and Anti-structural Force

According to al-Ghazālī (1058–1111), the disciple must be like the blind in the hands of the master.[106] Ibn ʿArabī goes further: the disciple must be like a cadaver in the hands of the corpse-washers.[107] Experiential knowledge and a symbolic exegesis imply another form of religious authority that often positions itself above the *ʿulamāʾ*s (religious authorities of the *sacra doctrina*). Accomplished Sufis, as 'friends of God', *walī Allāh*, are part of the elite, or *khāṣṣa*. Their authority concerns not only disciples; it concerns everybody, in that some Sufi saints can be *quṭb*, the pole of existence. This underlies the claim to metaphysical legitimacy.

This extraordinary authority also concerns the political dimension, as Vincent Cornell convincingly argued, pointing out that this ambivalence regarding temporal powers is found even in the etymology. In effect, *walī Allāh*, commonly translated as 'friend of God', has another signification. The word '*walī*' has a double meaning in Arabic: '*wilāya*' as love/proximity and '*walāya*' as authority.[108] We will see in the section that this ambiguity of meaning has served several political configurations over the centuries through the legitimation, possession or defiance of political power. This extraordinary authority and this special knowledge belonging to Sufis have laid the foundations for expanding into other geographic contexts as well as revivifying and modifying Islamic discourses and practices.

The famous *ḥadīth*, 'At the beginning of every century *Allāh* will send to this *umma* someone who will renew its religious understanding', is often used by Sufis to claim legitimacy as 'revivifiers' of Islam, not merely passive interpreters of the texts. This revitalisation, or *tajdīd*, is considered salutary, unlike the pernicious innovations defined as *bidʿa*. Of course, grasping what is *tajdīd* and what is *bidʿa* is, in general, problematic, remaining one of the major challenges in the history of Islam.

106 Even though this expression is probably older.

107 Knysh, *Sufism*.

108 Cornell, *Realm of the Saint*, xix.

In exploring the various meanings of 'mysticism' in the Christian religious context, then in the context of the human and social sciences, I sought to show that essentialist use in the twentieth century notwithstanding, this category is still relevant and effective. Instead of considering mysticism as a phenomenon separate from religion or as a grouping of marginal religious movements, I proposed considering it as a dimension inherent in religious phenomena. In reworking the analyses of Halbwachs, de Certeau, Turner, Sluhovsky and Bonaccorso, I described the dialectic between mysticism, or *scientia experimentalis*, and discursive tradition, or *sacra doctrina*.

This theoretical abstraction enables us to grasp some aspects – ecstatic experience, symbolic exegeses, orthopraxy, and linguistic and epistemological multiplicity and instability – as integral parts of religious life and not as the expression of exogenous influences such as Neoplatonism, New Age discourse, modernity, and so forth.

This theoretical abstraction proves useful in the description of Sufism, understood not as a 'purely mystical' phenomenon, but as participating in this dialectic between mysticism and tradition – *scientia experimentalis* and *sacra doctrina*.[109] In effect, we can ideally situate Sufi brotherhoods along this continuum. Having explored the mystical dimension of Sufism here, in the next section I will now examine its opposite: Sufism as a discursive tradition – *sacra doctrina* – the foundation of an epistemological, moral and social order.

Sufism as Discursive Tradition – *Sacra Doctrina*

Sufism is not limited to the rarefied atmospheres of Rūmī's poetry or the metaphysics of Ibn ʿArabī, instead relating to all social spheres, such as social and economic organisation, constructing political power and daily life. Understanding Sufism as a tradition thus enables us to the grasp the processes of institutionalisation, formalisation, dissemination and transmission of Sufi discourses and practices.

In addition, Sufi tradition is closely linked to constructing Islamic tradition in that it offers discursive knowledge around sacred texts and a foundation for the moral, social and political order. In this way, Sufism as tradition became

109 It should be noted that the mystical dimension described here is not limited to Sufism in Islam. In the history of Islam, other forms possess these characteristics, such as the philosophies of Mollā Ṣadrā Shīrāzī, Suhrawardī, Ismailism and *bāṭinism*.

a field of study at Al-Azhar University and thus a core part of Islamic theology. Sufis legitimated political powers; they were advisors to the sultans under the Ottoman Empire[110] and to the kings in Indonesia and Libya.[111] In some cases they even possessed this political power; take, for example, the 'colonising dervishes' at the beginning of the Ottoman Empire[112] or the 'brotherhood states' in Somalia, the Caucasus and Kurdistan.[113]

The strong relationship between Islamic tradition and Sufi tradition is also apparent in the vocabulary used. In the Maghreb, for example, many people are named after Sufi masters, whereas in Pakistan, 'be-pir', or 'without a Sufi master', means wicked. Islam and Sufism are so closely interwoven that it is sometimes impossible to distinguish between them, as is the case in Senegal, where 92 per cent of the population belongs to a Sufi brotherhood.[114]

It must be recognised that this 'social' Sufism is not 'less true' than 'mystical' Sufism. This clarification is necessary; over the centuries, several Sufi and non-Sufi intellectuals have developed a 'decadentist' model of Sufi history. The Sufi master al-Jullābī al-Hujwīrī (1009–77) was already reading the past through this lens in the eleventh century, as witnessed by his famous critique of the Sufism of his day: 'Sufism used to be a reality without a name whereas now it is a name without a reality.'[115]

The decadentist approach is also perceptible in the writings of the father of Arab sociology, Ibn Khaldoun, who criticised Sufi abuses, notably certain philosophical shortcomings of his time.[116] This 'Sufi decadence' was also described in various ways by European Orientalists: Marshall Hodgson portrayed the corruption of Sufi ideals in local forms of Sufism;[117] Arthur John Arberry distinguished between mystical Sufism and popular Sufism;[118] Henry Corbin

[110] Geoffroy, *Le soufisme voie intérieure de l'Islam*.

[111] Bruinessen, 'Les Soufis et Le Pouvoir Temporel'.

[112] Veinstein and Clayer, 'L'Empire Ottoman', 331.

[113] Veinstein and Popovic, *Les Voies d'Allah*, 18.

[114] Pew Research Center, 2012, *The World's Muslims: Unity and Diversity, Chapter 1 Religious Affiliation*, [online]. Available at <https://www.pewforum.org/2012/08/09/the-worlds-muslims-unity-and-diversity-1-religious-affiliation/> (accessed 6 January 2012).

[115] Al-Hujwīrī, *Kashf-ul-Mahjūb*, 44.

[116] Knysh, *Sufism*.

[117] Hodgson, *The Venture of Islam*.

[118] Arberry, *Sufism*.

separated esoteric philosophy from the social dimensions;[119] and Trimingham dissociated the golden age from its decadence.[120]

This decadentist model has been rethought using new historical approaches that maintain the complexity of the phenomenon and recognise both its social and metaphysical dimensions. After defining the concept of discursive tradition, I will describe the development of Sufism over the centuries, allowing us to the better characterise Sufism in Europe.

What is a Discursive Tradition?

The socio-anthropology of Islam reached a crucial turning point with the works of the American anthropologist Talal Asad, who turned attention from religious symbols to the production of knowledge and power. The initial hypothesis was that the 'religion' category arose in the European–Christian context and cannot be applied to Islam without reductionist consequences.[121] For Asad, religion – as a symbolic system, separate from the other spheres of social, political and economic life – is an exception stemming from European modernity.

Rather than collecting Islamic doctrines, practices, and symbols, Asad set out to analyse the discourses around the Qur'an and the *ḥadīths*.[122] To do this, he reused the concept of 'tradition' described by Alasdair MacIntyre[123] as a set of narratives and conventions defined and redefined over the course of history, in which *virtus*, ethics, is rooted. Tradition then becomes 'discursive' by borrowing points from Michel Foucault,[124] which makes it possible to link the ethical dimension to practices and power relationships.

Islam as a 'discursive tradition' instructs Muslims as to the proper aims and practices. These discourses influence the present, take their legitimacy from the past and project themselves into the future.[125] As a 'discursive tradition', Islam

119 Corbin, *L'imagination créatrice dans le soufisme d'Ibn Arabi.*

120 Trimingham, *The Sufi Orders in Islam.*

121 Asad, *Genealogies of Religion.*

122 Asad, 'The Concept of Cultural Translation in British Social Anthropology'.

123 MacIntyre, *Whose Justice? Which Rationality?*

124 Foucault, *Les mots et les choses.*

125 Asad, *Genealogies of Religion.*

possesses a specific rationality – that is, a form of reasoning[126] strictly linked to the authorities. This means that proper form-orthodoxy is not immutable; rather, it is influenced by religious, political and economic powers. As Brett Wilson argued, Asad's analysis resonates with Pierre Bourdieu's interpretation around *doxa*, the dominant right doctrine that determines how to think and speak about the world.[127]

It is not within this book's scope to analyse the merits and problematic questions in Asad's work and that of his successors, which touch upon several theoretical, epistemological and political knots. My aim here is to assert that the model of discursive tradition, which foregrounds power and orthodoxy, is incisive if used as a tool among others, but not as an exhaustive, totalising model. In effect, as Samuli Schielke[128] and Shahab Ahmed[129] have underscored, certain more nuanced aspects such as daily life, philosophy and mysticism, fall outside the Asadian model, which runs the risk of being juridic-centric. In keeping with Nadia Fadil,[130] I consider Asad's discursive tradition as an invitation to analyse rather than a closed system to be applied to my field of investigation.

In sum, we can conceptualise Sufism as discursive tradition or *sacra doctrina*, or *doxa* in Bourdieu's vocabulary,[131] capable of bringing order to the vivacity, multiplicity and indetermination of *scientia experimentalis.*

Sufism's Beginnings: Eighth–Ninth Centuries

Some historians situate the first forms of Islamic spirituality around *qurrā'* and *quṣṣāṣ*, respectively those who recite and those who narrate the prophetic message,[132] but the traces we find of ascetic–mystical movements in modern-day Iran, Iraq and Syria date back to the ninth century at the earliest. The most important figures in these movements were al-Ḥasan al-Baṣrī (642–727), ʿAbd

[126] Anjum, 'Islam as a Discursive Tradition'.

[127] Wilson, 'The Failure of Nomenclature'.

[128] Schielke, 'Second Thoughts about the Anthropology of Islam'.

[129] Ahmed, *What Is Islam?.*

[130] Fadil, 'De la religion aux traditions'.

[131] Bourdieu, *La distinction.*

[132] Saccone, *I percorsi dell'Islam.*

al-Wāḥid ibn Zayd (d. 750), Rābiʿa al-ʿAdawiyya al-Qaysiyya (717–801), Abū Sulaymān al-Dārānī (d. 830), ʿAbd Allāh ibn al-Mubārak (726–97) and Dhu'l-Nun al-Misrī (796–859).

This first form of spirituality was characterised by 'the practice of rigorous or even extreme asceticism'.[133] Hence the term *zāhid*, which can be translated by 'ascetic'. Early Sufism was only slightly formalised theologically and organisationally. Similarly, according to Sufi hagiographies, which narrate voyages and peregrinations, this initial Sufism seemed always on the move, involved in a constant pilgrimage. The first trace of a sedentary ascetic–mystical religious community is *ribāṭ*, a fortified convent founded by ʿAbd al-Wāḥid ibn Zayd in the city of Basra.

Historians have not arrived at a consensus on the relationship between asceticism and Sufism. Nile Green considers these movements as separate and competing,[134] whereas Alexander Knysh underscores their continuity.[135] These different positions are probably due to the divergent perspectives of the two authors, Green being more interested in social forms and power relationships (discursive tradition) whereas Knysh focuses on religious doctrines and experience (*scientia experimentalis*).

In the early Middle Ages, the religious borders between Judaism, Islam, Zoroastrianism and Christianity, in Arabia and Mesopotamia, were more fluid than one might imagine. This makes it especially difficult to grasp the genealogy of certain ideas and practices as well as the degree of reciprocal influence between the various religious movements active in these regions.

This porosity was interpreted by some Orientalists at the end of the nineteenth century as real proof that Sufism was a phenomenon separate from Islam, likely of Christian or Zoroastrian origin and thus Aryan rather than Semitic. They considered it closer to European populations, which, it goes without saying, made it 'more noble'.[136] Opposed to this 'Aryanisation' of Sufism, the new generation of Orientalists in the twentieth century, including Louis Massignon and Richard Nicholson, were quick to stress the Islamicness of Sufism, criticising the anti-Semitic bias.

[133] Gril, 'Les débuts du soufisme', 31.

[134] Green, *Sufism*.

[135] Knysh, *Sufism*.

[136] Renan, *Averroès et l'averroïsme*; Palmer, *Oriental Mysticism*.

Today, the supposed endogenous or exogenous origins of Sufism are no longer hotly debated by academics, but they still feed the arguments of anti-Sufi Muslims. From a historiographic viewpoint, as suggested by Nile Green, rather than debating the adaptations and borrowings between religions, we should speak of a 'semiotic *koine*',[137] a common language used by Muslims, Christians, Jews and others who lived at that time in the High Medieval Islamic context. This common language influenced Sufism but also Islam in general.[138]

Birth of Sufism between the Tenth and Twelfth Centuries

Between the tenth and twelfth centuries, Muslim spirituality reached a significant turning point: asceticism developed a metaphysical dimension. The most important figures of this period were Abū al-Qāsim al-Junayd (835–910), 'Alī al-Hakīm al-Tirmidhī (760–869), Ibn Manṣūr al-Ḥallāj (858–922), Abū Yazīd al-Bisṭāmī (804–74), and Abū Sa'īd al-Kharrāz (d. 890). This period was a time of formalising Sufism's fundamental principles, which were also influenced by Neoplatonism,[139] principles such as *ma'rifa* (Gnostic knowledge), *fanā'* (self-abnegation in God), *baqā'* (return to daily life after abnegation in God) and *walī Allāh* (friend of God, close to God), this last principle legitimising Sufism's religious power and later its political power.

This period also saw the formalisation of the relationship between master and disciple. The Sufi master could be called a sheikh, *murshīd*, *pīr*, *bābā*, *dede*, *efendi* or *mawlānā*. All these names evoke the master, the respect owed him, and his role as guide. Disciples, in turn, could be called *faqīr* (poor), *ṭālib* (student), *murīd* (aspirant), *sālik* (follower) or *darvīsh* (poor). The relationship between disciple and master was sealed by *bay'a*: pact, incorporation, initiation or allegiance.

Sufism's formalisation and institutionalisation were strengthened when several Sufis came into contact with the theologico-juridical school known as the Shāfi'ī, which had just emerged.[140] This school used the concepts of *ijāza* and *silsila*, which became permanent terms in Sufi vocabulary. The first denotes

137 Green, *Sufism*, 17.

138 Reynolds, *The Qur'an and Its Biblical Subtext*.

139 Sedgwick, *Western Sufism*.

140 Green, *Sufism*, 50.

the master's authorisation concerning several official activities, whereas the second denotes the transmission of knowledge from master to master, going all the way back to the Prophet Muhammad. This formalisation and institutionalisation enabled dissemination beyond Arabia and Mesopotamia.

This first metaphysical formalisation was not akin to organising a religious movement. These groups – which could be called *ṭāʾifa* (simply 'group'), *qawm* (tribe in the sense of spiritual belonging) or *khāṣṣa* (the elite) – still derived from fluid formations: '[Aside from] exceptions, a disciple's training involved successively or simultaneously frequenting several masters; distinct initiatic paths did not exist.'[141]

The spiritual vitality specific to this era was also expressed through the creation of other ascetic–mystical movements that varied widely. Futuwwa, or spiritual chivalry, highlighted the indissociable ties between ethics, war and spiritual purification. Then there was the Malāmatiyya, the 'way of blame', widespread among middle-class artisans and famous for its principle of dissimulating pity, which could flatter a disciple's ego. In addition to these was the Karrāmiyya, a religious movement that focused on ascetic practices and was mostly made up of the poorest classes of Khorasan.

Over the centuries, all these spiritual forms were incorporated into Sufism by figures such as the Sufi master al-Sulamī (942–1021)[142] who, according to Nile Green, set out to revamp Futuwwa. On this point as well, some historians emphasise the continuity of these phenomena,[143] whereas others speak of competing movements.[144] Once again, these divergences depend on how Sufism is defined, as discursive tradition or mysticism.

Institutionalisation of Sufi Brotherhoods between the Twelfth and Sixteenth Centuries

Starting in the twelfth century, these fluid groups began to consolidate. The masters, or more often the disciples, founded schools that transmitted the teachings and techniques specific to each master, whose name became that of the brotherhood, or *ṭarīqa* (*ṭuruq* in the plural form).

[141] Gril, 'Les Débuts Du Soufisme', 34.

[142] Al-Sulamī, *Futuwah*.

[143] Geoffroy, *Le soufisme voie intérieure de l'Islam*.

[144] Green, *Sufism*.

The organisational structure came to include hierarchies, giving rise to the *muqaddam* (one who introduces) and the *khalīfa* (vicegerent). It also established locations, such as the *zāwiya* (literally, 'corner'), *dargā*, *tekke* and *khānqā*, which could also house the tombs of Sufi saints. The relationships between master and disciple, and between disciples, were progressively strengthened and formalised. The mystical quest was systematised: 'He who has no master has *shayṭān* [the Devil] as his master,' said Ayn-al-Quzāt Hamadānī (1098–1131).[145] A new literature emerged around the conduct of Sufi aspirants that governed both daily practices and the spiritual approach. A good example is the *Kitāb ādāb al-murīdīn* of Abū al-Najīb Suhrawardī (1097–1168).[146]

The work of al-Ghazālī (1058–1111) bears witness to an important time in the institutionalisation of Sufism in the Middle Ages. The ecstatic inebriation and philosophical elements gave way to a sober Sufism, central to the production of Seljuk orthodoxy.[147] This institutionalisation continued with Ibn 'Aṭā'allāh al-Iskandarī (1259–1309), who in 1309 introduced Sufi sciences as a field of study at Al-Azhar University. This dissemination also spread in other directions, in the poetry of Jalāl al-Dīn Rūmī, 'Aṭṭār, Ḥāfiẓ, Yunus Emre and Maḥmūd Shabistarī (1288–1340), in the metaphysics of Ibn 'Arabī, and in the sciences of the occult.[148]

Institutionalisation also allowed branching into various geographic, cognitive, political, social and linguistic directions. This change was probably fuelled by the crisis in certain institutions destabilised by the Mongols' sacking of Baghdad in 1258, by the death of the last Abbasid caliph, by the *Reconquista* in Spain, and by the Crusades in the Holy Land.[149]

Sufi institutionalisation also led to Sufi participation in economic and political powers. The brotherhoods acquired agricultural land and ran religious centres in strategic locations for commerce.[150] Sufi discourses and Sufi masters with their *baraka* (grace, benediction, energy) also legitimised political powers. For example, in the Ottoman Empire and then during the Mughal

[145] Karamustafa, *Sufism, the Formative Period*, 116.
[146] Suhrawardī, *A Sufi Rule for Novices*.
[147] Green, *Sufism*, 72.
[148] Lory, 'Soufisme et sciences occultes'.
[149] Geoffroy, *Le soufisme voie intérieure de l'Islam*.
[150] Green, *Sufism*.

reign of Akbar (1542–1605), the doctrine of Ibn ʿArabī on the unity of existence was used to justify interreligious cosmopolitanism, framed by orthodoxy in the first case, and with syncretic consequences in the second.[151] In other cases, Sufis blessed and legitimised the creation of new political powers. For example, the Bahmani dynasty was supported by the Niʿmatullāhī brotherhood and the Timurid dynasty by the Naqshbandiyya. Sufis did not limit themselves to sacralising public power; in some cases, they even held political power, one example being the Bektāchīyya in the Balkans.

Sufism spread widely, not only geographically (in Africa, Europe and India), but also into all social classes. This expansion is explained by saint worship, which involved a large swathe of the population.[152]

This expansion and these interactions with other cultures and religions left their mark. New disciples often carried with them their cultural and religious references, influencing Sufi brotherhoods to various degrees; Hinduism impacted some Sufi brotherhoods in India, Christianity did likewise in some brotherhoods in the Balkans, and so forth. In rare situations, Sufi doctrines and practices were used, and sometimes still are today, by Hindus[153] and Jews[154] without conversion to Islam. In our time, this phenomenon has been reproduced in the West with New Age Sufism, which we will examine later.

These processes of dissemination and popularisation and these encounters with alterity led some Sufis to engage in profound self-criticism and to emphasise orthodoxy. A famous representative of this criticism is Ibn Taymiyya (1262–1328), probably himself a Sufi disciple. He criticised philosophical blunders and popular practices, but what he found most problematic was the ecstatic and metaphysical union with God. As he saw it, proper religious conduct should always be moderate and based on sacred texts and Islamic law. All the ecstatic, poetic and metaphysical explorations potentially fuelled innovation and hence sin.[155] In a way, Ibn Taymiyya's Sufism was only conceivable as *sacra doctrina*.

[151] Alam, *Languages of Political Islam in India 1200–1800*; Geoffroy, *Le soufisme voie intérieure de l'Islam*.

[152] Karamustafa, *Sufism, the Formative Period*; Green, *Sufism*.

[153] Dahnhardt, *Change and Continuity in Indian Sufism*; Boivin, *The Hindu Sufis of South Asia*.

[154] Bram, 'Spirituality under the Shadow of the Conflict'.

[155] Hoover, *Ibn Taymiyya*.

Renewal of Brotherhoods between the Seventeenth and Nineteenth Centuries

Controversies around orthodoxy, porous religious boundaries, as well as linguistic and epistemological instability have always been present in Sufism in the form of tension between *scientia experimentalis* and *sacra doctrina*. As for the renewal of brotherhoods that started in the seventeenth century, it was focused on ethical, juridical and theological dimensions to the detriment of ecstatic and metaphysical explorations.

A good example of those involved in this renewal is Aḥmad al-Fārūqī al-Sirhindī (1564–1624), who not only criticised Ibn ʿArabī's theory on the unicity of existence, but also stressed the differences between Muslims and Hindus, condemning the syncretism as well as the over-inclusiveness of some Indian Sufis.[156]

This renewal led researchers to forge the term 'neo-Sufism',[157] later abandoned by contemporary historians, who highlight both the differences and the continuity between Sufism in the Middle Ages and Sufism in the modern era.[158] However, the specificities of this time should be noted, particularly an increasingly developed structuration and the moral, cultural, political and military reaction to expanding European colonialism. This reaction may also have been fostered by millenarianism with the approach of the year 1000 of the Islamic calendar (1591 according to the Gregorian calendar).

Sufism continued its global dissemination, with new brotherhoods spreading widely in India, China, Russia and Indonesia. The links between Sufism and nation-building continued to strengthen. For example, in Morocco, Sufism became a state doctrine under the Saadi dynasty, with some Sufis going so far as to theorise their role as 'axis of the state'.[159]

Concerning their relationships with colonialism, brotherhoods used all available actions in the repertoires of contention, from armed conflict to collaboration to passive resistance. Sometimes sons made peace with the colonists their fathers or grandfathers were unable to overcome.[160] A good example

[156] Green, *Sufism*, 192.

[157] Rahman, *Islam*.

[158] O'Fahey and Radtke, 'Neo-Sufism Reconsidered'.

[159] Cornell, *Realm of the Saint*, 271.

[160] Green, *Sufism*.

of the armed opposition to colonialism is the resistance of Muḥammad ibn ʿAlī al-Sanūsī (1787–1859), a student of Aḥmad ibn Idrīs (1760–1837) and founder of the Sanūsiyya, which confronted Italian colonists in Libya as well as English and French colonists in Niger and Algeria. Sanūsī's grandson became the king of Libya, remaining in power until Gaddafi's revolution in 1969.

As we have seen, the first criticisms of certain Sufi practices and doctrines came from within the ranks of Sufism itself. Moreover, there are no doctrinal or sociological elements making it possible to definitively separate Sufism from Salafism, reformism and Islamism,[161] given that historical cross-over occurred several times. Being Sufi did not prevent one from being something else as well.

Another development was the arrival of Wahhabism in Arabia in the eighteenth century, which completely upset the balance on all sides. In fact, while Wahhabi criticism was not an absolute novelty (some Sufi practices were accused of being innovative, or *bidʿa*, and polytheistic, or *shirk*), ʿAbd al-Wahhāb (1703–92) and his disciples did not aim to reform Sufism in the way Ibn Taymiyya did. Rather, their objective was to eradicate Sufism from Islam, even if this meant resorting to violence by declaring jihad, or holy war. This explains why, in various countries around the world, Sufis are targeted to this day by jihadists.

Contemporary Sufism: Emergence of Global Trends

In the twentieth century, Wahhabis' frontal attack on Sufism was complicated by the opposition of colonial and non-colonial government institutions, which considered Sufi brotherhoods as a possible threat to political authority and an obstacle to modernisation, as in the case of Russia,[162] Algeria[163] and Turkey.[164] Reformist, nationalist and socialist Muslims and Muslim secular ideologues considered all Sufis as obscurantists who collaborated with colonial powers and, above all, were incapable of dealing with the challenges of modernity.[165]

161 Gaborieau and Grandin, 'Le renouveau confrérique'; Howell, 'Indonesia's Salafist Sufis'; Woodward et al., 'Salafi Violence and Sufi Tolerance?'.

162 Knysh, 'Sufism as an Explanatory Paradigm'.

163 Werenfels, 'Beyond Authoritarian Upgrading'.

164 Zarcone, 'La Turquie républicaine'.

165 Sedgwick, 'In Search of a Counter-reformation'.

These criticisms and attacks led some anthropologists, such as Clifford Geertz[166] and Ernest Gellner,[167] to diagnose a Sufi crisis in contemporary societies. They also endorsed theories on the process of secularisation that postulated religion's diminishing role in daily life and within institutions.[168] For these anthropologists, Sufism, associated with popular Islamic religion, would be swept away by the process of modernisation that was disturbing majority Muslim countries.

Despite these attacks and this terminal-phase diagnosis, Sufism succeeded in finding new energy in the twentieth century through new charismatic masters capable of attracting disciples both in the West, as shown by substantial scholarship,[169] and in majority Islamic countries.[170]

From its beginnings, Sufism was not only a transnational phenomenon, but also a vector of globalisation, with the first ascetic-Sufis travelling throughout Arabia and Mesopotamia and into India. Later on, brotherhoods became instruments of Islamisation in Africa, Asia and Indonesia.[171] This transnational dimension has intensified in contemporary Sufism, enabling us to speak of 'global Sufism',[172] a designation that does not take the place of previously described phenomena by representing a new category. Rather, it allows us to grasp the specifically global trends of Sufism.

In global Sufism, the processes of de-Islamisation and re-Islamisation exist side by side. A good example is Sufi Order International, founded by Inayat Khan (1882–1927) in the United States in collaboration with the theosophical esoteric current.[173] Islamic practices lost their importance in this brotherhood, replaced or accompanied by 'universal rituals'. However, in this de-Islamicised

166 Geertz, *Islam Observed*.

167 Gellner, *Muslim Society*.

168 Weber, *Sociologie des religions*; Acquaviva, *L'eclissi del sacro nella civiltà industriale*; Wilson, *Contemporary Transformations of Religion*; Berger, *The Sacred Canopy*.

169 Werbner, *Pilgrims of Love*; Westerlund, *Sufism in Europe and North America*; Geaves, *The Sufis of Britain*; Geaves, et al., *Sufis in Western Society*.

170 Quinn and Quinn, *Pride, Faith, and Fear*; Werenfels, 'Beyond Authoritarian Upgrading'; Bruinessen and Howell, *Sufism and the 'Modern' in Islam*.

171 Salvatore, 'Sufi Articulations of Civility, Globality, and Sovereignty'.

172 Piraino and Sedgwick, *Global Sufism*.

173 Dickson, *Living Sufism in North America*.

Sufism often designated as New Age, Islam did not completely disappear, returning later in the teachings of Khan's grandson, Zia Inayat-Khan (born in 1971). Given that both theosophical and New Age practices are not limited to the West, this de-Islamisation and this re-Islamisation do not solely concern European disciples. For example, the trend can also be seen in Pakistan.[174]

The de-Islamisation of Sufism is also palpable in some forms of aestheticisation,[175] such as the creation of a Jalāl al-Dīn Rūmī that is global, edulcorated, simplified and domesticated for a mainstream readership more interested in poetry than in an Islamic mystical path.[176] Nonetheless, the relationship between art and Sufism cannot be reduced to the process of aestheticisation, which brings something down to a commercial product. In fact, global Sufism is expressed through new cultural practices such as theatre,[177] rap[178] and the visual arts,[179] and does not necessarily lose its Islamic dimension nor the ascetic–mystical quest.

This hybridisation also concerns epistemology. In effect, several global Sufi masters and disciples are interested in the social and human sciences or the natural sciences, adapting and redeveloping their languages and categories based on these interactions.

Another characteristic of contemporary global Sufism is the incontestable presence of women, both as disciples and, rarely, as masters. By way of example, in several Turkish, Algerian, Moroccan, European and American brotherhoods, the question of women is under debate, sometimes in relation to metaphysics, sometimes in relation to social and political issues.[180]

Another crucial turning point has been the use of Sufism by nation states with a view to fighting Islamism. What only a few years ago was stigmatised

[174] Philippon, 'De l'occidentalisation du soufisme à la réislamisation du New Age?'; Dickson and Xavier, 'Disordering and Reordering Sufism'; Sedgwick, 'The Islamization of Western Sufism after the Early New Age'.

[175] Shapiro, 'Artification as Process'.

[176] Irwin, 'Global Rumi'.

[177] See the performance 'Sufi mon amour' of Hassan El Jaï and Haroun Teboul.

[178] Brigaglia, 'Eurapia: Rap, Sufism and the Arab Qaṣīda in Europe'.

[179] Cf. the works of the Franco-Algerian artist Rachīd Koraichi and his website. Available at <https://rachidkoraichi.com/> (last accessed 29 October 2023).

[180] Sharify-Funk et al., *Contemporary Sufism*.

as archaic, irrational and dangerous has rapidly become the good, traditional Islam. Fait Muedini describes this transformation occurring between the 1990s and recent years in Pakistan, Morocco and the United States.[181]

The processes of de-Islamisation and re-Islamisation, as well as cultural and epistemological hybridisation, must not lead us to believe that Sufism is no longer capable of representing and reproducing Islamic orthodoxy, or *sacra doctrina*. The forms of charismatic power that Sufi sheikhs exercise is not diminishing; on the contrary, it is on the rise. The Syrian sheikh Muḥammad al-Yaʿqūbī[182] (born in 1963) is founding new *zāwiya*s in both the Maghreb and Europe. Among other famous global Sufi *ʿulamā*'s are Hamza Yusuf and Abdal Hakim Murad, respectively based in the United States and the United Kingdom.

A final dimension of global Sufism is the renewal of a Sufism without brotherhoods – that is, without the permanence of their traditional organisational structures. Sufism has been a source of inspiration for intellectuals as well as religious and political movements, such as Jamaʿat al-Tabligh[183], the Gülen movement[184] and the al-Adl wa'l īḥsān (Justice and Spirituality) movement of ʿAbd al-Salām Yāssīn (1928–2012).[185] Among other forms of Sufism without brotherhoods, progressive and liberal movements and individuals use Sufi narratives without forming ties to any order. Omid Safi,[186] Sa'diyya Shaikh,[187] Abdennour Bidar,[188] Mohsen Hendricks[189] and Kahina Bahloul[190] illustrate in very different ways how Sufism can be interwoven with European philosophy, with the fight against racial discrimination and homophobia, and with secular thought.

[181] Muedini, 'The Promotion of Sufism in the Politics of Algeria and Morocco'; Muedini, *Sponsoring Sufism*.

[182] Muedini, 'Sufism, Politics, and the Arab Spring'.

[183] Reetz, 'Sûfî Spirituality Fires Reformist Zeal'.

[184] Hendrick, *Gülen*.

[185] Belal, 'Mystique et politique chez Abdessalam Yassine et ses adeptes'.

[186] Safi, *Radical Love*.

[187] Shaikh, *Sufi Narratives of Intimacy*.

[188] Hashas, 'Reading Abdennour Bidar'.

[189] Piraino and Zambelli, 'Queer Muslims in South Africa'.

[190] Bahloul, *Mon Islam ma liberté*.

Conclusions

The mystical dimensions described do not suffice for understanding the multiple layers of Sufi phenomena, making it necessary for us to introduce the concept of discursive tradition and analyse the historical development of Sufism over the centuries, in its social, political and cultural dimensions.

We have seen that over time, Sufi ascetic–mystical practices amalgamated, giving rise to religious movements possessing doctrinal coherence, organisational structures and canonical rituals. As a result, Sufism, as a discursive tradition, can be described as a subset and a sub-discourse of Islam. What gives the production of Sufi orthodoxy its specificity is that the discourses on sacred texts (Qur'an and *ḥadīth*s) have been supplemented by the authority of experiential knowledge of the divine possessed by the friends of God, that is Sufi masters.

The relationship between Islam and Sufism and between Islamic orthodoxy and Sufi orthodoxy has seen significant fluctuations in various sociogeographic contexts and over the centuries. At times, the two orthodoxies have almost coincided, making the difference between Sufism and Islam practically imperceptible, whereas in other contexts, they have been further apart.

Due to the unstable nature of the mystical dimension, these tensions have always been a part of Sufism, but factors from the nineteenth century on have substantially exacerbated them. For one thing, Wahhabism has tried to eradicate Sufi practices from Islam; for another, several Western intellectuals have imagined and created a universal Sufism by dissociating it from Islam. New Agers and Wahhabis have thus become unexpected allies. Nonetheless, as this book shows, these attacks and tensions have not prevented Sufism from propagating and proposing its own Islam.

2

SUFI PIONEERS IN EUROPE

The first forms of Sufism in Western Europe may date back to the Middle Ages, possibly taking shape in Sicily,[1] Andalusia[2] or France.[3] They may have been influenced by the doctrine around the mysticism of Ramon Llull[4] (1232–1315) or by Renaissance humanism. However, these subjects, no doubt fascinating, are not covered in this chapter. I do not aim to conduct an exhaustive analysis of the history of Sufism in Europe but seek instead to describe the religious movements that have influenced, and continue to influence Sufis in Europe – movements such as European esotericism, New Age or alternative religions, and the religious–intellectual stream known as 'Religionism'.

The pioneers of Sufism in Europe, or its 'ambassadors' as Pierre Lory[5] defines them, include lifelong Muslims such as Idries Shah, converts such as René Guénon and Eva de Vitray-Meyerovitch, and Christians and esotericists such as Henry Corbin, Louis Massignon and Georges Ivanovich Gurdjieff. This last group never converted to Islam but did dedicate several books to Sufism or Sufi practices, having a de facto influence on European Sufis.

[1] Barone, 'Islām in Sicilia'.

[2] Ebstein, *Mysticism and Philosophy in Al-Andalus.*

[3] Arkoun, *Histoire de l'islam et des musulmans.*

[4] Hillgarth, *Ramon Lull and Lullism in Fourteenth-century France.*

[5] Lory, 'Les ambassadeurs de l'Islam mystique'.

We should not consider these sources as isolated or static, but rather as reciprocally influential. I believe it necessary to maintain the distinctions between them because definitions of Sufism as 'Universalist',[6] 'Perennialist'[7] and 'Neo-Sufi',[8] which group together authors as diverse as Corbin, Guénon, Schuon, Shah and Gurdjieff in a single category, are not completely satisfactory. On the contrary, I consider it important to grasp the specific characteristics of these sources and to understand how they have created various methods to spread, imagine, build and experience Sufism. Finally, we should not give in to the temptation to mix these phenomena together in a comfortable but ineffective category, such as the 'esoteric mystical nebula'.[9]

These various influences have at times given rise to new rituals or new forms of Sufism, such as the de-Islamised New Age Sufism of Vilayat Inayat-Khan (1916–2004). There is also Guénonian–Traditionalist Sufism, which reproduces the practices, doctrines and organisational structures of European esotericism.[10] However, these influences are generally more nuanced, first of all because the distinctions between esotericism, New Age discourse and Religionism are often blurred. Secondly, most Sufi aspirant disciples who have discovered Sufism through the works of Guénon, Corbin and Shah are not very interested in the differences between these streams. What is certain is that the works of these authors often function as turning points[11] in the spiritual quest of many Sufi aspirants, among both converts and those raised as Muslims.

In this chapter, I will contextualise these religious phenomena and offer a specific reading of the New Age and esotericism, considered as religious discourses. Based on Marcus Morberg's classification of discourse analysis, there are three main approaches that share the social constructionist paradigm: (1) meta-theoretical reflections, (2) their contextualisation in religious

6 Geaves, *The Sufis of Britain*.

7 Hermansen, 'Hybrid Identity Formations in Muslim America'.

8 Hammer, 'Sufism for Westerners'.

9 Champion, 'Les sociologues de la post-modernité religieuse et la nébuleuse mystique-ésotérique'.

10 Zarcone and Vale, 'Rereadings and Transformations of Sufism in the West'; Piraino, 'Esotericisation and De-esotericisation of Sufism'.

11 Rambo, *Understanding Religious Conversion*.

environments and (3) research emphasising concrete examples/discourses.[12] According to Morberg's taxonomy, this book falls into the third category; hence I am following in the footsteps of other scholars who have worked on religious phenomena by focusing on the underlying discourses.[13]

Henceforth, we could identify a (religious) discourse as 'a set of meanings, metaphors, representations, images, stories, statements, and so on that in some way together produce a particular version of events'[14] and/or 'an overarching concept covering utterances (speeches) and textual, visual (imagery), symbolic or physical (gestures, body language) representations and practices embedded in them'.[15] In other words, a discourse is a worldview as well as social practices.

As a sociologist of religion who adopts an ethnographical approach, I am particularly interested in comprehending how a religious discourse shapes a religious movement, in terms of rituals, practices, organisational structures and politics. I want to stress that this bottom-up approach does not seek to describe conclusively what esotericism and the New Age are; rather, it is an attempt to describe what these discourses 'do' to specific religious movements. Finally, discourses are typologies and should not be confused with historical relationships, as has been argued by Granholm.[16] Rather, they should be empirically tested, to prove or disprove their heuristic value.

First Sufis: Migrants

It is clear that the first pioneers of Sufism in France and Italy were migrants from the Maghreb. However, in contrast to the other influences mentioned above, this history cannot be coherently described due to a lack of written sources, making this initial Sufism a 'hidden Islam'.[17]

It nonetheless seems possible and necessary to give this history a general frame. The first Algerian migratory flows began in the 1920s. For example, the first ʿAlāwī disciples arrived in France during this period; for the most part, they

[12] Moberg, 'First-, Second-, and Third-level Discourse Analytic Approaches in the Study of Religion'.

[13] Granholm, 'Esoteric Currents as Discursive Complexes'; Sutcliffe, *Children of the New Age*.

[14] Burr, *Social Constructionism*, 48.

[15] Erdogan, *Humanitarian Intervention and the Responsibility to Protect*, 5–6.

[16] Granholm, 'Esoteric Currents as Discursive Complexes', 53.

[17] Werbner, *Pilgrims of Love*.

were labourers of Kabyle descent.[18] Starting in the 1950s–60s, Algerian immigration evolved, the working periods lengthened, and many Algerians began to take up permanent residence in France.[19] It was during this time that the first *zāwiyas* took shape. Būdshīshī disciples of Moroccan origin arrived in France later, in the 1960s; they, too, were mostly labourers and factory workers.

A significant change occurred at the end of the 1980s, when the protagonists became new immigrants who were no longer labourers and factory workers but well-educated professionals. In addition, the sons and daughters of the first immigrants, the so-called second and third generations, started to climb the social ladder, attending university and becoming professionals. This new, more cultivated generation has contributed to Sufism's spread to a wider public, and continues to do so. I have already mentioned the Moroccan intellectual Faouzi Skali, and in the next chapters we will meet Sheikh Khaled Bentounes, indefatigable writer and lecturer, as well as Mounir al-Qādirī al-Būdshīshī, grandson of Sheikh Hamza al-Qādirī al-Būdshīshī and author of a thesis completed at EPHE (a prestigious French higher education institution known for its religious studies programmes) under the direction of Pierre Lory.

Immigration in Italy has been completely different. Up to the 1970s and 1980s, most of the few immigrants were university students. Starting in the 1990s, the flows of migrants increased considerably. Today, the Moroccan community is the largest majority Islamic community and the third largest migrant community in Italy, numbering around 400,000 people and positioned after the Romanian and Albanian communities.[20] Most of the immigrants hold working-class jobs and are concentrated in northern Italy. What is known as the 'second generation' has developed only in recent years[21] and has not yet produced public Sufi figures as in France.

The research on Sufi brotherhoods made up mainly of migrants, called 'transplanted brotherhoods',[22] describes ethnically homogeneous orders that

[18] Talbi, 'Immigration et intégration de la confrérie 'Alawiya en France depuis 1920'.

[19] Stora, *Ils venaient d'Algérie*.

[20] Di Corpo and Vannini, *Caritas/Migrantes: Dossier Statistico Immigrazione*.

[21] Frisina, *Giovani musulmani d'Italia*.

[22] Hermansen, 'Hybrid Identity Formations in Muslim America'.

reproduce the practices and structures in the country of origin and serve as a network for new immigrants,[23] as a 'welfare state', as a mediator in relation to the new society – in sum, as a sort of 'acclimatisation chamber'.[24] But we should not consider these brotherhoods to be static. In effect, over time the homogeneity and compactness of these transplanted brotherhoods have given way to interactions with new disciples (converts or migrants of other origins) and interactions with new cultural and religious influences, in a process of hybridisation that takes on completely different forms depending on each case. In this book, I prefer to focus specifically on this hybridisation process rather than on transplanted brotherhoods, which are already well documented in the academic literature.

Between Sufism and Esotericism: A Few Landmarks[25]

The heterogeneity of Sufism throughout its history discourages the use of a single descriptive category, such as mysticism, esotericism, asceticism, spirituality, popular religion or intellectual religion. All these categories can be either useful or misleading, depending on the specific context. Therefore, as argued by Simon Sorgenfrei, Sufism cannot be exclusively equated with esotericism.[26] Yet we cannot deny the existence of an Islamic esotericism, both in its medieval forms, such as *bāṭinism*,[27] and in its interweaving with contemporary esotericism. We must therefore start by clarifying the term 'esotericism'.

The term 'esotericism' did not come into use until the eighteenth century, as pointed out by Antoine Faivre and Jean-Pierre Laurant.[28] Faivre offers a very broad definition: 'a set of currents that have strong similarities and are historically connected'.[29] In other words, esotericism is a group of specific 'forms of thought' that are identified by 'four fundamental elements', namely, correspondence, living nature, imagination and mediation, and experience of

[23] Hermansen, 'What's American about American Sufi Movements?'.

[24] Schmidt di Friedberg, *Islam, solidarietà e lavoro*, 205.

[25] Parts of this sections have been published in Piraino, 'Esotericisation and De-esotericisation of Sufism in Italy'.

[26] Sorgenfrei, 'Hidden or Forbidden, Elected or Rejected'.

[27] Saif, 'What Is Islamic Esotericism?'.

[28] Laurant, *L'ésotérisme chrétien en France au XIXe siècle*.

[29] Faivre, *L'ésotérisme*, 10.

transmission.[30] This approach has been defined as functionalist by Wouter Hanegraaff,[31] who challenged Faivre's analysis, proposing instead a historical and genealogical examination.

According to Hanegraaff,[32] esotericism is a 'waste-basket category' that gathers together different fields of knowledge and practices perceived as 'incompatible with the normative concepts of religion, rationality, and science',[33] as they were defined by early Protestant religious thinkers and later by Enlightenment thinkers. This process of othering, which creates a sharp divide between what is rational, scientific and true, and what is irrational, archaic and superstitious, is at the heart of Western esotericism.[34] Hanegraaff's ground-breaking interpretation sheds new light not only on esotericism, but more broadly on the history of Western societies.

That said, Hanegraaff's work created a heated debate that is still ongoing. For example, Marco Pasi stresses that esotericism as a 'historiographic concept' has to sacrifice consistency and effectiveness in the analysis of esoteric contents. Furthermore, according to Pasi, the focus on rejection – on the process of othering – cannot be the only perspective on esoteric themes, because 'this tradition existed independently of rejection and stigma.'[35] Pasi and Olav Hammer[36] prefer a substantive definition of esotericism, returning to and elaborating on Faivre's approach to the field.

Completely different is the critique of Kocku von Stuckrad, who takes Hanegraaff's deconstruction of esotericism to its extreme. Even if these authors agree on the same genealogy for the category of esotericism, as a form of othering rooted in modern history, for von Stuckrad 'esoteric' becomes an adjective to qualify a discourse claiming higher or perfect knowledge: 'a vision of truth as a master-key for answering all questions of humankind'.[37] Von Stuckard's esoteric discourse, based on Western culture, is a counter-discourse in opposition

[30] Faivre, *Accès de l'ésotérisme occidental*.

[31] Hanegraaff, *Esotericism*, 337.

[32] Hanegraaff, *Western Esotericism*; Hanegraaff, *Esotericism and the Academy*.

[33] Hanegraaff, *Western Esotericism*, 13.

[34] Hanegraaff, 'The Globalization of Esotericism'.

[35] Pasi, 'The Problems of Rejected Knowledge', 210.

[36] Hammer, 'Deconstructing "Western Esotericism"'.

[37] von Stuckrad, *Locations of Knowledge in Medieval and Early Modern Europe*, 61.

to mainstream religious narratives. It entails a secrecy capable of bestowing status, prestige and symbolic capital on those who possess perfect knowledge.[38] As has been argued by Michael Stausberg,[39] the merit of this approach is that it moves away from a normative Christianity that defines and rejects esoteric phenomena, and towards a broad religious field where various actors intermingle. This shift has led to heated debate on the possible and necessary expansion of the category of esotericism beyond the Christian European context.[40]

The focus on esotericism as a discourse can also be found in the works of Hugh Urban.[41] By reworking the sociology of secrecy and Georg Simmel's secret societies,[42] Urban studies esotericism as an elitist, sectarian practice, legitimised by hidden knowledge. As an anthropologist–sociologist of religion, I am not inclined towards a conclusive definition of esotericism or Islamic esotericism. Similar to Brannon Ingram, I am more interested in what '"esoteric" does rather than what it is'[43] – that is, how 'esoteric' is understood and its implication in specific social and political spheres. I use esotericism in this context as a heuristic device shedding light on socio-political activities.[44] While I will use mainly the definition of esotericism as discourse, I consider it indispensable to link this analysis to other interpretations ('forms of thought' of Faivre and Pasi, and Hanegraaff's genealogical interpretation) by treating them as complementary.

Esotericism and Sufism: Continuities and Discontinuities

We can see resemblances and points of resonance between Sufism and esotericism, considered as all the forms of thought (after Faivre). Seven analogies stand out: (1) metaphysical knowledge can be compared with *maʿrifa*, or intuitive and spiritual knowledge; (2) perennial philosophy with *fiṭra*, the innate

[38] Urban, 'The Torment of Secrecy'; von Stuckrad, *Locations of Knowledge in Medieval and Early Modern Europe*.

[39] Stausberg, 'What Is *It* All About?'.

[40] Stausberg, 'What Is *It* All About'; Hanegraaff, 'The Globalization of Esotericism'; von Stuckrad, 'Ancient Esotericism, Problematic Assumptions, and Conceptual Trouble'; Faivre, 'Kocku von Stuckrad et la notion d'ésoterisme'.

[41] Urban, 'Elitism and Esotericism'.

[42] Simmel, 'The Sociology of Secrecy and of Secret Societies'.

[43] Ingram, 'René Guénon and the Traditionalist Polemic', 203.

[44] Urban, 'Elitism and Esotericism'; Asprem, 'Beyond the West Towards a New Comparativism in the Study of Esotericism'.

nature or original disposition present before birth, or with *dīn qaiyyama*, right religion; (3) elitism or sectarianism with *khāṣṣa*, the spiritual elite; (4) esoteric initiation with *bayʿa*, the initiatic pact; (5) esoteric transmission with *silsila*, the chain of transmission of sacred knowledge from master to master (going back to the Prophet Muhammad); (6) internal transmutation with *fanāʾ*, the annihilation of the ego in God; and finally (7) the difference between esoteric and exoteric can be compared with the difference between *ẓāhir* and *bāṭin*, visible and hidden teachings respectively.

Other points of resonance can be found based on the approaches of von Stuckrad and Urban. For example, several Sufi masters have laid claim to 'absolute knowledge', which implies elitism and sectarian organisational structures.[45] However, there remain differences and discontinuities that cannot be forgotten. European esotericism is often eclectic, using various sources from Christianity, Egyptian faiths, Jewish Kabbala and pagan religions, whereas Sufism is above all an Islamic phenomenon.

However, we have not yet arrived at the heart of the question: European esotericism is a marginal movement, in both its historical origins and its contemporary expressions. By contrast, Sufism is one of the core areas of Islam, in terms of theology, religion, politics and society. Finally, while esotericism for Wouter J. Hanegraaff and Kocku von Stuckard is 'repressed knowledge', a 'marginal discourse' within Western Christian religious pluralism, Sufism is not a discourse or a narrative, instead embodying a concrete historical–social phenomenon with institutions, hierarchies, practices, doctrines, rituals, and so on. Sufism is anything but marginal, having in reality played, and is continuing to play, a fundamental role in Islamic history. Hence Sufism requires several categories to be adequately described; the label 'esotericism' is only one way to do so.

René Guénon and Sufism[46]

René Guénon can be considered an essential figure both in European esotericism, which gave rise to the stream known as 'Traditionalism',[47] and in the

45 Urban, 'Elitism and Esotericism'.

46 Parts of this section have been published in Piraino, 'L'héritage de René Guénon dans le soufisme du XXIe siècle en France et en Italie'.

47 Sedgwick, *Against the Modern World*; Laurant, *René Guénon*; Bisson, *René Guénon*.

development of Sufism in Europe.[48] It would even be possible to assert that his work possesses a particular form of charismatic authority, related neither to the author himself, since he lived a very quiet life, nor to a specific religious group, which has never existed as such. Rather, his popularity is rooted in his writings. I refer here to what Zoccatelli describes as the 'charisma of the book'.[49]

During my fieldwork in various brotherhoods, Guénon was more often cited than the great Sufi saints. In effect, for numerous disciples, Guénon was a fundamental step in the process of converting to Islam or returning to Muslim religious practice. In addition, his thought led to Traditionalist–Guénonian Sufism, made up exclusively of European converts. This stream reproduces some forms of European esotericism.

René Guénon was born in Blois, France, in 1886, and grew up in a bourgeois Catholic family. In 1904, he moved to Paris, where he attended university and began to frequent the local esoteric milieu. In the course of a few years, he came into contact with occultism, Freemasonry and the Gnostic Church. His encounters with the 'East', including Hinduism and Islamic esotericism, were an important turning point in his life. Hinduism was the subject of his doctoral thesis and his first book,[50] and through the intermediary of the Swedish painter Ivan Aguéli, he joined the Sufi brotherhood Shādiliyya, took the Muslim name of 'Abd al-Wāḥid Yaḥyā, and later moved to Cairo, where he lived until his death in 1951.[51]

Guénon's area of study was especially vast. He studied and wrote commentaries on Greek philosophy, Gnosticism, Christianity, Celtic religion, Judaism and Kabbala, Islamic esotericism, Freemasonry, Hinduism, alchemy and Taoism. His all-embracing approach examined religious, spiritual, metaphysical and social phenomena. It enabled him to write a new history of the world that focused on

[48] Zarcone and Vale, 'Rereadings and Transformations of Sufism in the West'; Piraino, 'Esotericisation and De-esotericisation of Sufism'; Zarcone and Vale, 'Rereadings and Transformations of Sufism in the West'; Le Pape, 'Engagement religieux, engagements politiques'; Bisson, 'Soufisme et tradition'; Piraino, 'L'héritage de René Guénon dans le soufisme du XXIe siècle en France et en Italie'; Piraino, 'Esotericisation and De-esotericisation of Sufism'.

[49] Zoccatelli, 'AAA. Sociologia dell'esoterismo cercasi'.

[50] Guénon, *Introduction générale à l'étude des doctrines hindoues*.

[51] Laurant, *René Guénon*; Bisson, *René Guénon*.

the sacred and challenged twentieth-century mainstream European narratives, based as they were on the supposed superiority of a Western civilisation destined for inexorable progress.[52]

According to Guénon's interpretation, religions are composed of two dimensions, one exoteric, expressed by rituals, dogmas and cosmologies, and the other esoteric/metaphysical, conveying hidden supranational and universal truths: 'Metaphysics is the knowledge of universal principles, upon which all things necessarily depend, directly or indirectly.'[53] These truths or universal metaphysical principles are the reflection of a single 'Primordial Tradition',[54] the essence of all religions. All religions thus share the same metaphysical truth and only differ in their external forms. Among the various religions, some have more rigorously preserved the original primordial mould, whereas others have all but broken out of it, becoming 'simulacra'.

Of course, René Guénon was not the first to conceptualise a common religious source for all humanity. The *philosophia perennis* has been one of the hallmarks of Western esotericism since the Renaissance,[55] but Guénon was the first to connect this conceptualisation of religions with a critique of modernity and Western societies.[56] Guénon elaborated on Hindu eschatology, borrowing the idea of cyclical evolutions. The current cycle in which modern and contemporary societies find themselves is the *Kali Yuga*, the age of discord, or 'the Iron Age', marked by spiritual corruption, violence and destruction.[57] Western modernity is a 'perpetual carnival'[58] where all values are reversed. Guénon criticised materialist and scientific rationalism,[59] but also new religious forms, such as spiritualism, occultism, the Theosophical Society and the Jungian interpretation of religions, which he considered not only as new, but as the 'invisible engine' of corruption in Western societies.[60] According to Guénon's critique of

[52] Bisson, *René Guénon*; Accart, *Guénon ou le renversement des clartés*.

[53] Guénon, *Orient et Occident*, 51.

[54] Guénon, *Introduction générale à l'étude des doctrines hindoues*; Guénon, *Orient et Occident*.

[55] Hanegraaff, *Esotericism and the Academy*; Faivre, *L'ésotérisme*.

[56] Sedgwick, *Against the Modern World*.

[57] Guénon, *La crise du monde moderne*; Guénon, *Orient et Occident*; Guénon, *Le règne de la quantité et les signes du temps*.

[58] Guénon, *Symboles fondamentaux de la science sacrée*, 113.

[59] Guénon, *Le règne de la quantité et les signes du temps*.

[60] Guénon, *Le règne de la quantité et les signes du temps*, chapter 36: 'Pseudo-Initiation'.

modernity, modern political phenomena such as human rights conventions and liberal democracies are the fruit of the 'deification of the human being',[61] which challenges traditional hierarchies: 'This is the negation of all natural hierarchies and the lowering of all knowledge to the level of the limited, vulgar mind.'[62]

Guénon's thought reached a turning point in the 1930s, when the concept of initiation appeared in his work.[63] Esoteric initiation translated into access to supra-rational metaphysical knowledge, transmitted by the master since the creation of human beings. Initiatic transmission was the only path towards preserving this knowledge, an expression of the Primordial Tradition. According to Guénon, initiation also encompassed a dimension of accepting the external expression of religion; to practise Muslim esotericism, one had to be Muslim.[64]

To counter spiritual and material decadence and corruption, Guénon looked towards the East, where, he believed, religions preserved a deeper relationship with the Primordial Tradition, possessing an 'awareness of eternity'.[65] This protected them from the nefarious effects of modernity: 'Even if people from the East are forced to accept material progress to a certain extent, it will never entail a profound change for them.'[66] Ingram aptly describes how Guénon created 'a polarity between East and West that resonated with the Orientalist tradition: the East is anti-modern, medieval, feudal, static, unified, and monolithic, whereas the West is modern, democratic, always changing, and always divided'.[67]

However, this perspective must not be confused with advocating mass conversion. In his private correspondence, published in part, Guénon encouraged those who wrote to him to seek out esotericism not only in Sufism, but in other religions as well.[68] Guénon called for the birth of an elite to mirror metaphysical hierarchies. In particular, this elite would serve to re-establish the balance lost in the profane world: 'The masses, all while benefiting from this

[61] Guénon, *Symboles fondamentaux de la science sacrée*, 322.

[62] Guénon, *Orient et Occident*, 59.

[63] Guénon, *Le symbolisme de la Croix*.

[64] Guénon, *Symboles fondamentaux de la science sacrée*, 322. Guénon, *Aperçus sur l'initiation*.

[65] Guénon, *Orient et Occident*, 95.

[66] Guénon, *Orient et Occident*, 122.

[67] Ingram, 'René Guénon and the Traditionalist Polemic', 205.

[68] Laurant, *René Guénon*.

state of harmony, will not be directly aware of it, as it only concerns the elite.'[69] Nevertheless, according to Guénon, the elite remained strictly associated with an eschatological vision linked to the end of *Kali Yuga*; it prepared for the coming of a new era. Here, the interpretations of the role of the elite differ substantially; some focus on the symbolic aspect, whereas others transform the spiritual elite into a political elite.[70]

Guénon's thought developed between the two world wars, a period characterised by political instability, economic crisis and the perpetual threat of conflict. Europe continued its colonial expansion and considered conquest a natural right, in the name of the supposed superiority of European civilisation over 'primitive populations'. Guénon criticised this colonial vision, which was based on stereotypes of the East and often linked to a positivist paradigm. However, he did not truly step out of this framework, his representation of the East remaining just as monolithic and essentialised.

René Guénon and his intellectual work remain within the framework of Western esotericism for several reasons: first of all, because of his intellectual background and his relations with occultism and Freemasonry;[71] secondly, because of the content of his work (or 'forms of thought' to use Faivre's category),[72] which is identified with *philosophia perennis*, with the esoteric initiation transmitted from master to disciple, and with subtle correspondences that resonate with several esoteric phenomena.[73] Furthermore, as has been argued by Ingram, following on from von Stuckard's approach, Guénon is esoteric because he posited the existence of totalising, absolute knowledge in opposition to a profane understanding of reality. Finally, Guénon could also be labelled esoteric in keeping with Hanegraaff's conceptualisation; he reclaimed metaphysical knowledge rejected by Western societies, and like other esotericists he 'refuse[d] to accept the disappearance of incalculable mystery from the world'.[74]

[69] Guénon, *Orient et Occident*, 195.

[70] Guénon, *Symboles fondamentaux de la science sacrée*, 322.

[71] Sedgwick, *Western Sufism*.

[72] Faivre, *L'ésotérisme*.

[73] Faivre, *L'ésotérisme*; Riffard, *Nouveau dictionnaire de l'ésotérisme*.

[74] Hanegraaff, *Esotericism and the Academy*, 254.

René Guénon's Legacy in European Sufism

While the biographical relationship between Guénon and Sufism is clear, his belonging to Islam and the link to the exoteric dimension are not entirely obvious. We know from historical investigations that Guénon did not carry out Ḥajj (the pilgrimage to Mecca, one of the pillars of Islam), did not learn classical Arabic (the language of the sacred texts), and never became part of the Sufi milieu in Cairo. Guénon explains himself this way:

> I have never embraced the Muslim religion at any more or less recent time, contrary to what some claim, for reasons that escape my comprehension . . . the truth is that I have been affiliated with Islamic initiatic organisations for some thirty years, which is obviously very different.[75]

In 1948, Guénon reiterated this position by explaining that anyone aware of the 'unity of traditions' 'cannot be converted to anything whatsoever'.[76] Similarly, he explained that the exoteric dimension had to be adhered to so esotericism could be understood, and that this entailed spiritual interest rather than true belief. This 'non-conversion conversion' first served to legitimise non-Muslim Guénonians, then to support various interpretations of the relationship between Islam and Sufism.

Starting in the 1930s, the Guénonian interpretation of Sufism gave rise to Guénonian or Traditionalist Sufism, notably within the following brotherhoods: the Maryamiyya (Frithjof Schuon 1907–98), the 'Alāwiyya (Michel Valsan 1907–74, Titius Burckhardt 1908–84) and the Darqāwiyya (Roger Maridort 1903–77). These Sufi brotherhoods, independent and organised completely differently than the originating brotherhoods according to Zarcone,[77] reshaped the foundations of Christian and Masonic esotericism, fostering the intellectualisation and 'elitisation' of Sufism. For example, to participate in the brotherhood, the disciples of the Darqāwiyya of Maridort had to also join a Masonic lodge. In Chapter 6, this book will examine the last Traditionalist brotherhood, the Aḥmadiyya Idrīsiyya Shādhiliyya, founded by 'Abd al-Wāḥid Pallavicini (1926–2017) in Milan in the 1980s.

[75] Cited in Laurant, 'La "non-conversion" de René Guénon (1886–1951)', 134.

[76] Guénon, *Initiation et Réalisation Spirituelle*, 106.

[77] Zarcone and Vale, 'Rereadings and Transformations of Sufism in the West'.

Guénon's legacy has moved beyond the strictly esoteric frame, making him a key figure in the New Age scene (which he would not have appreciated), but also associating him with other spiritual seekers, such as Gurdjieff, Helena Blavatsky, Carlos Castaneda, and so on.[78] A figure who straddled these two worlds is Frithjof Schuon who, after founding his Sufi brotherhood, gradually assimilated the religious practices of Native Americans in search of the primordial experience. While for Guénon, Primordial Tradition was part of a metaphysical history, for Schuon the transcendental unity of religions was within reach.[79]

However, the most significant influence, at least for the purposes of this book, concerns the Islam of those brought up as Muslims. Guénon became a reference point for many children of Algerian and Moroccan migrants, who found in him an intellectual framework. For these disciples, Guénon was not to be understood literally; instead, a symbolic interpretation was called for. For them Guénon was a frame, a guide, or to use the words of his disciples, a 'vade mecum' (Malik, interview, Paris) and 'a pedagogy . . . a new intellectual orientation that changed things a lot' (René, interview, Paris). Guénon 'made it possible to find the words, to clarify what I could already feel in myself, and to define what seeking means, what initiation is, and what it isn't' (Malik, interview, Paris). These adepts are thus Sufi disciples first and Guénonians second:

> I'm not Guénonian, I'm Būdshīshī! Defining yourself as Guénonian in Paris means belonging to a certain cultural milieu. There are people who meet and do a real exegesis of the texts, who know everything by heart and are very critical of everyone (Jamal, interview, Paris).

Some of these disciples have undertaken a spiritual quest leading them to become interested in various religions: 'I looked at various traditions. Islam, or Sufism, was not a priority, so I also looked at others. When I rediscovered Islam, I found it had everything in it' (Tayob, interview, Paris). Another disciple said,

> I looked at most everything except Islam . . . I was really sure [about God], but I didn't know which path to take. [An old man in the train] said to me, 'You'll find your path in Islam', and the fact that a Catholic said that to me left me dumbfounded. He must have been a Guénonian. (Hadi, interview, Paris)

[78] Piraino, 'L'héritage de René Guénon dans le soufisme du XXIe siècle en France et en Italie'.
[79] Schuon, *De l'unité transcendante des religions*.

For many of these Muslims, Sufism is a way of rediscovering Islam, of 'converting back', of breathing new life into a religion with strong cultural and family connotations. For some of them, as for converts, Guénon became an intellectual orientation for starting their spiritual quest.

Similarly, Guénonian thought has enjoyed more or less official recognition by some Sufi brotherhoods in the Maghreb. As one of the former disciples of the Parisian Būdshīshiyya explained to me:

> The question as to whether Guénon was a saint has been settled. Why? Because outside the European Guénonian milieu, my own sheikh, *sīdī* Hamza, when the question was put to him, very clearly responded that Guénon was an *'Arif billāh*, what in Arabic we call someone who has knowledge through God. So *sīdī* Hamza answered a question someone had asked him more than ten years ago. (René, interview, Paris)

Sheikh Khaled Bentounes, of the 'Alāwiyya, wrote the following about Guénon:

> Nearly fifty years ago, René Guénon died in Cairo, discreetly, simply, a man whose work continues to provide food for thought to numerous men and women throughout the East and the West. Many of them have him to thank for awakening in them a spiritual fervour that led them back to Tradition at a time of great confusion, where the quest for a living spirituality remained uncertain. Let us pay homage to this son of the West, a true defender of the Universal Tradition.[80]

The influence of Guénonian traditionalism on Sufism and Islam has worked in both directions; several intellectuals from the Guénonian milieu who practise Sufism have gradually deepened their knowledge of Islamic doctrines and practices. In other words, they have been Islamised. A good example of this process is Michel Valsan (1907–74), who was initiated into Sufism through Guénon and later became the representative of the 'Alāwiyya Sufi brotherhood in Paris. Valsan learned and excelled in Arabic, translating the texts of Ibn 'Arabī. For Valsan, Guénon was the 'infallible compass',[81] a saint who can be credited with introducing the West to Sufism. Nevertheless, Guénon was

[80] Bentounes, *Soufisme l'heritage commun*, 349.

[81] Vâlsan, *L'Islam et la fonction de René Guénon*.

not his only intellectual reference, as Valsan enriched his study of Sufism with other classical authors.

These reciprocal influences have also changed the interpretation of Guénonian thought. The opposition between East and West, along with essentialist stereotypes, have lost their impact; the difference between these two worlds is no longer geographical, but symbolic. Furthermore, due to the participation of several Sufi brotherhoods in interfaith dialogue, and to the civic engagement in both Europe and the Maghreb, some of the criticism of the modern world, while still present, has lost the apocalyptic tone that characterises several of Guénon's works.

New Forms of Spirituality: The Coming of the New Age[82]

The definitions and boundaries of the New Age phenomenon and the 'cultic milieu'[83] are hotly debated in the academic literature.[84] Some have even argued that this category is so shape-shifting that its heuristic value is doubtful.[85] Others have questioned its effectiveness in contemporary societies, arguing that the New Age phenomenon belongs to the past, and that we should now focus on the 'Next Age'.[86] It is my belief that, despite its blurriness, the New Age category can be effective in describing contemporary religious phenomena, with the fundamental precaution of clearly stating how we are using this term.

We can make out two major approaches to this subject: (1) the historic–genealogical approach, aimed at contextualising the phenomena in Europe and North America from the 1960s to the 1980s through identifying fundamental doctrines; and (2) the approach focused on modes of belief, based on the concepts of individualism and the spiritual marketplace. I propose a third reading that considers the New Age as a discourse. As in the case of esotericism, it is not a matter of defining it once and for all, nor of delimiting the

[82] Parts of this section have been published in Piraino, 'Sufism Meets the New Age Discourse: Part 2: An Ethnographic Perspective'; and Piraino, 'Sufism Meets the New Age Discourse: Part 1: A Theoretical Discussion'.

[83] Campbell, 'Clarifying the Cult'.

[84] Lewis and Kemp, *Handbook of New Age*.

[85] Heelas, *The New Age Movement*; Hackett, 'New Age Trends in Nigeria'.

[86] Introvigne and Zoccatelli, *New Agen next Age*.

confines of this phenomenon. What interests me is understanding how New Age phenomena have influenced European Sufism – that is, understanding what these phenomena do, rather than what they are.

Historical Approach

The historical approach, perfectly embodied by Hanegraaff's seminal work,[87] describes the connections between Western esotericism and the New Age, in particular as regards the Theosophical Society of Alice Bailey (1880–1949). Hanegraaff clarifies the New Age, presenting it as a distinct phenomenon, only understandable in its historical context: Europe and North America in the 1960s–80s. The set of religious and spiritual doctrines and practices called New Age cannot be regarded as a new religion, but this term did mark a 'paradigm shift'[88] that rejected 'institutional religions'.[89] It was a new approach to religion, spirituality, culture and society that claimed a revolution was imminent, because 'Western society was corrupt without hope of a cure.'[90] In addition, this new approach questioned 'Enlightenment rationality'.[91] The New Age set of doctrines and practices is characterised by theological blurriness; in keeping with George Chryssides, the New Age phenomenon challenged the concept of religious monopoly employed by global religions, favouring instead a 'syncretic blend' of various ideas.[92] The believer is thus replaced by the spiritual seeker.

Hanegraaff also describes the main, most common doctrines disseminated in New Age culture: (1) channelling (communication between gifted people and spiritual entities); (2) the intertwined relationship between healing and spiritual growth, based on the conception that mind and body are both part of the same reality; (3) neo-paganism; (4) psychologisation of religion and sacralisation of psychology; and (5) reincarnation as a form of evolutionism.[93]

[87] Hanegraaff, *New Age Religion and Western Culture.*

[88] Hackett, 'New Age Trends in Nigeria'; Hanegraaff, *New Age Religion and Western Culture*, 60.

[89] Chryssides, 'Defining the New Age', 9.

[90] Hanegraaff, *New Age Religion and Western Culture*, 27.

[91] Hanegraaff, *New Age Religion and Western Culture*, 42.

[92] Chryssides, 'Defining the New Age', 19.

[93] Hanegraaff, *New Age Religion and Western Culture*; Hanegraaff, 'The New Age Movement and Western Esotericism'.

The historicist approach to Sufi studies is well represented by Mark Sedgwick, who describes how, over the course of the twentieth century, different elements such as the Theosophical Society, Traditionalism, the work of Georges Ivanovich Gurdjieff (1866–1949) and New Age culture have contributed to the shape-shifting phenomenon called 'Western Sufism'.[94] Even if Sedgwick does not offer a specific definition of the New Age, we could argue that for him, the New Age is a cultural and religious milieu that emerged in Europe and North America between the 1960s and 1990s, with ties to the hippie counter-culture movement. In particular, Sedgwick uses the category of New Age Sufism in describing the Dances of Universal Peace of Samuel Lewis (1896–1971) and the Sufi Order International of Inayat-Khan. Both were characterised by universalist doctrines and worship at the expense of Islamic practices and doctrines.[95] This New Age Sufism was later influenced by 'traditional' Sufi leaders, implying a process of re-Islamisation.[96] In the same vein, Marcia Hermansen,[97] Julia Day Howell[98] and Søren Christian Lassen[99] described the interactions between Sufism and the New Age milieu in Indonesia, the United States and Germany. In these contexts, the New Age is understood as a set of doctrines that encompasses Raja Yoga, Reiki, the Celestine Prophecy, crystal healing, and so on. These authors thus explain how Sufi and New Age doctrines came into contact.

Modes of Belief

Another approach to studying the New Age is to focus not on the historical context, nor on the doctrines, but rather on the modes of belief in this era of late capitalism and the market economy. From this perspective, New Age culture

> has become a 'spiritual supermarket' where religious consumers pick and choose the spiritual commodities they desire and use them to create their own spiritual combinations, 'fine-tuned' to their strictly personal needs.[100]

[94] Sedgwick, *Western Sufism.*

[95] Sedgwick, *Western* Sufisim, chapter 13.

[96] Sedgwick, 'The Islamization of Western Sufism after the Early New Age'.

[97] Hermansen, 'What's American about American Sufi Movements?'.

[98] Howell, 'Modernity and Islamic Spirituality in Indonesia's New Sufi Networks'.

[99] Lassen, 'Strategies for Concord'.

[100] Hanegraaff, 'The New Age Movement and Western Esotericism', 47.

This argument has been extensively explored, mainly by sociologists who have stressed the individualistic dimension and the atomisation of social bonds.[101] In this context, spirituality is regarded as one product among others to consume.[102] Sociologists have studied how this focus on individual experience has shaped new religious movements and faiths, characterised by organisational fluidity or even evanescence.[103]

These sociological analyses have polarised into two main positions. Some scholars have stressed New Age nebulosity, inconsistency and 'consumability', downplaying its value compared to different religious phenomena,[104] whereas others have defended the social and religious significance of the New Age phenomenon.[105] Both sides agree that the New Age, more than a mere set of doctrines, is an expression of modern or postmodern religiosity (depending on the use of these terms).

This debate has been brought into the field of Sufi Studies by Patrick Haenni and Raphaël Voix, who offer a specific definition of the New Age.

> 'New Age' is understood here as new modes of belief in which eclecticism dominates and the individual's well-being is the goal of a personal quest at the crossroads of spirituality and psychological therapies.[106]

These scholars describe how the Būdshīshiyya in Morocco has been influenced by New Age religiosity, underlining certain changes in this Sufi brotherhood, such as the accommodation of 'individualism, eclecticism, and relativism' and 'a modern attitude towards religious allegiance', since 'many of these bourgeois Sufi disciples participate in several *ṭarīqa*s simultaneously.'[107]

Marta Dominguez arrives at similar conclusions about the influence of postmodern religiosity on the Būdshīshiyya, proposing a different definition

[101] Lyon, *Jesus in Disneyland*; Possamai, *In Search of New Age Spiritualities*.

[102] Rindfleish, 'Consuming the Self'.

[103] Campbell, 'Clarifying the Cult'; Bainbridge and Stark, 'Client and Audience Cults in America'.

[104] Voas and Bruce, 'The Spiritual Revolution'; Bruce, *God Is Dead*; Carrette and King, *Selling Spirituality*.

[105] Heelas, *The New Age Movement*; Aupers and Houtman, 'Beyond the Spiritual Supermarket'; Hervieu-Léger, 'Le partage du croire religieux dans des sociétés d'individus'.

[106] Haenni and Voix, 'God by All Means . . .', 312.

[107] Haenni and Voix, 'God by All Means . . .', 250–1.

of the New Age phenomenon, comprising: '(a) channelling; (b) healing and spiritual growth; and (c) transpersonal psychology.'[108] The first point implies that some people are able to communicate with metaphysical entities, the second point stresses the fundamental connection between mind and body, and the last point 'may include ecstatic experiences, paranormal perceptions, and "altered states of consciousness"'.[109] By emphasising the New Age dimension in the Būdshīshiyya, these scholars describe the changes undergone by this Sufi brotherhood regarding its relations with religious otherness, religious norms and gender roles. The New Age designation becomes a synonym for modern religiosity, in which these Sufis participate.

Limitations of these Approaches

The historicist approach has the merit of describing specific movements, but it does not offer the instruments to analyse other Sufi phenomena in other historical and geographical contexts, where the boundaries between Islam and the New Age are more blurred. In effect, while Samuel Lewis was baptised 'the New Age in person',[110] leaving no doubt about the entanglements between Sufism and the New Age, it is more difficult to grasp if and how 'orthodox' Sufi brotherhoods with global reach in our times have been influenced by the New Age.

Focusing on the doctrines may reveal distinctions between the 'Old Age' and the New Age. However, while in some cases there is no doubt as to the origin of the doctrines, in others the difference is not at all clear. Furthermore, points of resonance exist between Sufi tradition and New Age culture, in the same way that assonances exist between Western esotericism and Sufism, a fact that facilitates the merging of these various phenomena. First of all, channelling other spiritual realities is similar to religious experiences with the *jinn* and angels that populate Sufi literature.[111] Secondly, alternative medicine has some assonances with prophetic medicine and *Ruqiyya* (which cures concealed illnesses caused by spirits), both of which are widespread in Islamic countries.[112] Thirdly,

[108] Dominguez-Diaz, *Women in Sufism*, 13.

[109] Dominguez-Diaz, 13.

[110] Available at <http://www.gnostic.org/murshidsam/forward.htm> (last accessed 2 November 2023).

[111] El-Zein, *Islam, Arabs, and the Intelligent World of the Jinn*.

[112] Saif, 'Between Medicine and Magic'.

the close relationship between mind and body described by New-Agers resonates with Islamic conceptions of healing and spiritual purification. As for an 'altered state of consciousness', it can be considered one of the pillars of Sufism, where experiential knowledge of God is paramount.[113] The following Islamic–Sufi categories and/or rituals may involve altered states of consciousness: *kashf* (unveiling), *ḥāl* (spiritual state), *'imāra* (divine presence), and *ḥaḍra* (divine presence). Finally, as regards the so-called relativism or universalism of the New Age, we find points of resonance in Sufism, which over the centuries has been influenced by other cultures and religions and, in some cases, has produced syncretic practices.[114] These similarities and points of resonance make distinguishing between the 'Old Age' and the New Age almost impossible.

As regards the modes of belief, the accent on the individual religious experience cannot be the sole criterion in understanding religious and especially mystical phenomena. This emphasis on the individual and intimate experience of God is a pillar of Sufism, but also of Christian mysticism. As has been argued by Danièle Hervieu-Léger, we should distinguish between the religious individualism that has long been part of Christianity and is characterised by the intimate relationship between the believer and God, and modern individualism, which translates into new religious forms characterised by the crises in institutional religions.[115]

Furthermore, identifying the New Age with (post)modern religiosity reduces its explanatory value. Are esotericism and the New Age the same thing? Do liberal and progressive values stem from the New Age? Is ecology the product of the New Age? In my opinion, a category that purports to explain everything loses its heuristic value. Such an approach would reproduce the dichotomy between tradition and modernity, which has been strongly challenged.

By exposing the heuristic limits of the New Age category, I do not wish to imply that we should abandon it; on the contrary, I think we can strengthen it by asking not only what the New Age is, but also what it does. In particular, I am referring to the social interactions and processes within the New Age that are often neglected, but before addressing the idea of the New Age as a 'discourse', I should briefly clarify how I intend to use this word.

[113] Knysh, *Sufism*.

[114] Veinstein and Popovic, *Les Voies d'Allah*; Green, *Sufism*.

[115] Hervieu-Léger, 'Le partage du croire religieux dans des sociétés d'individus'; Hervieu-Léger, *Le pélerin et le converti*.

New Age as Discourse

To propose an alternative reading of the New Age phenomenon as a discourse, I have drawn on the work of Steven Sutcliffe[116] around the New Age, and on the work of von Stuckrad[117] and Urban[118] around esotericism. I will start by describing the New Age as a discourse, then underline how it differs from the esoteric discourse.

Sutcliffe's *Children of the New Age: A History of Spiritual Practices* is the main academic work that considers the New Age as a discourse. In this book, Sutcliffe challenges the conceptualisation of the New Age as a movement, pointing to its historical development from the beginning of the twentieth century with the esoteric and theosophical quest of Alice Bailey (1880–1949). Bailey shaped New Age discourse, which tended to be 'ascetic, puritanical, and other-worldly' and which focused on 'supernaturalistic apocalypticism'.[119] Starting in the 1970s, this exclusive religious discourse developed into 'a humanistic idiom of self-realization in the here-and-now' that was 'emotionally expressive, hedonistic, and firmly this-worldly'[120] implying broad dissemination. This new religious discourse thus became one of several global religious discourses.

Despite the universal afflatus of New Age discourse, which lays claim to a new universal awareness that transcends every religion, Sutcliffe situates this discourse within the Anglo-American context. However, as we have shown, New Age discourse exceeds this geographical and cultural context, merging with other religious phenomena such as Sufism. Drawing on the analysis of Sutcliffe and others mentioned above, I will delineate the key elements of New Age discourse.

The New Age can be understood as a discourse around scattered sacred knowledge spread throughout every religious dimension and into the fields of psychology, psychoanalysis and quantum physics, in a process of sacralising

[116] Sutcliffe, *Children of the New Age*.

[117] von Stuckrad, *Locations of Knowledge in Medieval and Early Modern Europe*; von Stuckrad, 'Esoteric Discourse and the European History of Religion'; von Stuckrad, 'Western Esotericism'.

[118] Urban, 'Elitism and Esotericism'; Urban, 'The Torment of Secrecy'.

[119] Sutcliffe, *Children of the New Age*, 3, 112.

[120] Sutcliffe, *Children of the New Age*, 5, 3.

science. This conceptualisation of religious truth allows and promotes bricolage, which draws on various religious, epistemological and cultural phenomena. This bricolage includes not only doctrines, but also rituals and practices. As for the scattered sacred knowledge, it is now legible for 'those who seek' thanks to a new cosmic awareness – the New Age – that involves all of humankind. The New Age thus makes a universalist claim, as a 'collective development of human potential',[121] and as a 'new consciousness based on a holistic worldview and on the belief in a higher spiritual reality'.[122]

These elements imply a critique of established faiths that challenges and contests the borders of religious identities, doctrines and dogmas, and may even show disdain for 'institutional religion'.[123] Unlike esoteric discourse, New Age discourse is not absolute, limited to an initiated elite, but is 'at your fingertips'; virtually everyone is able to grasp and embody it. This implies that the dialectic of secrecy is not central to New Age discourse, where knowledge is virtually horizontal egalitarian. Spiritual seekers question institutional religions because they seek a more direct relationship with the divine: 'It is time for everyone to become a shaman, a metaphysician, a dream-weaver, a walker between worlds – each in our unique way.'[124] We could add 'a Sufi' to the list.

New Age discourse implies a change in focus, a shift from collective salvation to individual quest. Unlike the ideal types of 'convert', 'member' or 'congregant', 'the seeker is at the centre', in the sense that the spiritual quest is customised and adapted to suite their desires, needs and career plans. Seekers do not have to give anything up to enjoy their quest, meaning that they are 'largely preoccupied with the rational–functional application of spiritual skills'. This problem-solving approach emphasises 'short- and medium-term achievement of goals and the active creation of meaning in everyday life'.[125] An 'empiricised' spirituality such as this one has to prove helpful, rather than ring true.

All these elements contribute to shaping the organisational structures. New Age discourse moulds small groups with loose commitment that differ from

[121] York, *The Emerging Network*, 2.

[122] Höllinger, 'Does the Counter-cultural Character of New Age Persist?', 62.

[123] Sutcliffe, *Children of the New Age*, 12.

[124] Edwards, *Stepping Into The Magic*, 192.

[125] Sutcliffe, *Children of the New Age*, 221.

the ideal types of 'denomination' and 'sect'.[126] In fact, seekers can be involved in different religious movements, deciding on their own level of involvement. Of course, this does not imply the absence of power, which is still part of the equation, only instead of being held by professionals in institutional religious traditions, it belongs to new religious figures. This results in power struggles shaped by the long-standing rivalries among New Age groups.

To summarise, the key elements of New Age discourse are:

1. A discourse around scattered sacred knowledge that spreads to every religious dimension and beyond
2. Bricolage: reformulation of ideas and practices
3. A new awareness – a universalist claim
4. Contesting institutional religions – challenging religious identities, doctrines and dogmas
5. Egalitarian – horizontal
6. The seeker is at the centre: customisation/'empiricisation'
7. Small groups – loose commitment

New Age and esoteric discourses have important points in common. First of all, they share a claim to knowledge that presents an alternative to that offered by institutional religions, the dogmas and authorities of which they thus challenge. Secondly, neither of them is limited to specific religious traditions; they instead choose between various phenomena, creating an eclectic understanding of reality.

The most significant difference between these two discourses concerns the way religious truth is conceived of. In the esoteric discourse, religious knowledge is absolute, hidden and secret, limited to an initiated elite. In New Age discourse the reverse is true: each individual is their own master. These different conceptualisations of knowledge and power imply different organisational structures. Esoteric discourse favours a sectarian organisation fuelled by strong tension with the surrounding society and intense engagement, whereas New Age discourse favours the creation of small porous groups with loose commitment.

[126] Stark and Bainbridge, 'Of Churches, Sects, and Cults'.

Table 2.1 The key elements of the esoteric and New Age discourses

Esoteric discourse	New Age discourse
Absolute knowledge that is secret and hidden	Scattered knowledge available to everyone
	Bricolage
	A new awareness – a universalist claim
An alternative reading of institutional religions	Contesting institutional religions
Elitist	Egalitarian – horizontal
Knowledge is at the centre	The seeker is at the centre: customisation/'empiricisation'
Tense relations with society Sectarian organisational structures	Small groups – loose commitment

Sufism Meets New Age Discourse

Examples of the crossroads between Sufism, New Age discourse and esoteric discourse can be seen in the religious movements of George Ivanovich Gurdjieff and Idries Shah. Gurdjieff (1986–49), of Greek-Armenian descent, grew up in Kars in Transcaucasia, a region rich with diverse ethnicities, cultures and religions. The details of the first part of his life are clouded by the hagiography,[127] but what is certain is that his spiritual quest led him to travel across Asia. In 1921, already a refugee of the civil war, he founded the Institute for the Harmonious Development of Man in Russia, but fighting forced him to move to Georgia, then Turkey, and later England. He finally settled in France, close to Fontainebleau, where he remained until the end of his life. However, his travels did not end with his moving to France; in 1923, he left for an American tour with his 'dervish dances'.

Gurdjieff's thought can be partially understood through his books, rich in allegories, and through the works of his students, which nonetheless present non-negligible differences. As one of his students commented, 'Gurdjieff was a very great enigma in more ways than one. First and most obvious is the fact that no two people who knew him would agree as to who and what he was.'[128]

[127] Ouspensky, *In Search of the Miraculous Fragments of an Unknown Teaching*; Gurdjieff, *Meetings with Remarkable Men*; Bennett, *Witness.*

[128] Bennett, *Gurdjieff: A Very Great Enigma*, 7.

Ouspensky defined Gurdjieffian thought as 'esoteric Christianity',[129] whereas for Bennett, 'Gurdjieff was more than anything a Sufi.'[130] For Idries Shah, 'Gurdjieff's books were full of clandestine citations.'[131]

We should, however, try to elucidate this enigma. Gurdjieff's thought is based on seeking an awakening of self-awareness through specific practices. It views humans as 'asleep', machines without consciousness. Gurdjieff also developed the nine rules of the Naqshbandiyya, such as the consciousness of time and the repetition of divine names. This represents nothing new under the sun of spirituality, but matters become much more complex when examining Gurdjieff's theology and cosmology from the perspective of his student Ouspensky. His cosmology is very far from both Christianity and Islam, seeming closer to some Gnostic currents, but most of all, it reflects the originality of Gurdjieff's thought.

According to Ouspensky's Gurdjieff, there are various laws that govern the world, such as the 'Law of Three', which resembles the dialectical triad (thesis, antithesis, synthesis) and the 'Law of the Octave', which, through the musical scale, explains the continuity and discontinuity of reality. Moreover, human beings are subject to material and astral forces. But the real break from monotheistic religious traditions occurs around immortality. The 'machine man' in his unaware state 'has no future of any kind; he is buried and that is all. Dust returns to dust.'[132] Gurdjieff shocked his students by saying 'Nothing is immortal, even God is mortal. But there is a great difference between man and God, and, of course, God is mortal in a different way to man.'[133]

Gurdjieff's 'work', called the 'fourth way' by Ouspensky,[134] differs from that of the *faqīr* (asceticism), the monk (mystical rapture) and the yogi (intellectual quest). Gurdjieff also called it the path of the 'sly man', which underscores the detachment from all traditional religious forms. The accent is on the method's effectiveness and scientificity.[135] To add to that, Gurdjieffian thought seems to open the door to questioning religious morality; he himself was not looking

[129] Ouspensky, *In Search of the Miraculous Fragments of an Unknown Teaching*, 116.

[130] Bennett, *Gurdjieff: Making a New World*, 88.

[131] Shah, *The Way of the Sufi*, 40.

[132] Ouspensky, *In Search of the Miraculous Fragments of an Unknown Teaching*, 39.

[133] Ouspensky, *In Search of the Miraculous Fragments of an Unknown Teaching* 104.

[134] Ouspensky, *The Fourth Way*.

[135] Dickson, *Living Sufism in North America*.

for any form of saintliness, nor did he present himself as a saint. He affirmed, 'When crystallization [spiritual purification], is achieved renunciations, privations, and sacrifices are no longer necessary. Then a man may have everything he wants. There are no longer any laws for him, he is a law unto himself.'[136] The origins of his esoteric knowledge remain unknown, his thought like his life resembling a mosaic of various experiences.

This brings us to the heart of the question: is this Sufism, or rather something 'Sufistic'? As we have seen, Shah and Bennett expressed no doubts about the Sufi origin of his teachings. Gurdjieff himself claimed he acquired his knowledge from the Sarmoung Sufi brotherhood.[137] However, this brotherhood's name exists only in Gurdjieff's books, probably for pedagogical purposes. What then remains of Sufism in Gurdjieff's thought? We can find similarities between the dance of the 'whirling dervishes' and Gurdjieff's movements, and between his breathing exercises and Sufi *dhikr*, but given all the differences we have enumerated, qualifying Gurdjieff as Sufi would be an error.

And yet, how did the relationship between Gurdjieff and Sufism arise? First of all, the discourse is reflexive and circular: de-Islamised Sufis, namely Shah, Bennett, Coleman Barks, Murat Yagan and Samuel Lewis, reciprocally cite each other, creating and strengthening a certain idea of Sufism. Secondly, referring to Sufism may have been a way to gain legitimacy in the religious field, to certify the authenticity of their quest. Furthermore, the Naqshbandiyya *ṭarīqa*, in which we will clearly see the New Age influence, has acknowledged a partial affiliation with Gurdjieff, and some of its masters teach the enneagram (discussed in Chapter 5). In other words, it has appropriated Gurdjieff's legacy. Philippe de Vos, one of the Parisian Naqshbandi leaders, recounts the words of Sheikh Abdellah al-Daghestani, Sheikh Nāzim's master, addressed to Gurdjieff:

> Our coming together is blessed, but keep it a secret in your heart and divulge it to no one. 'Abd an-Nûr is your name with us. You are free to either stay or go, according to what your possibilities allow you. You are always welcome among us, having obtained security in the Divine Presence. May God bless you and give you strength in your work.[138]

136 Ouspensky, *In Search of the Miraculous Fragments of an Unknown Teaching*, 40.

137 Gurdjieff, *Meetings with Remarkable Men*.

138 Vos, *Genèse de la sagesse soufie*, 153.

De Vos also tells us that Gurdjieff transmitted his knowledge without permission from the sheikh, 'which undoubtedly explains some of his misadventures',[139] notably a serious car accident. Then there is the enneagram which, according to some Naqshbandi disciples, is a secret Naqshbandi Sufi technique that Gurdjieff disseminated. Other disciples consider the enneagram a Gurdjieffian invention unrelated to Sufism, but most have nothing to say about this technique and do not practise it. What is certain is that many Gurdjieffians have shown strong interest in Sufism, especially the Naqshbandiyya *ṭarīqa*. During my fieldwork, I met several disciples who began in Gurdjieffian groups or who participate in them as well as in Sufi brotherhoods. Damrel[140] confirms this, describing how, when Sheikh Nāzim arrived in London in 1974, many of the disciples of Bennett, who had recently died, joined the Naqshbandiyya Ḥaqqāniyya.

Idries Shah (1924–96), the son of a Scottish mother and an Indian Muslim father, grew up in England and was educated there. In 1956, he published his first work, *Oriental Magic*,[141] but his notoriety developed in the following decade, after he founded in 1960 the publishing house Octagon and released, in 1964, *The Sufis*,[142] which was very successful. Shah became the most widely read 'Western Sufi' of the twentieth century, with fifteen million copies sold.[143]

In the early 1960s, Shah met Gurdjieff's disciples,[144] particularly Bennett, who was in the process of delving into the Sufi sources of his deceased master's teachings. Shah succeeded in convincing Bennett that he was an emissary of the famous (but allegorical) Sarmoung Sufi monastery[145] and became the head of this group of Gurdjieffians. This experience was not a positive one for Bennett's group. They found themselves evicted from their property, which was then sold. Twenty years later, James Moore, one of Bennett's disciples, said they felt cheated.[146] And the controversies around Shah did not stop there.

139 Vos, *L'ennéagramme*, 28.

140 Damrel, 'Aspects of the Naqshbandi-Haqqani Order in North America'.

141 Shah, *Oriental Magic*.

142 Shah, *The Sufis*.

143 Sedgwick, *Western Sufism*, 209.

144 Pittman, *Classical Spirituality in Contemporary America*.

145 Bennett, *Witness*.

146 Moore, 'Neo-Sufism'.

For example, Shah presented himself as the master of an Asian brotherhood but did not specify which one. What is more, he claimed he was of Sharifian origin and thus a descendant of the Prophet Muhammad. Another controversy concerned a famous text, *Rubāʿiyāt* of ʿUmar Khayyām, which the Shah family had supposedly possessed for 800 years but had never revealed, which suggests it was a fake.[147]

The Sufism embodied by Shah is a Sufism without religious norms and practices, focused only on direct religious experience. In effect, Shah's Sufism is not a purification process in Islam, but mystical knowledge of humanity. Like the invisible masters of the theosophist Helena Blavatsky, for Shah the sources of sacred knowledge were hidden; thus, official Sufi institutions and scholars were of no interest to him. On the contrary, he adopted a truly antinomic posture, because he considered religious norms, traditional authority and cultural dimensions to be obstacles to the spiritual quest.

> Though commonly mistaken for a Moslem sect, the Sufis are at home in all religions: just as the 'Free and Accepted Masons' lay before them in their Lodge whatever sacred book – whether Bible, Koran, or Torah – is accepted by the temporal State. If they call Islam the 'shell' of Sufism, this is because they believe Sufism to be the secret teaching within all religions.[148]

This Sufism is non-confessional, based on the individual, as opposed to any religious law, norm or practice. Even Sufi rituals become automatic processes without value.[149] Shah's specificity lies not only in his doctrines but also in his practices. He underscored the therapeutic dimension of the stories–parables of Sufism and its surprising anecdotes. Shah thus transformed Mulla Nasreddin,[150] an allegorical figure in Islamic folklore known for his foolish acts, into a Sufi master who never existed. Finally, Shah showed a kind of creativity by appropriating (Gurdjieff), elaborating on (Mulla Nasreddin) and inventing ('Umar Khayyām) a Sufi tradition, which calls to mind the complex relationship between 'bricolage' and cultural 'poaching'.[151]

147 Elwell-Sutton, 'Sufism and Pseudo-Sufism'.

148 Shah, *The Sufis*, vi.

149 Shah, *Learning How to Learn*, 276.

150 Shah, *The Exploits of the Incomparable Mulla Nasrudin*.

151 Mary, 'En finir avec le bricolage . . .?'; Hervieu-Léger, 'Bricolage vaut-il dissémination?'.

Robert Ornstein, Shah's *khalīfa* in the United States and a researcher at Stanford University, translated the therapeutic dimension of Sufism into academic language. His book, *The Psychology of Consciousness*,[152] met with enthusiasm among some currents of American psychology.[153] Shah and his non-Islamic therapeutic Sufism has also had several admirers among artists and intellectuals. However, Shah has been severely criticised by academics such as Laurence Paul Elwell-Sutton, a professor at the University of Edinburgh who described Shah's works as pseudo-Sufism, centred on human beings rather than God.[154]

While the protagonists described here, including Gurdjieff and Shah, belong to the twentieth century, they remain relevant today. For example, the American poet Coleman Barks, a translator who has popularised and 'de-Islamized'[155] Rumi in English, acknowledges in his books the most important authors of this Sufism: Georges Ivanovich Gurdjieff, Idries Shah, Vilayat Inayat-Khan, Meher Baba and Sam Lewis.[156]

De-Islamisation is not the only common thread in these movements. Shah and Gurdjieff – like others not mentioned here[157] – made the religious norms, morality and authorities of Islam and Sufism into topics open to discussion. They went so far as to consider Sufi and Islamic orthodoxies as obstacles to spiritual realisation. A third common element lies in syncretism and eclecticism, which enabled these authors to develop and invent Sufi tradition without the constraints of tradition and the limitations of religious identities. Furthermore, in this de-Islamised New Age Sufism, the universal is not a vision of religious otherness, but can be personally experienced, here and now.

The experience of universalist religion, whether through the sly method of Gurdjieff, the psychology of Shah or the universalist faith of Inayat-Khan, leads to creating new religious forms with their doctrines, rituals and organisational structures. These actors no longer participate in transmitting a Sufi tradition, becoming actual religious creators.

152 Ornstein, *The Psychology of Consciousness*.

153 Hermansen, 'What's American about American Sufi Movements?'.

154 Elwell-Sutton, 'Sufism and Pseudo-Sufism'.

155 Irwin, 'Global Rumi'.

156 Barks, *Rumi: The Big Red Book*, 486.

157 Dickson, *Living Sufism in North America*.

The influence of New Age discourse on Sufism can also be understood through literature.[158] Doris Lessing is the most significant example. Winner of the Nobel Prize in Literature and a student of Shah, she contributed to bringing Sufism to the mainstream public. Lessing's novels and Shah's books influenced another author of best-selling spiritual novels: Paulo Coelho. In his books *Veronika Decides to Die* and *The Alchemist*,[159] the Brazilian author expresses the search for a sacred universal wisdom, which sometimes takes inspiration from, and uses expressive forms of de-Islamised Sufism.[160] This universal wisdom also supposedly exists in the works of Khalil Gibran, a Christian of Lebanese origin, considered in Europe and the United States as a classic figure of contemporary Sufism.[161]

As in the case of esotericism, New Age discourse in contemporary Sufism not only influences the creation of a new Sufism; it is also becoming widespread in various milieus, including the most orthodox. Many aspiring disciples in Europe come to traditional Sufism through the books of New Age Sufi authors, but in a way that does not disturb the traditional *ṭarīqa*. In this book, I do not cover de-Islamised Sufi brotherhoods, but we will see how the New Age influences brotherhoods considered to be orthodox (see Chapter 5).

Religionism: Between Academic Field and Religious Movement

The works of French intellectuals such as Louis Massignon, Henry Corbin, Eva de Vitray-Meyerovitch, and several others have gone beyond the academic frame and extended their influence to European Sufism. It is thus not surprising to come across European Sufi disciples who have embarked on Corbin's philosophical phenomenological path and reached its final stage, Sufi metaphysics, or to come across Moroccans who came to France to study at EHESS (School for Advanced Studies in the Social Sciences) and discovered Sufism through the books of Eva de Vitray-Meyerovitch. Furthermore, it is not

158 Sedgwick, 'The Reception of Sufi and Neo-Sufi Literature'.

159 Coelho, *Veronika décide de mourir*; Coelho, *L'alchimiste*.

160 For more details see Sedgwick, 'The Reception of Sufi and Neo-Sufi Literature'.

161 One need only enter 'Khalil Gibran Sufism' into a search engine to find various sites that speak to this point. The website Sufi Books lists his books among the classics of Sufism. Available at <http://sufibooks.info/2010/06/kahlil-gibran-poet-of-the-heart/> (last accessed 2 November 2023).

surprising for disciples studying Sufi metaphysics at EPHE (prestigious French higher education institution known for its religious studies programmes) to discuss the courses of Pierre Lory and Christian Jambet (heirs of Massignon and Corbin). This situation creates a paradoxical circle whereby the sociologist (myself), the research subjects (Sufis) and university professors study and study themselves.

The epistemological syncretism between the human sciences and the religious discourses of Massignon and Corbin are part of a movement called 'Religionism' by Hanegraaff, and more commonly known as the intellectual current that originated with Eranos.[162] Religionism is

> rooted in the impossible dream of a 'history of truth'. It can be defined as a project to explore historical sources in search of what is eternal and universal. The paradoxical nature of such an enterprise is obvious, and at least in its most sophisticated representatives, this sometimes gives Religionism an intellectual audacity that borders on heroism.[163]

Eranos arose from gatherings organised by Olga Fröbe-Kapyten (1881–1962) from 1933 to 1962[164] at Lake Maggiore in Ascona, Switzerland. These gatherings focused on spirituality, myth and symbology, bringing together the era's most eminent intellectuals, such as Heinrich Zimmer (1890–1943), Martin Buber (1878–1965), Raffaele Pettazzoni (1883–1965), Gershom Scholem (1897–1982), Daisetsu Teitarō Suzuki (1870–1966) Erwin Schrödinger (1887–1961), Mircea Eliade (1907–1986), Gilbert Durand (1921–2012), Antoine Faivre (1934–2021) and, of course, 'our' Louis Massignon and Henry Corbin.

Eranos's intellectual roots can be traced back to the German romanticism of Friedrich Schelling (1775–1854), but its guiding figures were Rudolf Otto (1869–1937), a theologian, and Carl Gustav Jung (1875–1961), a psychoanalyst, both interested, for different reasons, in establishing a comparative and unifying theory of religious phenomena. In particular, Jung set the language and the frame for several Eranos intellectuals by forging a form of psychoanalysis not intended as a separate discipline, but as the basis of all human and social

162 Hakl, *Eranos*; Wasserstrom, *Religion after Religion*.

163 Hanegraaff, *Esotericism and the Academy*, 296.

164 Gatherings that continue to this day but with a different focus.

sciences, including the history of religions.[165] Religious symbology was thus considered a tool for individual psychological and spiritual paths as well as for contemporary societies, as the individual unconscious is reflected in the collective unconscious.[166]

In early twentieth-century Europe, religious subjects, notably mystico-esoteric subjects, were less and less present in academic debates, swept away by a secularisation that was supposedly inevitable in the name of linear progress, whatever its form (positivist, Marxist or liberal). This made religion a subject of interest only for Orientalists, to better understand and dominate Eastern and African populations in the colonial empires.[167]

Eranos intellectuals were opposed both to the dogma of Western civilisation's superiority compared to other religious traditions, and to the disappearance of religious phenomena and mystery from the world. According to them, and in Jungian language, the religio-mythical dimension could only be eliminated from human societies through unpredictable resurgences of violence, such as the frenzy of war.

While most Eranos intellectuals agreed with the criticism that the excessive power of rationalist thinking undermined mythical language, and found fault with secularisation, Marxism and existentialism, this movement cannot be considered as simply anti-modernist. In effect, Eranos intellectuals did not advocate a return to tradition and religious orthodoxy as opposed to modernity.[168] On the contrary, they focused especially on marginal religious phenomena, often considered heretical. In addition, Eranos intellectuals converged in the hope of a different future where historical, psychological, philosophical and theological forms of knowledge could enter into dialogue. Finally, Eranos intellectuals represented the dominant current in the history of religions until the 1990s, working in the most prestigious universities, publishing in the major publishing houses, and enjoying the generous patronage of the Mellon Foundation.

Eranos intellectuals did not limit themselves to commenting on or analysing religious phenomena in their scientific frameworks, also acting as interpreters

165 Shamdasani, *Jung and the Making of Modern Psychology*.

166 Jung, *Collected Works of C. G. Jung, Volume 7*.

167 Said, *Orientalism*.

168 Wasserstrom, *Religion after Religion*.

and restorers of the religious message. More than mere historians or philologists, they were, to a degree, mystics and Gnostics, the bearers of higher sacred knowledge.[169] They did not content themselves with a description of religious phenomena, aiming instead to arrive at the essences of religions – an impossible aspiration, a 'heroic mission'.[170] This was heightened by a strong sense of eschatology.[171] However, unlike the apocalyptic Guénonian eschatology, their hope was a transformation of humanity, in the sense that their research might found a new humanism.

This higher knowledge at times sterilised the historiographic or sociological discussion, given that these intellectuals had a privileged relationship with their subjects of study: al-Ḥallāj was Massignon's spiritual master, as Suhrawardī was Corbin's. This criticism aside, philological and genealogical analyses were conducted alongside the study of correspondences, analogies and synchronicities, initiating discussion around the principle of causality. Intellectual deduction was accompanied by supra-intellectual intuition, expressed through poetry, visions and theophanies.

In this approach, there were no religious borders, or dogmas, or norms. Religious symbols were considered autonomous, beyond the frames of religious belonging, with intrinsic powers that were signs of another ontological dimension.[172] Monotheisms as well as polytheisms participated in the expression of a sacred Beyond, of *philosophia perennis*, or of the collective unconscious. Scholem's expression – 'my secularism is not secular'[173] – indicates the distance taken, from both religious orthodoxy and secularisation, in the study of religious phenomena.

While the quality of the magistral analyses and translations of Eastern works by Eranos intellectuals cannot be contested, their limitations from an academic standpoint cannot be ignored, even though these limitations are not covered here for reasons of concision. Once again, what interests us is the influence on Sufism in Europe.

[169] Hanegraaff, *Esotericism and the Academy*, 311.

[170] Mosès, *L'ange de l'histoire*.

[171] Hakl, *Eranos*; Hanegraaff, *Esotericism and the Academy*.

[172] Wasserstrom, *Religion after Religion*, 90.

[173] Scholem, *On Jews and Judaism in Crisis*, 46.

Louis Massignon

Louis Massignon (1883–1962) was an eclectic figure. A professor at the College of France (higher education research and teaching establishment) with a military background, he was also a diplomat and a spiritual figure sometimes seen as a saint.[174] In his youth, he was an emissary of French colonialism, but later he became a detractor of the so-called French mission to civilise. Massignon can be included among the fathers of French and European Islamic Studies, having conducted novel research and developed refined linguistic and philological knowledge of Arabic. Massignon never set his spiritual quest in opposition to the social sciences, unlike many of his Eranos colleagues, but he did share with them a penchant for heretical figures.

Massignon considered himself 'at the crossroads, in the field of spiritual contact between Christianity and Islam'.[175] Pope Pius XI grasped this liminality between Islam and Christianity, qualifying Massignon as a 'Muslim Catholic',[176] in the same way that Professor Ibrāhīm Madkūr (1902–95) of Al-Azhar University described him as 'the greatest Muslim among Christians and the greatest Christian among Muslims'.[177]

A spiritual, psychological and physical crisis struck Massignon in 1909 when he was in Iraq conducting fieldwork. He was accused of spying but was saved by his Muslim hosts, who risked their lives for him. This unexpected gesture of hospitality was concomitant with 'La visitation de l'Étranger' (Visitation of the Foreigner) and the 'tout Autre' (Complete Other) (probably a reworking of the category of Rudolf Otto and Karl Barth[178]), which grew out of the fundamental impact these events had on him. He viewed Islam and Christianity as interwoven, in that his conversion to Catholicism was realised through the 'mirror of Islam'[179] – that is, Muslims played a role in the Socratic method by which he rediscovered Christian faith.

[174] Pénicaud, *Louis Massignon*.

[175] Moncelon, 'Sous le signe d'Abraham'.

[176] Pénicaud, *Louis Massignon*, 16.

[177] Pénicaud, *Louis Massignon*, 9.

[178] Raphael, *Rudolf Otto and the Concept of Holiness*.

[179] Pénicaud, *Louis Massignon*, 74.

Starting from this reflective conversion, Massignon developed a 'religion of hospitality', a moment of knowing and sharing in otherness. He advocated a form of universalism whose guiding figure was Abraham.[180] In this way, Massignon focused on the convergences between Abrahamic religions, both in his scientific research and his spiritual life. In 1934, he founded with Mary Kahil in Alexandria the prayer group Badaliya, which was dedicated to peace between Muslims and Christians, and which spread across Europe and the United States. In 1954, he organised an interreligious pilgrimage to the city of Vieux-Marché (Brittany) where the local Catholic worship of seven saints ideally aligned with the Seven Sleepers of Ephesus mentioned in the eighteenth sura of the Qur'an. Hence Sidney Griffith's conclusion that Massignon was 'perhaps the single most influential figure in regard to the church's relationship with Islam'.[181]

> May we never tire of repeating that Christians, Jews, and Muslims must pray together for the coming of this much-desired peace, for which we have waited so long. Any attempt at agreement in the economic or even the cultural field, if it is not based on a sincere movement of hearts united in the Faith of the God of Abraham, the father of all believers, will only serve to frighten the Third World and relegate it to the camp of professional Atheists.[182]

For Massignon, these convergences between monotheistic religions did not imply the foundation of a new syncretic religion that would only find its sublimation in the eschatological moment. On the contrary, Massignon remained a Catholic loyal to the Catholic Church, without defying its norms, doctrines or dogmas. This put him at a remove from several Eranos intellectuals, who took their distance from official religions. Nonetheless, a degree of ambiguity subsists concerning his liminal position between Islam and Christianity. For example, Massignon considered the Qur'an as non-created divine speech and fasted in a manner very similar to Ramadan. In addition, he recited *al-fātiḥa*, the first sura of the Qur'an, while facing the crucifix during the Badaliya prayer. This ambiguity was not transmitted to his disciples Vincent Monteil and Eva de Vitray-Meyerovitch, who converted to Islam while continuing the quest, both scientific and spiritual, of their master.

180 Massignon, *Les trois prières d'Abraham*.

181 Griffith, 'Sharing the Faith of Abraham', 193.

182 Massignon, *Sur l'Islam*, 127.

Massignon's liminal position, like the centrality of the mystical quest, was reflected in his academic analyses. For example, the Sufi al-Ḥallāj was not merely the subject of his doctoral research; he became a spiritual master who was present, capable of influencing him across the distance of a thousand years. Their proximity led Massignon to Christianise al-Ḥallāj who, according to this initial analysis, died as a Catholic. Massignon later abandoned this analysis to recognise al-Ḥallāj's Islamicness and, more generally, to recognise the Qur'anic sources of Sufism in an era – that of Orientalism in the twentieth century – where Sufism was often reduced to exogenous influences (Zoroastrianism, Christianity, Gnosticism, Hinduism, Neoplatonism, and so on).[183]

Massignon's impact was probably more direct on Islamophilic Catholics than on Muslims. However, it should be noted that his works on al-Ḥallāj remain a reference point for all Francophones, including Muslims, as has been publicly recognised by Skali, the Būdshīshī intellectual,[184] and Abdelhafid Benchouk, a local Naqshbandi leader. A further sign of his legacy is the Islamo-Christian Seven Sleepers pilgrimage, which he founded and in which Sufi 'Alāwī disciples participate regularly. Finally, Massignon contributed in his own way to developing a universalist discourse centred on hospitality which, as we have seen, is a recurring theme in European Sufism.

Henry Corbin

Henry Corbin (1903–78), a student of Louis Massignon and Étienne Gilson (1884–1978), was a French philosopher, philologist and translator. In 1954, Corbin succeeded his master and friend Massignon as research director at EPHE in Islamic Studies, inheriting from Massignon his 'soul of fire'[185] – that is, a passion for research on religious phenomena so far beyond the historiographic frame and categories that it turned into a mystical quest. Corbin was also affiliated with the French Institute of Istanbul and founded the Iranology department at the French Institute of Tehran. In 1974, he founded a research centre for comparative religions in Jerusalem.[186]

183 Rocalve, *Louis Massignon et l'islam*; Laude, *Pathways to an Inner Islam*.

184 Skali, 'La passion de Hallâj', *Le Matin.ma*, 22 May 2020. Available at <http://www.lematin.ma> (last accessed 2 November 2023).

185 Corbin and Jambet, 'Post-scriptum biographique à un entretien philosophique', 41.

186 Granger, 'In Mémoriam Henry Corbin'.

His interests ranged from Christian mysticism (Meister Eckhart, 1260–1328; Emmanuel Swedenborg, 1688–1772) to European philosophy (Friedrich Hegel, 1770–1831; Edmund Husserl, 1859–1938; Martin Heidegger, 1889–1976), but it was in the translation and interpretation of Sufi works,[187] Islamic philosophy[188] and Shiite spirituality[189] that Corbin's thought reached its summit.[190] However, it is impossible to distinguish between Corbin's interest in European philosophy and his interest in Iranian metaphysics, from a chronological or epistemological viewpoint. In fact, Corbin saw Husserl, Heidegger, Ibn 'Arabī and Suhrawardī as part of the same discourse on existence.

As for most Eranos intellectuals, the tension between scientific research and the Gnostic quest was probably one of the drivers of Corbin's intellectual life. He was more than the point of reference for French Islamic studies; in effect, '[Corbin] was not averse to wearing the "metaphysician's hat" on some occasions, or even the hat of the "Gnostic" or the "theosopher".'[191] As in the case of Massignon's al-Ḥallāj, Suhrawardī was not only an object of study, but an invisible master.

Unlike Massignon, Corbin considered historiographic–sociological analysis to be opposed to profound metaphysical comprehension. According to him, the social sciences were destined for arid reductionism. This criticism is also found in Guénon's writings, but in Corbin's case, it did not imply the idealisation of an alternative history relative to its official equivalent.[192] The opposition lay between social facts, as ephemeral contingencies, and transhistorical and atemporal essences.

In Corbin's works, we can see the influence of Jungian psychoanalysis. For the French theosopher, religious symbols were not 'dead signs', anchored in specific historical contexts, but were always alive, imbued with transformative power in communication with transcendence.[193]

[187] Corbin, *L'imagination créatrice dans le soufisme d'Ibn Arabi*.

[188] Corbin, *Histoire de la philosophie islamique*.

[189] Corbin, *L'homme de lumière dans le soufisme iranien*.

[190] Jambet, 'Le soufisme entre Louis Massignon et Henry Corbin'.

[191] Bisson, *René Guénon*, 403.

[192] Bisson, *René Guénon*.

[193] Jung, *Reponse à Job*.

Syncretic thought that harmonises philosophies, religions and esotericisms is not an absolute novelty in the history of Islam. Corbin was following his spiritual master Suhrawardī who, in twelfth-century Persia, tried to bring Islam, Zoroastrianism and Neoplatonic philosophy into convergence. Studying other Muslim thinkers, such as Mulla Sadrā (1571–1640) and Ibn Ṭufayl (1105–85), Corbin showed the interdependence between philosophical and religious thought, and he went so far as to ascribe to philosophers 'the rank of minor prophets'.[194]

Unlike others, Corbin was not interested in founding a religious movement, seeking instead to find correspondences and analogies between various symbols, religions and discourses. That said, for Corbin, as for most of the authors cited in this chapter, the discourse on the correspondences and convergences between different religions found its full expression in an eschatological tension. In his quest for correspondences and analogies, Corbin identified universal archetypes that could be found across different religions: angels, paths to purification, the imaginal interstitial world between mind and body, sacred texts, the perfect human, the prophets, eschatology, *philosophia perennis*, and so on.

One of the specificities of Corbin's thought is its focus on subjective experience, namely personal imagination, beyond the borders of religious orthodoxies. For Corbin, *individuum est ineffabile* – that is, religion, as a collective phenomenon, is secondary to personal transcendent experiences: '[T]he vertical dimension is individualisation and sacralisation, whereas the horizontal dimension is collectivisation and secularisation.'[195] The pre-eminence of the individual over the collective encompasses an opposition to religious norms, the so-called 'legalism'[196] that hides true metaphysical religion. His expression on this subject is famous: 'Heretics of all religions, unite!'[197]

Corbin influenced several Muslim intellectuals in Iran in the 1960s and 1970s when he was teaching in Tehran. Daryush Shayegan, one of his students, recounted how Corbin succeeded in transmitting Iranian mystical heritage to

[194] Shayegan, *Henry Corbin*, 107.

[195] Corbin, *L'homme de lumière dans le soufisme iranien*, 78.

[196] Basset, 'Henry Corbin', 4.

[197] Moncelon, 'La foi de Henry Corbin'.

young Iranians, lost between an Islam they did not understand and a Marxist–existentialist Europe that was out of their reach.

> Old ideas appeared wearing a sparkling new dress . . . The Iranian world was paradoxically resuscitated in Descartes's clear language; transmuted into elegant French, these ideas were almost modernised . . . Corbin became, without specifically seeking as much, the bridge between the Iran of Sohrawardi and the West of Heidegger.[198]

We can also see Corbin's influence among Sufi intellectuals in Europe and the United States, such as Eva de Vitray-Meyerovitch, Seyyed Hossein Nasr, Éric Geoffroy, Faouzi Skali and Philippe de Vos (we will return to the last four over the course of this book). A good example of Corbin's impact beyond the academic frame comes to us from Skali (Chapter 3), who recounts the revelations he received in dreams while he was reading Corbin:

> While I was reading Corbin's *L'imagination créatrice dans le soufisme d'Ibn 'Arabī* ['Creative Imagination in the Sufism of Ibn 'Arabi'], I started to dream a great deal and saw the master whom I would later meet. [*Sīdī* Hamza? I ask.] Yes. *Sīdī* Hamza, that's right. I saw him in a dream. At a time when I didn't know him, I didn't know who he was (Skali, 2018 interview, Fez).

Eva de Vitray-Meyerovitch

Eva de Vitray-Meyerovitch (1909–99), a human science researcher at the French National Centre for Scientific Research (CNRS), discovered Islam at the age of forty-five through the work of the Pakistani poet and philosopher Mohammed Iqbal (1877–1938). She embraced this religion, in both her academic work and her personal life. During the years that followed, she translated several of Iqbal's works, notably *Reconstruire la pensée religieuse de l'Islam* (1955). She also translated the works of Rūmī, including *Le Livre du Dedans* and *Masnavi-I Ma'navi*, to cite only the most significant texts, and made this poet the subject of her doctoral thesis. De Vitray-Meyerovitch also bore witness to her love for Rūmī in her final wish: to be buried near him in Konya.

De Vitray-Meyerovitch's work is also recognised outside European academia. From 1969 to 1973, she was invited to Al-Azhar University in

198 Shayegan, *Henry Corbin*, 33–4.

Cairo to teach comparative religion. In 1987, she received the title of doctor *honoris causa* from Selçuk University (Turkey) for her translations of Rūmī. In the 1980s, she met Skali, with whom she wrote a book on Jesus.[199] Skali also introduced her to the Sufi master Sheikh Hamza al-Būdshīshī, with whom she made the *bay'a*, the initiatic pact. However, in an interview, she admitted that she turned for spiritual guidance to the master of the 'Alāwiyya, Khaled Bentounes, closer to her geographically and linguistically. 'Alāwiyya and Būdshīshiyya disciples played a crucial role in her final years, and they honour her memory through their association Les amis d'Eva de Vitray-Meyerovitch (Friends of Eva de Vitray-Meyerovitch), which continues to organise conferences and gatherings to this day.[200]

De Vitray-Meyerovitch, like Massignon and Corbin, did not see boundaries between the various religions and philosophies. In her work, there are several references to Plato, Victor Hugo, Marcel Proust, Blaise Pascal, and Western philosophy in general. But more important is the link between religion and contemporary science. In fact, de Vitray-Meyerovitch saw in the work of Rūmī, and in Sufi mysticism in general, a strong correspondence between the contemporary science of quantum mechanics, on one hand, and intuitive Sufi revelations, on the other. Consequently, for her, *ḥīyrat*, meaning the awe of believers in response to beauty and mystery, strongly resembled the awe of researchers.[201]

Unlike most Religionist intellectuals, de Vitray-Meyerovitch did not reject the importance of religious orthodoxy. She did not identify with mystical heterodoxy, aligning her approach with Islamic tradition instead.[202] Furthermore, unlike Massignon and Corbin, who were active interpreters of the religious message, de Vitray-Meyerovitch preferred to remain in the background. For example, when a journalist asked her theological questions about the Beyond, she responded humbly, '[I] am not a religious authority.'[203] This did not prevent

199 Skali and de Vitray-Meyerovitch, *Jésus dans la tradition soufie*.

200 The website of Les amis d'Eva de Vitray-Meyerovitch is available at <http:// eva-de-vitray.blogspot.com/> (last accessed 2 November 2023).

201 De Vitray-Meyerovitch et al., *Islam, l'autre visage*.

202 De Vitray-Meyerovitch et al., *Islam, l'autre visage*.

203 De Vitray-Meyerovitch et al., *Islam, l'autre visage*, 38.

her from examining the question of universality, which she situated not in theosophy, nor in hospitality, but once again in the Islamic tradition:

> I had the sudden impression that it had answered all my questions. I found in it this much longed-for Universalism, this idea that fundamentally, the Revelation can be nothing other than one, that two plus two equals four everywhere, and that these figures always encompass a single truth, whether it be in Aztec, Chinese, or Arabic script. Yes, a single truth. The Qur'an says nothing else.[204]

This dialogue between Islamic orthodoxy and universalism also enabled her to articulate her relationship with religious norms, thereby underlining her European identity, her freedom of thought and even her feminist engagement:

> Headscarves and Islamic clothing are wholly ridiculous in Europe. The habit does not make the monk. We should not ape traditional customs or take superstitions as so many truths. As a woman, the possibility in Europe to practise an Islam not weighed down by custom is a terrific privilege! I remain European all while being Muslim, with my freedom of thought and my capacity to think critically. Sometimes I even celebrate this with my little feminist refrain! And none of that contradicts Islam.[205]

Legacy of Religionism in Contemporary Sufism

Of course, this is not the place to discuss the legacy of Religionism in the social sciences. Yet it should be noted that some authors, like Corbin and Massignon, are today criticised for their methodologies, their essentialist biases and their tendency to consider mystical phenomena more authentic than institutional religions. This healthy criticism notwithstanding, their works should be contextualised and we should recognise that they were among the first to elucidate unknown phenomena, criticise the supposed authority of Western civilisation, and relativise the methods and epistemologies of the social sciences by anticipating the questions around the 'ontological turn' spoken of today.[206]

Concerning their influence on contemporary Sufism, the works of Massignon, Corbin and de Vitray-Meyerovitch are a source of inspiration for several

[204] De Vitray-Meyerovitch, *Universalité de l'Islam*, 32.

[205] Rocher and Cherquaoui, *D'une foi l'autre*, 104.

[206] Holbraad and Pedersen, *The Ontological Turn*.

current-day Sufi intellectuals. Massignon's Abrahamic harmony, Corbin's quest for correspondences and analogies, and de Vitray-Meyerovitch's universalism are still of interest for Sufis such as Nasr, Geoffroy, Bentounes and Skali. In addition, these intellectuals initiated a fundamental discussion around the possible convergences between rational–scientific research and the intuitive–mystical quest – convergences that, as we will see in this book, are considered crucial by Sufis who profess hybrid hermeneutics and epistemologies (Chapters 3, 4 and 6).

Finally, the opposition between Sufism and 'legalistic Islam', between heterodoxy and orthodoxy, as seen in Corbin's work and that of other Religionist intellectuals like Jung and Scholem, seems to have lost its significance. Following on from de Vitray-Meyerovitch, the question of universalism is no longer conceptualised as heretical, esoteric and elitist knowledge, but rather knowledge that is articulated in Islam.

Conclusions

Esotericism, the New Age and Religionism share several common elements, namely: (1) criticism of Western modernity; (2) imminent eschatology; (3) the call for sacred knowledge as opposed to the dominant materialism; (4) universal sacred knowledge that surpasses the limits of religious identities; and (5) criticism of institutional religions.

These common elements make it hard to identify the borders between these various streams. Some figures, such as Schuon and Gurdjieff, can be considered to straddle esotericism and the New Age. Furthermore, while Guénon's analyses were deemed anti-scientific by his professors at the Sorbonne, resulting in his expulsion from academia twenty or so years later, similar ideas appeared in Corbin's Religionism. Unlike Guénon, Corbin found a mentor (Massignon), colleagues (Eranos) and a patron (Paul Mellon) who were interested in and open to his 'heterodox' ideas.

Although it may be impossible to dissociate all these streams once and for all, we do not need to content ourselves with a nebulous description where all phenomena are equal. In fact, we can grasp significant differences, such as: (1) the relationship with orthodoxy and religious norms and (2) the various forms of universalism. For Guénon and several Traditionalists, it is crucial to adhere to religious orthodoxy, or at least its narrative, because in the Guénonian frame, the good spiritual seeker subscribes to an orthodox esoteric and exoteric tradition descending from the Primordial Tradition (Judaism, Islam, Christianity, Hinduism, and so on). All non-traditional spiritual forms are accused of parody, the action of the Antichrist.

Orthodoxy's conceptualisation in the New Age and Religionist contexts is completely different, since religious norms lose their reason for being. The Sufism of Shah, Gurdjieff and Corbin is 'sharia-free', in that it needs no frameworks, norms or religious structures to be experienced. This difference has significant consequences for knowledge production, the conceptualisation of religious authority and organisational structures.

While the question of what is universal is the through-line for all the authors mentioned in this chapter, the conceptualisations vary considerably. For Guénon, the concept of 'Primordial Tradition' highlights the fact that all orthodox religious forms share a common origin. Believers have no other choice than to practise an orthodox religion. On the other hand, for authors such as Shah, Gurdjieff and Schuon, religion's universality is not a limit concept; rather, it is expressed in the practices and doctrines within reach. The universal can be experienced here and now, through the application of a master's teachings. The universal according to Massignon and Corbin differs in yet another way, amounting to the analogies, correspondences and atemporal symbols found in various religions. In any case, these different conceptualisations provide no indications on how to practise religion or which spiritual master to follow.

Except for the Sufism practised by the first wave of Maghrebi migrants, which is unfortunately difficult to access due to a lack of data, the first forms and representations of Sufism in twentieth-century Europe were significantly shaped by the esoteric, New Age and Religionist streams. In these intellectual–religious currents, Sufism was described, imagined and experienced in a form very different from its 'traditional' form. In effect, these currents have integrated Sufi discourses, practices and organisational structures into their own. However, I do not wish to suggest an opposition between the 'authentic' Sufism of Arabs and Turks and the 'counterfeit' Sufism of European converts. First of all, the interaction between these various discourses has been made possible through significant points of resonance between them. In addition, as we have seen in the opening chapters, Sufis who declare themselves as non-Muslim or as esotericists seeking universal interreligious harmony, are not absolute novelties (see Suhrawardī and the Jewish Sufi Abraham ibn Musa Maimonides).

Making distinctions is even harder today, given that esoteric, New Age and Religionist streams have undergone a gradual process of Islamisation. For example, we have seen that Guénon went beyond the European esoteric frame, becoming a point of reference in Islamic orthodoxy. Similarly, some New Age Sufi movements are in the process of re-incorporating Islamic narratives.[207] In sum, the question I am asking is not whether Sufi brotherhoods in Europe are hybrid, but how Sufi tradition has entered into contact with other religious discourses: what forms of hybridisation has this interaction produced?

[207] Sedgwick, 'The Islamization of Western Sufism after the Early New Age'; Philippon, 'De l'occidentalisation du soufisme à la réislamisation du New Age?'.

3

QĀDIRIYYA BŪDSHĪSHIYYA

Entering the Brotherhood: Dinner with the Master

I first came into contact with the Būdshīshiyya brotherhood through a colleague, one of its disciples, who invited me in my role as a sociologist to the seventh edition of an international Sufism conference, 7ème Rencontre Mondiale du Soufisme, held concomitantly with *Mawlid al-Nabawī* in 2013.[1] This invitation was made possible by the absence of my thesis advisor, Enzo Pace, initially scheduled to speak but finally unable to attend. I thus stepped in for him, benefiting from all the advantages this situation offered. As a guest of honour, I had a particular vantage point from which to see this brotherhood, as an organisation capable of coordinating an event with professors, imams and *'ulamā*'s from all over the world, not to mention hundreds of thousands of disciples and sympathisers.

On 21 January 2013, I arrive at the airport of Oujda, in eastern Morocco, close to the Algerian border. Right away, at the security checkpoint, the police officer is pleased that I am participating in *Mawlid*, which surprises me. How could he know this? Then I realise that the Būdshīshī *Mawlid* dominates all the cities in the area during these days, including their airports. This means that any foreigners can only be there for the celebration.

[1] *Mawlid* is the celebration of the birth of the Prophet Muhammad.

A taxi is waiting for us (myself and other invitees who arrived at the same time) and drives us to Madagh, a small village around 60km from Oujda. During the trip, I get to know university professors from France, Tunisia and Senegal. At midnight, we reach Madagh, where a meal awaits us before the ride to our hotel. The food is served under a big-top tent, close to the *zāwiya*. There are about 100 of us. Many introduce themselves, and I am immediately struck by the variety of ethnicities and nationalities I encounter in the space of a few minutes.

We start by eating the famous *tchicha* soup that gave its name to this brotherhood (according to the hagiography). Suddenly, everyone turns their attention to the arrival of an elderly man, whom I later learn is *sīdī* Jamal, the son of Sheikh Hamza and the future spiritual guide of the brotherhood (after his father's death in 2017). Everyone rises in salutation, and those closest to him move to kiss his hand, which he withdraws as an expression of humility, while others kiss his shoulder.

Sīdī Jamal decides to sit next to me, out of some 100 people, but only later will I understand the significance of this. Everyone is watching him, and watching me, to figure out who I am. Thus begins a pleasant conversation with *sīdī* Jamal, who asks me my first name, my origins, and so on. Within a minute, there is no longer any room at the table, because everyone wants to be close to Jamal. He then asks me to change tables so we can continue our conversation. It is worth mentioning that Jamal, the most important person after Sheikh Hamza, is not interested in the professors or *'ulamā'*s, seeming more inclined to speak with the young people.

Within a minute, a large platter of chicken and vegetables is brought to the table. We eat in the Moroccan way, taking food with our hands from the platter placed in the centre. *Sīdī* Jamal offers me a piece of chicken with his hands, but I decline, thanking him and explaining that I have already eaten. Suddenly, seeing the expressions of those around me, I realise that I am about to commit a serious error, so I accept the chicken and thank him. In the Būdshīshiyya, food is not only nutritionally and socially important; it is also spiritual medicine, even more so when it is offered by someone spiritually elevated. The food of the *zāwiya* helps cleanse the soul of the defects of the ego.

During the dinner, I also speak with a young Moroccan man sitting next to me. He tells me he was 'converted' to Sufism by a 'purebred' Italian disciple named Francesco. When I tell him Francesco is also my name, he is amazed. 'It's a sign!' he exclaims.

Around two in the morning, a taxi drives us to the hotel. The first evening was not only a total immersion in Moroccan Sufism; it also offered a surprising opening, in that the gesture *sīdī* Jamal made to me was seen by some disciples as a sort of blessing acknowledging and authorising my research. This had a positive impact on my relations with the Būdshīshiyya in Morocco as well as in France and Italy. A few weeks later, in Paris, a disciple said to me, 'Ah! You were invited to Madagh? You must be an eminent professor!' 'No, not really! I was there by chance,' I replied, explaining my fortuitous invitation. Concluding our conversation with a smile, he said, 'There's no such thing as chance.'

Qādiriyya, 'Living Saint' and Reasons behind a Global Dissemination

> *Sīdī* Hamza is impressive; he invokes [God] even while asleep. You can see his mouth moving (Abdel Ghafur, aged fifty, Moroccan-Italian disciple).

The Qādiriyya is one of the most widely disseminated brotherhoods in the world. Founded by the Iranian 'Abd al-Qādir al-Jīlānī (1077–1166), it spread from India to the Maghreb. The name 'Būdshīshiyya' appeared in the eighteenth century, according to hagiographical accounts, when *sīdī* 'Ali Qādirī, nicknamed 'Būdshīshī', founded an independent branch in the Beni Iznasen region of north-east Morocco. The hagiography also offers us two narratives as to the meaning of this name. According to the first, during a famine that struck the region, the *zāwiya* of *sīdī* Ali 'became a refuge for the starving locals, who were served cracked wheat, called *tchicha*'. The second version tells us that a Sufi saint transmitted his knowledge and his *baraka* to *sīdī* Ali, designating him as his spiritual successor, by means of the *tchicha* soup. Historians prefer to associate the birth of this brotherhood in 1952 with Abū Madyan Munawwar Būdshīshī (d. 1955), known to the disciples as *sīdī* Boumediene.[2]

Concerning the complex history of the Būdshīshiyya between the eighteenth and twentieth centuries, I refer to the article by Rachida Chih,[3] who described this brotherhood's fight against French colonialism, the succession of

[2] Sedgwick, 'In Search of a Counter-reformation'.

[3] Chih, 'Shurafā' and Sufis'.

various sheikhs, and the possible shared genealogy between the 'Alāwiyya and the Būdshīshiyya. According to some sources, Abū Madyan Munawwar Būdshīshī was the local *muqaddam* of Aḥmad ibn Muṣṭafā al-'Alawī (1869–1934), founder of the 'Alāwiyya. This shared genealogy is not recognised by Būdshīshī disciples, perhaps to underscore the brotherhood's Moroccan origins, or to highlight the Būdshīshī lineage.

For the purposes of this book, it is enough to know that until the 1970s, the Būdshīshiyya was a small brotherhood, tending towards elitism and conservatism and focused on ascetic and meditative practices.[4] This moral and political conservatism is confirmed by the presence of 'Abd al-Salām Yāssīn (1928–2012), a Būdshīshī disciple and the future founder of the Islamist al-'Adl wa al-Iḥsān, or 'Justice and Spirituality' movement.[5] This 'problematic presence' led to strict monitoring by the Moroccan government – the *makhzan* – until the 1990s.

Starting in the 1990s, the Būdshīshiyya saw widespread dissemination. From the small village of Madagh, it brought together thousands of people in Morocco and even attracted people from France, the United Kingdom, the United States, Latin America and Canada.[6] According to Idris, the Parisian *muqaddam*, there were 3,000 people at the 1990 *Mawlid* and 200,000 at the event in 2012. These numbers are plausible; the researcher Dominguez estimates that there are some 400,000 disciples and sympathisers in Morocco alone.[7] The hagiographical narratives tell us that this exponential dissemination was only possible though Sheikh Hamza, the living saint who revolutionised not only the Būdshīshiyya but also contemporary Sufism,[8] transformed into a 'Sufism for all'.

The designation of 'living saint' is not commonly used in classical Sufi language. Furthermore, the interpretations of its meaning change from disciple to disciple. For the most 'moderate', 'living saint' indicates that the teachings of Sheikh Hamza have a new energy, a renewed strength and powerful

[4] Tozy, *Le prince, le clerc et l'Etat*.

[5] Elahmadi, *Le mouvement Yasiniste*; Belal, 'Mystique et politique chez Abdessalam Yassine et ses adeptes'.

[6] Dominguez-Diaz, *Women in Sufism*.

[7] Dominguez-Diaz, *Women in Sufism*.

[8] Ben Driss, *Sidi Hamza al-Qâdiri Boudchich*.

baraka. His brotherhood is thus not *tabarrūk* – a vehicle of good graces – but rather a vehicle of divine presence. Youssuff, the Padua *muqaddam*, explained to me that 'the living master is the one who possesses the secret for renewing the path.' By contrast, the most enthusiastic disciples consider Sheikh Hamza to be *quṭb*, the pole or axis – that is, the perfect man, *insān al-kāmil*, who guides the hierarchy of the saints, the vehicle of ontological existence itself. Isa, a young Parisian disciple, told me, '*Sīdī* Hamza is the master of the saints! The saint of saints! The greatest saint in all History!' To use Weberian language, we could say Sheikh Hamza was not a routine sheikh but was instead a vehicle of prophetic charisma.[9]

Reconstructing how Sheikh Hamza's charisma developed is a difficult exercise, primarily due to the lack of books, articles and videos. All we know has come to us through the disciples.[10] The rare videos that can be found on YouTube of Sheikh Hamza show *samāʿ*, or sacred music. Finally, in the *zāwiya*s, whether they are made up of French converts or recently immigrated Moroccans, no documents, such as videos or manuscripts, can be found. The only things that count are *dhikr* and the word-of-mouth accounts of the disciples.

The charisma of Sheikh Hamza does not seem based on a discursive narrative, a specific vision of the world. It instead seems to derive from his non-verbal language, body language, physical presence and gaze. The disciples, especially those who have been his followers for a long time, describe a man of incredible physical and spiritual power – a 'true lion'.[11] When I saw him, he was ninety-two, making this power difficult to perceive. The centrality of the sheikh's body has been effectively highlighted by the researchers Mouna and Hlaoua:

> His body is a point of articulation between the profane world and the sacred world, the social realm and the religious realm, popular culture and scholarly culture. The sheikh's body serves as an intermediary between the visible and invisible worlds.[12]

[9] Weber, *Sociologie des religions*.

[10] We will see that in most other brotherhoods, the sheikhs write books, give interviews, and so on.

[11] '*Hamza*' means 'lion' in Arabic.

[12] Mouna and Hlaoua, 'Du corps incarné au corps identitaire', 24.

Moreover, Sheikh Hamza only spoke Arabic; verbal communication with his Francophone and Anglophone disciples was thus more than limited. This, however, has not prevented Europeans from entering the brotherhood. As for the 'living saint' construct, it includes accounts of miracles, especially among Moroccan disciples. Sheikh Hamza is seen as capable of curing any disease with his supernatural powers.

Sheikh Hamza's charisma was not the only factor explaining the expansion of this brotherhood. His sainthood has legitimised the ardent proselytism that has succeeded in reaching all social classes, including the Moroccan elite. The Būdshīshiyya has thus expanded beyond rural milieus, counting among its members such international public figures as the Moroccan intellectual Faouzi Skali, the French musician Abd Al Malik, the French politician Bariza Khiari, the Moroccan religious affairs minister Aḥmad Tawfīq and the Moroccan anthropologist Zakia Zouanat.

This openness to Moroccan society, and the subsequent openness on a global scale, has been defined by disciples as a 'pedagogical turning point' or a 'spiritual reorientation'.[13] According to Būdshīshī disciples, the brotherhood has moved away from the path of *jalāl* (pride, majesty) – characterised by asceticism and rigour – and towards the path of *jamāl* (beauty) – characterised by love and gentleness. Interestingly, this shift has tempered Sufi ascetic practices but has not affected narratives concerning the Islamity of the brotherhood, which aligns itself with Maliki orthodoxy. According to the disciples, this newfound openness is due to the figure of Sheikh Hamza, bestowed with a special spiritual authorisation.

> The first point is the notion of spiritual authorisation. In the history of Sufism, some spiritual masters have an *idhn* for initiating only one disciple in extreme cases. Others have a much broader *idhn* [in terms of the number of disciples], as in the case of *sīdī* Hamza who was gifted with several privileges. (Idris, Parisian *muqaddam*).

The disciples told me that in Boumediene's time, at the beginning of the twentieth century, the brotherhood included around forty disciples, who were

[13] Ben Driss, *Sidi Hamza al-Qâdiri Boudchich*, 17; Voix, 'Implantation d'une confrérie marocaine en France'.

subjected to rigorous tests, such as remaining standing all night to practise *dhikr*. Some of them even placed onions on their eyes to keep from falling asleep. The sheikh ordered those disciples of noble descent to shave their beards, a distinctive sign that carried great importance at the time. 'Sheikh Boumediene said, "I prefer having a handful of bees than a sack of flies." In his time, Sheikh Hamza gave this response: "I prefer both."' This is according to Tayob, who explained to me how Sheikh Hamza changed the pedagogical method:

> He starts by illuminating a disciple's heart; then he moulds him . . . The master seeks the disciple, whereas before it was the disciple who sought the master. This was a test of sincerity. Today, society is so materialistic that the test of sincerity is to live in the world.

This turning point not only implies the loss of asceticism, which 'is not of our time' according to Tayob; it also has political and cultural consequences, given that Sufism is regaining a central place in contemporary societies. The Būdshīshiyya is becoming the favoured partner of the Moroccan government in controlling the religious sphere, in opposition to Islamist movements.[14] This has led Mark Sedgwick to speak of the 'counter-reformation'[15] of Būdshīshī Sufism, as opposed to the reformism of modernists and Islamists. In addition, the dissemination of this brotherhood is also due to its structure, which is both solid, to guarantee homogeneity in various contexts, and malleable, as seen in its success in incorporating disciples of diverse social, cultural, religious and ethnic backgrounds.[16]

In summary, we have seen that the global dissemination of the Būdshīshiyya is due to several factors: (1) the charisma of the masters, (2) an inclusive pedagogy that has led to intense proselytism, (3) collaboration with the Moroccan government in its search to find anti-Islamist narratives and (4) organisational structures that are both solid and malleable, capable of adapting to various contexts. All these factors concern the macrosociological dimension. At this point, we can examine the dissemination of the Būdshīshiyya from a microsociological perspective, from the bottom up – that is, by asking ourselves

14 Muedini, *Sponsoring Sufism*; Werenfels, 'Beyond Authoritarian Upgrading'.

15 Sedgwick, 'In Search of a Counter-reformation'.

16 Dominguez-Diaz, 'The One or the Many?'.

what the new disciples have found in this brotherhood. In this regard, I will show that fellowship and the centrality and intensity of rituals have played a crucial role.

Organisation of the Būdshīshiyya in Morocco

The Būdshīshiyya is organised in various ways according to the geographical context. In Morocco, where this brotherhood has hundreds of thousands of disciples, the Būdshīshiyya has significant political, cultural and economic power. In Europe, where the disciples are much less numerous, the Būdshīshiyya takes the form of small groups. Despite enormous differences between these forms, the brotherhood maintains a degree of stability and solidity, guaranteed by hierarchies embodied by local *muqaddams* who are selected by the sheikh.

This brotherhood, like many others, is organised in concentric circles. At the core lies the Būdshīshī family, with Sheikh Hamza, his son Jamal and his grandson Mounir defined as 'the youth of God, in direct proximity with God' (as advised by Mourad, a French convert). Around these three figures orbit other family members and the closest disciples, who live in Madagh or Naima. Around this circle are the disciples who do not live in the *zāwiya* but are dedicated to the community practices. They probably comprise a few thousand people. The third circle, the largest, is made up of those who participate in the major events, such as *Mawlid*, drawn by Sheikh Hamza's aura of saintliness. They also come seeking *baraka* and/or miracles (*karāmāt*).

From a social–economic standpoint, the brotherhood in Morocco is an important force in the local economy. It owns large agricultural properties and manages many donations. Functioning as a 'welfare state', it takes care of disciples facing difficulties, orphans, widows, and so on. The brotherhood also pays salaries to some *muqaddams* in charge of large *zāwiyas*. In addition, it offers summer courses on Arabic grammar, Islamic law, and so forth.[17]

From a political–social standpoint, the brotherhood is interconnected with the powers of the Moroccan government, both locally and nationally. Būdshīshī disciples can be found among politicians, journalists and professors, but also among authorities exercising Islamic religious power. Using sociological

[17] Tozy, *Le prince, le clerc et l'Etat*.

categories, we can describe the Būdshīshiyya through the ideal type of the church[18] or the denomination.[19] This means that the brotherhood has a symbiotic relationship with the surrounding society, and thus with religious and temporal powers. This accommodating relationship with society and its authorities also explains how the Būdshīshiyya has become, for some, a sort of 'social elevator', allowing them to develop a political, economic and social network.

Organisation of the Būdshīshiyya in Europe

In Italy, the Būdshīshiyya comprises three *zāwiya*s in the north of the country: Biella (Piedmont), Milan (Lombardy) and Padua (Veneto). The disciples have told me that there are other centres in southern Italy, but there is no contact between the north and the south. The *zāwiya*s in Biella (around thirty disciples) and Padua (around fifteen disciples) are the oldest, established at the end of the 1990s and the start of the 2000s; the Milan *zāwiya* was established in 2005 (around ten disciples). Several Moroccan disciples had to leave Italy starting in 2008 because they lost their jobs following the economic crisis. I frequented the Milan *zāwiya* from November 2013 to March 2014, spending every Saturday evening with the disciples for the spiritual meeting. In addition, I was able to speak with and interview the disciples and the *muqaddam* of the Padua *zāwiya*.

To describe the Milan Būdshīshiyya, one could use the category of a 'transplanted'[20] brotherhood, which highlights Moroccan ethnic homogeneity, the reproduction of organisational structures in the home country, and the role of an acclimatisation chamber for new immigrants.[21] The disciples are middle- or working-class, employed as cultural mediators, labourers, factory workers, or set up as small-scale entrepreneurs. In addition, entering the Italian Būdshīshiyya is only possible through direct relations with the disciples (friendship, work or family ties). The brotherhood lacks promotional and proselytical tools such as lectures, seminars or a website.

The absence of a promotional system (well developed in France, as we will see) is not explained by doctrinal reasons. This lack of openness stems not from

[18] Weber, *Sociologie des religions*.

[19] Martin, 'The Denomination'.

[20] Hermansen, 'What's American about American Sufi Movements?'.

[21] Schmidt di Friedberg, *Islam, solidarietà e lavoro*.

a choice but from linguistic and logistical limits; the disciples do not have a perfect command of Italian (it was often easier to speak in French). The limits are also logistical, given that the Milanese disciples do not have a *zāwiya*. Each spiritual meeting is organised in the home of a disciple, hence the difficulty of being open to strangers.

The Padua *zāwiya* differs substantially from the others due to the presence of two disciples in particular: a university professor – Khalid Rhazzali – and an intercultural mediator. These disciples, here again of Moroccan origin, have facilitated opening the brotherhood to non-Moroccans. Thus, in Padua, we also find Italian coverts, Bengalis and Somalians. Furthermore, the cultural skills of the Padua disciples make it possible to organise lectures, seminars and concerts around Islam and Sufism. Despite the choice to remain discreet, the Paduan *zāwiya* has played and continues to play a significant role in the local Islamic community and in its relationship with public institutions.

The French Būdshīshiyya comprises 1,000 to 1,200 disciples located in major French cities, even though most disciples are in Paris, with around four hundred disciples organised for several reasons into five *zāwiya*s: Argenteuil, Nanterre, Aulnay-Sous-Bois, Saint Denis and Bagnolet. To avoid conflating Sufi Islamic practices with Moroccan culture, Sheikh Hamza made the choice to create a *zāwiya* specifically for French disciples in Bagnolet. However, this division is not a rule and exceptions are possible.

The first Būdshīshī *zāwiya* in Paris was founded in 1973 in Argenteuil, around a group of Moroccan working-class followers without authorisation to spread the path, except for Eva de Vitray-Meyerovitch and a disciple named René. *Idhn* came in 1987 with Faouzi Skali, a Moroccan intellectual who graduated from the Sorbonne and performed the first *bay'a*, or initiatory pacts. At the start of the 1990s, the first group of converted disciples began meeting in each other's homes. A few years later, they formed the Bagnolet *zāwiya*. Skali served as the bridge or 'isthmus' (the name he would later give his Sufi association in Paris) between traditional Sufism and the intellectual Sufism as conceived by Francophone intellectuals who drew their inspiration from Guénon, Schuon, Corbin, and so on.[22]

The 1991 and 1992 visits of Sheikh Hamza to Paris strengthened the ties between the Bagnolet *zāwiya* and the master. In 1994, Mounir, the grandson

[22] Piraino, 'Sufi Festivals as a Social Movement'.

of Sheikh Hamza, moved to Paris to complete his PhD and later taught at the Paris Dauphine University. He also became the *muqaddam* in Argenteuil. Finally, the language used in the brotherhood is *dārija*, the Moroccan dialect.

I chose to observe the Bagnolet *zāwiya* from February to October 2013. To begin with, it was the first contact that presented itself to me (I had met a Bagnolet disciple in Madagh). Secondly, even though the Bagnolet *zāwiya* is smaller than the one in Argenteuil, it made it possible for me to observe the processes of conversion and of rediscovery of Islam by French followers of Algerian descent. Before discussing the structures of the Bagnolet *zāwiya*, I should mention the differences compared to Argenteuil that the disciples pointed out.

> It's the same brotherhood, the same teachings . . . but with different functions; for us, to receive young people who are not Muslim, with less *dhikr*. We have also almost eliminated the Maghrebi cultural side . . . Their life habits and appearance differ from ours; they wear the *djellaba* and the women wear headscarves all the time . . . They often speak in Arabic, and the classes are in Arabic. (Nicolas)

In addition to the cultural dimension, there is the question of rituals; in Argenteuil, the practices are more frequent (almost every evening) and more intense. There are not appropriate for beginners, René tells me, the only French convert in Argenteuil.

While the Milanese Būdshīshiyya was formed by working-class followers, the Bagnolet *zāwiya* comprises mostly upper-middle-class members; I encountered university professors, architects, engineers, public officials, entrepreneurs, and so on. Most of them had university degrees and spoke several languages. Their average age was forty to fifty.

As we have seen, in Milan, the only way to contact the brotherhood is by knowing a disciple directly. In contrast, in Paris, there are several ways to get in touch with the disciples, for example through their websites.[23] But the Forum 104 meetings held every other month are the primary means of contact. Forum

[23] Available at <https://www.saveurs-soufies.com/> and <https://www.soufisme.org/> (last accessed 3 November 2023).

104, in the centre of Paris, is 'a space for cultural and inter-spiritual exchange',[24] a place for dialogue, lectures and interrelation between religions, spiritualities and philosophies. The Forum 104 evening events costs €4, and both male and female Būdshīshīs participate. Presentations by disciples range from Sufi doctrines to personal experience on the path (impressions and life histories). Whether the tone is more personal or more doctrinal depends on the person and the characteristics of the event. After the lecture, collective *dhikr* is conducted with the audience and generally lasts ten minutes. According to the disciples, this '*lā 'ilāha 'illā-llāh*' *dhikr* is basic, not requiring the conversion of the participants.

The audience, around thirty people, is upper-middle class in make-up, consisting of Parisian 'spiritual seekers'. The atmosphere is relaxed. The women Būdshīshīs only wear headscarves during the ten minutes of *dhikr*. Dress is informal. The goal of these Sufi events is to provide a theoretical framework for Sufism, but above all to transmit direct, personal experience of the brotherhood. The Bagnolet Būdshīshiyya organises another spiritual event every other month that is open to the public and called '*Portes ouvertes*' (open house). It is organised at the *zāwiya* or in the disciples' homes, but unlike Forum 104, those who attend are friends of friends, limiting the participation of people outside the path. Finally, the Argenteuil and Bagnolet *zāwiya*s have given rise to the associations Isthme[25] and VSMF[26] (Valeurs et Spiritualité Musulmane de France), which organise concerts and workshops.

Despite these forms of promotion, over eight months in Bagnolet and five months in Milan I only witnessed two conversions, and only in the Parisian *zāwiya*. This means that the promotion of the Būdshīshiyya exists but is limited (we will see that in the Naqshbandiyya there were several dozens of conversions). We could thus speak of 'soft' proselytism, at least in Europe. 'Talking about the path with anyone whose quest is profound and sincere'[27] is one of

[24] The Forum104 website is available at <https://www.forum104.org/> (last accessed 3 November 2023).

[25] The website of the French Būdshīshiyya is available at <https://www.soufisme.org/> (last accessed 3 November 2023).

[26] The website of the association VSMF is available at <http://vsmf.fr/> (last accessed 3 November 2023).

[27] Ben Driss, *Sidi Hamza al-Qâdiri Boudchich*, 203.

the principles of the brotherhood.[28] Entering it is relatively simple and does not require a long training period. *Bay'a* is given by the *muqaddam* after a few meetings and discussions.

The mechanism that seems to regulate the entry of new adepts is not selection at admission; newcomers are greeted with openness and availability (such as the flexibility regarding sharia, as we will later see). What regulates the entry of new members are the rituals. I heard it said several times: 'What holds us together and protects us is *dhikr*'; but I initially thought this to be a rhetorical statement on the importance of *dhikr*. In reality, this affirmation is an important sociological truth – that is, the centrality and intensity of the religious practices discourage all those who turn to Sufism to socialise or discuss Guénon and Gurdjieff.

The organisation in the Bagnolet *zāwiya* is well structured, with an organisation chart assigning everyone with a task: economic, logistical and library tasks; relations with neighbours; travel; meetings; and so on. In the *zāwiya*, despite the importance of the *muqaddam* and the 'major brothers' (more advanced on the path), equality reigns. Everyone has the right to speak, and decisions are made collectively. This equality can also be seen in economic matters, such as maintaining a set price for participating in the *zāwiya*, to which everyone adds what he can/wants to for extraordinary expenses. This equality in organisation and management strengthens the ties between disciples, who all bear responsibility for meeting common needs.

The local leader in the Būdshīshiyya is chosen by the sheikh. He guides the rituals, and his charisma is strictly tied to his role. Both Idris in Paris and Muhyiddin in Milan wear the same clothes and are treated in the same way as the other disciples. In other words, they are responsible for representing the sheikh, have the final say in practical matters and manage the rituals. But ultimately, they are disciples like the others. During my field studies, I saw the *muqaddam* serve food like the others and sleep in his sleeping bag like the others. As a result, in the rituals the *muqaddam* does not interpret *dhikr*; he directs its execution. When the Būdshīshī *muqaddam* is absent, the activities are conducted in the same way. Finally, the *muqaddam* is not a confidant. For example, David told me that when he asked the *muqaddam* for help in

[28] The other principles are sharia, *dhikr*, science (sunna, *ḥadīth*), generosity and fellowship.

personal matters, the response was: 'Are you saying *dhikr* correctly? Because everything is *dhikr*.'

Both in France and Italy, the Būdshīshiyya is organised according to the instructions of Sheikh Hamza, separating male and female disciples. There are many reasons for this. First of all, the gender separation ordained by sharia–*fiqh* must be observed. Secondly, it is a matter of space, given that the European *zāwiyas* are small and cannot bring together large numbers. Finally, according to some disciples, the simultaneous presence of men and women is discouraged for ecstatic rituals. Unfortunately, I did not have the opportunity to speak with women disciples; the French *muqaddima* was not interested in meeting with me. My interactions with women disciples were thus limited to public gatherings, such as the workshops and lectures in Paris. Concerning Italy, there were not enough women for spiritual meetings and gender segregation was even more pronounced, due to a more conservative view of Islam. Finally, the wives of the disciples were mostly housewives and had limited logistical means for getting to meetings.

Ecstasy: Feeling the Divine Presence

Dhikr*: Between Individual and Collective Practice*

'God Himself makes his appeal within you,' said Sheikh Hamza,[29] making explicit the process of purifying the soul and the concomitant divine presence in the disciple who practises *dhikr*. This is the process of deification/dehumanisation that was explained in Chapter 1, on Sufism as mysticism.

Rituals are central to the Būdshīshiyya brotherhood. To give an estimation (which can vary according to the disciple and the *zāwiya*), the individual practices of a Būdshīshī disciple in France, beyond the five canonical daily prayers, consist of 15,000 '*lā 'ilāha 'illā-llāh*'[30] per day, in addition to *wird*, a personal *dhikr* given to the disciple by the master or by the *muqaddam*. This means that a Būdshīshī disciple prays up to three hours a day, depending on the speed of recitation. Concerning the Milanese Moroccans, their practices appear to be even more intense, according to what Jafar told me. In addition to the practices already

[29] Sheikh Hamza, quoted in the *Classeur des nouveaux arrivants*, an internal document of the Parisian *zāwiya* for newcomers, 64.

[30] The first part of *shahāda* – that is, 'There is no god but God.'

explained, there are two *ḥizb* from the Qur'an,[31] plus a prayer on the Prophet from the *Dalā'il al-Khayrāt*, written by Muḥammad al-Jazūlī (1404–65). Finally, the Italian-Moroccan disciples told me that many of them practise supererogatory rituals, such as the sixth prayer, *ṣalāt al-nafil*, or weekly fasts.

> There is a *ḥadīth* that says that if you succeed in saying '*lā 'ilāha 'illā-llāh*' once in your life with your heart, you will go to heaven. We say it 15,000 times a day, so who knows! We hope that one of these will be true. (Jafar, aged thirty-five, Italian disciple)

The disease is *nafs* – the egoistic soul – whereas the medicine is *dhikr* and the physician is Sheikh Hamza, who reminded his disciples over and over that '*dhikr* is the food of the heart' and that one must be regular in one's invocation. The spiritual force of *dhikr* is not found in the etymological and rational meanings of the words. Rather its power comes from the 'living saint', from his spiritual authorisation:

> The divine name draws its influence and its power from *idhn* (authorisation); if the word 'potato' had *idhn*, it would become a divine name.[32]

> Every man is a slave to something, except for men who are free internally. Invoke God so that you may become free.[33]

> The only things that remain after death are your acts and your *dhikr*.[34]

The centrality of *dhikr* is justified by the fact that, in this brotherhood, the teachings are not rational–discursive, but rather communicated 'from heart to heart'. Youssouf, the Padua *muqaddam*, tells us that '*sīdī* Hamza taught through *dhikr*.' This explains the lack of books and the emphasis placed on the rituals.

The centrality of the rituals does not solely concern the disciple's private life, but also life in the *zāwiya*. Participation in collective events is thus strongly encouraged. This includes attending prayer meetings, making pilgrimages to Morocco, going on spiritual retreats and, more generally, sharing and dialogue between disciples – that is, fellowship.

[31] The Qur'an is divided into thirty-three *ḥizb*; two *ḥizb* are thus 2/33 of the Qur'an.

[32] Sheikh Hamza, quoted in the *Classeur des nouveaux arrivants*, 46.

[33] Sheikh Hamza, quoted in the *Classeur des nouveaux arrivants*, 61.

[34] Sheikh Hamza, quoted in the *Classeur des nouveaux arrivants*, 61.

Prayer meetings are held according to the availability of each *zāwiya*. For example, in Madagh, the rituals almost never stop; there is always someone reciting and/or praying. In Milan, where there are few disciples, one spiritual meeting is held per week, unless something unexpected comes up. In Paris, this depends on the *zāwiya*; the one formed by French converts and French disciples of Algerian descent in Bagnolet organises four meetings per week (two for women and two for men). In contrast, the *zāwiya* formed by Moroccans in Argenteuil organises meetings all week long.

Weekly Meetings

Spiritual meetings take different forms and comprise various rituals. Rather than listing the rituals, I prefer to describe an evening in the Parisian *zāwiya* of Bagnolet, formed by converts and by Franco-Algerians who were raised as Muslims.

At around 7.30 p.m., I take the stairs of a small building in the Paris suburbs that has no distinctive features. The disciples are on the third floor in an apartment measuring around 650 square feet. I am a little late, but the door to the apartment is always partway open. I enter the *zāwiya* silently, as I do not want to disturb anyone. In a little antechamber I take off my shoes, then use the light of my cell phone to find a place among the cushions, arranged in the Moroccan way on the floor and on the sofas. The curtains are completely closed, and the disciples are seated facing Mecca. They are engaged in *tahlīl*, the silent repetition of '*lā 'ilāha 'illā-llāh*'.

The only sound that can be heard is the rustling of *tasbīh*, the prayer beads used to count the number of recitations. This murmur is sometimes interrupted by *aḥwāl*, ecstatic states (*ḥāl* in the singular) described as 'electric shocks', moments of contact with the divine presence that cause the disciples to cry out, weep, laugh or jump.

> Sufis define the spiritual state (*hal*) as a sensation that emanates from deep within one's being, arising furtively and uncontrollably. After plunging the mystic into a state of nostalgia (*shawq*), reverential fear (*hayba*), and opening up (*bast*), *hal* disappears as rapidly as it appeared.[35]

Ḥāl is among the specific characteristics of the Būdshīshiyya. Even though these states exist in all the brotherhoods, they are more present in the Būdshīshiyya

[35] Ben Driss, *Sidi Hamza al-Qâdiri Boudchich*, 37.

and are expressed the most freely. Over time, I came to recognise disciples by their *ḥāl*. David broke into a powerful '*ALLAH*!', sometimes frightening the others. Another got up and started to jump while calling out '*sīdī* Hamza!' Idris made guttural sounds. Another whistled in a way that made me think of science fiction films. Abdel Haqq broke the ecstatic tension with 'Hop! Hoppepy!', whereas Adam sat still, always seeming about to jump up. Beyond the particular sounds, in most cases the movements of the facial muscles revealed the moments of tension and liberation following this jolt, this divine presence.

Adab, or proper conduct, dictates that these *aḥwāl* should be eliminated or controlled by the disciple, but Muhyiddin, a Moroccan immigrant in Italy, explained that 'sometimes, it is impossible to prevent them.' I have noted that *aḥwāl* are more frequent in the *zāwiya* of converts in Paris compared to *zāwiya*s where the brothers were raised as Muslims (Milan, Paris, Madagh), probably due to stricter discipline regarding etiquette during rituals.

After around an hour of *tahlīl* (silent repetition of '*lā ʾilāha ʾillā-llāh*'), the disciples turn on the lights and change positions. We form a circle and start the repetition of the name of God, '*Allāh*', aloud. The rhythm is rapid; there seems to be no time to breathe, and there is still another hour of intense practice to engage in afterwards. Over the course of the evening, the number of disciples increases; during *tahlīl*, when the meeting began, there were about a dozen of us, but the little room gradually fills, and I count around thirty disciples.

We have arrived at the heart of the spiritual meeting: *waẓīfa*, the recitation out loud of a set of names for God, such as *Allāh* (The God), *al-Laṭīf* (The Subtle One), *Huw* (He) and *al-Ḥaqq* (The True One). Parts of Qur'anic verses are also recited, as well as entire suras such as Sura Yasin (36). This invocation, composed by Sheikh Hamza, changes from time to time. The last time was in 2011, when it was lengthened, 'probably as a result of the Arab Spring', to protect the populations, according to Adam, a Parisian convert. Before *waẓīfa*, handbooks are distributed with the transliteration into the Latin alphabet since the recitation is rapid and some parts are difficult to learn by heart.

The *muqaddam*, Idris, sets the rhythm of the ritual, indicating when it is time to speed up or slow down. He also uses his prayer beads to count the number of invocations, signalling like an orchestra conductor the transition from one invocation to another. The rhythm of *waẓīfa* consists in a series of peaks – moments of ecstatic tension, followed by slower interludes.

After *waẓīfa*, the 'class' lasts around fifteen minutes, led every week by a different disciple. This class is a form of instruction and self-instruction, in that the disciples must learn to study and express the spiritual theological themes specific to Sufism and Islam. The principle of equality is explicit; all participants are called upon to participate in the teaching. On several occasions, the disciples admitted to me that they used the class notes of the women because they were better. The content of the classes can vary significantly in the form they take; 'more classical' disciples prefer to quote the great Sufis, while others focus instead on their own experience. Every two months, the *zāwiya* organises a 'long class' that lasts around two hours, where one disciple knowledgeable about Islamic theology and the great scholars of Sufism gives an intense, more integrated lesson.

Once the short class is finished, other handbooks are distributed to the disciples. They provide transliterations of the sacred songs, known as *samāʿ* in Arabic. The *muqaddam* gives us the page number and the disciples sing for about twenty minutes. Unlike *dhikr* and *waẓīfa*, *samāʿ* is more relaxed; the ecstatic tension seems to have fallen away.

On the other hand, *samāʿ* is the ritual where another practice may manifest itself, *ḥaḍra* – literally, the (divine) presence. In the Būdshīshiyya, this is expressed by rhythmical movements, little hops, a kind of dance – movements accompanied by chanting or abrupt guttural sounds: 'HU, HU, HU'. They serve to set the rhythm, like the basses in an orchestra. Above these 'basses', other disciples sing the sacred music. The results of the *samāʿ–ḥaḍra* ritual vary enormously depending on the occasion and the ambiance. *Samāʿ* can take place without *ḥaḍra* because the latter is not entirely formalised. 'It happens when it happens,' Nicolas told me.

However, when there are many disciples, or an important event such as the presence of the sheikh, the manifestation of *ḥaḍra* is practically ensured. The Parisian disciples are not really gifted as singers, as they are well aware, often making fun of their own performance. By contrast, when I was in Madagh for *Mawlid*, *samāʿ–ḥaḍra* had a lasting impact on me. The basses and the guttural sounds of thousands of people made the ground shake, and the best singers threw themselves into their song, leaving everyone amazed.

The evening ends with a meal, prepared each time by a different pair of brothers who complete the rituals before the others. Plastic and paper tablecloths are spread out on the ground, and we eat from large platters in the centre, using forks. The quality is always excellent, as is the variety; the mix of nationalities ensures a wide range of recipes.

During my first Būdshīshī evening meeting in Paris, because I was a little worried about missing the last metro, I thought I would leave before the meal. But Tayob pointed out with a smile: 'Be careful, eating together is part of the evening.' This reminded me of the importance of meals, given that they are one of the spiritual medicines. Community meals also occasion the rediscovery of the body for some. For example, David told me he was used to eating with luxurious silverware and that eating with his hands in Morocco 'was a wonderful discovery'.

In this evening meeting that I have just described, I did not take into consideration the canonical Islamic prayers, *ṣalāt*, which take place in the evening at the appointed times and change with the seasons. My account also lacks another ritual, namely the salutations between disciples, which may take place several times in the same evening, at the end of each 'major' ritual like *waẓīfa*. The salutation involves trying to kiss another's hand while they attempt to kiss yours at the same time. The disciples withdraw their hand before the other can kiss it. The disciple then places his open hand on his heart with a smile and says, '*Salām 'alaykum*!' or 'Good evening *sīdī*!' This gesture expresses the humility of both the disciple attempting to kiss the other's hand and the disciple who pulls his hand away. During these spiritual meetings, the salutations are also a moment of relaxation and happiness, during which the disciples make jokes and show signs of affection.

The spiritual meeting I have described in the Bagnolet *zāwiya*, commonly called *waẓīfa* (the most important ritual of the meeting), is carried out on Saturday evenings. Another spiritual meeting takes place on Monday evenings at the Bagnolet *zāwiya*, during which *latīf* is carried out. I have never observed this ritual, as it is reserved for the most advanced disciples. Idris, the *muqaddam*, explained to me that it would be disrespectful to allow me, 'the sociologist', to participate, while other disciples are still excluded. Based on what I surmised from the disciples' accounts, *latīf* is completely different. The doors of the *zāwiya* are closed at the beginning of the ritual, a white sheet is placed the ground, and water is placed in the centre of the circle formed by the disciples. This water, 'loaded' with *dhikr*, is one of the spiritual–physical medicines. Each of the disciples must interiorly and silently recite a precise number of invocations, which will be added to the *dhikr* of the others. During *latīf*, there is no place for states of *ḥāl*; everyone must remain focused on *dhikr*. This ritual seems to require greater attention and discipline. Finally, to carry out this ritual, a minimum of twelve disciples is required.

The disciples in the Milan region practise only *waẓīfa* on Saturday evening, because there are too few of them to perform *latīf*. Unlike their French counterparts, the Italians (Moroccan immigrants in reality) do not need handbooks; they know everything by heart. In addition, the rituals are faster, the recitation going so quickly that Muhyiddin, the *muqaddam*, must sometimes make signs to slow the pace and calm the other participants.

Moreover, there are fewer *aḥwāl*, probably due to greater attachment to ritual etiquette on the part of the Moroccans. We have seen that *aḥwāl* are part of the Būdshīshiyya, but one must, of course, learn to control them. The second explanation is linked to the number of disciples. In other words, spiritual meetings involving seven or eight people (Milan) may thus generate less 'effervescence'[36] or 'energy'[37] compared to a spiritual meeting in which some thirty disciples participate (Paris).

The centrality of *dhikr* in Būdshīshī Sufism is even more evident in the Milanese *zāwiya*. For these disciples, every moment is right for practising *dhikr*. My first meeting with the Milanese Būdshīshiyya, in December 2013, is a good example of this. I had arranged with a disciple to leave Milan together and travel by car to the home of another brother who lived in the Milan suburbs.

I climb into the car and introduce myself. This is the fifth time I have entered into contact with a brotherhood, so I know what to expect in terms of questions about my research, my religiosity, and so on. But the two disciples show little interest in sociology. They greet me as if I were a brother, and are delighted to learn I went to Madagh, that I even met and dined with *sīdī* Jamal. They do not ask me any questions and get started with *dhikr*, which lasts around twenty minutes as we travel down the highway towards our destination. Once *dhikr* in the car is over, the brother starts to say *du'ā'* in Arabic, or a prayer of supplication, and I am prompted to say '*āmīn*' with each phrase.

[36] Durkheim, *Les formes élémentaires de la vie religieuse*.

[37] Collins, *Interaction Ritual Chains*.

In the trips I went on with these Milanese disciples in the following months, there was always a time for prayer but also a time to chat. That said, I want to emphasise that the prayer time is not limited to established rituals. This means that the separation between profane and sacred moments is difficult to determine, not least during times of exchange between the disciples. Similarly, during the spiritual meetings, both in Milan and Paris, children were at times present, and played or spoke during some of the rituals. Mystical experience is not separate from the everyday. Any time is a good time to think of God, in a totalising sacralisation of life, as we have seen in the characteristics of *scientia experimentalis*, or mysticism.

> The goal is divine love; it can come from the sheikh, or it can come from the disciples. Ultimately, I would say that God should be seen in all things. Really everything. See, for me, God is as present in a bar as in a mosque. [I looked at him incredulously and he replied] Really! Of course, young people may be more or less focused on God, but God is everywhere. (Malik, Franco-Algerian disciple, aged forty)

Khalwa: *Spiritual Retreat*

Once or twice a year, the Parisian *zāwiya* in Bagnolet organises a spiritual retreat in the countryside that lasts three to four days. In Sufi language, there is the term *khalwa*, which refers to a spiritual retreat involving prayer and silence. But in the French Būdshīshiyya, this retreat is anything but silent. It is, on the contrary, a time of joy and exchange that I will attempt to describe below.

The retreat, in which I participated in June 2013, is held in a fifteenth-century castle belonging to a brother of aristocratic descent. The castle is not completely renovated, so several parts of it cannot be used. Though we sleep in sleeping bags on mattresses, this does not detract from the castle's charm or the bucolic atmosphere.

I arrive with the Paris disciples for the evening's activities and, as always, I am warmly welcomed. Around forty-five people are present. During the dinner, the atmosphere is relaxed, and we laugh over stereotypes about various nationalities. Everyone participates in the housework: setting the table, preparing the food, washing the dishes, and so on. Even Nicolas, who owns the castle, and Idris, the *muqaddam*, work incessantly.

The retreat schedule includes spiritual exercises that are more intensive than usual. The disciples carry out all the rituals we have seen (*tahlīl*, *waẓīfa*, *latīf*, *ḥaḍra*, *samāʿ*, personal invocations, classes), adding the recitation of some surahs from the Qur'an. The retreat starts at 3.45 a.m., before dawn, with *ṣalāt al-fajr* (pre-dawn prayer) and the first *waẓīfa*. But most disciples do not have to get up, since they have spent all night singing, practising *dhikr*, or simply talking with the other brothers. The entire day is dedicated to prayer, with a few rare breaks after meals. However, at the end of days filled with ten hours of intense rituals, the disciples do not seem tired, but rather full of energy. Finally, on Saturday, after lunch, a football match is organised between France and the rest of the world.

The intensity of these days is also accompanied by a degree of tranquillity, as the rituals are not obligatory and no one is checking up on them. For example, except for the five ordinary prayers (*ṣalāt*), there is a measure of liberty in the practice of the other rituals. I see disciples practise *dhikr* while walking in the countryside or sunbathing. The two or three brothers who smoke find a corner out of the way, which is not to say they are hiding, even though in the Būdshīshiyya, as in most Maghrebi brotherhoods, smoking is frowned upon.

The rituals, as tools to feel the divine presence and acquire a sacred inner knowledge of God, exceed static formalisations. Each moment is opportune for remembering God, each act is a form of prayer. This sacralisation of daily life has a degree of spontaneity and creativity, and other forms of prayer arise. For example, during a break, a few disciples and I were exploring the grounds and the castle when suddenly we caught sight of a baby grand piano. We entered the room and one of the disciples, also a musician, began to play some jazz. Within a few minutes, the room filled with disciples and someone began making requests. Bachir jokingly asked for some *samāʿ*. The result was a sort of 'jazz-*samāʿ*', musically compelling, but even more compelling from a sociological standpoint. The disciples started to sing to this bizarre 'jazz-*samāʿ*', and I could see in their faces both the solemnity of the sacred music and the joy, fun and irony of this spontaneous rendition.

On several occasions, I was witness to this joyous approach to mystical experience. For example, I happened upon the disciple Abdel Haqq by himself in a room, reading the *waẓīfa* transliteration handbook. Although he is of Algerian descent, he does not speak Arabic and probably wanted to learn *waẓīfa* by heart. At one point, he broke into laughter and laughed heartily for several minutes. Enjoyment and playfulness seem to be important aspects of the Būdshīshiyya, especially in Bagnolet, where the code of conduct is more relaxed. Another example is that of David, who told me that during his first visit to the *zāwiya*, he asked the disciples what they thought of laughter, since for him joy and laughter are inseparable from the spiritual path. The disciples all laughed exuberantly in response.

Visitations: Ziyāra *and* Mawlid

One ritual I did not have the possibility of participating in is *ziyāra*, the religious journey to Naima in Morocco, where Sheikh Hamza lived. These journeys are organised every two months and last around a week. The disciples told me that the rituals are even more intense in Naima compared to the spiritual retreat I participated in. They described the same energy and joy, but unlike at the castle, in Morocco it would be out of place to play football, sing 'jazz-*samāʿ*' or leave the others to smoke a cigarette. The Moroccan context seems to involve more rules and formality.

In Sufism, *ziyāra* is notably associated with veneration at the tombs of saints. The disciples told me that in Madagh there are tombs that give off *baraka* – that is, energy, grace and blessings capable of spiritually nourishing the disciples. Some are even the site of *karāmāt*, or miracles. However, in the accounts of Būdshīshī disciples I met, the importance of the tombs seemed relative, because all the discourses were focused on the presence of the 'living saint', Sheikh Hamza.

Another form of pious visitation takes place during *Mawlid al-Nabawī* (*moulud* in the Maghrebi dialect) – that is, the celebration of the birth of the Prophet Muhammad. This celebration takes place on the twelfth of the Islamic month of Rabīʿ al-Awwal, which in 2013, when I participated in it, fell on 24 January. As I have already mentioned in the introduction, the celebration of *Mawlid* in Madagh is organised as part of the Rencontre Mondiale du Soufisme, the international Sufism conference that lasts three days. The conference, which attracts intellectuals from around the world, is important from a political–cultural standpoint, but *Mawlid* is above all a religious celebration.

The conference was attended by 200 to 500 people, in addition to television crews and journalists. These numbers are significant when you consider the location of the conference – that is, under a big-top tent in the province of Oujda. However, for the celebration of *Mawlid*, the numbers are much more surprising; I watched as this little village overflowed with people. The brotherhood reported 120,000 participants, and although it is difficult to calculate the exact number, there must have been tens of thousands of people. The following year, the Moroccan newspaper *Le Matin* gave the figure of 150,000 disciples.[38]

It was also difficult for me to attend the many rituals and events that accompanied *Mawlid*. I was among the guests of honour and had the pleasure of sharing a meal with the other professors in the home of *sīdī* Jamal. Yet I realised that what was happening outside was just as interesting. As a result, I went back and forth between the guests of honour and the crowds of disciples. Looking for my colleague, a Būdshīshī disciple, I found myself in the building for the disciples who had come from abroad, mostly Europeans. They were singing, and the atmosphere was so festive that they drew me into their songs, even though I did not know the melodies or the words. Finally, I left to find my colleague, who, when I found him, led me with his group of 'Italian' disciples to the mosque for prayers (in reality, there were two Moroccans, one Somalian and two Italians). The mosque was enormous, but still under construction so the walls were bare. In this mosque, I heard *samāʿ* sung by dozens of disciples, accompanied by rhythmical *ḥaḍra*; they resembled an orchestra. Before leaving the mosque, we were interrupted by a man whom my friend introduced to me as a *majnūn*, a 'holy madman' – according to Sufi vocabulary, one who has been burned by divine love and has not returned to earth. With contagious joy, this *majnūn* told me that he spoke the 'English of Adam', babbling something that ended with '*ṭarīqa Qādiriyya Būdshīshiyya is good*!' He burst into laughter, and we joined him.

I went with the group of 'Italians' to pay a visit to Sheikh Hamza. I would have had the possibility to see him with the other guests of honour, but I preferred to see him with the crowd of disciples. The line was interminable. We were in the area facing the home of *sīdī* Hamza as we waited to see him. There were thousands of people waiting in the January rain and wind. They were singing and practising *dhikr*. Despite the large number of people and the poor weather conditions, everything went smoothly. After three hours of waiting in line, we reached the building of the sheikh, climbing a stairway that opened onto a large room. It was silent despite the crowd. On the right was a

[38] Sbaï El Idrissi, 'Lahsen Sbaï El Idrissi, porte-parole de la Tariqa Boutchichiya', *Le Matin.ma*, 13 January 2014. Available at <https://lematin.ma/> (last accessed 3 November 2023).

small wooden barrier that separated, at least symbolically, the 'sacred zone' from the mass of disciples. In the sacred zone were rugs and a bed piled with cushions. From where he was seated on the bed, Sheikh Hamza looked at us serenely. White was the dominant colour in the room, matching his clothing and beard.

Disciples surrounded him in the sacred zone, where two men near the wooden barrier were holding black plastic sacks in which the disciples left their offerings. We could only glimpse Sheikh Hamza for a few seconds; other disciples in charge were gently pushing us towards the exit. My friend spoke with one of these disciples, telling him something in Arabic so that I would be able to approach the sheikh. They told me to take off my shoes, since one must walk barefoot in the sacred zone. I did so, not really understanding what I was to do. Offer a salutation? Kiss his hand? But I was too slow in taking off my boots, and one of the disciples in charge motioned me towards the exit. Once again, this visit demonstrated to us the importance of Sheikh Hamza for his disciples, who were willing to wait in the rain and wind for hours and hours, only to catch a glimpse of him for a few seconds.

The closing ritual of *Mawlid* took place in the mosque, completely full of people, while outside the doors thousands tried to hear whatever they could. The big night-time event started at 11 p.m. and lasted until 4 a.m. the next morning. In the middle of the stage, Sheikh Hamza sat on a bed, dressed entirely in white. Around him were the most important figures (his family, *muqaddams*, politicians and professors). Then, a little further away, still on the stage, the conference participants sat comfortably on low chairs. At the edge of the stage was a security line, formed by bodyguards, and beyond them were television crews, then a bevy of photographers. Beyond this security line stretched the mass of disciples who were pushing forward in an attempt to see Sheikh Hamza. Women looked on from the second floor.

Unfortunately, my scant knowledge of Arabic made it difficult for me to understand the speeches of the esteemed scholars. Among the orators were Mounir, Jamal, *'ulamā'*s from Al-Azhar University and the imam of Al-Aqsa Mosque, Abū al-Hounoud. Some of the professors I stood next to told me that these speeches were invocations, blessings and recitations from the Qur'an. The speeches gave way to *samā'*, first performed by children and then by the Būdshīshī choir.

The atmosphere was solemn and ceremonious. During the invocations, a disciple who was older and a guest of honour began *ḥaḍra* by himself. The others watched him, smiling. It was not until *samāʿ* that everyone gradually started *ḥaḍra*. Even those who, up until that point, had been the most serious broke into song and began to dance. But the real performance was happening behind us, where the crowd of thousands of people punctuated the singing with guttural sounds. The mosque shook with these 'HUW! HUW! HUW!' I was in the last row of the guests of honour, so I could see the faces of those at the front of the crowd. Many wept, others cried out. Most of them danced and sang in unison. The bodyguards turned their back to the stage and watched the crowd, their eyes peeled to keep everything under control.

Mawlid in Madagh was focused on the figure of Sheikh Hamza; this celebration could also be seen as the exhibition of his sacred body. Because he was the 'living saint', the power of his *baraka* (blessing–spiritual energy) was such that it eclipsed the importance of the tombs of the saints, part of the history of Sufism. The three days of *Mawlid* took place as a continuous ritual that never stopped.

The disciples, especially the Europeans, had the opportunity to practise the principles of the path, including humility and fellowship. Only the conference participants and a few other people had the status of guests of honour. The European disciples were part of the crowd and slept in sleeping bags in the mosque or in the building facing the home of *sīdī* Jamal. The disciples shared not only their lodgings, the prayers and the rituals, but also the work. For example, before I was introduced at the conference, a young man served me a cup of coffee. Once everyone had been served, he began to sweep the tent. I then discovered that this disciple was a young physician from Lyon, who helped the brotherhood by cleaning the tent and serving coffee.

During spiritual retreats and even more so during *Mawlid*, the disciples have the possibility to experience a feeling of sharing, fellowship, equality and humility. To use the category of Victor Turner, they embody the '*communitas*'.[39] Below is the enthusiastic account of Mourad, a French convert, describing his first experience at Madagh:

> I went to Madagh for two weeks by myself, not with the Bagnolet group. I didn't know anybody. I was surrounded by Moroccans, young people from

[39] Turner, *Dramas, Fields, and Metaphors*, 1987.

> the countryside, real *fuqarā'* who don't have very much, not at all like the bourgeoisie in the home of *sīdī* Jamal. I slept in the mosque with a labourer who didn't even speak French. It was great! We hardly spoke. But there was some kind of back and forth, it was magical. I can still see those *fuqarā'* today. 'Wow! How are you?' We spoke with our hearts. That's what really struck me! The path [Sufi order] got me like that!

To summarise the complexity of the rituals described, I would like to highlight the following points, and first of all, the centrality of the rituals, which take up most of the time the disciples spend together. The *zāwiya*, whether in Paris, Madagh or Milan, is not a place to socialise, but rather a place of prayer. The friendships I saw in the brotherhood developed outside the *zāwiya*. In this regard, Sheikh Hamza recommended that the disciples 'should not talk too much during spiritual meetings', according to Muhyiddin, the *muqaddam* in Milan.

The second point concerns the experience of *communitas*, whereby mystical rituals become a sort of common language capable of linking disciples from various countries, cultures and social classes. But this does not imply an absence of organisational structure. Furthermore, this sense of equality in humility must not be confused with the closeness one feels with family members and friends. The disciples use the term '*sīdī*' for everyone, including sociologists, a term that can be translated into English as 'sir'. Equality thus comes with a form of respect and deference. This is somewhat less true in the Parisian *zāwiya* of Bagnolet, where the levity is like that found among family and friends, in contrast to respect and deference.

The third point, which we have seen in the ecstatic states – *aḥwāl*, in *samā'* and in *ḥaḍra* – is a kind of expressive liberty, a sort of creativity. Even though the rituals are formalised, the disciples' enthusiasm leads them to express and experience contact with the divine in unique ways. We have seen how in *ḥaḍra*, *aḥwāl* differ from disciple to disciple; there is also the example of 'jazz–*samā'*'. This liberty is expressed in the possibility of showing one's emotions by crying; during *Mawlid*, I saw several people in tears during the speeches, as a sign of joy.

Būdshīshī Doctrines and Pedagogy

While ecstatic practices predominate over discourses – several disciples repeatedly said that '*sīdī* Hamza taught through *dhikr*, from heart to heart' – this does not mean doctrine is not transmitted within the brotherhood. Reading the Qur'an and *ḥadīth* is strongly recommended for all disciples, as is reading the classical texts of Ibn ʿAshir (on sharia) and al-Nawanī (on *ḥadīth*). Concerning Sufi books, Ibn ʿAjība (1747–1809) and Ibn ʿAṭā' Allāh are often cited, as are Emir Abdelkader and René Guénon, though to a lesser degree, and primarily in France. Based on the disciples' narratives, I identified the most important doctrines, which give priority to a perspective that encompasses doctrinal discourse applied to daily life.

Before discussing the content of Būdshīshī discourses, I would like to highlight a meta-narrative element, concerning the form of Būdshīshī narratives. At a meal in Madagh during *Mawlid*, David, a French convert, told the participants how he experienced ecstatic states only when with his brothers. However, when he was with other people unaware of his conversion, he never experienced these ecstatic states. David, a university professor, concluded that God chooses the right time for these divine electric shocks. The other participants, almost all Maghrebi Muslims, told him that autosuggestion probably also played a role.

This anecdote shows us how, in this path, the faculty of reason is not set aside. The narratives and magnifications of the brotherhood and the master exist and are significant, but at the same time, certain attitudes that may seem inappropriate are discouraged. This is a matter of *adab* or proper conduct; disciples should be solemn in both their ecstatic states and their accounts.

The Living Saint and His Physical and Oneiric Presence

The most important narrative in this brotherhood, in all the *zāwiya*s, is that of the 'living saint'. We have seen that there are various interpretations, the most enthusiastic of which do not hesitate to refer to Sheikh Hamza as *quṭb*, the axis of existence, at the summit of the hierarchy of saints. David told me that he was a Muslim 'for *sīdī* Hamza', because if Hamza was of another religion, he himself would be of that religion. He added, '*Sīdī* Hamza is the living example, the prophet himself.' Amin, a Moroccan-Italian disciple, carries a photo of *sīdī* Hamza in his wallet. He told me, 'Anyone who has this photo with him cannot be afraid.'

Another French convert explained that '*sīdī* Hamza is the best and the Būdshīshiyya is the greatest brotherhood.' But the reactions of the disciples diverge; some agree, while others are embarrassed by these statements. Among the disciples is another representation of *sīdī* Hamza, in which:

> The sheikh is a teacher, and the brotherhood is a school. The sheikh is a normal person, but he is someone who has worked hard to be closer to God. The sheikh is not the prophet. He is someone who has arrived at the truth. (Jafar, Milanese disciple)

Similarly, Faouzi Skali, in a lesson given to the Bagnolet disciples which I attended, said, 'The master is like a mirror; he helps you become aware. It's like the Socratic method.' Malik, a Parisian disciple, is particularly distrustful of any exultation of the master. For him, first and foremost, 'The sheikh is not a master of a way of thinking, but rather a way of de-thinking.' Secondly, even the Prophet Muhammad was a man who, beyond his prophetic revelations, could make mistakes.

Among the Moroccan disciples, stories concerning miracles are more common. Abdel Ghafur is around fifty years old and moved to Italy to work as a labourer thirty years ago. His experience with the brotherhood started in Morocco, where he grew up in a large family of modest means. During his adolescence, Abdel Ghafur was not engaged in a religious quest and practised only sporadically. At the age of twenty, he suffered from a serious illness that upended his life, but he continued his university studies, among other things, despite his health problems. The first epiphany took place in the hospital, where he dreamed of a white light that told him, 'You must pray!' 'But I let it go,' he recounted. The second epiphany occurred through a friend who told him about the Būdshīshī disciples:

> I saw beautiful faces, they were so filled with light. I had never seen people like that. They were disciples. First of all, I asked them to show me the ablution. I couldn't remember it anymore; it had been years . . . The same night I had visions, they were like a purification. My blood changed. Bad blood went out and good blood came in. And I saw this man in white. I was at his feet, crying out, 'You can't let me go, you have to help me.' He said to me, 'First go and see this man, then come to my home.'

The man in the dream, whom Abdel Ghafur would learn was *sīdī* Hamza, sent him to pray at the tomb of a Sufi saint near where he lived (in the dream, he is referred to as 'this man'). The following morning, he felt much better.

His illness had disappeared. According to Abdel Ghafur's account, his physicians could not believe what they saw. A few days later, Abdel Ghafur met *sīdī* Hamza in the flesh:

> I sat down near him and there was so much light that I couldn't look at him. Now I can look at him, but at that point . . . He leaned toward my ear and asked me, 'How is your health?' 'Better,' I told him. 'Stay with the disciples and you will no longer have anything to fear!' That's what he told me. *Allāh 'aʿlam*, that's how I learned about the brotherhood.

Hamza's presence in Abdel Ghafur's accounts is continuous. The master guided him during his immigration to Italy, helped him find a job, and helped him start a family.

> Hamza is my salvation. I will always be grateful. Both here and hereafter [both in life on earth and life after death]. Even if he asked me for an eye, I would give it to him. I swear to you, after what I experienced, what I escaped from.

Sheikh Hamza guided the disciples even in their dreams. For example, a widespread story involves dreaming of Sheikh Hamza before meeting him physically for the first time, even before becoming a disciple or converting to Islam. These dreams become milestones for disciples in their quest; they offer metaphysical confirmation of their cognitive journey. Like the other ecstatic rituals, dreams are part of the history of Sufism and Islam[40] and have a formalised dimension (with common modalities and narratives) as well as a creative dimension, where disciples express themselves freely. Tayob explained the difference he sees between '*le songe*' and '*le rêve*', both of which translate into English as 'dream'.

> I immediately began having very powerful dreams. In Islam, a distinction is made between '*le rêve*' and '*le songe*'. '*Le songe*' is a kind of revelation; it has another dream quality, and the veracity of the dreams cannot be challenged. And it's really a personal experience. I didn't know there was a sheikh. I had been to the meetings twice, and I dreamed of the sheikh all week. He came into my *songes* and this was the first time I saw the face of Sheikh Hamza. I had never seen his face in reality. After a week or two, the disciples showed me the sheikh's face, and I said to myself, 'Oh yes, that's him!' For me, there was no

[40] Ewing, *Arguing Sainthood*.

> question, it seemed natural. Along the path there are signs. It's a good thing if you don't pay much attention to the signs, it's better not to focus on them too much. But, in any case, there are signs. (Tayob)

Brotherhood, Baraka *and Fellowship*

Sheikh Hamza's *baraka* extends over the brotherhood and the brothers. Everything touched by this *baraka* benefits from its energy and protection. The Milanese disciples told me that even though I was not Muslim, I myself, and my thesis (I presume my book as well), would all benefit from this *baraka*. The reason for this is that one need only talk about the brotherhood to benefit from it. In other words, fellowship is one of the founding principles of the Būdshīshiyya.

> Fellowship is love that circulates between us. *Sīdī* Hamza says that we are taught through fellowship. Fellowship is this circulating secret. (Locqman, aged forty, French convert)

> Non-judgement among brothers preserves the love we have for each other, because judgement impairs the love in our hearts. In our conduct, we must avoid excessive annoyance and joking, which can result in making judgements or hurting others. This aims to preserve the love between brothers, because this love carries us.[41]

Fellowship is an occasion for pedagogy; in the Būdshīshiyya, the brother is the mirror in which we see our flaws. Among themselves, the brothers learn to 'distinguish between people and acts'. They learn that 'judgement is a subtle disease' (Adam, French disciple). While fellowship is related to sunna – religious norms stemming from the life of the Prophet Muhammad – the Būdshīshī disciples accentuate the jovial dimension. During my field research, both in Paris and Milan, I always saw the disciples' enthusiasm, for any time was a good time to sing *samāʿ*, to laugh, to be together. For these disciples, Sufism is always a joy. At the end of the spiritual retreat, before leaving, Mourad said to me, 'We're replenished, we come back replenished, like peaceful warriors!'

> For me, Sufism is always a party! As soon as I joined the brotherhood, I [had] joy in my heart! (Muhyiddin, Milanese *muqaddam*)

[41] Sheikh Hamza, quoted in the *Classeur des nouveaux arrivants*, 57.

Between Law (Sharia) and (Truth) Ḥaqīqa

> Haqiqa and sharia are two primordial dimensions of Islam. Even though the Law (sharia) depends on the Truth (haqiqa), these two dimensions are experienced in a complementary way, between occult Truth and apparent Law.[42]

A discourse that is widespread among Būdshīshī disciples, beyond geographical and cultural differences, concerns the fact that Sufism cannot exist without Islam, which is to say that sacred experience cannot exist without rules and a framework. In other words, Sufism cannot exist without sharia. However, understanding what sharia is, and what role it plays, is far more complex.

In the disciples' accounts, religious law has a propaedeutic function; it is the framework for the quest, the rod for standing upright, the cork in the bottle containing the sacred drink. Sharia is the point of departure, not the point of arrival along the spiritual path. Abdel Haqq, a Franco-Algerian disciple, describes this aspect:

> You see, when I went to the mosque, they told me, 'You must do this, you must do that. They mentioned a lot of prohibitions. You come here and you understand with your heart, then you understand the meaning of sharia.'

Sharia that is propaedeutic must also be adapted to the level of each disciple:

> We can't ask someone who's just arrived to adhere to everything, to suddenly break with their entire life. A gradual change must be encouraged, and above all it must be voluntary. Because it's important to understand the value of the rules . . . The risk is an upheaval that can cause psychological damage and block the spiritual path (Charif, French disciple who converted many years ago).

Idris, the Parisian *muqaddam*, explained to me that 'the practice of *dhikr* makes it much easier to apply sharia.' He also told me about his experience of being converted:

> As for me, when I made the pact, I knew nothing about Islam, nothing at all. I practised *dhikr*, and then little by little, I began to perform the ablutions, I began to pray. And that's what *sīdī* Hamza teaches us, that this . . . should not

[42] Ben Driss, *Sidi Hamza al-Qâdiri Boudchich*, 26.

> be a chore, a constraint, something that weighs on you. Instead, it should be applied progressively, the person should know it's indispensable but should progress at their own pace.

Once we have realised both the importance of sharia and its propaedeutic function along the religious–spiritual path, what remains to be understood is which sharia is involved – that is, how it is translated into *fiqh*, the juridical dimension. There is no univocal interpretation.

The Parisian disciples in Bagnolet have a broad view: 'Sharia is not limited to juridical schools, but is the physical law itself, governing the movements of the planets, of nature' (Tayob). Regarding the practical dimension, sharia concerns the five pillars of Islam (profession of faith, alms, pilgrimage, prayers and ritual fasting); it also governs the form these rituals take (ablutions, times, and so on), and prohibitions such as pork, alcohol and the use of drugs. Finally, sharia prohibits sex outside of marriage.

> Sharia defines *muʿāmalāt*, all the rules concerning social life, marriage, inheritance, divorce, and so on. I have no problem with that, because sharia also says that those who live in a non-Muslim country must follow that country's laws. And that's something *sīdī* Hamza tells us regularly: follow the laws of the [French] Republic! Apply the laws of the Republic! Then there's *ibāda*, the acts of individual adoration: ablutions, prayer, fasting during Ramadan, food, and the fact of not having sexual relations outside of marriage. A lot of rules like that, and we follow them totally. (Idris, Parisian *muqaddam*)

We thus see how sharia, in the Bagnolet *zāwiya*, is understood as a framework governing rituals and proper conduct, based on a separation between what concerns the individual and what concerns social life. Living according to partial sharia, which concerns only the personal sphere, does not seem to be a problem for the Parisian disciples, as Tayob, French with Algerian parents, tells us:

> We are lucky to live in France, where there are no doctors of the law in the government. So, in the end, we do what we want. We have freedom of thought. There's no point in following rules just to follow rules . . . [That's what] Jesus said when he addressed the Pharisees. You follow the letter, but what about the spirit? Rules for the sake of rules are a nightmare!

In the Milan *zāwiya*, made up exclusively of Moroccan immigrants, the notion of sharia and its translation into *fiqh* are stricter and not limited to the personal sphere. Rédha told me that he wanted to send his ten-year-old daughter back to Morocco, so she would grow up in a country where it is easier to apply sharia. He also told me that when he bought a house with the help of a bank loan (prohibited by sharia), his life began to go badly, and he had to sell the house to return things to normal.

For all the Būdshīshī disciples I spent time with, sharia is a tool, not an end in itself. This approach, based on the spirit and not the letter, is aligned with the orthopraxy that characterises mysticism. It should not be confused with the Sufi anomie described by some Orientalists.

However, in the Būdshīshiyya, several stances exist on how to apply this tool. For most Europeans, whether converts or those raised as Muslims, sharia is limited to the personal sphere. For those with a more recent history of immigration, the question is much more complex, a matter of striking a balance between following the laws and customs in the new country and following religious rules.

Finally, several times I heard *ijtihād* mentioned – that is, the individual effort of interpretation necessary for clarifying contradictory or ambiguous situations. Others consider *ijtihād* to be the potential for a new interpretation of certain religious laws. Take, for example, the case of the inheritance of women according to the Maliki *fiqh* to which the Būdshīshiyya adheres. Some disciples see this religious norm as no longer in keeping with the spirit of the Qur'an. The fact that daughters inherit only the half of what sons inherit makes sense in a society where sons are obligated to take care of their sisters before their marriages, but in a contemporary society, where this obligation no longer exists and where women even work, this discrimination, previously considered fair, loses its value.

However, *ijtihād* remains taboo for most Būdshīshī disciples, who are cautious, saying only that they do not have the capacity for such complex theological and juridical reasoning. The ʿAlāwī disciples, as we will see in the next chapter, are more audacious, claiming that *ijtihād* is a necessity.

Sufism as a Code of Ethics in Daily Life

> Because when I began on the path I clearly didn't know what I was looking for, I was looking despite myself, it was more a matter of dissatisfaction, of not

> finding answers . . . Later, when you're on the path, you call out for help, the answers you find are not really what you were expecting. In the end, the answers are [instead] in how you feel, in your experience, in the change in conduct, in the change in how you see things. (Nicolas, aged fifty, Parisian Būdshīshī)

In a famous *ḥadīth* often cited in the Būdshīshiyya, the Prophet Muhammad says to his disciples, 'I was sent to perfect good character.' Similarly, according to a Sufi saying, 'He who goes beyond you in conduct goes beyond you in Sufism', highlighting the fact that the path of spiritual purification is in vain if it is not reflected in one's conduct.

The narrative of proper conduct is among the most important in the Būdshīshiyya. Proper conduct concerns everyone, beyond any ethnic, religious, class, gender or other differences. It relates to universal values such as humility, justice, not judging others and equality before God. The Moroccan-Italian disciples also note the importance of respecting one's parents and one's family: 'The requirements for entering the brotherhood are to have a saint in your family [ironic], or respect for your parents' (Abdel Ghafur).

The path of purifying the soul is expressed in proper conduct. In other terms, 'There can be no purification of the soul if it does not manifest itself in daily life, with your wife, your children, and your co-workers. Islam has to be applied!' Tayob declared. He also explained the difference between a sect (in its common rather than its sociological meaning) and the brotherhood: 'A sect wants to turn everyone into the same person, whereas in Sufism, we want everyone to become themselves.' According to Sheikh Hamza, even the dissemination of Islam should not use apology and proselytism, but rather set a good example:

> Communicating the path by example is, in my opinion, the most elevated way. This is the way Islam spread and the Prophet communicated. The Prophet did not preach, did not lecture on such and such a doctrine, but rather attracted people through his sublime conduct.[43]

In the Būdshīshiyya, I heard explanations several times on how Sufism can be incorporated into daily life and how it can improve relations between friends, family members and co-workers.

[43] Sheikh Hamza, quoted in the *Classeur des nouveaux arrivants*, 58.

In this regard Mourad's example is apposite. Mourad is a French man around thirty-five years old, a part-time musician and an IT technician. He grew up in a non-practising family and, in his adolescence, he completely abandoned religion, rediscovering it later in hallucinogenic mushrooms and LSD, as he tells us: 'I had mystical experiences. I could see into the universe, as if I was becoming part of human consciousness in its very essence. These were powerful experiences.'

Based on these mystical–psychotropic experiences, he became interested in the Kabbala and in magic. He frequented shamans, then Santo Daime, a new Brazilian religious movement that uses ayahuasca, a hallucinogenic beverage made from vine extracts. He went on to take an interest in Islam and Sufism, after marrying a Muslim woman of Moroccan descent who practised shamanism with him. Then he came into contact with the Būdshīshiyya, which changed his life. Over time, he gave up alcohol, cigarettes and marijuana 'naturally' and became increasingly involved in the brotherhood. Mourad changed not only the form of his experiences, but also the substance. The Sufism he practised enabled him 'to go back to work on Monday' and to understand that the experience of God can also be a part of daily life.

> The more I moved towards a more complete [Islamic–Sufi] practice, the more anchored and materialist I became and was not as involved in the ecstatic side. On the contrary, I went from very ecstatic experiences with shamanism to a very basic, material spirituality. It's a little like, 'Come on, it's time to come down from your thing. You saw that God exists, you saw it with your own eyes! Now come down and see that God also exists in material things!' And that you can also raise them up, these material things. But with God in these material things.

This new approach to religion, more 'materialist', to use his word, implied 'a peaceful life' that was more balanced. His relations with his family, friends and work improved.

> I'm less impulsive than before, less authoritarian, less aggressive. I've improved my conduct and follow the rules, now I buy my metro ticket. When things are prohibited . . . I obey the law.

Applying Sufism in daily life also means applying it in society. For example, Aziz, a craftsman and carpenter, told me how Sufism enabled him to understand his work more profoundly, both in terms of aesthetics and his relationship with the materials. Sheikh Hamza encouraged young people to study, build their careers and get involved on all levels. It would be an exaggeration to revisit Weber and his Protestant work ethic, but in a way, the Būdshīshiyya encourages professional success and wealth.

During the spiritual retreat, Aziz and I admired a beautiful Maserati parked near the castle. He told me, 'On our path, we say, if you have the money to buy two cars, then buy them! This is not an ascetic path, but a way of giving things value.' Suleyman, a Milanese disciple, told me, '*Sīdī* Hamza tells us to have the best clothing, to eat the best food. Always without wasting!' On this subject, Faouzi Skali wrote:

> In principle, no incompatibility exists between moving along the path and professional success, and success in the professional realm can even be considered the reflection of spiritual advancement, enabling personal development and growth in all areas.[44]

Accounts of success are also found in the immigration stories of the Moroccan disciples in Milan. They describe how the brotherhood pushed them to study, work, integrate and, in general, achieve material success in life. I heard many success stories concerning immigration. Some disciples told me that they left Morocco with nothing, or even that they came as illegal immigrants and worked as street vendors, but after a few years of sacrifice, they succeeded in building a decent life, with permanent employment and a decent home.

> All of us were poor when we got here, and we'd come from very modest families in Morocco. But we have all made a little money, a nice life. All of us have children. (Muhyiddin, Milanese *muqaddam*)

Universality of Islam and Sufism

In the first chapter introducing Sufism as mysticism and as a discursive tradition, I showed that within Islam we can observe a dialectic between universal and particular narratives. In response to the questions 'Who is the infidel?' and 'What is the relationship between Islam and other religions?', Muslims and Sufis have given very different answers over the centuries, depending on various relationships with alterity. We have seen how in the twentieth century,

[44] Skali, *Le souvenir de l'être profond*, 166–7.

Sufism was influenced by esoteric, New Age and religionist cultural–religious currents that foregrounded universalist dimensions, sometimes at the expense of religious norms and sometimes in a process of reinventing Sufism.

The first manifestation of Būdshīshī universalism is in the context of Islam – that is, in expanding beyond various cultures and ethnicities, between Arabs, Berbers and converts of European descent. As highlighted by Faouzi Skali, Sufism is 'neither Eastern nor Western'.[45] By contrast, Dominguez-Diaz[46] describes a degree of distrust and scorn on the part of Moroccan disciples regarding European disciples that can go as far as challenging the authenticity of their conversion to Islam. Over years of field research, I have never observed this attitude. On the contrary, the Moroccans living in Italy always told me that converts carry 'a lot of *baraka*'. But I have conducted my fieldwork in Europe whereas Dominguez-Diaz has focused on Morocco.

Būdshīshī universalism can also be seen with regard to other religions. The disciples did not want to convert me, or affirm the superiority of their religion. Similarly, they wished me 'Merry Christmas' and 'Happy Easter'. This ecumenical approach is also reflected in daily life. For example, I observed a discussion between David and other disciples on the conflict between him and his Catholic wife, who had not accepted his conversion to Islam and who considered the brotherhood a dangerous sect. David felt torn between his blood family and his spiritual family, resulting in an intense marital crisis. Nonetheless, the disciples advised David to remain with his wife and do everything possible to resolve the crisis. We will see that, in similar situations in other brotherhoods, the *muqaddam*s and the masters advise or even impose a separation.

Būdshīshī universalism also manifests itself through communication, during interviews and long discussions with disciples. Both the converts and those raised as Muslims translate Allah by 'God' or 'the God', underscoring that their God is no different from 'mine'. Universalism is also in the code of conduct. Racism and discrimination are not only discouraged; they are considered inadmissible. Muhyiddin, the Milanese *muqaddam*, told me:

> If you want to detest someone, detest your *nafs* [ego]. We love everybody: believers, non-believers, Buddhists, Catholics, Jews and Muslims. We love everybody . . . As soon as you want to hurt someone you are cut off.

[45] Skali, *Le souvenir de l'être profond*, 109.

[46] Dominguez-Diaz, *Women in Sufism*.

The causes and forms of this Būdshīshī universalism are many. We can link it to the esoteric universalism, New Age influences and religionism that characterise the quest of several disciples, especially converts. For example, several Parisian disciples came to Sufism through Guénon and use the concept of 'Primordial Tradition' to frame the relations between religions. Others come from a quest more focused on ecstatic experience and have little interest in theoretical formalisations, because what they are looking for is intimate experience with God.

Universalist discourses also arise out of the curiosity and thirst for knowledge that I saw among many disciples. I met a number of them, from all social classes, who wanted to study and compare other religions. This can be explained by the presence of converts or by the context of countries with liberal democracies and a majority of Catholics. For example, Tayob, who is French of Algerian descent, told me that, in his spiritual quest, Islam was not the only choice:

> I looked at various traditions. Islam, or Sufism, was not a priority, so I also looked at others. When I rediscovered Islam, I found it had everything in it, that everything was perfectly coherent. And it wasn't in opposition to other religions.

Similarly, Malik, also French of Algerian descent, explained that the universal dimension present in the Būdshīshiyya served as an anchor in his intellectual and spiritual quest.

> Two things I discovered were, firstly, the spiritual dimension of the religion and, secondly, the openness towards other traditions. You can be part of your tradition, but by taking an interest in other spiritual religious traditions you understand the common points. All of them are aimed at the same objective: the love of God, divine love, love for creatures, and peace . . . Up to that point, the Islam I had known had been more of an Arab Islam, a Maghrebi Islam. I had never had the opportunity to meet Western Muslims. Knowing Western Muslims in the 'Alāwiyya and Būdshīshiyya *ṭarīqa* proved that Islam is, in fact, universal. It addresses humanity and isn't cultural.

This universalism thus cannot be reduced to exogenous influences; rather, it is based on Sufi practices and discourses. The Moroccan disciples in Italy, often new working-class immigrants, have not been exposed to esoteric or New Age discourses, but they express universalist discourses centred on their religious experience.

A good example is Muhyiddin's singular pilgrimage to the tomb of Saint Emilianus in the province of Brescia. Muhyiddin, the Milanese *muqaddam*, had dreamed of Saint Emilianus, a Christian saint 'of the same period as the Prophet Muhammad, *ṣallā Allāhu 'alayhi wa-sallam*'. The saint had invited Muhyiddin to visit him. According to Muhyiddin, the deacon of the church across from his small grocery store also had a dream. He saw Muhyiddin and his wife, Qur'an in hand, praying towards the mountain where Saint Emilianus had his tomb.

A few days later, Muhyiddin and the deacon recounted their respective dreams and decided to visit the saint together. Muhyiddin explained to me that he prayed at the tomb of the saint only with his eyes, in order not to disturb the other believers. He also explained that there is a *ḥadīth* that says you must visit and honour the saints of the area where you live. Given that Muhyiddin lives in Italy, Christian saints are the saints to be honoured. Because there is only one God, a common sainthood links all religions.

Finally, it was a dream – the vision of the saint; that is, direct contact with sacredness – that legitimised the value of this remarkable pilgrimage. Muhyiddin is known among his brothers as having extraordinary sensitivity; he often experiences intense ecstatic states and even prefers to have someone else guide *waẓīfa* because the ecstasy is too powerful for him. In this case, what blurs religious boundaries is not a specific understanding of religious phenomena, but rather direct religious experience – the *scientia experimentalis* of Muhyiddin with the saint. Muhyiddin explained to me that this entailed 'finding beauty everywhere. What is important is how you see things; you have to see light everywhere.'

Abdel Ghafur, a Moroccan Būdshīshī disciple who lives near Milan, told me a similar story, that of a Milanese disciple who was 'Sharifian and the niece of *sīdī* Hamza'. Following recurrent dreams of a saint named Anthony, this disciple, the wife of the Moroccan consul, decided to visit the sanctuary in Padua dedicated to Saint Anthony.

> She went by car with some other people, but the sanctuary was closed. However, they opened it so she could visit the saint's tomb. She's the niece of *sīdī* Hamza! But you know, *sīdī* Francesco, those people, we are not worthy, even of talking about them. We talk about our very simple lives. Like them, we live only through *dhikr*. (Abdel Ghafur)

This universality also works in the other direction. The disciples are not only the vehicles of universalism; they also 'receive it'. Abdel Ghafur told me that during his first days in Milan, in the early 1980s, he looked for work with an organisation managed by the Church. In their offices, a sister asked for his documents. While getting them out, Abdel Ghafur removed the photo of *sīdī* Hamza that was next to his identity card:

> The sister saw the photo and asked me, 'Who is that?' I answered, 'My father.' 'No! That's not true! This man is a saint!' *Allāh 'a'lam*. With God as my witness. I don't know if she was a hidden saint. When she told me that, I got goosebumps!

A few days later, Abdel Ghafur continued, he returned to the office and the sister presented him to Father Ferdinando, saying, 'This man is one of us.' According to Abdel Ghafur, she was referring to faith that transcends religious identities. In his story, Abdel Ghafur shows us that his universalism is also reflected in the beliefs of other religions. The sister and the priest recognised him, with his religion and his spiritual master. After listening to the accounts of Muhyiddin and Abdel Ghafur, Jafar, who grew up in the brotherhood, told me a Sufi parable:

> There was once a Sufi master who told one of his bad students to find someone worse than he was, or else risk expulsion. The student searched among his brothers but couldn't find anyone. So, he found a Jew, feeling sure of himself. 'He isn't even Muslim!' The bad student took the Jew to the master, who recognised the Jew as a saint. The student was sent away.

Finally, I would like to underscore that these disciples, such as Muhyiddin, Abdel Ghafur and Jafar, are unfamiliar with René Guénon, Gurdjieff and Theosophy. Their universalism is based on other ideas. In addition, they tend to be conservative concerning gender roles, raising children and applying Maliki *fiqh*. Their universalism is not linked to liberal ideas.

The universal discourses described here do not imply the absence of Islamic particularism. In this way, despite the idea of a common truth that runs through monotheistic religions, Islam is – according to these disciples – the best expression of it, being its most recent revelation. Similarly, the Qur'an is the most well-preserved holy book, compared to other holy books, which have been modified over the centuries. Finally, the idea of a common metaphysical truth does not exempt the disciples from following the religious norms of sharia, even though, as we have seen, there is disagreement as to the practical application of these norms, namely, *fiqh*.

Of course, in the Būdshīshiyya as in each religious movement, various approaches to other religions exist side by side, with each believer imagining alterity differently. Moreover, the presence of an Italian sociologist brought up in Catholicism may have favoured putting universalist narratives on display.

Finally, this universalism does not prevent the presence of exceptions – that is, severe criticism of other religions or apologies of Islam or Sufism. For example, on one occasion, I heard a French convert espousing conspiracies concerning Jews and the 11 September 2001 attack on the Twin Towers, and concerning Daesh, supposedly a marionette created by Israel. However, these accounts seem to originate in the counter-culture and/or New Age milieu, which has given rise to several conspiracy theories.[47] They are very rare and generally criticized in the *zāwiya*.

For example, during a *waẓīfa* evening in Paris, Samir took advantage of the *muqaddam*'s absence and that of more experienced brothers to ask me some questions. Assuming that because I was Italian I was also a Catholic, Samir wanted to get into a theological discussion on Christianity. Taking an unpleasant, provocative tone, he asked me, 'What do you think of the trilogy [*sic*]?', referring to what he considered one of the most problematic aspects. I did not even have time to respond; the other disciples immediately stepped in to defend me. Bachir asked him, 'What? The *Star Wars* trilogy?', highlighting Samir's error in confusing 'trinity' with 'trilogy'. Everyone started to laugh, but Samir corrected himself and continued. He asked me what I thought of the prohibitions in Islam, and without giving me the chance to respond, he began to assert the Qur'an's superiority over the Bible. Then he asked me about Jesus's divinity. Malik said this attitude was disrespectful towards me, adding, 'If this had been my first evening here, I would not have come back.' Tayob affirmed that 'all religions make it possible to join with the absolute' and that to compare theologies, one needed to have instruments, to have knowledge. Another disciple cited the Qur'an and how one should 'argue only in the best way with

[47] Asprem and Dyrendal, 'Close Companions? Esotericism and Conspiracy Theories'.

the People of the Book'.[48] But Abdel Haqq delivered the *coup de grâce*, telling Samir, 'You, you're criticising the trinity, but what do *you* know about theology?! Would you like to tell us about the time you said Hamza was God?' 'But that was in a moment of ecstasy, I don't know . . . I wasn't myself,' answered Samir. Another disciple brought the debate to a close: 'So every foolish thing you've said has been inspired by God? And it isn't your fault? Is that it?' Samir, mortified, apologised to me then, and once again, during the following meeting.

Submission and Relationship with 'One's Time'

A fundamental topos of Sufi literature is submission to divine will and acceptance of the life we are 'destined' to live. The primary effort, *jihād al-akbar*, does not concern one's 'outer' life, but rather the fight against one's own ego, or *nafs*. Against this backdrop, Mahdi's story is telling. Mahdi, a Moroccan man around fifty years old who emigrated to the United States, told me about his conversion. It occurred when he was able to submit to divine will, even if it meant his own death. His illumination and 'reconversion' to Islam–Sufism took place in a dramatic situation – Mahdi was on the verge of drowning in a lake. He went through three phases: 'rage', stemming from the idea of losing his family, his house and his prestigious career. He then experienced a feeling of 'penitence', concerning his lack of piousness and a life focused on material things. Finally, he arrived at 'acceptance', saying to God, 'Take me, I am ready.' He explained to me that 'when you accept existence in its unity, you can receive mercy. Prayer is never for oneself, it's only to grow closer to unity.' This life-changing experience initiated his spiritual quest, which led him to the Būdshīshiyya.

Accepting the divine will also means accepting the society we live in. This attitude of openness to others and society in general expresses itself through the relationship with 'time' – that is, the historical context in which each disciple lives. In this regard, the disciple René cited al-Ghazālī: 'God is time, don't insult time, this is the time desired by God', which refers to a similar *ḥadīth*: 'Do not vilify time, for Allah is time.' Sheikh Hamza thus encouraged a positive attitude towards 'time': 'It is [as an] impure heart that you misunderstand time.' As another Sufi adage goes, 'The Sufi is the son of the instant.'

This openness to 'one's own time' conflicts with the Guénonian anti-modernism of some converts, such as René. This former student of Michel

[48] Q.29: 46 (translation by M. A. S. Abdel Haleem).

Foucault went through an 'intellectual drama', which led him to study Guénonian esotericism and then convert to Islam. At the beginning of his quest in Sufism, his view of Islam was influenced by anti-modernism, but meeting Būdshīshī disciples changed his perspective and his way of experiencing Islam.

> Sufism is the son of its time. The Moroccan disciples, who were working class, realised that here in the West, they were like fish in water. They never felt hostility towards the outside. They never complained of racism. And their attitude towards the Western world was almost positive. They didn't adopt a critical stance like Guénonians, who are always critical. And I realised this gave them what you could call an enormous advantage, even though the word is regrettable, in terms of integration. They felt at home here! No problem! The wisdom of this always surprised me. I've asked myself a lot of questions, but I've realised that on the spiritual path, it's best to develop true spontaneity, joy in being here . . . We shouldn't judge young people, we should be clear about things, what is good, what is evil, but we shouldn't judge young people. As for them, they didn't judge. '*Kuffār*! Miscreants!' Never!

This attitude towards society includes another expectation: 'The *faqīr* [Sufi disciple] must be a good citizen.' The disciple must not only obey the laws of the country where he lives; he must also be active and positive in his social context. The Būdshīshī singer Abd Al Malik wrote a book, *Qu'Allah bénisse la France* ('May Allah bless France'), in which he tells his life story, recounting his conversion to Islam and later to Sufism, and in which he reveals his passion for French culture and the values of the French Republic.

Muhyiddin, the Milanese *muqaddam*, did not write a book, but he often recites *du'ā*, or prayers, during which he asks God for the end of the Italian economic crisis. Youssuff, the Paduan *muqaddam*, best expresses this discourse:

> A *faqīr* has to be integrated. A *faqīr* is, by definition, openness, tolerance and integration. He is the definition of *taṣawwuf faqīr ibn wāti*; he is the son of his time. This is also true in Morocco. I learned this from *sīdī* Hamza . . . He teaches why loving is not easy, is not simple, is not for everybody. Love becomes spontaneity.

This engagement in social relations is 'politics with a capital P; it isn't limited to the left or the right,' says Idris, the Parisian *muqaddam*. For the French and Italian disciples, being a good disciple, being a good citizen means changing society from the inside, starting with one's daily relations with others. This positive relationship with society, with the 'times', does not mean an absence of criticism, or acceptance of the *status quo*. Finally, this idealistic, utopian approach (without any pejorative meaning) also poses concrete political challenges which I will discuss below.

Religion and Politics

In Morocco: Bastion of Tradition and/or Counter-reformation?

This brotherhood is both so widely disseminated in Europe and so closely linked to Moroccan society that it cannot have a univocal political position. Yet it is possible to discern two forces within this Sufi order. The first is conservative, defending 'traditional' Moroccan society and closely associated with the figure of the king, the *makhzan* and the Maliki rite. The second emphasises questions of gender equality, ecology, religious pluralism, and so on. These two tendencies must be considered not as separate but as open to each other, with mutual influence. Although I will focus on the humanist dimension, more widespread in Europe, a brief look at the conservative dimension is necessary to contextualise this Sufi brotherhood.

The conservative dimension of the Būdshīshiyya can be seen in its fidelity to the Moroccan monarchy and to the ʿAlāwī dynasty, which has governed Morocco since the sixteenth century.[49] The king of Morocco is *amīr al-mu'minīn*, commander of the faithful; his role is both political and religious. This association between the Būdshīshiyya and the king of Morocco is accentuated by some Moroccan disciples who assert that the Būdshīshiyya has remained faithful to the king, even under the reign of Hassan II, who opposed the brotherhood.

King Muḥammad VI has promoted a Moroccan Islam steeped in Sufism, in opposition to the Islamist and Salafist tendencies of contemporary Islam.[50] The relationship between the brotherhood and politics is taboo in the Būdshīshiyya. Both in books[51] and in the personal accounts of disciples, it is common to hear disciples insist, 'We are not interested in politics.' Nonetheless, the Būdshīshiyya has been co-opted by the Moroccan government. There are many journalists,

[49] Cornell, *Realm of the Saint*.

[50] Spadola, *The Calls of Islam*.

[51] Ben Driss, *Sidi Hamza al-Qâdiri Boudchich*; Skali, *Le souvenir de l'être profond*.

professors and government representatives among its disciples, the most important being Aḥmad Tawfīq, Minister of Islamic Affairs, and Ahmed Abbadi, director of Rabita mohammadia des oulémas, an organisation created by the Moroccan government whose mission is to promote tolerance and openness in Islam.

The Būdshīshī political strategy has been described as maintaining an 'engaged distance'.[52] To this effect, the brotherhood has an ambivalent relationship with the Moroccan government, cultivating important relationships with Moroccan authorities while presenting itself as uninvolved with politics. This apparent distance disappeared in 2011, during the so-called 'Arab Spring', when Sheikh Hamza asked his disciples to demonstrate in Casablanca in favour of the king and the new constitution, contested by the February 20 Movement.[53] In this regard, Mark Sedgwick[54] has described the Būdshīshiyya as supporting a counter-reformation that has brought the criticisms of both Salafist reformers and secular intellectuals into the discussion.

Civic Engagement in Europe: Discourses

Despite a limited number of members, this brotherhood plays a significant role in Italy as in France. Indeed, the conservative force described in Morocco seems less present in European disciples, probably due to a plurality of factors, such as the presence of converts and the disciples' daily negotiation with European culture.

In Morocco, the Būdshīshiyya has been co-opted in political life, in support of the king's political–religious right to reign. In contrast, the discourses in Europe concern the universalism described above, the Islamity of democracy and religious pluralism. 'The values are the same; the desires are the same', as asserted by Slimane Rezki, invited to speak at an event organised by the Būdshīshiyya in Paris in 2018.

In this regard, both Būdshīshī intellectuals and disciples highlight historic examples of religious and cultural pluralism within Islam, such as the Andalusian *Convivencia*, Ottoman cosmopolitanism, and the House of Wisdom (*bayt al-ḥikma*) in ninth-century Baghdad. The history of pluralism in the history

[52] Heck, 'The Politics of Sufism'.

[53] Desrues, 'Mobilizations in a Hybrid Regime'.

[54] Sedgwick, 'In Search of a Counter-reformation'.

of Islam shows, according to Būdshīshī disciples, that secularism is not only compatible with Islam; it is truly Islamic. They maintain that the constitution of Medina advocated by the Prophet Muhammad in 622, which established the rights and responsibilities of the various religious communities, was nothing less than a form of secularism *ante litteram*. Consequently, the tensions between Islam and secularism, palpable in contemporary France, are not related to fundamental principles, resulting instead from literalist interpretations of Islam or from Islamophobic instrumentalisation.

It follows, then, that the oft-mentioned 'clash of civilisations' is nothing more than a 'clash of stupidity' because, according to Rezki, the clash involves an ossified Islam and a Europe caught up in a crisis of values, consumed by individualism and consumerism. 'How can there be a clash of civilisations when civilisations no longer exist?' Others are more optimistic, noting how religion, and notably Islam, should contribute to democratic life.

> I think that both democracy and secularism are good things, but there is a risk of veering off course. We shouldn't be naive. Someone said democracy is not ideal, but it's the best system human beings have invented, which is not to say God invented it. I thank God I live in a secular country. (Malik)

As Malik effectively explains, God did not invent democracy. It is a system invented by human beings, but it is compatible with Islamic values. In any case, several disciples assert that democratic practices cannot be considered an end point because the 'real work' concerns the ego and one's love for others.[55] In the next section, I will show how these discourses are embodied in the activities of this brotherhood.

Civic Engagement in Europe: Practices

Concerning Italy, the Milan *zāwiya* is still too small to host activities, and the disciples do not speak Italian well enough to organise cultural events. The Padua *zāwiya* is much more active. It holds intercultural and interreligious events, drawing on the talents of various disciples. Youssef, the *muqaddam*, works as an intercultural mediator for the Italian Ministry of the Interior, and has played a role in migrant emergencies in the Mediterranean. In addition, he

[55] Piraino, 'Les politiques du soufisme en France'.

founded an association to help immigrants in Padua, regardless of ethnicity, religion or nationality. Having earned an Islamic sciences degree in Morocco and a social sciences degree in Italy, he is well positioned to mediate between Paduan Muslim communities and public institutions.

Khalid Rhazzali, the friend who helped me gain access to the Būdshīshiyya, is a researcher at the university in Padua. He is one of the founders of Master degli studi sull'Islam d'Europa, which promotes research and dialogue and organises events for both academics and the general public. The Italian Būdshīshiyya is not an active, identifiable political player because the disciples hone their political–social involvement without using the 'Sufi' label. That said, the spirit of Islamic humanism is evident in the activities they organise. The choice not to use the 'Sufi' label in these political–cultural activities could be interpreted as a calculated strategy for maximising the dissemination of their ideas. Rather than as a marketing strategy, I interpret this approach as being tied to a view of religion less focused on identity and more focused on the ethical and experiential dimensions.

The commitment of Būdshīshī disciples to peacefully living together is not necessarily linked to a public, identifiable engagement, but as in the Italian case, it often takes the form of a silent, solemn commitment that does not make declarations, manifesting itself instead in daily life.

> Sufism changes society not with direct activism, although this is not excluded in certain cases. It instead works silently, making improvements from within, in relationships . . . [This is a] silent revolution . . . If we really want to follow the prophetic model, we should be revolutionaries, progressives, as was the Prophet, *ṣallā Allāhu ʿalayhi wa-sallam*. Think about what he did in the social sphere, for orphans, for the poor and for women. (Malik, Franco-Algerian disciple)

Although the other disciples do not have the same revolutionary values as Malik, most of them believe that Sufism will play a role in achieving peace and reconciliation in French society. In the words of the Parisian *muqaddam* Idris:

> I sincerely hope a time will come in which Sufism will play a really important role, especially in what is referred to as the problem of the suburbs.[56] In fact, I'm positive this moment will come.

[56] This refers to the tensions in the suburban areas of Paris, which reached a peak in the 2000s due to social injustices, unemployment, segregation and criminality.

This message of love, deeply rooted in Islam but going beyond the Islamic religion, and this brotherhood's cultural diversity imbue its disciples with a sense of responsibility for French society. The mercy shown by the 'living saint' has indeed inspired a form of accountability in some disciples. What concrete forms does this take in French society? First of all, it translates into prayer – that is, *dhikr*. This was the case after the terrorist attacks that struck Paris in 2015; the brotherhood organised evening prayer events dedicated to protecting the city. The Būdshīshiyya has also participated in public demonstrations against terrorism, such as the '*Marches républicaines*', held on 10–11 January 2015. The sense of responsibility towards French society is also expressed through organising cultural activities.

The grandson of Sheikh Hamza, Moulay Mounir al-Qādirī al-Būdshīshī, promoted the association Valeurs et Spiritualité Musulmane de France (VSMF) in Argenteuil, whereas in Bagnolet the association Isthme was created. Even the names of these associations express the intention of linking various cultures and religions, an isthmus being a strip of land that joins two seas. As for VSMF, it highlights the plurality of 'values' shared across various cultures. These two associations also have shared objectives in terms of the activities they have organised: (1) promoting Sufism and another image of Islam, beyond the negative representations in the media; (2) encouraging interreligious dialogue, especially with Jewish and Catholic communities; (3) advocating new ways of living together; (4) building awareness around ecological questions and the religious dimension of respecting nature; (5) developing activities to enrich young Muslims (similar to the Boy Scouts); and (6) organising Sufi concerts.

Būdshīshī discourses around the importance of pluralism and democratic practices, similar to the promotion of Sunni Islam as being both traditional and open to modernity, do not constitute specific political positions; nor do they give specific instructions on the rules to follow or contest. The objective instead seems to be the building of a space for dialogue between various, apparently irreconcilable, positions. For example, they posit the importance of sharia and its spiritual value, without explicitly indicating how to interpret *fiqh*.

I observed a good example of this inclusive, conciliatory approach in Brussels, during an evening event organized by VSMB (Valeurs et Spiritualité Musulmane de Belgique) on 'Women in Muslim spirituality'. During the event, researcher Malika Hamidi and Būdshīshī radio journalist Yousra

Dahry engaged in a dialogue with the public on the role of women in Islam. A disciple presented them by highlighting the paradox from the start, noting that these women were 'entirely feminine, if not to say feminist, entirely traditional, entirely modern and entirely intemporal'.

In the discussions, all the various positions came up. Some participants underscored the importance of fighting against the patriarchy, citing the African American communist activist Angela Davis, while others put forward an Islamic feminism focused on embracing maternity, in some cases at the expense of pursuing a career. Still others promoted liberal positions. The participants wore a variety of clothing, from hijab to headwraps inspired by African Americans to no head covering at all. Everyone agreed that women must be free to choose how to live.

This inclusive, conciliatory approach runs the risk of upsetting some; conservatives may be disappointed in the progressive discourses that question so-called 'tradition', whereas progressives may be disappointed in the lack of systematic criticism of religious norms.

This tension, which could potentially give rise to dialogue between the Maliki Sunni tradition and modernist discourses, such as feminism, has led to fractures in the French Būdshīshiyya. For example, the French intellectual Abdennour Bidar left the brotherhood after criticising it fiercely.[57] Bidar has become the champion of a 'self-Islam' that promotes discussion around religious norms and even certain practices. On the other hand, some disciples mistrust the cultural and political engagement of the Būdshīshiyya, wondering if it would be better to focus exclusively on prayer. This is the case of Omar Van den Broeck, a well-known Belgian Muslim intellectual who, in a 2018 interview, explained to me:

> From the moment you put your ego on display, you are in contradiction with Sufism. *Sīdī* Mounir voices a paradox by almost saying the opposite. He says, you're the ones who think about always fighting your ego, so you're the victims of your ego [you don't think about others]. Those who work to do good in the world are those who actually fight their ego. Who's right? I think we're in a new phase of Sufism. Personally, I don't want to take sides.

[57] Bidar, *Self islam*; Bidar, *Un islam pour notre temps*.

Some Būdshīshī disciples engage in a much more visible, ostensible way. This is the case of the Socialist politician, Bariza Khiari, and the rapper, Abd Al Malik. They promote an open and progressive Islam, drawing criticism from some more conservative disciples. But this criticism does not prevent them from being officially supported by the brotherhood.

Senator Bariza Khiari

Bariza Khiari, born in Algeria in 1946, is the first Muslim woman senator in France (Socialist Party). She was the Vice-President of the Senate from 2011 to 2014 and is a judge in the French High Court of Justice. She is also a Knight of the French National Order of Merit. I had the opportunity to interview her at the Senate building in 2013. Senator Khiari told me how, at the start of her career, the religious dimension was personal, but when Islam began to be a political subject, she decided to speak out:

> In all my actions, I staunchly defend the French Republic and am comfortable with my Muslim identity. I don't hide who I am. Those who hide who they are eventually need a psychiatrist! (Khiari, 2013 interview)

She went on to clarify her position and present an Islam that is not in opposition to the values of the French Republic, such as secularism and democracy:

> I am a Sunni Muslim, of the Maliki rite and the Sufi tradition. And our Islam, like that of most Muslims in France, is entirely peaceful, open and tolerant, in keeping with the French secular tradition.[58]

The discourses of this Franco-Algerian senator clearly display progressive thinking. She works for social justice, the rights of women, personal liberties, and tolerance between diverse religions and cultures. That said, her discourse does not call for reform, in that she does not want to revolutionise Islam. On the contrary, she expresses the desire to rediscover a forgotten past:

> Because Islam has never been as strong, powerful, intelligent, beautiful, aesthetic or poetic as when it interacted with other religions. Look at the Andalusian period, when the Sufis dominated with their Jewish and Christian friends. They were very creative . . . Becoming creative again can also happen through Sufism. (Khiari, 2013 interview)

[58] Marie Lemonnier, 'L'islam n'est pas en rupture avec le christianisme', *L'OBS*, 17 December 2009.

Khiari's socialism and her Sufism are linked to her love for others and her idea of justice. The senator relates the story of her parents – who were Muslims and socialist activists, fighting against French colonialism in Algeria, and who had lived through torture and imprisonment – to her own political engagement: '[I entered] socialism through the door of justice.' Similarly, her life is interwoven with Sufism:

> The question of justice is a backbone in Sufism. There is no incompatibility between my socialist vision and my Sufi vision. Because my socialist vision is to serve those who have entrusted me with a public office . . . Always more justice, always more emancipation for the men and women of this country. And Sufism brings me peace in facing inner conflict. It's a backbone for inner peace. Which helps me remain centred . . . Emir Abdelkader said something very true: 'Politics involves carrying the destiny of others on your shoulders.' (Khiari, 2013 interview)

The link between Sufism and Khiari's socialist ideals reminds us of the possible links between Sufism and the theology of liberation:[59]

> I had a dream. If Muhammad Iqbal, Imam Shamil, and Emir Abdelkader were with us today, they would be feminists, because a nation cannot move forward by depriving itself of half the energy of its vital forces; they would advocate for a social ecology . . . they would advocate for a social economy . . . they would be democrats . . . they would move toward modernity without rejecting tradition, instead embracing it to better surpass it . . . Yes, Emir Abdelkader, Imam Shamil, and Muhammad Iqbal would have had this courage . . . and you!!![60]

In 2015, Senator Khiari was named Director of the Institut des Cultures d'Islam (ICI),[61] which includes a cultural centre and a mosque in the eighteenth arrondissement of Paris. It organises various activities linked to Islam in its cultural manifestations (for example, language courses in Arabic, Kabyle, Wolof, and so on). Khiari, who dreams of an Islamic and Sufi humanism, also

[59] Geoffroy, *L'islam sera spirituel ou ne sera plus*; Khiari, *Le soufisme*; Khiari, 'Le soufisme et engagement citoyen'; Mériboute, *La fracture islamique*.

[60] Khiari, 'Le soufisme et engagement citoyen'.

[61] The website of the Institut des Cultures d'Islam (ICI) is available at <https://www.institut-cultures-islam.org> (last accessed 3 November 2023).

shared her concerns about the conflict with fundamentalism, a conflict she characterises as an actual war:

> There is a spiritual Islam that is being killed. There is a war, a real war, which has led to the destruction of mausoleums of saints in Mali, Mauritania and Tunisia. The war is on. Between spiritual Islam and legalistic Islam.

She is also concerned by an abusive form of secularism that is instrumentalised for political and Islamophobic purposes. But she admitted to me that it is not always easy to connect politics and faith. For example, she had to think carefully about the question of gay marriage, oscillating between moral–religious doubts and political reasoning, finally deciding, with some difficulty, to vote in favour of gay marriage.

Among Būdshīshī disciples, there is a normative tendency, well represented by Khiari, that at times rehabilitates the Orientalist antinomy of Islamic 'legalism' in opposition to 'Sufi Islam'. And in her account of how the Būdshīshiyya got involved in 2011 in Morocco, the brotherhood was supporting the king to save the country from the protesters of the February 20 Movement, described as the expression of Islamic radicalism, a position which discredits a heterogeneous protest. For Khiari, 'Sufism is the bastion against radical Islam.' Sufism is the solution, an expression resonant with a well-known Islamist slogan.

The Rapper Abd Al Malik

Abd Al Malik, born in Paris in 1974, spent his early childhood in Brazzaville, Congo, where his parents were from originally, before returning to Strasbourg in France a few years later. He recounts his particularly difficult adolescence in his autobiographical book, *Qu'Allah bénisse la France*,[62] which led to a film by the same name. His parents divorced and his mother raised him and his six brothers and sisters alone. Abd Al Malik, who at the time went by the name Régis, rapidly fell into petty crime, namely pickpocketing and selling drugs. But Régis was at the same time a model student, seeming to lead a parallel existence.

At age sixteen, he converted to Islam, an Islam he describes as obsessed by the *ḥarām–ḥalāl* (illicit–licit) opposition, fuelled by 'total hatred of the West'.[63]

[62] Abd Al Malik, *Qu'Allah bénisse la France!*

[63] Abd Al Malik, *Qu'Allah bénisse la France!*, 96.

This 'protest-driven'[64] Islam did not enable Abd Al Malik to resolve his inner conflict and merge his parallel lives. On the contrary, after discovering his passion for music and his musical talent, he felt even more torn. In the ultra-conservative Islam he practised, music in general was frowned upon, particularly rap. Music, which would turn him into an international star, became for him a 'shameful disease'.[65] Similarly, his passion for philosophy and literature was considered to contradict his faith.

That was when the singer discovered another Islam, Sufism, first through the classical works of al-Ghazālī and Ibn 'Arabī, then through the contemporary works of Faouzi Skali and Éric Geoffroy. In 1999, he came into contact with the Būdshīshiyya: '[The] gaze of Sidi Hamza met mine; for a fraction of a second, I was transported by this vision of an ocean of love.'[66] Inspired by this spiritual and existential reconciliation, Abd Al Malik entered a new artistic phase. He became a mainstream star, his success resulting in several awards.

What makes Abd Al Malik special and gives him his artistic force lies in the diversity of styles, languages and experiences that the singer expresses. His music has a rap base, but also reveals the influence of jazz, as in the song 'Gibraltar' (2006), which tells of his first encounters with Sufism. We can also hear the influence of Francophone singer-songwriters, such as Jacques Brel. This comes through in the song 'Juliette and Romeo' (2008) which he sings with Juliette Greco.

In his lyrics, Abd Al Malik tells of his Catholic Congolese origins, his difficult adolescence and the 'gangster' world he frequented. The rapper–disciple is also in a position to refer to 'high culture', citing the writer Albert Camus and the philosophers Spinoza, Deleuze and Derrida. His music and lyrics can also be interpreted as a 'manifesto for social integration',[67] a manifesto advocated by a singer who defines himself as 'breaking down ghettos'.[68] Not limiting himself to music, Abd Al Malik has become a public persona. He is regularly invited to television shows to talk about Islam, Sufism, secularism,

[64] Roy, *Globalized Islam*.

[65] Abd Al Malik, *Qu'Allah bénisse la France!*, 120.

[66] Abd Al Malik, *Qu'Allah bénisse la France!*, 171.

[67] Bourderionnet, 'A 'Picture-perfect' Banlieue Artist' 153.

[68] Abd Al Malik, 'Grand Corps Malade & Abd Al Malik – On n'est pas couché' [video], *YouTube*, 27 December 2008. Available at <https://www.youtube.com/watch?v=dNeayxVhzvI> (last accessed 3 November 2023).

democracy, integration, and so on. The principle he primarily highlights in his work and his discourses is that of reconciliation. The universalism he defends is the fruit of both his personal experience and his view of spirituality: 'Our differences are a gift . . . which *sīdī* Hamza teaches me every day, so I can be a universal man, filled with love for humanity, for creation.'[69]

This Islam is not disconnected from politics; the artist espouses the concept of 'spiritual democracy' of Stéphane Hessel and the Dalia Lama[70] and affirms, '[I have] realised how much French republican values are vehicles of spirituality.' This position does not mean he makes no criticisms of French institutions; take, for example, his criticism of the caricatures of Muhammad published in the satirical magazine *Charlie Hebdo*. According to him, they 'contributed to spreading Islamophobia, racism, and mistrust toward all Muslims'.[71] Abd Al Malik thus supports French republican values, but calls for their rediscovery and reformulation:

> This is an unprecedented time we have the opportunity to live in, a time in which it is possible to reinvent ourselves, a time in which we have the opportunity to correct and then rewrite our collective history . . . [a time in which] we are called upon to start dreaming again.[72]

His lyricism also extends to French republican values; he often says, 'France is beautiful!' 'I love France' as in the song 'C'est du lourd' (2008).

> While the word 'fraternity' may seem old-fashioned today and without real significance for many of us, it's because we've forgotten, purged from our memory that France is not a country, it's not a chain of mountains, it's not a climate or a group of rivers. In fact, France isn't even a people or a nation. And if France is still all these at once, it's above all because France is a mother, and the worst of it is that we've made her forget her own role.[73]

[69] Abd Al Malik, cit. Piraino, 'Les politiques du soufisme en France', 10.

[70] Hessel and Dalaï-Lama, *Déclarons la paix!*.

[71] Bénabent and Pascaud, 'Abd Al Malik: 'L'islam est méconnu, par les musulmans eux-mêmes et par les autres,' *Télérama*, 8 December 2020. Available at <https://www.telerama.fr/livre/abd-al-malik-l-islam-est-meconnu-par-les-musulmans-eux-memes-et-par-les-autres,123130.php> (last accessed 3 November 2023).

[72] Abd Al Malik, *L'Islam au secours de la République*, 175.

[73] Abd Al Malik, 'Abd Al Malik répond à Guillaume Pelletier' [video], *YouTube*, 10 February 2012. Available at <https://www.youtube.com/watch?v=uVptpTYlfuI> (last accessed 3 November 2023).

Abd Al Malik's artistic contents and political messages reveal a hope for reconciliation, faith in human beings and in society, and a utopian dream of a peaceful, harmonious society, where religious, cultural and social differences are instruments for personal and collective development.[74] Abd Al Malik shows openness even in the face of criticism. He never seems to lose his patience, responding to his detractors with kindness. This peaceful attitude, along with his utopianism, have often been fiercely criticised. Abd Al Malik has been accused of being 'self-righteous', 'too nice' and 'too much the good little boy'. Jacques Denis, in the newspaper *Le Monde Diplomatique*, defines his music as 'domesticated'.[75] He has often been criticised in the world of French rap for being too optimistic and naive in his political views.[76] To his critics, Abd Al Malik always responds firmly:

> I want to say something. My point of view is that an artist has to be subversive, and I would say that subversion is something that varies with the times. For me, being subversive today means being capable of shifting from the individual to the collective . . . We need to be together, we need to show this marvellous diversity, we need to say that alone, we accomplish nothing! . . . Reconciliation is important.[77]

The spiritual–political utopia of the French rapper inevitably draws criticism from those who are distrustful of Islam. It draws criticism from those who consider French political structures incapable of implementing the values they claim to serve. Finally, it draws criticism from those who do not accept the idea of a multicultural society.

Public institutions like the media, in their desperate search for models of the 'positive Muslim', of 'successful integration', run the risk, in beatifying[78] Abd Al Malik, of polarising the discussion. The danger is to create, on one hand, the

[74] Abd Al Malik, *Place de la République*; Abd Al Malik, *Le dernier Français*.

[75] Jacques Denis, 'Rap domestiqué, rap révolté', *Le Monde Diplomatique*, September 2008. Available at <https://www.monde-diplomatique.fr/2008/09/DENIS/16290> (last accessed 3 November 2023).

[76] Jouili, 'Rapping the Republic'.

[77] Abd Al Malik, 'Grand Corps Malade & Abd Al Malik – On n'est pas couché' [video], *YouTube*, 27 December 2008. Available at <https://www.youtube.com/watch?v=dNeayxVhzvI> (last accessed 3 November 2023).

[78] Abd Al Malik was named 'Chevalier des Arts et des Lettres' (knight of arts and literature) by the French Minister of Culture. He was also named a patron of the Institut des Cultures d'Islam and a patron of the 'Vivre ensemble' (living together) event put on by the mayor of Paris.

'good Muslim' who loves France and, on the other, the 'bad Muslims' who do not. The danger is to forget that constructive criticism and non-constructive criticism come from both sides. And the danger is to reduce the complex questions of integration, multiculturalism and racism down to a single and overly simplistic question: 'Do you love France?'

It is interesting to see the reactions to Abd Al Malik's liminal position. The Būdshīshī *zāwiya* in Bagnolet likes this rapper–disciple, who made the initiatory pact with the lodge's *muqaddam*. In addition, I have met disciples who were drawn to Sufism because of his work. However, some disciples told me that not everybody likes him, particularly in conservative circles, because of his progressive positions. All the same, he is often invited to Madagh to speak at the international Sufi conference, Rencontres Mondiales du Soufisme. The brotherhood thus officially supports him.

The philosopher Pierre Tévanian, in a provocative article entitled 'Pierre écoute un disque de slam . . . et vomit',[79] which plays on the title of a song by Abd Al Malik,[80] argues that the cultivated citations of the rapper–*faqīr* represent his 'desire for distinction at the expense of the proletariat, the indigenous, and other elements of "suburban youth"'. The bitter criticism of the philosopher targets another song, 'C'est du lourd' (2008), calling it a 'reactionary manifesto', because it champions the values of family, work, tolerance and the French Republic.

The sociologist Jeanette Jouili does not use Tévanian's aggressive style, but her criticism is pointed in the same direction. According to Jouili, Abd Al Malik's political–religious perspective implies the exclusion of religion from the public sphere. Furthermore, she considers the rapper's calls for effort and individual responsibility to promote neo-liberal individualism and values. In fact, Jouili considers his universal–utopian rap incapable of designating and defying power structures and consequential forms of injustice. Even his music has become 'the sound of the status quo'.[81]

[79] Pierre Tévanian, 'Pierre écoute un disque de slam . . . et vomit', *lmsi*, 14 February 2009. Available at <https://lmsi.net/> (last accessed 3 November 2023).

[80] 'Gilles écoute un disque de rap et fond en larmes' ('Gilles listens to a rap album and breaks into tears', giving rise to Tévanian's 'Pierre listens to a slam album . . . and vomits'), on the album *Dante* (2008).

[81] Jouili, 'Rapping the Republic', 76.

The criticisms of Tévanian and Jouili open a debate that goes far beyond Abd Al Malik because we can witness the same utopian–humanistic engagement and the same theoretical issues in several Sufi brotherhoods in Europe and elsewhere. This utopian–humanistic engagement thus poses several questions: what is the origin of this utopia? Is it Islamic or secular? Is it a blunt weapon incapable of criticising those in power? Is this utopia a form of 'false consciousness', a superstructure of neo-liberal and individualistic thought? Doesn't this utopia push us towards the polarisation between the 'good Sufi' and the 'bad Muslim'?[82] Given the cross-cutting dimension of these questions, which implicate many of the protagonists in this book, I prefer to wait until the concluding chapter to make an attempt at answers. For now, I would like to underscore that no answer is clear-cut, because the same discourses can have various applications, and significant discrepancies can exist between theory and practice. I am thus as distrustful of the 'good Sufi' apology as I am of its opposite: the denunciation of 'domesticated Sufis'.

Conclusions

Sheikh Hamza, the living saint, and the discourses linked to this extraordinary figure, have generated a real renewal in the Būdshīshiyya brotherhood, which has taken on a global dimension. The living saint has legitimised intense proselytism, 'a Sufism for all', which abandons ascetic and elitist practices and opens the way for everyone, including potential European converts.

This global dissemination has been helped by the collaboration with the Moroccan government (interested in better controlling the religious field) and by the recruitment of intellectuals, politicians and artists who have given the Būdshīshiyya a new image and new languages (the rap of Abd Al Malik, the human sciences and European esotericism of Faouzi Skali, and the civic engagement of Bariza Khiari).

In addition to these macrosociological explanations, there is another microsociological explanation: the Būdshīshiyya promotes a religious practice strongly focused on ecstatic rituals and fellowship, which has attracted new disciples from all social and cultural milieus. This accent on *dhikr*, on

[82] Safi, 'Good Sufi, Bad Muslims'; Philippon, '"Bons Soufis" et "mauvais Islamistes"'.

mystical and ecstatic practice, has created cohesion both locally and internationally. Finally, all these dimensions – the living saint, global dissemination, new languages and prioritising ecstatic practices – have contributed to creating and spreading universalist narratives, which in turn form the basis for political engagement.

4

ʿALĀWIYYA DARQĀWIYYA SHĀDHILIYYA

> Our contribution, through our teachings, is to participate in a universal consciousness. Let's return to what is human so that the divine can reveal itself in us. This is in keeping with tradition. (Bentounes, interview conducted in 2014)

Entering the Brotherhood

It is a sunny Saturday afternoon in May and I am waiting for the ʿAlāwī disciples at the Aulnay-Sous-Bois train station in the Parisian suburbs. Contacting the ʿAlāwiyya of Khaled Bentounes was relatively difficult; I made several unsuccessful attempts. This, it turns out, is a paradox, given that the ʿAlāwiyya is strongly present in the public sphere of contemporary Sufism and is known to be an open, tolerant brotherhood. The difficulty I had is not unique to me; other disciples and brotherhoods have tried to contact this brotherhood as well, but to no avail. Only later will I understand that this is not a form of elitism but stems from the priorities of the path; the ʿAlāwī focuses most of its efforts on cultural, social and political activities, rather than on proselytism.

Two disciples come to meet me: Quentin, a retired French physician, and Afif, a young Algerian man completing an internship in France. We greet each other warmly, my Italian and Venetian background once again serving to break the ice. On the way to the *zāwiya*, we discuss the relations between Algeria and the Most Serene Republic of Venice, along with colonialism and politics.

Strangely, they do not seem particularly intent on presenting the brotherhood to me, nor on discussing Islam or Sufism.

We reach the *zāwiya*, an attractive house with a nice yard. In the street and the yard are some fifty disciples who are greeting each other and talking, creating a joyful atmosphere. They introduce themselves with a simple 'Bonjour' (hello), followed by two kisses on the cheeks, which I receive from men as well as women. Camilla, president of AISA Paris (International 'Alāwī Sufi Association), smiles at me and says, 'Don't be alarmed! They call us the kissing brotherhood!' Often, physical contact between men and women (such as greeting kisses and handshakes) is frowned upon by conservative Muslims, but as we will see, the 'Alāwiyya is characterised by its challenging of the numerous principles that underlie women's roles and gender segregation.

We enter the house and find ourselves in a small antechamber where a flight of stairs ascends to rooms on the upper floor and a door opens onto the large basement where the rituals are practised. This temporary *zāwiya* is the home of one of the disciples, the son of the last *muqaddam* (local leader).

The first sacred ritual takes place in the antechamber. All the disciples remove their shoes and put on a djellaba. White is the predominant colour, a symbol of purity. As for the women, they cover their heads with a white veil. Quentin goes about finding me a djellaba, which he calls '[my] work uniform'. The *zāwiya* basement, measuring around 860 square feet, is covered with rugs. On the white walls are three small frames: a photo of Sheikh Aḥmad ibn Muṣṭafā al-'Alawī, founder of the brotherhood; a photo of the last local Parisian leader; and a drawing of the 'Alāwī *silsila* (spiritual lineage). There is also a small bookcase.

When it is time to enter the *zāwiya*, the joyful effervescence observed in the street and outside the home suddenly vanishes, replaced by an ambiance of silence and concentration. Whereas people were making eye contact a few seconds before, their gaze is now directed towards the ground. The *muqaddam*, seated with his back to the wall and flanked by the other elderly disciples, looks out into the room. Now the religious salutations with the *muqaddam* begin: the standing disciple kisses the head of the seated disciple, who places their right hand on the right foot of the standing disciple. They then kiss each other's hands while saying, '*Salām 'alaykum*'. Seated in one of the rows, I take in my first 'Alāwī spiritual meeting. Once it is over, I approach the *muqaddam* to explain my research and ask him for permission to participate in the brotherhood's activities. Old, seriously ill and fatigued, Lyès nonetheless has enough strength to direct the meeting. I speak to him, but he cannot hear me, as he is deaf in one ear. I have to get close to him, as if in a confessional; then I restate the reason I have come. He smiles and says:

> Welcome! I want to tell you, though, that you can stay with us or go into all the *ṭuruq* [brotherhoods] in the world, but Sufism is in you . . . Sufism is not only a faith, it's also a quest . . . I hope I have answered your question.

Although I had not asked any questions, his response satisfied me. I was delighted to have contacted this brotherhood and to begin my fieldwork with the 'Alāwīs.

Birth of the 'Alāwiyya

> Our elixir is a very old wine. Sealed before Adam! We are drunk with it, O dear friend. Since a time before time![1]

This brotherhood's non-conformist character and its ardent, at times provocative, spirit came into being with Sheikh Būzīdī, master of Aḥmad ibn Muṣṭafā al-'Alawī and the sheikh of the Darqāwiyya Shādhiliyya brotherhood in Mostaganem, a city in western Algeria. According to the hagiography, Būzīdī shocked Algerians at the end of the nineteenth century by entering brothels to educate the sex workers. He went so far as to exhort unmarried disciples to take them as their wives. According to him, 'There is more merit in bringing creatures out of hell than in preaching to good men.'[2]

Aḥmad ibn Muṣṭafā al-'Alawī was born in Mostaganem in 1869. His spiritual education started with the 'Isāwiyya brotherhood where he learned to charm snakes and walk on burning coals, practices he would later describe as instructive for 'exalting the ego'.[3] At the age of sixteen, he left the 'Isāwiyya to devote himself to the teachings of the Darqāwiyya Shādhiliyya of master Būzīdī.

Būzīdī left this world in 1909 without designating a successor. However, the hagiography has it that Būzīdī gave his disciple a sign: 'You're like a lion.

[1] Al-'Alawī, cited by Geoffroy, *Un éblouissement sans fin*, 92.

[2] Bentounes, *La fraternité en héritage*, 31.

[3] Bentounes, *Soufisme l'heritage commun*, 136.

Wherever you lay your hand, you'll be master.'[4] The image of the lion (already present in the hagiography of Sheikh Hamza as mentioned in Chapter 3) captures the idea of powerful charisma. And the charismatic aura of Sheikh al-ʿAlawī did indeed attract thousands of disciples throughout the Maghreb, which led him to found his brotherhood in 1911. In discussing this phenomenon, Martin Lings refers to a 'overflowing faith',[5] whereas the Orientalist Augustin Berque relates how the French colonial authorities, not without alarm, took a particular interest in the 'conversion' of thousands of people, leading them to accuse the sheikh of hypnotism.[6]

The definitive consecration of the brotherhood in the Sufi milieu came with public recognition by the master's grandson, al-Darqāwī.[7] Concerning the number of disciples, the Orientalist Probst-Biraben gave the figure of 100,000 disciples in 1949,[8] whereas Éric Geoffroy and Talbi have spoken of 200,000 disciples.[9] It is extremely difficult to give an accurate number, since the brotherhood spread rapidly with each voyage of Sheikh al-ʿAlawī. Most of the disciples were in the Maghreb, but there were others in Palestine, Syria, Saudi Arabia and Yemen, not to mention the United Kingdom and Europe. In this way, the ʿAlāwiyya became the Sufi brotherhood of several European Guénonians seeking initiatic knowledge.[10]

The key to understanding the charismatic power of Sheikh al-ʿAlawī lies in his multifaceted figure. He was the defender of an Islam and an Arab culture under attack by French colonialism. Metaphysician[11] and poet,[12] he was also a man of his time who took an interest in the technological advances and philosophy coming out of Europe, as we will see below. Some have pointed out that the spread of the ʿAlāwiyya was made possible by the support

[4] Bentounes, *La fraternité en héritage*, 34.

[5] Lings, *A Moslem Saint of the Twentieth Century*, 120.

[6] Berque, 'Un mystique moderniste'.

[7] Bentounes, *Soufisme l'heritage commun*.

[8] Probst-Biraben, 'La Tariqa Alawiyya', 79.

[9] Talbi, 'Immigration et intégration de la confrérie ʿAlawiya en France depuis 1920'; Geoffroy, *Un éblouissement sans fin*.

[10] Sedgwick, *Against the Modern World*.

[11] Carret, 'Dans l'intimité du Cheikh al-Alawi'; al-ʿAlawī, *L'Arbre aux secrets*.

[12] Al-ʿAlawī, *Extraits du Dīwān*.

(or at least the non-opposition) of the French colonial government,[13] although other authors have shown the divergence of opinion among colonial authorities, in that Sheikh al-ʿAlawī was at times seen as a precious ally and at others as a formidable enemy.[14]

According to disciple accounts, the sheikh's charisma was first and foremost physical, and secondarily intellectual. This is but one example of the charismatic Sufi sheikhs considered in this book, who drew disciples to themselves with a magnetic attraction described as inexplicable. Saintliness is a phenomenon that moves through the body before its expression in language; it is experienced 'in the flesh and in the bones' according to a verse of Sheikh al-ʿAlawī's poetry.[15] The sheikh recounted how, in writing commentary on the Qur'an, he experienced the same physical phenomena as the Prophet during the revelation.[16]

The charisma of the ʿAlāwiyya's founder went beyond ethnic and national boundaries, bringing together disciples from diverse backgrounds, who were often politically opposed. In the 1920s, within the Mostaganem ʿAlāwī *zāwiya* were Arabs, Berbers and Europeans. Moreover, several Europeans saw in al-ʿAlawī a 'Christic' dimension,[17] recognised by the brotherhood and in keeping with Sufi tradition, which allowed that saints could possess the characteristics of prophets.[18] Sheikh al-ʿAlawī was thus seen as a 'Christic' saint – that is, possessing some of the characteristics of the prophet ʿĪsā ibn Maryam (Jesus, son of Mary).

The openness to alterity concerned not only ethnicity but also religion. We know that Sheikh al-ʿAlawī showed openness and curiosity regarding the Aḥmadiyya and the Bahá'ís as well as Christianity.[19]

> If I could find a group to be my interpreter in the European world, everyone would be surprised to see that nothing divides the West from Islam.[20]

[13] Sedgwick, 'The Making of a Sufi Saint of the Twentieth Century'.

[14] Dieste, 'Sufi Sainthood, Modernity, and Reformism'.

[15] Bentounes, *Thérapie de l'âme*, 127.

[16] Geoffroy, *Un éblouissement sans fin*, 118.

[17] Vâlsan, *L'Islam et la fonction de René Guénon*; Lings, *A Moslem Saint of the Twentieth Century*; Carret, 'Dans l'intimité du Cheikh al-Alawi'.

[18] Ibn al-ʿArabī, *Le livre des chatons des sagesses*.

[19] Probst-Biraben, 'La Tariqa Alawiyya'.

[20] Al-ʿAlawī, cited by Bentounes, *Soufisme l'heritage commun*, 156.

The dialogue that French physician Carret reported having with al-ʿAlawī shows us a spiritual master not interested in proselytism or in demonstrating Islam's superiority. Based on the discourse reported by Carret, the sheikh underscored common points with atheists and agnostics, telling his interlocutor, 'It is a pity that you will not let your Spirit rise above yourself. But whatever you may say and whatever you may imagine, you are nearer to God than you think.'[21]

Sheikh al-ʿAlawī's openness and curiosity also applied to so-called 'modernity'. According to the hagiography, he was interested in Henri Bergson's philosophy as well as Albert Einstein's science.[22] He was the first Algerian in Mostaganem to have a telephone and a car. In addition, he redefined the role of women in the culture of his day, a subject that was to remain a constant in this brotherhood. He gave women the esoteric initiation through a blessing and a glass of water, and taught his adopted daughter, Kheira, to swim and ride horseback.[23]

> The Muslim religion is very liberal and recommends instruction and science in Muslim countries as well . . . Pasteur, I am told, was a religious man, but this did not stop him from making major contributions to humanity through his marvellous inventions. No! Religion does not prevent man from reaching the highest summits of science, for religion is merely a guide . . . If God had wanted to leave man to fend for himself, he would not have revealed to his numerous prophets the New Testament, the Talmud, the Bible, and the Qurʾan to guide man to the right path.[24]

Sheikh al-ʿAlawī was also present in the public sphere. In 1923, he founded the newspaper *Lisān al-dīn*, which would be repressed by the French colonial government. In 1926, he bought a printing press (still on display in the Mostaganem *zāwiya*) and founded another newspaper called *Balāgh*. The articles in these newspapers spoke of subjects such as colonialism, materialism and communism, not to mention Islam. Moreover, the sheikh organised a conference every year in Algiers, open to all Muslims, in view of 'unifying Muslims to resist the acculturation and ignorance imposed by colonial authorities'.[25]

[21] Al-ʿAlawī, cited by Lings, *A Moslem Saint of the Twentieth Century*, 33.

[22] Berque, 'Un mystique moderniste'.

[23] Bentounes, *La fraternité en héritage*.

[24] Al-ʿAlawī, cited by Berque, 'Un mystique moderniste', 771–2.

[25] Bentounes, *Soufisme l'heritage commun*, 164.

Sheikh al-ʿAlawī was a defender of Sunni Islam, Sufism and Arab culture against the political and cultural dictatorship of the French. However, his firm but peaceful political engagement against colonialism, also characteristic of his successors, was not synonymous with shutting out Christianity or new knowledge from France. On the contrary, the sheikh encouraged learning French along with other foreign languages. From this perspective, encountering the Other did not impede self-realizstion, but rather furthered it.

From a theological point of view, the sheikh criticised the presupposed heterodoxy of some Sufi practices (magic, exorcism, mortification, and so on), but he defended the value of pilgrimages to the tombs of saints,[26] called into question by Wahhabism.[27]

Finally, Sheikh al-ʿAlawī is considered a *mujaddid*, someone capable of revivifying the Islamic religion. This is how he is viewed in all the brotherhoods I visited. The Mostaganem sheikh is also unanimously recognised among the Sufi disciples I met as being *quṭb* in his day. As a pioneer in both the Sufism of migrants (Algerians in France and Yemenites in the United Kingdom) and in Guénonian Sufism, he is an even more important figure in European Sufism.

After the death of Sheikh al-ʿAlawī in 1934, there was no one with his charisma who could step in and bring together different ethnicities, nationalities, cultures and languages as he had done. Subgroups emerged and created brotherhoods: the Būdilmiyya Habibiyya, the Maryamiyya and the ʿAlāwiyya Madaniyya. However, the ʿAlāwiyya brotherhood continued on its path with ʿAdda Bentounes, who was appointed sheikh by the Council of Sages in 1934. He was also married to Kheira, the adopted daughter of al-ʿAlawī.

Sheikh ʿAdda Bentounes continued the effort to disseminate the brotherhood, which spread to Senegal and grew stronger in Europe. Sheikh ʿAdda lacked his sheikh's magnetic charisma, but he established himself through humility and sharing. Here is what he said in an interview published in the newspaper *El Morchid*, which he had founded in 1944:

> Brothers! It is not Sheikh ʿAdda who invited you to this conference. It is the fakir, your brother, to whom you gave the mission to continue the work of the Great Master . . . I am but a servant of the Alawi tariqa, at your command.

[26] Dieste, 'Sufi Sainthood, Modernity, and Reformism'.

[27] Al-ʿAlawī, *Lettre ouverte à ceux qui critiquent le soufisme.*

> I accept your judgement but be advised if you decide to allow me to continue on the path that I know and have found to be straight . . . So you all have a duty to perform: helping me along this path . . . [The work of the ʿAlawīs is] in service not of fuqara nor Muslims, but rather all men, fallen humanity in its entirety, which is veering off the path of faith and which we have an obligation to help.[28]

Sheikh ʿAdda developed the brotherhood's social dimension, creating a football team for young Mostaganemers, reintegration programmes for juvenile offenders, and schools for learning how to write and speak Arabic. In this way, he continued his master's battle to defend the Arabic language and Arab culture.

Sheikh ʿAdda also shared the universalist enthusiasm of Sheikh al-ʿAlawī. He engaged in interfaith dialogue to promote peace and reciprocal understanding. In 1948, he founded the association Les amis de l'Islam (Friends of Islam) in which people of diverse religious backgrounds played an active role.

It is worth noting that the language of interfaith dialogue was not yet a given at that time, particularly in occupied Algeria. This openness led some to accuse Sheikh ʿAdda of syncretism and of being a Freemason.

> What does it mean to be a friend of Islam? It means being a true Christian, or a true Israelite, or a true Buddhist, or a true Muslim; in short, someone truly in search of Truth, accepting all those who wish to love God and serve Him, without concern for the origins of his brother . . . Do not believe, my sisters and brothers, that the prophets (may blessings and peace be upon them), Moses as well as Jesus and Muḥammad, came to divide us or serve their own interests. No, truly, they came only for the good and in sole interests of the world, to bring all hearts of this world to the path of God, to the Way of Truth.[29]

Sheikh ʿAdda died in 1952. The Council of Sages then selected his son Hadj al-Mahdī Bentounes whose deep spirituality and devotion to studying the Qur'an set him apart from an early age, according to the hagiography. By age eleven, he had already made the pilgrimage to Mecca, hence the title of *Hadj*.

Sheikh al-Mahdī guided the brotherhood during a period of political instability. He participated with his disciples in the Algerian War and was even taken

[28] Bentounes, *Soufisme l'heritage commun*, 226.

[29] Bentounes, 'Editorial', 2–3.

into custody and later subjected to house arrest. During this war of liberation, the *zāwiya* provided shelter and medical care. At the end of the war in 1962, the brotherhood resumed its activities. In 1967, Sheikh al-Mahdī founded a Qur'anic school and had a mosque built in the Tigdit district of Mostaganem. He continued the work of his masters, who had been committed to Algerian society, by offering a societal model that was neither capitalist nor Socialist, 'but rather rooted in its millennial culture [Islam]'.[30]

The newfound tranquillity in the Mostaganem *zāwiya* was short-lived. Starting at the end of the 1960s, the brotherhood was accused of being an anti-nationalistic association, a 'State within the State', and a spy network abetting foreign powers, most likely due to the unusual presence of European converts. In 1970, suspected of spying, Sheikh al-Mahdī was arrested and tortured and the property of the brotherhood confiscated: its bank account, its land and the *zāwiya*. The sheikh's eldest son, Khaled, crossed Morocco and fled to France. Often considered a 'martyr' within the brotherhood, Sheikh al-Mahdī died in 1975 at the age of forty-seven years old. The Council of Sages appointed his son Khaled to take the reins.

Khaled Bentounes: An Iconoclastic Sheikh who Rejects Charisma

Khaled Bentounes was born in Mostaganem in 1949 and received a traditional education in the *zāwiya*, studying the Qur'an, the *ḥadīths*, and *fiqh*. In addition to his Islamic education, Khaled took an interest in such European classics as Karl Marx's *Capital* and Jean-Paul Sartre's *The Devil and the Good Lord*, even though he considered these works to be vaccines[31] and highlighted their problematic dimensions.

In 1968, he fled to Europe to escape possible retaliation by the Algerian regime which, as we have seen, feared the ʿAlāwiyya. He initially went to Oxford to study, but rapidly left England for Paris. There, in 1972, he opened an artisanal clothing shop and met his future wife, Evelyne, a Catholic from Normandy who even wore miniskirts.[32] The disciples, the *zāwiya*, Mostaganem, Sufism and political problems seemed far away for Khaled, who wanted

[30] Bentounes, *Soufisme l'heritage commun*, 269.

[31] Bentounes, *Le soufisme, cœur de l'Islam*.

[32] Bentounes, *La fraternité en héritage*.

to lead another life: '[Because] I felt a distance from all of that. Something pushed me to invent my own life, to refuse an overly traditional destiny for my freedom-loving soul.'[33]

His Parisian life was upended by the premature death of his father al-Mahdī in 1975. At age twenty-six, he was appointed sheikh of the 'Alāwiyya brotherhood, a decision he did not initially believe: '[They] made me dress in the white djellaba of the Sheikh. And in this instant, I became the Sheikh for everyone, except for myself.'[34] Sheikh Khaled suffered from this decision by the Council of Sages:

> [At] night, I couldn't sleep and was covered in sweat. During the day, I vomited constantly and my chest felt like it was on fire.'[35]

After initially refusing his role, he did not feel worthy of being the sheikh. He went through an interior struggle, both spiritual and physical:

> I had to fight a long battle against myself to accept my fate.[36]

Sheikh Khaled did not accept his fate as spiritual guide passively, instead leading the brotherhood to a significant turning point in terms of both form and content. Khaled manifested a particular kind of charisma: 'the rejection of charisma'. In his books, he presents himself as a man like any other and provides biographical information at odds with building the aura of a Sufi master. For example, he tells of how, as a child, he skipped Qur'anic classes to play football behind the mosque. He even recounted his doubts and fears upon being appointed as spiritual guide: '[I] do not feel I am one of these seekers of God privy to sacred knowledge. I am not a mystic.'[37]

Sheikh Khaled deconstructed the image of the Sufi master; he did not wear a beard, married a French Catholic woman, and only wore traditional clothing for rituals. Quentin, a disciple from the Parisian middle class, acknowledged that the sheikh was not very interested in his image. He described how the

[33] Bentounes, *La fraternité en héritage*, 98.

[34] Bentounes, *La fraternité en héritage*, 105.

[35] Bentounes, *Le soufisme, cœur de l'Islam*, 40.

[36] Bentounes, *La fraternité en héritage*, 12.

[37] Bentounes, *La fraternité en héritage,* 71.

master was dressed in a T-shirt, Bermuda shorts and flip-flops during one of his visits to see him: 'He looked like a German tourist' (Quentin).

> Sheikh Khaled is not a spiritual man of the twenty-first century, he's already in the twenty-second century! Even Sheikh al-'Alawī was criticised, whereas today no one would dare to do so. (Antoine, aged thirty, French disciple)

The deconstruction of the classical figure of the Sufi sheikh has changed the relationship between the master and the rest of the world. Sheikh Khaled has exposed himself to various situations liable to highlight his weaknesses, such as television interviews where journalists press him on current political and religious matters. The sacred space, which protects Sheikh Hamza of the Būdshīshiyya and Sheikh Nazim of the Naqshbandiyya both physically and symbolically, is something Sheikh Khaled seems to reject, viewing it instead as a limitation. In his relationship with his disciples, he dislikes signs of deference, preferring, for example, to shake hands rather than undergo the hand-kissing salutation. Furthermore, he dislikes discourses and narratives that magnify his person. Add to that his view that the miracles of sheikhs are not an argument in conversation because 'they feed the ego' (Karim).

This rejection of charisma and the saintly aura are part of his pedagogical–theological vision, as we will see. Sheikh Khaled often shocks his disciples by saying, 'I'm not your sheikh; that's something you must find within yourself.'

> Finally, allow me to add that we must be wary of masters, beginning with myself. This wariness must subsist until the relationship is firmly established in candour, loyalty, friendship, devotion and total love. Before reaching this level, we do not yet have a master. The master is nothing more than a mirror in which the disciple contemplates their ugliness and their beauty. And stay close to those masters who say, 'I know that I do not know.' And God is the most learned. And He is the one we return to.[38]

We can take an example from my fieldwork: when I interviewed Sheikh Khaled in this home near Grasse (southern France), a disciple gave me an ashtray because he had seen me smoking previously. However, during the three-hour interview that followed, I chose not to smoke, aware that in

[38] Bentounes, *Le soufisme, cœur de l'Islam*, 222–3.

Maghrebi brotherhoods, smoking is considered disagreeable. Even though some disciples smoke regularly, no one would dare to smoke in the presence of an elderly disciple, not to mention the sheikh. But at that moment, in the master's home, it was more important to make me comfortable than it was to preserve the sacred space around the sheikh. A similar situation, the consequences of which are clearly different, took place with the Būdshīshiyya in Madagh. After eating lunch in a restaurant, I went out and stood opposite the building so I could smoke a cigarette. A few moments later, Sheikh Hamza's grandson, Mounir, stepped out to make a phone call. At that point, two disciples quickly approached and took me by the arm, kindly but firmly, to distance me from Mounir, so that the smoke from my cigarette would not disturb him.

These two examples show us how, in the Būdshīshiyya as in other cases we will see, the disciples and the brotherhood have built a sacred space around the master (and sometimes his family), made up of subsidiary rituals (salutations, distance and deference) and narratives of saintliness, which contribute to constructing the figure of the Sufi master and to protecting him. In the ʿAlāwiyya, Khaled Bentounes has deconstructed this space. This does not lessen the figure of this sheikh; what changes is the narrative the disciples build – that is, Sheikh Khaled has become for his disciples an emblem more important than being sheikh of the ʿAlāwiyya, in that he has become a spiritual reference, a source of hope for all those who wish to live in peace.

> He is not pulling away because he no longer wishes to be the sheikh, but because he is becoming something more important, not only for us, but for everyone. (Quentin, aged fifty, French disciple)

This rejection of charisma, the saintly aura, and the protective sacred space is, in and of itself, proof of Sheikh Khaled's saintliness for some disciples. For them, his humility is proof of his self-realisation: 'Among the signs of being *quṭb* is the fact of openly saying one is not *quṭb*' (Abdel Sabour, aged forty, French of Kabyle descent).

> The sheikh is a theophany, he's not God because God is everywhere, but he is his expression on Earth! (Abdel Hay, aged fifty, Franco-Algerian disciple)

Khaled Bentounes, despite his particular charisma (the rejection of charisma), has succeeded in spreading ʿAlāwī Sufism in Europe and now even in Japan.

It is especially through books, lectures and interviews that Khaled Bentounes has succeeded in connecting with new audiences. Others have interpreted this rejection of charisma as a form of excessive modernisation or a form of inferiority, compared to past masters, and have left the brotherhood as a result. The metamorphosis embodied by Sheikh Khaled Bentounes concerns not only his role but also the functioning of the entire brotherhood. We will see in this chapter how this change affects the brotherhood's discourses, activities and organisational structures.

Organisation of the 'Alāwiyya: Between Confraternity and Post-Confraternity

It is decidedly difficult to estimate the exact number of 'Alāwī disciples. We have seen that when al-'Alawī was the sheikh, there were around 200,000 disciples and sympathisers, but the brotherhood underwent significant fragmentation after the founder's death. As a rough estimate, in 2009 during the centennial celebration, the brotherhood was considered to have around 6,000 participants.

The presence of 'Alāwī disciples in Paris began in the 1920s with the first wave of Algerian immigration. The 'Alāwīs were thus among the protagonists in the beginnings of Islam in France. They built the first halal slaughterhouse and participated with the sheikh in inaugurating the mosque in Paris.[39] The migration of disciples increased in the 1950s, then once again in the 1970s.

There are around 600 French disciples, and the Parisian *zāwiya* is made up of 200 disciples who are members of the Association International Soufi Alawiya (AISA; International 'Alāwī Sufi Association). However, at the weekly rituals I attended in 2013, I never saw more than seventy disciples together at once.

It is not easy to retrace the history of the Parisian *zāwiya* because, since the 1920s, it has regularly changed locations. During my interviews, *zāwiya*s in Bobigny, Drancy and Ivry-sur-Seine, among others, were mentioned. Until the end of the 2000s, the *zāwiya* was based in Drancy, in the Île-de-France region around Paris. Bentounes then decided to sell the building it had used until that time, to 'get young people involved', in the words of Abdel Sabour. For a few years after that, the disciples used the home of one of their brothers,

[39] Talbi, 'Immigration et intégration de la confrérie 'Alawiya en France depuis 1920'.

in Aulnay-sous-Bois, where I frequented them in 2013. In 2014, the Parisian disciples inaugurated the new *zāwiya*, once again located in Drancy.

Algerian-Kabyle families form the core of the Parisian brotherhood. It is currently possible to come across 'fourth-generation' Parisian disciples. That said, there is a significant number of converts. Concerning social class and education, the brotherhood is highly heterogeneous. It includes university professors, physicians and architects, as well as those in working-class jobs. Of course, this heterogeneity breaks down along generational lines; those in working-class jobs are often Algerian immigrants who came to France in the 1950s and are today retired, whereas the newer generations exercise more prestigious professions.

The internal hierarchies of the brotherhood are based on spiritual advancement or, from a profane perspective, the age of the disciples. One of the particularities of the ʿAlāwiyya is how sheikhs and local leaders are chosen. They are not chosen by the sheikh but are instead elected by the elders, considered the community's 'sages' and guided through dreams, visions and divine signs. In the case of the local leader, the sheikh simply confirms the decision of the Council of Sages. Another ʿAlāwī particularity relates to the sheikh's family, who does not benefit from any special treatment, such that the other Bentounes are considered simple disciples like the others.

The characteristics described up to this point are part of the history of the ʿAlāwiyya, but the changes in the past ten years have led to a Sufi organisation that can be described as no longer centred on the brotherhood. This, in turn, has led to what Éric Geoffroy, an ʿAlāwī professor and intellectual, describes as a case of 'post-confraternity-ism'.[40]

> [Post-confraternity-ism] does not result in a loss of original principles, which are always to transmit this inner teaching and seek a balance between the horizontality of the world and the verticality of the eternal world. (Bentounes, interview conducted in 2014)

Both Bentounes and Geoffroy note that Sufism cannot be identified with the brotherhood model. The forms of Islamic spirituality can change over time, in that the brotherhood is just one of the various possible forms. This is not to say that the post-confraternity Sufism of the ʿAlāwiyya is an alternative model;

[40] Geoffroy, *L'islam sera spirituel ou ne sera plus.*

rather, it proposes a return to 'original Sufism', in which the Islamic spiritual quest was more fluid, not yet formalised.

> Things are going to become more subtle, as they were in the beginning, but in a different way. (Geoffroy, interview conducted in 2013)

Before explaining post-confraternity-ism, we need to clarify what has been called the 'disease of confraternity-ism'. As explained by Geoffroy, this entails a hardening of the brotherhood system which, for some disciples, becomes the only possible way: 'Outside my brotherhood no salvation is possible.'[41] This hardening has not spared the 'Alāwiyya. According to Abdel Sabour, love for the sheikh and the brothers can become pride and vanity. To illustrate this, he told me about disciples who asserted in the 1930s that:

> If you touch someone who is not in the brotherhood, you lose your ablutions. If you lack water or stones to perform them, you need only touch another brother. There were even disciples who prayed in the direction of Mostaganem.

Other disciples have recognised Sheikh al-'Alawī as not only *quṭb* – the pole of existence – but as the Mahdī himself, the eschatological redeemer.[42] Sheikh Khaled, Geoffroy and the Parisian leader often stress the importance of not falling into these egotistic forms related to Sufism. However, Bentounes' action is not limited to simply curbing possible forms of degeneration; it also seeks to revitalise the forms of Sufism.

The first element of discontinuity is the role of the sheikh, who is no longer in Mostaganem or Paris to guide the rituals, impart teachings or advise the disciples. Publishing books, participating in conferences, and all the other activities to which Bentounes has devoted himself have considerably reduced the time he has available. Some disciples say he is 'retired, making it more and more difficult to see him, which some disciples have a hard time accepting' (Quentin). As a result, making an appointment to see the sheikh is sometimes difficult. Likewise, some disciples participate in the cultural activities for the sole reason of seeing him and speaking with him. Concerning his traditional role, the sheikh participates in major celebrations such as *Mawlid*, the national

[41] Geoffroy, *L'islam sera spirituel ou ne sera plus*, 189.

[42] Dieste, 'Sufi Sainthood, Modernity, and Reformism'.

meeting at the end of the year, and extraordinary events, but his home is no longer 'the' *zāwiya*. Antoine describes the relationship with the sheikh this way:

> We rarely see him. I'd like to see him more often, but the last time I saw him, I had nothing to say to him. Everything had been said. The more we want to be close to him, the more we show that we haven't understood the teaching. The sheikh is not a crutch we [can] lean on. Spirituality also teaches us to be an adult – responsible, mature and independent. He carries you on his shoulders but in another way. (Antoine)

> An authentic sheikh makes the disciple autonomous. (Karim)

> You also have to know how to kill the sheikh, so that the inner sheikh can come into being. (René)

The accent on dialogue and living together harmoniously has shifted the balance of the ʿAlāwiyya, which is more focused on external activities than on promoting itself/proselytism. This means that despite its coverage in the media, contacting the ʿAlāwiyya is not easy. In my case, it took two months to find the right contact person, probably a consequence of this indifference to proselytism. Furthermore, several disciples told me that obtaining *bayʿa* (the initiatic pact) is even more difficult; they had to wait years before making the pact with Sheikh Khaled. This long wait, compared to other brotherhoods where access, conversion and the pact are immediate (cf. the Naqshbandiyya in Chapter 5), has caused some potential disciples to give up and continue their Sufi quest elsewhere.

Sheikh Khaled has sought to rethink the brotherhood based on the idea and image of a circle and not a pyramid.[43] For instance, all the disciples are called upon to work and share responsibilities; everyone must contribute to the well-being of the brotherhood. On this account, the sheikh encourages an independent local organisation with the capacity to propose ideas and activities, whereas the sheikh's role is to set guidelines and inspire the disciples to take action. This decentralisation and fostering of independence have spurred the creation of other organisational forms, such as associations,[44] institutions,[45] local discussion

[43] Bentounes, *Thérapie de l'âme*.

[44] The website of the association *Conscience soufie* is available at <https://consciencesoufie.com/> (last accessed 8 November 2023).

[45] The website of the META Institute is available at <http://meta-com.ch/accueil.html> (last accessed 8 November 2023).

groups, private foundations[46] and NGOs.[47] It follows that instead of a single heart and a single decision centre, the brotherhood has several.

The largest ʿAlāwī organisation is the Association Internationale Soufie Alawiya (AISA),[48] which perpetuates the work of ʿAlāwī associations founded by former masters, such as Les Amis de l'Islam. AISA is the association responsible for most of the activities conducted by ʿAlāwī disciples. Founded in 2001, this association is a federation of various national AISAs that remain independent (in France, Belgium, Germany, Canada and Switzerland) and that, in turn, comprise local committees. For example, there are eight cities/*zāwiya*s in France, and thus eight committees, in addition to the national committee. Each year, the General Meeting is held to make a joint assessment of the brotherhood's situation. The decisions are debated together: 'One person, one vote.' Even though all members of AISA are ʿAlāwī, the activities are intended for everyone, which led the UN to recognise AISA in 2014 as an NGO with a special advisory status.

Another element of Khaled Bentounes's post-confraternity-ism is the centrality of the role played by women and young people in the brotherhood. In Paris, the curtain that used to separate men and women has been removed. Likewise, it is now possible to hear female disciples singing during *samāʿ*, not only the refrains, but as the principal voices. Finally, women are extremely involved in the brotherhood's activities, in which they play key roles.

While certain elements, such as the centrality of women's roles and the proliferation of other organisational forms, seem well accepted by most disciples, others, such as the sheikh's different role, have not been greeted favourably by all disciples. More specifically, I met disciples who had left the ʿAlāwiyya due to the prolonged 'absence' of Sheikh Khaled from the *zāwiya*. One disciple, Edith, explained to me that the sheikh had been categorical on more than one occasion: 'If the brotherhood doesn't follow me, I have no problem with that. I'll work with non-believers.'

[46] The website of the Adlania Foundation is available at <http://www.fondation-adlania.ch/vision.html> (last accesed 8 November 2023).

[47] The website of the NGO AISA is available at <http://aisa-ong.org/> (last accessed 8 November 2023).

[48] The acronym AISA calls to mind the name of Jesus in Arabic (ʿĪsā or Aīssa), highlighting the Christic dimension of the founding sheikh as well as the ecumenical dimension.

During my fieldwork, I could also sometimes feel the tension between the 'traditional' Sufi brotherhood and the new 'post-confraternity' forms. For example, in 2013, I was fortunate enough to participate in the AISA General Meeting, organised in the city of Orléans in north-central France. Beyond the annual report on local, national and international activities, the major question for the 2013 meeting concerned the formalisation of a new status. What the President of AISA France proposed would dispense with any religious reference. The reason for this de-Islamisation of AISA's status was due to the limits imposed by the French government on religious associations concerning public funding. The president also pointed out that every time AISA had to take out an insurance policy for a public event, the 'Islam' label multiplied the price of the coverage. Finally, the president noted that this change was only a formality, that the Islamic spirit and ethics would remain intact. The participants' reaction was virulent; only two people (out of eighty) seemed to agree with the new status. Others openly showed their disapproval, including the man sitting next to me, who spoke of a 'schizophrenic situation'.

This rejection of the new status is not merely a legal or bureaucratic issue; it symbolises the internal tension between the brotherhood and the association AISA, between the confraternity and the post-confraternity, between a Sunni Islamic dimension and a universal dimension based on the promotion of 'living together harmoniously', which Sheikh Khaled often reiterates. This shows that, despite universal narratives and the focus on interfaith dialogue, the 'Alāwiyya is, in its daily operations, strongly influenced by Sunnism, which is centred on observance of Maliki *fiqh*, especially among the generation of elderly disciples.

Post-confraternity-ism also poses problems: 'Many disciples are upset,' says Quentin. Many view Sheikh Khaled and his innovative leadership in a positive light, but at the same time they compare the brotherhood to how it used to be with a degree of nostalgia. The era of Sheikh al-'Alawī remains in the minds of many an incomparable time:

> I was born into the brotherhood, you could say, I was born into a very deep and very spiritual Islam that was nonetheless highly rigoristic. The disciples in the time of my grandfather were youngsters who couldn't live in today's world. Today's Salafists would kiss their feet and they'd be unable to live up to their pious standards . . . They lived through war and famine, they lost children,

> they were confronted with hardship. But at the same time, if they spoke of this period, they'd say, 'We experienced days that maybe won't exist in heaven. We were constantly in the divine presence and witness to miracles.' They lived their lives with intensity – the veil had been drawn back! (Abdel Sabour)

Finally, one might expect this tension to weaken the brotherhood, but this is not the case. While some disciples have objected to these changes and have left the brotherhood, others have joined the path. As a result, the 'Alāwiyya remains one of the most important Sufi brotherhoods in the Maghrebi and Francophone public sphere.

Between Ecstasy and Discipline: Rituals

Despite the strong ethical, political and intellectual dimensions of the 'Alāwiyya, the rituals have a fundamental role in this brotherhood: '[Praying] is like breathing,' wrote Bentounes.[49] The collective religious practices of the Parisian 'Alāwiyya take place twice a week: Saturday afternoon in Aulnay-Sous-Bois,[50] the most important meeting characterised by its solemnity, and Friday evening in the homes of two disciples (one to the north of Paris and the other to the south), where the atmosphere is more relaxed.

Concerning the individual rituals, they last thirty to forty minutes and are performed twice a day, at dawn and sunset. They comprise divine names – *dhikr* – along with the repetition of parts of the Qur'an and other prayers – *wird*. Unlike in the Būdshīshiyya, the sheikh does not highlight the importance of individual practices, but most disciples seem to adhere to them.

Individual and Collective Practices

The Saturday afternoon meeting starts outside the *zāwiya*, in the narrow street it sits on, where the disciples greet and kiss each other. The standard French greeting of 'Bonjour' intermingles with '*Salām 'alaykum*'. We then enter the antechamber where everyone puts on a white djellaba and takes off their shoes. The salutations resume, only this time they are more solemn and sacred and begin with the *muqaddam* and the older disciples. We kiss the seated person

49 Bentounes, *Le soufisme, cœur de l'Islam*, 31.

50 Even though, as mentioned above, the *zāwiya* has been moved to Drancy.

on the head, and they touch our right foot with their right hand. Then both of us mutually kiss each other's hand. After the salutations, we sit down.

In the first row sit the *muqaddam* and the older disciples, with their backs to the wall and their gaze directed out into the room. In the second row, facing the older disciples, sit the two *musammiʿūn*, or singers, and the other disciples. The last rows are made up of the women and children.

Once everyone is seated, silence sets in, replacing the joy and happiness of the salutations with an atmosphere of calm and concentration. It is impolite to arrive late and disturb the meeting, and it is unlikely that a telephone will ring, since even the youngest show great respect for this gathering.

The ʿAlāwī rituals in the *zāwiya* are highly formalised; I have mentioned clothing, times, silence and positioning, but posture is also important. It is impossible to stretch out your legs; the only accepted positions are to be seated on your knees or with your legs bent and crossed.

The *muqaddam* directs the meeting, making nearly imperceptible signs to the *musammiʿūn*, or singers, defined as 'the pillars of *jamāʿ* (spiritual meeting). Everything starts with *wird* which, according to the hagiography, was created by the famous master Shādhilī and modified by Sheikh al-ʿAlawī. Made up of Qurʾanic verses and other prayers, ʿAlāwī *wird* is psalmodised with great speed, producing a psalmody that, unlike the recitation of the Būdshīshī *waẓīfa*, is strikingly rhythmic and musical, seeming almost sung. The speed and rhythmic complexity[51] of *wird* does not overwhelm the disciples, who seem to know everything by heart, even those who do not speak Arabic. Newcomers are given an explanatory sheet on *wird* with the transliteration of the Arabic into the Latin alphabet along with the French translation.

Once *wird* is over, the *muqaddam* signals to the singers to start *samāʿ*, the distinctive sign and point of culmination of the ʿAlāwiyya. *Samāʿ* is based on the poetry of Sheikhs al-ʿAlawī and ʿAdda Bentounes. Abdel Karim explained to me that there are more than 800 airs. The structure divides into the main melodies of the singers and the refrains sung by all disciples. It is particularly difficult to capture in words the musical beauty of ʿAlāwī *samāʿ*, which is due in part to the influence of 'Arab-Andalusian music'.[52]

[51] *Wird* are often psalmodiaed with odd time signatures that are very long (for example, 20/8).

[52] Geoffroy, *Un éblouissement sans fin*, 236.

Samāʿ gradually transforms into *dhikr*, the complex melodies and rhythms progressively giving way to linear, accelerating rhythms and melodies. The divine names, repeated in an increasingly intense atmosphere, gradually turn into guttural sounds. Some words end up as nothing more than aspirated Hs. In time with the rhythm, the disciples move their heads back and forth or right and left. At this point, the ecstatic tension emerges, controlled by the *muqaddam*, who knows the right moment to amplify it and the right moment to tone it down. He then starts the *mudhakara*, or teaching, which lasts around twenty minutes. Lyès provides no definitions of Sufism or Islam like the ones we are likely to hear among the Būdshīshiyya. Nor is his discourse intended to attract young people, as that of the Naqshbandiyya is. Lyès's teaching is instead aimed at raising religious questions by contextualising them in daily reality. Rather than reassuring the disciples, he questions their certitudes: 'Are you sure that [I myself] am following the advice I give to you?' he asks.

Lyès also highlights the importance of correctly executing the rituals: punctuality, *adab* (proper conduct) in the *zāwiya*, rhythm, correct pronunciation in Arabic, spiritual discipline and the importance of attending collective spiritual meetings.

> The meeting is the essence of mercy . . . There is no excuse for missing *jamāʿ*. What could be more important than a meeting attended by angels?[53] (Lyès)

Right before the *muqaddam*'s discourse, one of the disciples gets up to serve mint tea, while another collects donations. Once the *mudhakara* is over, *samāʿ* resumes, but this time the female *musammiʿāt* sing. The spiritual meeting ends with salutations; we form two concentric circles that rotate so that everyone is included. We kiss the right shoulder and say a few words.

On specific occasions, such as annual celebrations or when the energy level is particularly high, *samāʿ* and *dhikr* transform into *ḥadra* or, according to other definitions, *ʿimāra*, 'the presence' or *dhikr al-ṣadr*, 'the invocation from the chest'.[54] In this ecstatic ritual, the disciples stand and hold hands; they

[53] Here the *muqaddam* is referring to a famous *ḥadīth* that says, 'Whenever any people gather to recite and study the Qur'an, *sakīna* (tranquility) descends upon them, they become engulfed in mercy and the Angels surround them and Allah mentions them by the Angels . . .' (Sahih Muslim, *ḥadīth*s 6793 and 6795).

[54] Geoffroy, *Un éblouissement sans fin*, 241.

form concentric circles with the *musammiʿūn* or the *muqaddam* at the centre, setting the pace. They sing not with the tongue, but rather with the throat, producing the H of *Ḥuwa* (Him). In time with the ever more intense 'HUW!' sounds, the disciples move their heads and torsos, which bend and lift forward and back. The disciples' faces express joy as well as tension. Everyone participates in *ʿimāra* with enthusiasm.

> We've seen seventy-year-olds, who walk with a cane, becoming young again as soon as they engage in this dance.[55]

> *ʿImāra* makes fear and anxiety go away. You feel more dynamic, with heightened sensitivity and tenderness. All your sensations are more intense – your entire body is vivified.[56]

Unlike in the Būdshīshiyya, the ecstatic dimension experienced in the ʿAlāwiyya is more focused and controlled in *ʿimāra*. *Aḥwāl*, or ecstatic states, are rarer and more contained. This is undoubtedly due to Sheikh Khaled's desire to control ecstatic energy and the enthusiasm of the disciples.

The Friday evening meeting, which takes place in the disciples' homes, immerses us in a totally different atmosphere. It starts around 7 p.m. in Drancy. All the disciples bring something to eat, which will be shared over the course of the evening. Participants are greeted warmly, and several families are in attendance. The rituals are not different in themselves, aside from the fact that everything is much more relaxed. There is no austere *muqaddam* imparting the teachings, and some disciples smoke cigarettes, which would be impossible in the presence of the elderly disciples. In place of the palpable tension on Saturdays is the joy of being together in the name of Sheikh Khaled and the brotherhood. The music extends far beyond *samāʿ* which, once finished, is followed by Algerian and French songs. Sometimes, these meetings even seem like a gathering of friends.

The changes made by Sheikh Khaled, described above as post-confraternity-ism, impact not only organisational structures (the sheikh's role, the emergence of new social forms and the role of women), but also the rituals, since

[55] Bentounes, *Le soufisme, cœur de l'Islam*, 150.

[56] Bentounes, *Soufisme l'heritage commun*, 191.

'the sheikh keeps us focused on the essential' (Geoffroy, interview conducted in 2013).

The disciples explain to me that the spiritual meetings have been reduced in frequency and duration. During my fieldwork (2013), the evening spiritual meetings took place twice a week and lasted between two and three hours. In the past, they lasted longer and occurred more frequently. However, not only did the quantity change, but also the intensity, given that this change affected *ḥaḍra* or *'imāra*, literally 'the presence' – that is, *dhikr* in song and dance that often leads to ecstasy: '[*'Imāra*] is like a drug, according to Bentounes' (Geoffroy, interview conducted in 2013). Khaled Bentounes wanted to unsettle the brotherhood and the egos of his disciples by touching their hearts, which has meant making Sufism's ecstatic dimension – *ḥaḍra* – secondary.

> We mustn't get stuck on form. Form is a guide. We have reached a point where we no longer perform *'imāra*. When we said no *ṭarīqa* without *'imāra*, we were saying that *'imāra* is at the heart of *jamā'* (spiritual meeting). It's the core of everything, what the meeting fuels. The sheikh says to us, 'You don't know how to perform *'imāra*.' The sheikh always breaks the idol, he breaks the form. But he comes back to us, he possesses *raḥma* (mercy), he is dear to us. He takes a big swing at the ego, and he always challenges you. Once you think you're on firm ground, that you're doing what you should and feeling kind of proud of yourself, he wipes everything away. He's going to make you doubt. (Abdel Sabour)

Sheikh Khaled has sought to de-emphasise the ecstatic dimension, which was central to the 'Alāwiyya, not only to 'break the idol' of traditional Sufism, but also to focus the disciples' energy on social causes, as we will see below. A good example of this reorientation (from ecstasy to good works) can be found in the account of Abdel Rahman, a Moroccan disciple living in Brussels whom I met during a *khalwa* (spiritual retreat) near Paris. During a visit to Sheikh Khaled, Abdel Rahman asked for 'more *dhikr*', to augment daily religious practices, because he did not feel satisfied. But the sheikh did not prescribe other prayers for him. Rather, he advised him to volunteer with his 'Alāwī brothers in an ecological project in Algeria. Abdel Rahman followed this advice and told me how this journey and his activities had profoundly changed his life.

This profound change did not mean abandoning the ecstatic dimension or Sufi rituals in the 'Alāwiyya of Khaled Bentounes. Despite the reduction/reorientation described here, the 'Alāwī rituals are much more frequent and intense than in other Sufi brotherhoods that we will examine later (the Naqshbandiyya in Chapter 5 and the Aḥmadiyya in Chapter 6). In this way, Sheikh Khaled has not eliminated ecstasy, but he has asked his disciples for a commitment that is no longer limited to inner work and that concerns society.

Khalwa, *the Spiritual Retreat*

Khalwa is a fundamental time in the religious life of the ʿAlāwī disciples. According to Éric Geoffroy,[57] it was one of the reasons Sheikh al-ʿAlawī founded the brotherhood. In theory, *khalwa* lasts between three and forty days, but to my knowledge, the French ʿAlāwīs organise *khalwa*s lasting three or four days, four times a year, in various cities.

Although *khalwa* is limited to disciples who have made the *bayʿa*, Sheikh Khaled granted me permission to participate in the June 2013 *khalwa*, during the month of Ramadan. The location of this retreat has been the Clarté-Dieu Franciscan Monastery in Orsay (near Paris) for many years. A place of silence and peace, it has extensive grounds and numerous rooms for prayer. As Abdel Karim tells us, 'You can feel it's a place of prayer.' The collective rituals are thus an opportunity for the ʿAlāwiyya to highlight its ecumenical role.

During the three days at the monastery, it is fully possible to speak with the monks and other Christians of diverse backgrounds. The disciples told me that, during the previous year's event, they had even sung *samāʿ* for the monks. Nevertheless, the main goal is prayer, with everyone's energy focused on *dhikr*, leaving little time for discussion.

Attending *khalwa* requires the authorisation of the sheikh, who controls and confirms the list of participating disciples. Only a limited number may participate. In 2013, there were only nineteen of us, comprising ten women and nine men. The disciples ranged in age from twenty-five to fifty, with a concentration around the age of forty.

We wake at 4.45 a.m., have breakfast, and by 5.30 a.m. we are ready to begin the spiritual day. After *ṣalāt al-fajr* (dawn prayer), we start with *wird* and move on to a *dhikr* provided for this occasion by the sheikh. The divine names are *al-Raḥmān*, *al-Raḥīm* and *al-Salām* (Clemency, Mercy and Peace), which are repeated 300 times each (each lasting ten to fifteen minutes). The rhythm accelerates, the divine name is inspirated and aspirated slowly, but the rhythm

[57] Geoffroy, *Un éblouissement sans fin*, 218.

never reaches *'imāra*, the paroxysm, the aim of this retreat being introspection and peace.

Once the recitation of the three divine names is finished, we start with the 'supreme name', *Allāh* – God – which is inspirated and aspirated slowly to the point of elongation spanning several seconds. Omar, the *muqaddam* of the *khalwa*, explains to us that 'we have to feel it in our legs, arms, chest, mouth, everywhere!' Moreover, unlike other *dhikr*, which have a specific cadence, the supreme name does not have a specific rhythm or intonation. The only common feature is the low tonality of all the voices. On the first day, this supreme name *dhikr* lasts thirty minutes, on the second day forty-five minutes, and on the last day sixty minutes. The effect of all these voices deeply respiring this name is striking, totally different from all the other *dhikr* in which I have participated.

The other sessions take place at 2 p.m. (*ṣalāt* + *dhikr*), at 6 p.m. (*ṣalāt* + *dhikr*), at 9 p.m. (*ṣalāt* + *dhikr*) and at 11 p.m. (*ṣalāt* + *wird* + *dhikr*). Religious practices thus take up most of the day (between eight and nine hours), requiring intense concentration and a certain kind of physical stamina, especially when Ramadan is also taking place. During free time, the disciples rest; some sleep, others read, while still others walk the monastery's grounds.

Everyone participates in all the rituals and if anyone is missing, the *muqaddam* goes out to find them and invite them 'gently but firmly', according to Omar, to partake in the prayers. During *khalwa*, no one is allowed to make phone calls or leave the monastery, a rule that also applies to me as a sociologist. However, this temporary isolation from the outer world and the pursuit of introspection, peace and silence are not experienced as a constraint by the disciples, but rather as a time of joy. Edith, a French convert, describes *khalwa* as 'so much fun, like drinking champagne, a party! What a joy!'

Women wear headscarves only during the rituals. In addition to the mixing of the genders, which is normal for this brotherhood during *khalwa*, all differences between men and women are set aside during this retreat. They are no longer physically or symbolically separated. The rows include both men and women. The disciples even told me that a few years ago, a woman *muqaddam* led the retreat.

The final observation we can make about this *khalwa* concerns the fasting for Ramadan. As we will see, Bentounes authorises reducing the fasting time to twelve hours for those in Northern European countries, where daylight lasts most of the day during the summer. Thus, during these three days of *khalwa*, Ramadan ended at 7 p.m., at the time set for eating in the monastery's refectory. Some disciples (four or five), however, preferred to observe the standard times for Ramadan and prepared their dinner separately. This difference was not viewed as problematic, as everyone was free to interpret *fiqh* without fear of being judged by the others.

Pilgrimages

Sheikh al-ʿAlawī was not in favour of certain so-called 'popular' Sufi practices, such as charming snakes, using psychotoxic substances and self-flagellation. Concerning so-called 'tomb worship', the approach preferred by ʿAlāwīs is a 'moderate' one, given that the tombs of saints are considered to possess strong spiritual energy, or *baraka*. They may even have miraculous effects, or *karāmāt*. However, Sufi tombs are always secondary to the living teaching of masters and disciples. Visiting and praying at a Sufi tomb is seen as positive, but we will not see in the ʿAlāwiyya the effervescence and enthusiasm found in other brotherhoods.[58]

For example, when I visited Algeria for the Féminin – parole aux femmes conference on women's roles and voices, we visited the Mostaganem *zāwiya* and its grounds, but the visit to the tombs of the Sheikhs al-ʿAlawī, ʿAdda Bentounes and Mahdī Bentounes was optional. Even so, I was able to visit them with some Parisian disciples. The building was very modest, and the room containing the masters' tombs was very narrow, as was the adjacent mosque. This demonstrates that the brotherhood does not want to embellish the mausoleums or focus on pilgrimages to tombs.

The ʿAlāwiyya does, however, organise other types of pilgrimages. We will see that the Muslim Scouts, founded by this brotherhood, set up trips for Muslims with reduced mobility as part of ʿUmra (off-season pilgrimage to Mecca). The brotherhood also organises pilgrimages to showcase and celebrate the richness of European Islam (Andalusia, Sicily and Albania).

[58] In 2010, I had the opportunity to visit the mother *zāwiya* of the Chishtiyya in Ajmer (India). In this *zāwiya*, the tomb of the founder–master was the heart of the brotherhood, at the centre of all its activities. This intense relationship between brotherhoods and tombs seems more pronounced in the Sufism of South Asia (cf. Werbner, *Pilgrims of Love*).

Other pilgrimages and gatherings are organised with the idea of bringing together various brotherhoods and breaking through internal identity barriers, thus 'fighting' the 'disease of the brotherhoods'. For example, pilgrims travel to Uzbekistan to meet the Naqshbandiyya and to Turkey to meet the Mevleviyya. In this context, pilgrimage becomes a communication tool, for interreligious and intra-religious dialogue.[59]

As we saw with the Būdshīshiyya, pilgrimages can be 'spontaneous' in that they are not organised by the brotherhood but reflect an inner need of a given disciple. This is the case of Abdel Rahman, who made the pilgrimage to Santiago de Compostela and told me he was prompted by his curiosity about the Other and by his belief in the unicity of God. 'The truth is that God is the same!' he said. He completed this spontaneous interfaith pilgrimage with an Italian Catholic he met along the way. Praying in the churches, he performed *raka'āt* (prayer movements) with his eyes 'in order not to disturb anyone. Where should I have gone? [A church] is still the house of God, isn't it?'

Abdel Rahman's universal vision remained intact even when he saw 'Santiago the *Matamoros* [he who kills Muslims in Spanish], with the skulls of *moros* at his feet . . . This is not a nice thing to see, but I can understand that people needed a symbol for the war at that time.' Like the Būdshīshī Muhyiddin, Abdel Rahman was around forty years old and from a working-class family. Their Sufism is entirely Islamic, in that they follow the religious norms and rituals and align with the discursive Islamic tradition as instructed by its religious authorities. Their universalism does not seem based on Traditionalism and/or New Age discourses. Abdel Rahman was following another form of universalism, centred on the discourses of Sheikh Khaled Bentounes, which we will examine below.

Doctrines and Pedagogy

My goal in this section is to reconstruct the discourses and doctrines of the 'Alāwiyya brotherhood, based on the books of, and my interviews with, Sheikh Khaled and Éric Geoffroy, an eminent intellectual and member of the brotherhood. In this reconstruction, I will also consider the narratives of the disciples I met during my fieldwork in the Parisian *zāwiya*.

[59] Piraino, 'Pilgrimages in Western European Sufism'.

A Negative Islamic Theology: Truth between the Relative and the Absolute

While the Būdshīshiyya, between the end of the twentieth century and the beginning of the twenty-first century, opened up to the general public, letting go of ascetic and elitist practices to move beyond ethnic, cultural and national differences, resulting in what I described as a 'Sufism for all', in the 'Alāwiyya this opening up took place in the 1920s with Sheikh 'Alāwi, the founder. The 'Alāwiyya opened up beyond religious frontiers, since the Sufi–Islamic message 'is intended for Muslims, Christians and non-believers; above all, it speaks of the principle of unity that concerns every being' (Bentounes, interview conducted in 2014).

> [This message] is aimed at improving humanity's condition. It may be very pretentious to say so, but through this work we're bringing together young people and representatives of different religions for the purposes of mutual enrichment. We're trying to offer a vision of synergy. No one possesses the whole, everyone has a part of it. Let's put the parts together for a world that is better for all. To live together. To live together more harmoniously. (Bentounes, interview conducted in 2014)

This narrative of openness to alterity, which may at first seem similar to forms of de-Islamised Sufism (cf. Chapter 2), is in fact grounded in Islam in both the practices and the doctrinal sources. Moreover, it should be noted that this openness, promoted by Sheikh Khaled, is part of the very history of the brotherhood, as illustrated by his grandfather, Sheikh 'Adda: 'Do not ask someone what their religion is; ask them which truth they are seeking.'[60]

This narrative of openness to alterity arises from the tension between the universal and particular dimensions, a tension specific to Islam and Sufism (cf. Chapters 1 and 2). We can sum up this tension through the following questions: who is the infidel?[61] What is the definition of a Muslim? Are they simply those who are subservient to God, or do they follow the indications of the Qur'anic revelation? The 'Alāwī response oscillates between these two poles. To explain this paradox to me, which seems to echo the *coincidentia oppositorum*,

[60] Bentounes, *La fraternité en héritage*, 170.

[61] Piraino, 'Who Is the Infidel?'.

Éric Geoffroy, in a 2013 interview, cited Jalāl al-Dīn Rūmī, noting that the Persian master was very rigorous in his practice of Islam:

> For I do not recognize my own self. I am neither Christian, nor Jewish, nor Zoroastrian, nor Muslim. I am neither from the East nor the West, neither of the earth nor the sea. I come from neither nature nor the skies in their revolution.[62]

A concrete example is provided by Abdel Sabour, a thirty-five-year-old disciple who grew up in the brotherhood and is from one of its most important Sharifian families.[63] Plus his grandfather was the *muqaddam* under Sheikh al-ʿAlawī. He practises a Sunni Maliki Islam and, despite his young age, he demonstrates an in-depth knowledge of the Qur'an, the *ḥadīth* and Sufism. Nonetheless, his definition of Sufism is unusual:

> When you say 'Sufi', it's synonymous with 'spiritual' for me, it's not us, not the ʿAlāwiyya, not Muslims. A journalist asked the sheikh, 'How many of you Sufis are there in the world?' The sheikh laughed and said, 'The number of Sufis we don't know about is enormous!'

ʿAlāwī universalism implies the redefinition of the concept of *kāfir* (infidel), who is no longer the non-believer, the atheist, the polytheist or – for the most exclusivist interpretations – all those who are not Muslims. The infidel, then, becomes a state of mind:

> One who is incapable of gratitude, who rejects the divine dimension that dwells in every individual. Considering oneself superior or better than others is the road to *shayṭān*, the one who did not recognise the divine dimension of the human being. (Karim, aged fifty, Franco-Algerian disciple)

While the openness towards religious alterity is common in European brotherhoods, it is only in the ʿAlāwiyya that we find a discourse open to atheists. Karim tells us that 'religion is not the only path' and adds that atheists 'are halfway along the path because they have understood half of the *shahāda*' (that is,

[62] De Vitray-Meyerovitch, *Anthologie du soufisme*, 262.

[63] Descendants of the Prophet Muhammad.

'*lā 'ilāha*', or 'there is no divinity'). This perspective was shared by several of the disciples I interviewed.

ʿAlāwī universalism does not mean the absence of Islamic particularism – that is, the characteristics that mark Islamic identity (Qurʾan, sunna, rituals, and so on). Bentounes's books contain countless Qurʾanic citations, but what characterises the ʿAlāwī theological discourse is a conception of religious truth that is at once absolute and relative.

For example, during our interview, Sheikh Khaled explained that, in the Qurʾan, what is commonly translated as 'order what is right and forbid what is wrong'[64] is not correct; it should be translated as 'what is recognised by everyone as right and reject what is recognised by everyone as wrong' (Bentounes, interview conducted in 2014). In fact, *al-maʿrūf* means the 'common good', which surpasses religious and cultural differences. According to the sheikh's interpretation, absolute truth then consists in what is 'recognised by everyone as right'. Truth is also relative:

> No one has a monopoly on truth, whether they be a monk, a mystic, a theologian or a scientist . . . We are only fragments of the truth, and the path of Sufism is only a permanent quest to revivify it.[65]

> [The truth] is absolute, but at the level of the divine. At the human level it is always relative. The person who says they hold absolute truth divinises themselves. They are no longer a person; they are God. (Bentounes, interview conducted in 2014)

Sheikh Khaled does not pretend to have access to absolute truth; in the same way, he does not encourage his disciples to seek it. On the contrary, he warns them about the perils of absolute truths:

> Don't seek the truth because you'll end up constructing it. Seek peace, and maybe there you'll also find truth. (Anna, aged forty-five, Franco-Algerian disciple)

I also heard among several disciples the narrative of perpetual seeking, of this truth that continues to elude us. Lucien, a twenty-five-year-old French disciple,

[64] Cf. Q.3: 104–10; 7: 157; 9: 71 (translation by M. A. S. Abdel Haleem).

[65] Bentounes, *La fraternité en héritage*, 178.

spoke to me of the 'mystery of Allah . . . You know, we don't know everything, the same concept of God, nobody possesses it. God is a big question mark.' And Karim noted, 'Nothing belongs to us, not even faith.'

This approach to religion could be described as apophatic – that is, religious knowledge is not based on discursive arguments on the attributes of God; rather, it is based on direct religious experience and proceeds by subtraction. An 'Islamic negative theology' is not an absolute novelty in the history of Islam; rather, it has its roots in medieval Islam and was influenced by Neoplatonism.[66]

This Islamic negative theology implies putting values into perspective. As Sheikh Khaled often says, 'Both the saint and the murderer find what they seek in the Qur'an.' Within this meaning, Islamic values must be experienced from within to be understood.

> We should start by noting that Islam, even its exoteric side, is eminently based on the *via negativa* . . . It is not in vain that Islam originated in the desert; *One knows God through the void, because the void is plenitude.*[67]

This negative theology implies a reconceptualisation of right and wrong, concepts not seen to be radically opposed but rather rooted in the natural dialectic of the world. Evil and the devil enable us to improve ourselves, to test our qualities. *Shayṭān* (Satan), with his temptations, prompts us to make our way towards God. The devil is not a dangerous, aggressive and dark figure in 'Alāwī narratives. Rather, both good and evil are the expression of God's will. The 'Alāwī path thus leads one to overcome duality, to accept this dialectic. When I asked a disciple about the ways of fighting evil, she answered me as follows:

> That's so Manichean! What's there to fight? There's nothing to fight. There's a need to appease, to seek reconciliation, to learn to live with things as they are. The inner combat, or jihad, is appeasement, it's consciousness. It means accepting this dark side we have, which is important to recognise. That's the middle ground. It's a dynamic equilibrium. (Edith, aged fifty, French disciple)

This reconceptualisation is also reflected in the views on heaven and hell. Lucien told me that 'there is no real separation between what happens before, during

[66] Kars, *Unsaying God*.

[67] Geoffroy, 'Les voies d'accès à la réalité dans le soufisme', 198. Italics added.

or after life.' As for Karim, he explained that 'rather than places, heaven and hell are spiritual states we experience in the world. What happens after death? Honestly, I don't know.' Some disciples, like Antoine, go further, giving heaven and hell a totally symbolic meaning: 'Heaven and hell are entirely inside you, like positive and negative.' He asserted that it is impossible to understand life after death, 'which is like explaining the physical world to a foetus in their mother's womb'. Hence, for Antoine, a thirty-year-old French disciple, the conception of heaven as the physical place of rewards 'is like Santa Clause for children'.

Khaled Bentounes, referring to Ibn 'Arabī in *Fuṣūṣ al-ḥikam* (*The Bezels of Wisdom*), explains that heaven and hell are steps towards God. The flames of hell are not eternal damnation, but rather a moment of purification:

> In this moment, because we can only access the superior world as pure consciousness, our soul frees itself of anything negative received in this life. This is where the symbolic notions of heaven and hell come into play; they are, in fact, stages for accessing Ultimate Reality . . . Through a purifying fire, these souls realise that '*there is no other God than God.*'[68]

During my interview with Sheikh Khaled, I hoped to delve into the conceptions of heaven and hell and clarify them, but he wanted to centre the discussion on the present day, on this hell on earth that many men and women experience on a daily basis.

> Let's start by speaking of our hell, before we talk about the hell that lies beyond us. And let's start with all we can contribute to make this life heavenly and peaceful. Because what does heaven represent? Tradition tells us that it's a place where all human desires are fulfilled, where nobody lacks for anything. Heaven is *dār salām*, the house of peace. (Bentounes, interview conducted in 2014)

From this perspective, one of the goals of the brotherhood is to attain a degree of heaven on earth – that is, to contribute a degree of peace. The question of what lies beyond, of life after death, is not only considered secondary; it may even become a form of hidden idolatry. In the words of Bentounes, we can discover the spirit of the eighth-century saint Rābiʿa al-Adawiyya, who wanted

[68] Bentounes, *Le soufisme, cœur de l'Islam*, 205. Italics added.

to set fire to heaven and pour water on hell so as to love God only out of love, and not in view of a reward or by fear of punishment.

> If I go to heaven what good will that do me? I leave that in God's hands. He created me so he'll manage on his own! (Bentounes, interview conducted in 2014)

'Going Outside Religion': A Negative Pedagogy

'Negative' theological discourse is not limited to the intellectual and theoretical sphere; it is an actual pedagogical instrument. Éric Geoffroy tells us of 'a negative theology as an antidote to nihilism', citing Henry Corbin,[69] but it is also as an antidote to the ineluctable calcification of the Islamic faith. Similarly, I heard several disciples speak of 'going outside religion'[70] – that is, rediscovering Islamic religious values and forms in their inner meaning, in their universal meaning. In other words, negative pedagogy aims to lead disciples out of cultural or ethnic Islam, or Islam based on family tradition, to discover its 'true' spiritual and universal dimensions.

> The fear of losing my identity . . . What is my primary identity? It's *fiṭra*![71] . . . [Identity is] ego *par excellence*. We make our own God. God becomes something made in our image, after our likeness, and not the other way around. (Bentounes, interview conducted in 2014)

'Going outside religion' means going outside a religious identity that sets limits, that puts up barriers between human beings, that has 'become an ideology, an instrument for manipulating the population'.[72] The challenge, according to Bentounes, is 'to assemble without resembling each other' and 'to debate without beating each other up' (interview conducted in 2014 and notes in 2018).

> Sufism is the quest for truth that blows up every preconceived idea. Young people turn to religion to find preconceived ideas and pre-packaged truths, to

[69] Corbin, *Le paradoxe du monotheisme*, 181.

[70] This position must not be confused with that of Abdennour Bidar's book, which promotes a drastic reformism of the Islamic religion. Cf. Bidar, *Comment sortir de la religion*.

[71] The soul's natural state before birth.

[72] Bentounes, *Le soufisme, cœur de l'Islam*, 31.

> bring blessings on themselves. No, Sufism sweeps everything away. 'My religion is the best, my master is the best' – all that serves the ego! 'I'm right, me, me, me.' In Sufism there is no longer me, there's the Other. We call the outer part exotericism: 'I'm me and you're you', whereas in esotericism: 'You're me and I'm you.' And after that there's another stage: 'There's no longer you and me; there's only Him!' All of this is scary, too, since there's a loss of power (Antoine, aged thirty, French disciple)

It is only by understanding this negative pedagogy that I was able to grasp the provocations of Lyès, the Parisian *muqaddam*, who said, 'There is no "we Muslims", "we 'Alāwīs".' He often provoked the disciples by affirming:

> *Taṣawwuf* is the path that leads you to union, it's the path of the messenger, *ṣallā Allāhu 'alayhi wa-sallam*, it's the path of the brave, the courageous, the reckless . . . Our path is the path of lions, but pigs and monkeys can also follow it. Pigs don't want to get rid of the vileness of their souls, and monkeys only know how to imitate.[73]

Lyès also remarked that the Sufi quest is never over: 'This is not a combat that lasts a month, this is not a combat that lasts a year, it lasts your entire life!' Several times, I heard this old Parisian *muqaddam* ask distraught disciples if it was worth it to pursue the rituals and activities of Sufism and repeat them again and again over the years.

> Maybe I'm wrong, maybe advancing *taṣawwuf* as has been transmitted until now is wrong. Maybe this is the fruit of the ego . . . Maybe disciples today should express themselves in another way. But how? What do you think? (Lyès, Parisian *muqaddam*)

The following anecdote may help us better understand this complex dialectic between the universal and the particular. The protagonist, Moussa, nearly sixty years old, comes from Mostaganem and is an English teacher in a school in the Parisian suburbs. During an interview, Moussa told me that one of his students was absent from school for three months. When he came back, the student told him that he had spent his time at the mosque and that the imam

[73] The disciples told me this was a citation of Sheikh al-Darqāwī. Unfortunately, I was unable to find the source.

had told him: 'Those in mixed classes at school, with both male and female students, go to hell.' Moussa did not tell the student he was a Sufi disciple or a Muslim. He instead let him believe he was Jewish (the name Moussa is used by both Muslims and Jews). In the way of a response, Moussa suggested that the student read the Qur'an more closely and in greater depth, especially concerning the prohibitions the imam had peremptorily cited. The student was then able to return to school all while continuing to deepen his faith thanks to help from his 'Jewish teacher'. According to his account, Moussa chose not to oppose 'his' Sufi Islam against Salafi Islam. Nor did he choose to use his authority as a teacher against the authority of the imam. Rather, he allowed the student to learn using the Socratic method, without pitting one truth against another.

Deconstructing Islamic identity to reconstruct it also means questioning religious forms. Edith's anecdote on this subject is insightful. Edith, a French woman who converted to Islam fifteen years ago, was becoming, at this stage of her life, 'a little demanding, judgemental, dogmatic, a little hardened . . .', she told me. Sheikh Khaled advised her to stop praying. 'But Islam is five prayers a day!' she responded, overcome. The sheikh retorted, '[Now] it's prayer that leads you, rather than the other way around.' Edith then stopped praying for a few days. The result was positive; she felt calmer and found peace again. She then went back to praying normally. Until that time, Edith never would have thought that a Sufi master would advise her to stop praying. 'Sheikh Bentounes is an iconoclast,' she said. 'It's unbelievable, this man is unbelievable.'

Of course, total deconstruction of identity in this way is not possible. Otherwise, one could not talk about the 'Alāwiyya as a brotherhood. Moreover, this negative theology and pedagogy, which aim to deconstruct pride around Sufi identity, can sometimes become an argument for asserting this pride. More specifically, we have seen over the course of this chapter how some disciples see Master Bentounes's humility as proof of his saintliness and thus his superiority with regard to other Sufi brotherhoods.

Sufi Ethics

The adage we heard in the Būdshīshiyya – 'He who goes beyond you in conduct goes beyond you in Sufism' – is also very commonly heard in the 'Alāwiyya. In addition, the hagiography tells us that the founding master, al-'Alawī, stressed that 'Sufism is entirely proper conduct.'[74] A widespread discourse among the disciples encourages not judging others, whatever the characteristics of each person.

> How human beings judge what is right and wrong is often a result of their upbringing and the effect of an emotive reaction when they find themselves in conflict with others. But we must temper our judgements because they will always be more or less influenced and biased. And this is normal; we are only human, after all.[75]

One anecdote I heard several times in the *zāwiya* has as its protagonist Sheikh 'Adda. After being turned away from several mosques, a man came to the Mostaganem *zāwiya* to request the burial of his friend, a sex worker. This request provoked a heated debate among the disciples until Sheikh 'Adda stood up and said, 'I'll do it!' The disciples then went to the brothel, took the woman's body, and went out singing, '*Lā 'ilāha 'illā-llāh*!' Sheikh 'Adda had this to say in conclusion: 'I've understood why I came into this world: my task was to bury this woman' (Jawad, aged sixty, Franco-Algerian disciple).

What characterises the 'Alāwī ethical discourse is the notion of balance between divine concepts. We have seen how right and wrong are experienced in this brotherhood, as interdependent and part of a permanent dialectic. Ethical conduct is balanced conduct. The universal man is not he who has eliminated negative characteristics, but he who succeeds in mastering them: 'That's what a sheikh is for me, someone who carries all the divine names within, who carries the name of Allah' (Lucien).

Forms of Knowledge: Between the Religious and the Secular

According to Camilla, President of the Parisian branch of AISA (International 'Alāwī Sufi Association), 'Everything is God, even science. There is no scientific discovery that is not the work of God!' To illustrate this, she recounted that Sheikh al-'Alawī was very interested in Albert Einstein's scientific discoveries.

[74] Geoffroy, *Un éblouissement sans fin*, 175.

[75] Bentounes, *Thérapie de l'âme*, 208.

The relationship between scientific knowledge (both in the hard and human sciences) and religion is extremely positive for most disciples I met. For example, Sheikh Khaled Bentounes and most French disciples support the theory of evolution, considering some verses of the Qur'an to suggest its validity.[76]

The brotherhood also encourages the disciples to form research groups, potentially open to all, in which the Qur'an, the *ḥadīth* and Sufism are discussed. This research uses a hybrid methodology, between Qur'anic exegesis (*tafsīr*) and the use of social science methodologies. This approach can create paradoxes which, as we have seen, are not lacking in this brotherhood. For example, Omar, who participated in the Qur'an research group, explained to me how the Qur'an is both an uncreated sacred text and a created historical text that must be contextualised historically to be fully understood.

Here again, this is not simply a capitulation of Sufism in the face of modernity – in this case, European historiographical reason – but rather the encounter between historical–discursive reason, which also has protagonists in the Muslim world (cf. Ibn Khaldun, Averroes, Avicenna, Iqbal, and so on), and intuitive reason which, in the words of Éric Geoffroy (drawing on Guénon), is not irrational, but supra-rational.[77]

We have already encountered this type of hybrid epistemology (aimed at uniting rational and intuitive knowledge) in the religionist discourses of Louis Massignon, Henry Corbin and Eva de Vitray-Meyerovitch (cf. Chapter 2). In this vein, Éric Geoffroy is continuing the quest for a hybrid epistemology in the wake of Eranos, by bringing into dialogue the 'open rationality' of Edgar Morin,[78] the post-positivist epistemology of Gödel, Heisenberg and Prigogine, as well as classical Sufi metaphysics.[79] This hybrid epistemology, which is sometimes called 'Islamic humanism', should be a vehicle for rational and intuitive knowledge, and thus capable of interacting with all fields without ever being definitive: 'Islamic humanism is apophatic because the essence of human beings

76 Q.21: 30; 24: 45; 71: 13–14.

77 Geoffroy, 'Les voies d'accès à la réalité dans le soufisme'.

78 Morin, *La Méthode*.

79 Geoffroy, 'Les voies d'accès à la réalité dans le soufisme'.

could never be circumscribed or objective.'[80] Finally, Geoffroy underscores that it is not only a matter of introducing discursive rationality into religion, but also the sacred into the sciences. This entails 'seeing with both eyes'.[81]

> By trying to use this integral method, we could perhaps – author and reader – contribute to the 're-enchantment' of the epistemological field and, beyond that, the human experience.[82]

Feminine and Masculine Divine Energies: Body and Gender

The deconstruction and the reconstruction of ʿAlāwī religiosity also entails the 'education of the senses' which are a 'source of irremediably ambivalent knowledge; while being necessary to the development of our being, they participate in veiling Reality'.[83] In the teachings of Bentounes, the body is not the source of evil and of uncontrollable passions. Similarly, it is not the prison of the soul. The body is not something to be combatted: 'It is erroneous to speak of a fight against its nature because its real nature is one of health.'[84] Bentounes encourages finding the balance between the various energies, not repression. Sex, for example, becomes something positive, in the context of marriage:

> There is nothing blameworthy in sexuality itself. It is a meritorious and fully acknowledgeable act if it is part of the relations among spouses and within society. The only thing Islam requires is transparency.[85]

Karim shared with me, not without a degree of reticence, the sheikh's words during a marriage: 'When the tongues of the spouses embrace, *raḥma* [mercy] is set in motion.' Karim added: 'In the union between a man and a woman, there is the experience of *tawḥīd* – naturally, for those who have an elevated [spiritual] level, and always in the context of marriage.'

Balance is sought in the complementarity between the masculine energy and the feminine energy, which are expressions of the divine. Geoffroy tells

[80] Geoffroy, *L'islam sera spirituel ou ne sera plus*, 61.

[81] Geoffroy, *L'islam sera spirituel ou ne sera plus*, 94.

[82] Geoffroy, *L'islam sera spirituel ou ne sera plus*, 13.

[83] Bentounes, *Thérapie de l'âme*, 55–6.

[84] Bentounes, *Le soufisme, cœur de l'Islam*, 71.

[85] Bentounes, *Thérapie de l'âme*, 64.

us that Sheikh al-'Alawī sang the praises of God using the feminine pronoun, 'She'. The balance between masculine and feminine energies concerns both the individual and the society as such.[86] Therein lies a mission that seems to be among the most important for the brotherhood: to rebalance the role of women and the feminine in society. This is so important that the sheikh has said, 'Women are the future of Islam' (interview conducted in 2014).

Many 'Alāwī activities are aimed at the so-called 'liberation of women', in both the Arab–Islamic and European contexts, where women are often the victims of various forms of patriarchy.

> In the Islamic tradition, women are prisoners of a social order, but men are also locked inside local and ancestral customs that go against the Qur'an, whose sacred message is above all a message of liberty.[87]

For Bentounes, this 'liberation of women' must take place in the context of the rediscovery of Islamic history. He speaks of 9,000 female theologians forgotten by Islamic societies (interview conducted in 2014). Gender equality in religion as in society is thus not an invention, but part of a forgotten Islamic culture.

> Take the example of the University of al-Qarawiyyin in Fez. It educated promising young men who went on to become theologians, scholars and mathematicians. Even the Jewish philosopher Maimonides studied there. The person who created this university was a woman [Fatima al-Fihri]. In the history of Islam, we have had women scholars, imamas, queens, great mystics, great philosophers, great physicians and engineers. But all these women have, in some sense, been forgotten. From some point on, this entire history became hidden, especially the role of women at the beginnings of Islam.[88]

Camilla, President of AISA Paris, explained to me that the importance of women in Islam, even though systematically forgotten, is directly visible in the Qur'an where the Virgin Mary and 'Imran (Moses's mother) received '*wahi*,

[86] Geoffroy, *Allah au féminin*.

[87] Bentounes, *La fraternité en héritage*, 100.

[88] Magassa-Konaté, 'Khaled Bentounes: 'Les femmes sont vecteurs de paix', *Saphirnews.com*, 9 October 2014. Available at <https://www.saphirnews.com/Khaled-Bentounes-Les-femmes-sont-vecteurs-de-paix_a19649.html> (last accessed 8 November 2023).

the revelation. Only prophets receive the revelation ... [These women] are prophets by rights.' Rediscovering women's role also means understanding that 'sharia was written by men' (Camilla). But as we have shown above, the balance of masculine and feminine energies is a necessary step for both human beings and society.

> It's something that affects everybody ... all societies and all religious faiths. This history of women disturbs Christians as much as Muslims. Jews as well as Buddhists, anyone you can think of! So, it's quite revolutionary, but in any case, that's not my experience. In my opinion we're behind, that's how I see it. It's high time to re-establish women, to give them their rightful place once again! ... What are we waiting for, for the world to blow up? We need to rebalance ... Because human beings are made up of two essences, one feminine and one masculine, and having completely crushed and flattened a part of ourselves ... We can't live like that. That's why we pollute the earth, that's why there are mothers who kill their kids ... (Camilla, French *faqīra* of Kabyle descent)

The question of homosexuality is intimately linked to the masculine and feminine dimensions, an issue I had the opportunity to discuss with both the disciples and the sheikh. Karim told me, without being sure, that one of the disciples was possibly a homosexual. Once again, the disciples were reluctant to judge in this matter but did not really know what to say. Is homosexuality a sin? In this particular case, the sheikh is, as Quentin put it, 'a step ahead of his disciples'. Bentounes did, in fact, explain during our interview that 'what is part of human nature must be supported rather than condemned. What is natural is not a sin.'

He also explained that even in some expressions of *fiqh*, homosexuality is taken into consideration. For example, homosexuals have a specific place in the mosque and are exempted from fighting in wars. In this way, they are excluded neither from society, nor from religion. The fear and condemnation of homosexuality in the Islamic world is a modern invention. Furthermore, a male Moroccan disciple acknowledged to me during the Féminin – Paroles aux femmes, a conference on women and the feminine in 2014 organised by the brotherhood, that the sheikh wanted to discuss the question of homosexuality. However, this was not possible because the Algerian authorities were opposed to it; in Algeria, homosexuality is still considered a crime. While I was unable to verify this information, there is no doubt as to openness of the brotherhood to homosexuality, which was confirmed by Geoffroy during our interview.

The discourse on the balance of feminine and masculine energies is also found in the conversion or 'reconversion' narrative of several disciples, as in the case of Aïcha, born in Algeria in the early 1960s. Despite the illiteracy of her parents, Aïcha was an extraordinary student and went on to study at the prestigious Sciences Po University in Paris. Her upbringing was exceedingly strict when it came to religion, which Aïcha totally rejected: 'Simply put, I refused any and all religious practices. I was an atheist.'

Aïcha identified Islam with how her father had raised her: 'On a psychological level, since my father was very, very strict, there was a parallel between my father and God, and because I didn't like my father, I didn't like God either!' Aïcha did not call into question the existence of God, but rather the form of the Islamic religion which, according to her upbringing, was without any source of joy or love: 'There was fear, a lot of prohibitions, which were related to this denied sexuality. It was hidden and you weren't supposed to talk about it.'

> My father never ate with us, never talked to us, he never explained anything or took us to a movie. My mother was illiterate, my father was illiterate, nobody explained anything to us . . . We were like plants, they gave us water and left us to grow on our own.

In Paris, Aïcha completely gave up religious practice, but she was reluctant to tell her parents and her Algerian friends, on one hand, and she felt the need to delve into the religious dimension, on the other. She admitted to me that she was ready to convert to Protestant Christianity. Parallel to her spiritual search, Aïcha developed a passion for politics, which posed other questions with regard to religion:

> I've always been a Marxist and I'm a Marxist to this day, in the economic sense of the term. I'm not an activist, but I am part of an extreme-left group around the struggle of workers.

The Sufism of the ʿAlāwiyya brotherhood, which she discovered around twenty years ago, brought together all these apparently irreconcilable aspects: religion, social engagement and pacification with the masculine gender. Her contact with the Parisian ʿAlāwiyya was the first form of her reconciliation with her religion, especially regarding Muslim men, whom she had considered arrogant or solely interested in sex.

> But in the ʿAlāwiyya brotherhood we're not seen in this way . . . And they don't try to find out if you're married or not . . . That reconciled me a little with men, whereas in my childhood there was a strong link between Islam and men, between Islam and domination by men. I had associated Islam with the all-powerfulness of men, who could do as they pleased.

Aïcha began to frequent the brotherhood, but it was at the tomb of Sheikh al-ʿAlāwi that she experienced an epiphany:

> I knew there was a tomb, and I don't know why, but I started to cry. I had to make an invocation even though I was an atheist and not a practising member of any religion. I had to make an invocation and say to him, 'Please help me!' I left with the conviction that I had to change my profession. So I returned to Paris, quit my job, and then my daughter was born.

ʿAlāwī Eschatology: The End of the (this) World

The eschatological dimension is essential for understanding contemporary Sufism. Several Sufi brotherhoods propose narratives related to the imminent end of the world.[89] These eschatologies take various forms, based on Islamic doctrines but sometimes also influenced by Guénonian esotericism and New Age discourses. Here again, the ʿAlāwiyya surprises us, by proposing a completely different eschatology.

The ʿAlāwiyya do not seem interested in classical Islamic eschatology, according to which the end of the world is heralded by signs, such as the inversion of the natural order and a war between the forces of good and evil. In this regard, the sheikh cites a verse from the Qur'an that says, only God knows the Hour (Q.7: 187). When I posed this question to Lyès, the Parisian *muqaddam*, he replied:

> The end of the world is when you die, isn't it? When you die, the world dies, your time dies. Think about how infinitesimal your life is! Your lapse of time in the world.

[89] Conner, 'From Amuq to Glastonbury'.

When I described to Sheikh Bentounes the eschatology I had heard in the Naqshbandiyya (cf. Chapter 5) and in the Aḥmadiyya Idrīsiyya Shādhiliyya (Chapter 6), which are characterised by a dark view of a world in the process of dissolving, Bentounes proposed an end of the world that was optimistic, even luminous:

> The coming of Mahdī creates an atmosphere of hope; it's as if the believer is immersed in this divine mercy. It's the hope that one day Mahdī will return and re-establish justice. It's a qualitative leap in universal consciousness. So it's not at all negative.

Furthermore, another eschatology is present that does not concern the end of the world, but instead the end of a world. This eschatology does not elicit fear; on the contrary, it is a vehicle for hope and joy. While there is no clearly defined, systematic vision, there is a strong feeling that the tensions, wars, upheavals and injustices of the contemporary world will give way to a renewed world.

> [The sheikh] often says not to get tied up in the negative, not to focus on catastrophes and crises. For him, all of that is very positive. It's like a woman in labour, she's in pain, but everything must change, all the seeds are there. We have to change the paradigms, but everything is there. There are a lot of organisations, a lot of willing young people. Everything is already in place. The future economy, the future politics, the future society and living together harmoniously are already there! (Abdel Sabour, aged forty, Franco-Kabyle disciple)

The world that is dying is the decadent world of the divinisation of the individual, of the all-powerful market value. This world is in a 'crisis of humanist values', is the 'individualistic and egotistical culture of "me"'.[90] The world that is dying is the world of inequality, of ecological and economic unsustainability. In this frame of reference, religion becomes a simulacrum, a refuge during a time of crisis around identity.

This vision of the world does not imply despair; on the contrary, Bentounes sees the 'renaissance of a planetary consciousness' in the near future, a renaissance that would concern all human beings.[91] On this subject, when I

[90] Bentounes, *La fraternité en héritage*, 171–2.

[91] Bentounes, *La fraternité en héritage*, 168.

interviewed him in 2014, the sheikh had just returned from a conference with French imams during which he was moved by the openness, intelligence and preparation of the new French imams. Likewise, on several occasions, as during the event on Eva de Vitray-Meyerovitch (2013), Bentounes asserted that fanatical, fundamentalist Islam was losing ground to spiritual, free Islam.

The action of the ʿAlāwiyya would seem to consist precisely in guiding us towards this new world: 'We have the responsibility to sow the seeds of a better future' (Karim). What exactly does this new world comprise? No one really knows. Karim maintained that it is not a 'return to tradition' but rather a 'projection towards the future'.

Between Rhetoric and Practice: A Sufi Reformism?

The iconoclastic character of this 'liberating' and 'negative' brotherhood is subject to religious norms; it is not a matter of 'self-Islam',[92] where the only judge is the self. On the contrary, in the ʿAlāwiyya (as in the Būdshīshiyya), religious norms play an important role, even if they must be understood in their inner sense.

First of all, Khaled Bentounes and Éric Geoffroy often remind disciples and the general public that a distinction must be made between sharia, commonly translated as Islamic law, and *fiqh*, the understanding of this law – that is, its theological–juridical formalisation. Although these terms are often superimposed, they are profoundly different. Sharia is the entire path towards God that everyone, individually and collectively, undertakes based on the Qur'an and the *ḥadīth*. This path has been formalised by scholars according to various *madhāhib*,[93] or juridical schools (Maliki, Hanafi, Hanbali, Shafiʿi, and so on). The criticism of Bentounes and Geoffroy targets the 'hypertrophy of Muslim law',[94] which has phagocytised and hardened the plurality of paths towards God.

> Let's talk about rituals rather than sharia. Because the word 'sharia' has come to be used in an unbelievable way. You are faced with a system, as if it were a manual you consult to do this or that. A ritual is not a manual. If sharia becomes a manual, it's over. Sharia is a ritual. It's a ritual that teaches us . . . To move from a profane space to a sacred space . . . There's a way of doing

[92] Bidar, *Self islam*.

[93] *Madhab* in the singular.

[94] Geoffroy, *L'islam sera spirituel ou ne sera plus*, 96.

> it. I do my ablutions, it's a ritual I have to perform. (Bentounes, interview conducted in 2014)

Khaled Bentounes has highlighted that *fiqh* comes from human beings: 'God said . . . No! No! No! It was the *'ulamā'*!' (interview conducted in 2014). He has also pointed out that the doors of *ijtihād* – the effort to interpret sharia – are always open.

> *Fiqh* is always open. That's where the entire question of the future of Islam resides. Muslims must accept reform; there is no other alternative . . . Who closed [the doors]? Let's review history. And we'll see that it was the political authority . . . But he was a *khalīfa* among *khalīfās*, because it was politically advantageous to him. Let's open up history. And stop lying to ourselves. It's a lie! (Bentounes, interview conducted in 2014)

The 'Alāwiyya – at least the French branch – is calling for a discussion on the closure of Muslim juridical schools and for a renewed effort to comprehend sharia in the contemporary world. Éric Geoffroy assures us that this proposition is not very revolutionary: 'Even the UMF,[95] which is more conservative, says that a European Muslim rite is necessary, so this is not spectacular progress' (interview conducted in 2013).[96]

Nevertheless, the 'Alāwiyya is not satisfied with mere juridical reform achieved by imposing a new juridical code; rather, Sheikh Bentounes's discourse aims at rethinking the relationship between faith and law, calling for sense and the spiritual dimension to prevail over the juridical dimension. In this context, the *fiqh* of the *'ulamā'*, like the interpretations of the Sufi masters, become precious suggestions, but are in no way constraints. And clearly, the concept of 'State sharia' loses all meaning. The path to God cannot be established once and for all, for all human beings, and for all times. Khaled Bentounes and the 'Alāwiyya thus participate in the perpetual philosophical, theological, juridical and social debate around contemporary Islam as to the use of *ijtihād*.[97]

> Reading the Qur'an in a spiritualistic, multidimensional way ensures comprehensiveness because it offers a view unifying both the letter and the spirit of

[95] Union des Mosquées de France (Union of Mosques in France).

[96] Unfortunately, I was unable to confirm this information.

[97] Kersten, *Contemporary Thought in the Muslim World*.

> the letter, both reason and supra-reason. It is 'revolutionary' in the sense that it activates a permanent revolution in human beings; nothing is gained once and for all in our relationship with the Text.[98]

Openly questioning the power of the juridical schools and their defenders has led to much criticism inside and outside this brotherhood, even among some scholars,[99] which begs the question: how can this Islam be changed? Furthermore, what are the practical consequences of this spiritual *ijtihād*? What juridical norms are the 'Alāwiyya disrupting?

Concerning rituals, they are mainly Maliki with only a few Hanafi rituals. Most disciples I have met respect the prohibitions around alcohol and pork, even though a few French converts admitted to drinking in moderation on special occasions, such as a ceremonial toast. It should be noted that in almost all religious groups, there is a range of members who are more or less disciplined.

Adjusting the hours of fasting during Ramadan is more relevant when Ramadan occurs in the summer. Sheikh Bentounes asserts that Ramadan serves to purify; it should not be intolerable. It may be modified in Northern Europe if the time spent fasting is excessive. So those who wish to may limit it to twelve hours.

The more significant elements of reform concern women; Sheikh Khaled encourages training them as *'ulamā'* and imams. While the history of Islam offers several examples of learned women in Islamic jurisprudence (even though they are less present today), the idea of an imama is considered as heterodox in the general Sunni sense. During my fieldwork, women imams were more of a potential discourse than a reality, and while it is true that the rituals are performed in mixed-gender groups and that the disciples spoke of a woman guiding *khalwa* (spiritual retreat) on one occasion, I nevertheless did not see any women imams officiating.

That being said, on 21 February 2020, an 'Alāwī disciple, Kahina Bahloul, organised the first collective prayer in the new Fatima Mosque in Paris. This mosque is presented not as Sufi but as open to all Muslims with a liberal, progressive approach. Bahloul is not only a doctoral candidate in Islamic studies

98 Geoffroy, *L'islam sera spirituel ou ne sera plus*, 130.

99 Haenni, 'Le centenaire de la confrérie Allaouia'.

at EPHE (one of France's most prestigious higher education institutions), she presents herself as an imama and a *fiqh* reformer. At the time of this writing, the Bahloul's Fatima Mosque is taking its first steps, after being slowed down by the COVID-19 pandemic. It thus remains difficult to determine the reach of these phenomena beyond the French media frenzy around 'good Muslims' and the concomitant obsession with 'bad separatist Muslims'.

Other cases of breaking with Maliki *fiqh* exist, notably concerning marriage between a woman Muslim and a non-Muslim man, and concerning the concept of apostasy. This is due to the reconceptualisation of the idea of the infidel, mentioned above. Women's inheritances constitute another break with Maliki *fiqh*, because it dictates (according to several conditions) that they should amount to half those of men. 'Alāwī disciples consider this interpretation valid in the medieval context, where men were financially responsible for women and where women could keep this wealth for themselves. Conversely, in the context of contemporary societies, where women often work and contribute economically to family life, this rule has lost its value.

In the 'Alāwiyya, several discourses call into question the obligation and even the value of the 'Islamic headscarf', and the NGO AISA even organised an exhibit on the religious headscarf in the three monotheistic religions, showing its cultural dimension as preceding its religious dimension. Similarly, I heard several discussions within the brotherhood that challenged the obligation to wear a headscarf. Finally, the 'Alāwī call for allowing women the freedom to choose whether to wear a headscarf, since the principle of modesty takes precedence over its application, which may vary according to context and personal sensibilities.

> The headscarf is the headscarf! And Islam is Islam! Associating the headscarf with Islam doesn't make any sense. It has no basis! Is there a sixth pillar that makes women wear a scarf on their head? We have to stop the lies . . . I was born into a Kabyle family, my mother didn't wear a headscarf, my grandmother didn't wear a headscarf. No one would wear a headscarf in Kabylia! Kabyles are colourful. They wear little scarves, not headscarves, because it's very hot. Very colourful. You see Tuareg men with a headscarf, but not Tuareg women. (Camilla)

Several of the breaks with *fiqh* described here can be seen in the daily life of other Sufi brotherhoods in Europe, like the question of women's inheritance, wearing headscarves, and marriage between a Muslim woman and a non-Muslim man. The difference between the ʿAlāwiyya and these other Sufi brotherhoods seems then to concern the rhetoric around *fiqh* more than its application. We have seen in the Būdshīshiyya, and we will see it with the Aḥmadiyya Idrīsiyya Shādhiliyya (Chapter 6) as well, that there are several accommodations with regard to *fiqh*, but the disciples, and especially the masters, prefer to avoid the question of a possible reform or the use of *ijtihād*.

The disconnect between rhetoric and application of sharia–*fiqh* reaches its peak with the Naqshbandiyya Ḥaqqāniyya in Italy (Chapter 5), where many disciples hold ultra-conservative views on the sultanate as a political model, 'State sharia', polygamy, rigid segregation of the sexes and women's freedom of movement. However, these ultra-conservative positions do not result in fixed realities in the daily lives of most of the disciples, who often follow a Sufism customised according to their needs and desires. In sum, sharia here becomes a rhetorical discourse, an ideal dimension with few consequences in reality.

This disconnect between rhetoric and practice reveals the complex relationship between the sharia–*fiqh* religious principles and norms, which cannot be reduced to dichotomies such as orthodox/heterodox or tradition/modernity. All the Sufi brotherhoods interpret and adapt religious norms to suit their context, negotiating with religious authorities, namely *ʿulamā'* and *mufti*. What is specific to the ʿAlāwiyya is not its adaptation of *fiqh*, but rather its reformist call to rethink the relationship between norms and spiritual values. This may be seen as audacious, arrogant or courageous, according to the various interpretations of Islam.

Religion and Politics

Relations with Political Powers in Algeria and France

The relations between the ʿAlāwiyya and the Algerian government have changed profoundly over the twentieth and twenty-first centuries. The non-opposition to French colonialism, sometimes amounting to collaboration, facilitated the development of this Sufi order, even though it was considered a security threat and monitored due to the number of its disciples and the charisma of its leaders. Between the 1960s and the 1980s, the new Algerian government repressed this Sufi order due to its collaboration with the former French regime, and also for doctrinal reasons. More specifically, according to

Arab nationalism, Sufism was seen as an archaic Islam and an obstacle to the process of modernisation. Opposition to Sufism ended in the 1990s, when the Algerian government, seeking new religious legitimacy to counter the growth of Islamism, began to look for allies in the religious field.[100]

Today, the Algerian government presents Sufism as the good Islam, both traditional and authentic. In 1991, the Union nationale des zaouias d'Algérie (UNZA, National Union of Zaouias of Algeria) was founded by Omar Mahmood Chalal and officially supported President Bouteflika.[101] When Chalal stopped supporting Bouteflika, another association suddenly appeared, the Organisation nationale des zaouïas (ONZA, National Organization of Zaouias), founded by Abdelkader Bassine and loyal to President Bouteflika.

Sheikh Khaled, like other Algerian Sufi masters, considers these so-called Sufi associations as 'empty shells' (2018 field notes). This does not mean there are no relations between the ʿAlāwiyya and the Algerian government. We could describe the relationship between this brotherhood and the Algerian nation state using Markus Holdo's definition, and thus as 'conditional cooperation and mutual legitimization'.[102] It is not surprising, then, that Bentounes obtained the prize of the Algerian National Order of Merit, awarded by Bouteflika, the former Algerian president. In addition, the 'International Day of Living Together in Peace', declared by the United Nations General Assembly, was presented by the intermediary of the Algerian government. Finally, numerous events organised by the ʿAlāwiyya in Algeria benefit from ministerial patronage.

This cooperation and mutual legitimation does not imply co-optation (which we saw in the Moroccan Būdshīshiyya); Bentounes and the ʿAlāwiyya do not participate in party politics. Their approach is always conciliatory, avoiding sensitive subjects like elections or violation of human rights in Algeria. They prefer to discuss general matters, such as religious pluralism, the environment and gender equality, while avoiding direct confrontation with the authorities of the nation state. Finally, even though the ʿAlāwiyya, like many other Sufi brotherhoods in Algeria, has abstained from adopting strong positions against the regime, it expressed its support for the demonstrations in February 2019. In fact, numerous disciples took to the streets.

[100] Werenfels, 'Beyond Authoritarian Upgrading'.

[101] Joassin, 'Algerian "Traditional" Islam and Political Sufism'.

[102] Holdo, 'Cooptation and Non-Cooptation', 10.

Despite significant differences between the French and Algerian contexts, some continuities do exist. In 2016, the French Minister of the Interior decided to influence the Islamic field by creating the Fondation Islam de France (Islam Foundation of France) which promotes a liberal (and often Sufi) Islam in opposition to Salafism.[103] In this way, the French government promotes Sufi brotherhoods by sponsoring activities such as the exhibit on Emir Abdelkader (1808–83), organised by the ʿAlāwiyya in 2018. And the French government has recognised Bentounes; in 2017, French president Emmanuel Macron made him a Knight in the French National Order of Merit. In keeping with the Algerian situation, Bentounes's approach in France is conciliatory and non-conflictual. That is, criticism of the French normative system, sometimes discriminatory,[104] as seen in the growing Islamophobia in French society, is almost entirely absent.

Islam as Liberation from Idolatry

> Sufis are not revolutionaries in the way we understand this word today; rather, they renew, they revivify.[105]

To understand the political–social vision of the ʿAlāwiyya, it is necessary to grasp how disciples and masters experience the Islamic message. Islam is considered as a universal message of liberation from idolatry, a message of openness to the Other. Submission to God's will must not be identified with the social constraints of religion: '[The] therapeutic approach of Sufism proposes to educate human beings so that they regain their original liberty.'[106] This message of liberation implies responsibility and an active involvement in society:

> [The sheikh] is the community's guardian and cannot shirk this responsibility by saying: 'I only deal with spirituality, so good luck with the rest of it!' This attitude is not in keeping with the traditional attitude.[107]

103 The website of the *Fondation de l'islam de France* (FIF) is available at <https://fondationdelislamdefrance.fr/nos-missions/> (last accessed 8 November 2023).

104 Fernando, 'Reconfiguring Freedom'.

105 Bentounes, *Le soufisme, cœur de l'Islam*, 32.

106 Bentounes, *Thérapie de l'âme*, 277.

107 Bentounes, *Le soufisme, cœur de l'Islam*, 87.

This proactive engagement (as in the Būdshīshiyya) could be described as 'Islamic humanism' because it focuses on the value of human dignity beyond any differences in religion, ethnicity, politics, gender or sexual orientation (this subject will be explored in greater depth in the Conclusions). Bentounes considers accepting and promoting pluralism and alterity to be inherent in Islam and its history:

> It's divine will that wants this plurality! You could even call it the principle of unity, in its absolute form, but in its embodied form, it's multiple. God is one, but he's also multiple. (Bentounes, interview conducted in 2014)

> I always tell my students, especially my Muslim students who want to defend Islam, that Islam was rich and spread very rapidly at first because it was very plural, there was a pluralism and a wealth of opinions that were incredible! And to some degree that's what the 'Alāwiyya brotherhood is for me. (Geoffroy, interview conducted in 2013)

This conception of Islam as freeing human beings from idolatry and power recalls the Christian liberation theology in South America, which was a spiritual reform as well as a political one. Éric Geoffroy, following on from Zidane Meriboute,[108] has asked if an Islamic liberation theology is needed and what the relationships would be between this theology and Sufism.[109] However, when I asked Sheikh Bentounes directly if his Sufism is comparable to liberation theology, his response was rather cold; he would only speak of a 'free and accountable' Islam. The sheikh probably does not want to use this category because it is too loaded with meaning.

There remains, however, the current conceptualisation of Sufi Islam as liberation of the oppressed, liberation from both theological rigidities and power structures. In this vein, Sheikh Bentounes offered the example of an Iranian Sufi master of the tenth century:

> The story of al-Ḥallāj is a political story. Why does the story of al-Ḥallāj keep coming up? Because his trial is not over. Because in Muslim history, there's something unique about al-Ḥallāj. Society has not digested it and it keeps

[108] Mériboute, *La fracture islamique*.

[109] Geoffroy, *L'islam sera spirituel ou ne sera plus*.

> coming up. Al-Ḥallāj was a martyr for the truth, but first and foremost a political martyr. Because he made those in power uncomfortable. Al-Ḥallāj was on the slaves' side, and his disciples took up arms against the Abbasids. (Bentounes, interview conducted in 2014)

This perspective was shared by the Parisian disciples I met, whether they were of Arab, Berber or French descent. Here are the words of Quentin, the physician we spoke of at the beginning of this chapter:

> Do you know why people fight Sufism throughout the world? Because Sufism is freedom, freedom [in the face of] political power: the state, the sultanate and the economy. Because the Sufi is linked only to God.

The Sufi as 'Son of the Instant': Islam, Human Rights and Democracy

Another discourse shared by the 'Alāwiyya and the Būdshīshiyya is the Sufi as 'son of the instant', which, as we saw in the previous chapter, highlights a constructive position relative to modernity and its challenges. 'Who are we to criticise the work of God? How can we allow modernity to be criticised?' (Camilla, Franco-Algerian disciple, aged fifty-five). Éric Geoffroy goes beyond his Guénonian and anti-modernist origins by affirming that 'the Sufi should always be "modern", if we look to the ancient Greek etymology of the term "modernity", which means "today".'[110] But what is modernity? Bentounes does not consider it a moment in history but rather a 'state of consciousness':

> When [human beings] overcome their fear . . . The capacity to be conscious, to seek, to understand the mystery of life. To no longer live in fear that the sky is going to fall on our heads, to no longer fear power . . . It's primarily a matter of freeing human beings from their fears. This capacity makes it possible to be, and to be able to say, 'I'm capable of transforming my life, my society, I'm capable of building, of healing.' All these things are the consequences of this initial attitude. (Bentounes, interview conducted in 2014)

The humanist discourse of the 'Alāwiyya implies adhering to democratic narratives and human rights. However, these values and practices are understood as being truly Islamic. For example, Karim told me how the French welfare

[110] Geoffroy, *L'islam sera spirituel ou ne sera plus*, 145.

state inaugurated by Napoleon (concerning orphans, invalids, and so on) was inspired by contact with Islam during the Egyptian campaign (1798–1801).[111] Likewise, all the disciples I met shared the idea that *shūrā*, or 'consultation', is aligned with the principle of participative democracy.

Similar to the Būdshīshiyya, Bentounes and his disciples situate pluralism and democratic values in the history of Islam, as in the celebrated case of the Andalusian *Convivencia*. While some historians question this narrative and consider it an exaggerated utopian thought imposed on history,[112] Bentounes does not take this to heart and replies, 'What does it matter if this is a myth? That doesn't stop us from using it as a model!' (Bentounes 2018, field notes).

Beyond interpretations and arguments that may be more or less valid historically, ʿAlāwī disciples affirm that Muslims contributed to building Europe not only as an enemy – as Christian Europe's alter ego – but especially through the influence of art, science, philosophy, music, medicine, poetry and religion.

Concerning secularism, several disciples explained to me that the principle of respect and the freedom of various religious faiths has always existed in the Muslim world. Despite displeasing many Muslims, the sheikh often reiterates that in the constitution of Medina, Christians and Jews were considered to be part of the *umma*. In this regard, Geoffroy explains that Islam is a vehicle of the 'ethics of discord'[113] and adds, citing Massignon, that Islam is an 'egalitarian and secular theocracy'.[114]

The values of tolerance, respect, plurality, equality, fraternity and freedom are not, from this perspective, specific to Europe; rather, they are part of humanity and thus part of the Islamic religion. According to this perspective, Islam does not need reform; it does not need to go through centuries of Enlightenment to understand democratic values. On the contrary, this is the same Islam that is coming to the aid of the French Republic as it struggles with a crisis of values. In this way, Islam revivifies democracy: 'Islam has a rendezvous with France,' says Khaled Bentounes, and adds, 'Islam needs France,

[111] Unfortunately, I was unable to find any bibliographic references to check this hypothesis. That said, we are not interested here in the historical truth of this affirmation, but rather in the development of democratic and secular values. Historical truth is secondary.

[112] Fernández-Morera, *The Myth of the Andalusian Paradise*.

[113] Geoffroy, *L'islam sera spirituel ou ne sera plus*, 54.

[114] Bouamrane and Gardet, *Panorama de la pensée islamique*, 185.

in the same way France needs Islam' (interview conducted in 2014). Muslims thus become 'citizens par excellence' (Bentounes, interview conducted in 2014). The sheikh always advises his disciples to participate in their country's political life, advice that, as we will see, translates into actions that drive the activities organised by the brotherhood.

Nevertheless, this attitude of openness towards modernity is not synonymous with accepting all the forms it may take. For instance, the sheikh is very critical of modernity when it comes to the neo-liberal economy, the exploitation of human beings, pollution, the commodification of women's bodies, and so forth. But the conciliatory approach favours pacificatory rather than critical discourses.

Finally, this humanist approach, mixing religious and secular discourses, is too progressive and liberal for some disciples, especially in the Maghreb. For example, one of the *muqaddams* in Morocco was so disconcerted by the progressive positions of his master that he cut ties with the brotherhood (according to disciple accounts), and even attempted to appropriate the *zāwiya* and its disciples.

Activities of the Brotherhood

> Work in this world as if you will live eternally and work for the other world as if you will die tomorrow.[115]

> If you do not find God among human beings, you will find him nowhere.[116]

> The ʿAlāwiyya is a path of meditation and action. Through action, we meet the Other and ourselves. (Antoine)

The social dimension has always been a pillar of the ʿAlāwiyya, since the time of its founder, Sheikh al-ʿAlawī. But it has reached its peak with Sheikh Khaled Bentounes, who inspires and develops a considerable number of activities. I have classified ʿAlāwī activities into six themes: (1) transmission of heritage, (2) ecology, (3) an alternative power structure, (4) civic engagement, (5) women and (6) interfaith and intercultural dialogue. The brotherhood also supports

[115] Bentounes, *Le soufisme, cœur de l'Islam*, 140.

[116] Al-ʿAlawī in Bentounes, *Soufisme l'heritage commun*, 277.

charitable projects for those in need, including the creation of a women's cooperative in Indonesia after the tsunami in 2004.

Before I describe the various activities, it should be noted that Bentounes does not manage them himself. He provides inspiration but leaves the disciples to carry them out. Likewise, the activities are open to all, in terms of their use, organisation and planning, an openness aimed at spreading 'Alāwī ideals.

> I am entirely aware today that being a representative of the Alawiya tariqa makes me one of the fortunate of this world, and I fully accept this spiritual responsibility. But this does not make me a chosen one. I never forget that I was given a duty, for a fixed timeframe, and for a specific goal: to protect in order to transmit.[117]

The transmission of Islamic–Sufi culture, religion and spirituality is one of Sheikh's Bentounes major priorities. In 1978, returning from the United States, he founded the 'Institut Alif' to train young people and bring information technology to 'third-world countries'.[118] It was, in fact, the Institut Alif that produced the first digital versions of the Qur'an and the *ḥadīth* in 1984. Another of the brotherhood's projects is building a museum around Sufism, which will be available in an online version as well.

While waiting to interview the sheikh, I had the opportunity to meet disciples and discuss with them their digitisation of old Arab astrology and mathematical manuscripts. Other disciples and the scientific community will be able to study these books once they are digitised. Bentounes encourages this kind of historical research on Islam and Sufism, making the relationship with the academic world particularly fruitful. As already noted, there is no opposition between religious reason and discursive reason according to Bentounes. This research, initially intended for disciples, has a wider scope, beyond the brotherhood's frontiers. At the time of my 2013–14 fieldwork, three research groups of disciples existed around the Qur'an, the *ḥadīth*s, and the relationship between faith and reason.

Sheikh Bentounes stresses the importance of an eco-sustainable economy and society. In concrete terms, the brotherhood offers an awareness-building and educational campaign in Algeria centred on the environment. In addition, the

[117] Bentounes, *Le soufisme, cœur de l'Islam*, 142.

[118] Bentounes, *Soufisme l'heritage commun*, 109.

agricultural land of the brotherhood in Mostaganem has been transformed into a Jannat al-ʿĀrif (Garden of the Gnostic) where biodiversity and bio-agronomy are fostered, creating a place for gathering and education.

Islamic humanism, as a form of liberation, criticises the conception of power. All pyramidal forms of power are called into question, including the brotherhood's structure, as we saw in the concept of post-confraternity-ism. In opposition to the image of a pyramid is that of a circle, where decisions are made in common and where pluralities and freedoms can be fully realised. Based on this teaching, META (Management, Ethics, Tradition, Alternatives) was founded by Philippe Mottet, a disciple of the Swiss ʿAlāwiyya, who was inspired by the seminars of Khaled Bentounes on 'Therapies of the Soul'.[119]

> The Institut META International [International META Institute] promotes a personal and societal metamorphosis where each individual is free and accountable and can thus participate in a common project centred on living together harmoniously.[120]

Alma, an ʿAlāwī disciple around thirty-seven years old and a statistics researcher at the University of Paris, has been collaborating with META over the past few years. During our interview, Alma explained to me that this tool is applicable to all decision-making contexts, beyond cultures and religions. This method has no Islamic–Sufi hallmark, at least for non-experts in this type of system. META has thus been used by the offices of the Mayor of Paris to improve work organisation as well as the quality of relations between employees. The French bureaucracy has thus benefited from a method inspired by Islam! Although META has no signs of the Islamic religion and is intended for all human beings, Alma illustrated how this universalism is utterly Islamic and concluded by affirming, 'META's logo is the universal man . . .The universal man is Muhammad, who is beyond tradition and religion.'

In 1991, Khaled Bentounes founded the Muslim Scouts of France. In addition to traditional scouting activities (camping, education, games and prayer), this association offers civic and social engagement. For example, each year the Muslim Scouts organise travel for Muslims with reduced mobility as part of

[119] Seminars that led to Bentounes's book *Thérapie de l'âme* ('Therapy of the Soul').

[120] The website of the META Institute is available at (<https://meta-com.ch/accueil.html> (last accessed 8 November 2023).

ʿUmra, off-season Islamic pilgrimages to Mecca. In 2009, they organised the Flamme de l'espoir Méditerranéenne, an event promoting dialogue between Mediterranean religions and cultures:

> History bears witness to the fact that East and West knew, at one point, how to come together, develop complementary and harmonious exchange, and found a common heritage. The Flamme de l'espoir Méditerranéenne grew out of this historical perspective. It enables real dialogue between young people, while also developing fruitful exchange through scouting practices. We must be attentive to the needs and desires of each individual.[121]

This intercultural and interfaith dialogue continued in 2010 with the Flamme de l'Espoir Compostelle – Cordoue', linking Santiago de Compostela and Cordova, two cities symbolising Catholic and Muslim Europe. The scouts also organised visits to Sicily, Andalusia and Turkey, to promote a better understanding of the history of Islam in Europe. In 2011, the scouts organised the Flamme de l'Espoir Citoyen, which aimed to:

- Re-establish among young people the sense of belonging to the French nation and to Europe
- Foster understanding of the importance of this engagement to build the future
- Encourage young people over 18 to vote
- Raise awareness among elected officials of the considerable electoral potential represented by young people, of the importance of being attentive to issues that matter to them, of the urgency of providing concrete solutions for improving their lives, and of the need to appease their sense of uncertainty about the future
- Restore the universal meaning and virtues of the motto of the French Republic – 'Liberty, Equality, Fraternity' – in order to defend social cohesion in both France and Europe.[122]

[121] The website of the Muslim Scouts of France is available at <https://scoutsmusulmans.fr/la-flamme-de-lespoir/> (last accessed 8 November 2023).

[122] Schildböck, 'Les Scouts musulmans de France ont allumé "La Flamme de l'Espoir Citoyen"', *EuroScoutInfo.com*, 12 May 2011. Available at <http://euroscoutinfo.com/2011/05/12/les-scouts-musulmans-de-france-ont-allume-la-flamme-de-lespoir-citoyen/> (last accessed 8 November 2023).

The Flamme de l'Espoir Citoyen took the form of a bus that stopped in fifteen 'large French cities and their suburbs' to remind young people of democratic values.

> In **France with its wealth of diversity** and where, by the power of its republican laws, each individual has the guarantee that their rights and convictions will be respected, we have the duty to protect and defend '***Living Together Harmoniously***' which all those who fought for liberty, equality and fraternity have passed down to us.[123]

We have seen how republican and democratic values are understood and promoted as truly Islamic. Through these activities, Bentounes's aim is to encourage French Muslims to participate in political life, by fighting both Islamophobia and Islamism. This political–cultural objective is not sought in the name of Sufism or against Salafism and the Muslim Brotherhood. Bentounes tries not to use or create labels that could cause division, although this may be experienced differently in practice.

The scouts are a good example of this conciliatory approach. Several disciples told me that over the years, the Muslim scouts were monopolised by Salafists and that, for this reason, one of the disciples even took his son out of the organisation. By contrast, other disciples think that the Salafists who participate in the scouts are currently changing thanks to the sheikh's show of mercy.

> For ten years, the sheikh let the bearded brothers[124] do what they wanted, but it was a good thing. They were the ones who gave in. Many of them changed their attitude. (Abdel Sabour)

The narrative of the ʿAlāwiyya does not posit a simple identity opposition between Sufism and Salafism. But in following the idea of 'going outside religion', it has developed an intra-religious dialogue to spread the values of fraternity and tolerance.

[123] The website of the Muslim Scouts of France is available at <https://scoutsmusulmans.fr/la-flamme-de-lespoir/> (last accessed 8 November 2023). Bold added.

[124] Those described by their beards, or 'barbus', accord a great deal of importance to appearance.

The narratives on the importance of women and the feminine in contemporary societies is at the centre of several activities organised by the association AISA. In 2014, in the Algerian city of Oran, I participated in the Congrès International Féminin – Paroles aux femmes, an international conference giving voice to women's experience. During this three-day event, where the languages used were Arabic and French, more than 3,000 people participated from around the world – including researchers, journalists and Islamic religious authorities – alongside high-profile representatives of the Algerian government.

The ʿAlāwiyya and AISA wanted to avoid imposing one perspective over another, hoping instead to open the debate on women and the feminine. To this end, the conference speakers addressed the question of women according to several approaches, such as those of agnostic Socialist feminists, *ʿulamāʾ* discussing women in the Qurʾan, historians such as Mohammed Talbi, and disciples sharing views on women in Sufism. Some women wore headscarves of various styles and some did not. Psychological, juridical, sociological and religious questions co-existed and intermingled.

> What we hope for with this conference and with the work we will carry out in more than fifteen workshops is to implement a pedagogy that enables us to find gender harmony between the feminine and the masculine. To reconcile the masculine and the feminine. To not pit them against each other, but rather to find their synergies.[125]

There have been numerous activities favouring interfaith and intercultural dialogue, both locally, with each *zāwiya* attempting to build good relations with other religions, and nationally or internationally, with such demonstrations as the Marche du Vivre Ensemble (March for Living Together) in Cannes, which brought together thousands of people.

Listing all these activities would not, in my opinion, further the understanding of their purpose. I have thus made the choice to present a detailed account of one of these events, the 1er Festival du Mawlid al-Nabawī de Bruxelles

[125] Magassa-Konaté, 'Khaled Bentounes: "Les femmes sont vecteurs de paix"' *Saphirnews.com*, 9 October 2014. Available at <https://www.saphirnews.com/Khaled-Bentounes-Les-femmes-sont-vecteurs-de-paix_a19649.html> (last accessed 8 November 2023).

(1st Celebration of the Birth of the Prophet Muhammad in Brussels), organised by the association AISA in February 2013. The event brought together around 600 people in a theatre in a Brussels suburb. The subtitle of the *Mawlid* – 'an assembly without resemblance' – as well as the evening's programme can be interpreted as a real manifesto for the brotherhood.

The evening starts with a chorale of disciples from the Muridiyya brotherhood, followed by an 'Alāwī chorale with the presence of female singers. In addition, Sheikh Hassan Dyck of the Naqshbandiyya is participating, rounding out the inter-brotherhood dialogue. Also performing is the Congolese-Belgian gospel choir 'African Joys',[126] which garners an extremely favourable response from the audience. Before I was familiar with the 'Alāwiyya, I never would have thought I would see Muslims singing gospel and rhythmically clapping their hands during *Mawlid*. And other surprises await me this evening. To start with, a group of young Belgians (aged fifteen to twenty) comes on stage to put on a breakdancing performance. And the audience remains very enthusiastic. The evening reaches its peak with Sheikh Hassan Dyck who, through his music and poetry, casts a spell, making everyone dance. Bentounes concludes the evening by thanking the participants and the audience, stressing that we should not be afraid of the future.

On this evening, the audience is very diverse, including young people of all ages and numerous families. Some of them are wearing traditional clothing, while others wear Western attire. Nearly the entire audience is made up of Muslims of Algerian and Moroccan descent, and among them are the ambassadors of Morocco and Algeria.

The difference between the Būdshīshī *Mawlid* and the 'Alāwī *Mawlid* is clear. The Būdshīshī event in Madagh, celebrated over three days, focused entirely on Sheikh Hamza and his brotherhood, and the ecstatic tension was palpable at all times. By contrast, in Brussels, even though the 'Alāwiyya organised the event, neither their name nor that of Bentounes were listed on the programme, and the sheikh only went on stage for the final acknowledgments.

The 'Alāwī *Mawlid* was a celebration between the sacred and the profane. The profane dimension was evident in the festivity, structured as a theatrical

[126] The website of the chorale 'African Joys' is available at <https://www.africanjoys.be/> (last accessed 8 November 2023).

and musical performance (presenters, artists, tickets, and so on), and in the fact that neither gospel nor breakdancing are part of Islamic or Sufi culture. Nonetheless, the event was sacred, not only because of the Sufi music (the chorales), but above all because of the ʿAlāwī mission: interfaith and intercultural dialogue. This celebration was, in fact, a way of fostering communication between various *ṭuruq*, in the spirit of post-confraternity-ism, and between various religions (gospel music), while putting a spotlight on and engaging new generations (breakdancing).

Conclusions

The spread of the ʿAlāwiyya started with a charismatic man, Sheikh ʿAlāwi, considered by his disciples as the saint, the pole of existence. *Scientia experimentalis* – reflected in Sheikh ʿAlāwi's intimate, experiential knowledge of God – was the basis for his mystical authority, expressed in the doctrinal dimension as much as in the social and political dimensions.

Sheikh ʿAlāwi wrote poetry and metaphysical texts that renewed Sufi language. Moreover, despite the French colonial presence and the prohibitions regarding Arab–Islamic culture, he started a process of openness towards alterity (religious, gender-related and epistemological otherness). At the same time, Sheikh ʿAlāwi continued to transmit Islamic and Sufi *sacra doctrina* – that is, the transmission of Islamic discursive knowledge related to Qur'anic exegesis, *ḥadīth*s and *fiqh*. The balance between *scientia experimentalis* and *sacra doctrina* enabled him to attract disciples from various milieus, cultures and religions, including Guénonian intellectuals in search of the Primordial Tradition, erudite Muslims steeped in the Islamic sciences, as well as 'non-believers' in search of miracles and *baraka*.

Scientia experimentalis remains visible in the ʿAlāwiyya of the twenty-first century. We have seen how the intimate, bodily knowledge of the divine guides these disciples and enables them to cultivate new doctrinal, cultural and social forms. Starting in the 1990s, Sheikh Khaled Bentounes focused attention on the ethical dimension. While not eliminating the ecstatic dimension, he channelled it into social activities related to intra-religious and interreligious dialogue, ecology, balancing the feminine and the masculine, and civic engagement. According to this perspective, the purification of the soul necessarily involves contact with the Other.

The humanism of Bentounes, Geoffroy and the ʿAlāwiyya is first and foremost based on Islamic–Sufi heritage, the Qur'an, the *ḥadīth* and the teachings of Sufi masters. It is also open to the epistemological hybridity of religionism, where the human, social and natural sciences converse with the divine revelation and mystical intuition. Other elements that may have influenced this humanism are Guénonian perennialism and the daily contact with the Other. It should not be forgotten that Sheikh Bentounes married a French Catholic woman, and that this brotherhood includes several mixed couples. This Islamic humanism thus centres on the question of alterity, calling into question all its forms – around identity and faith along with cognitive and organisational alterity.

Raising questions in this way is at times more rhetorical than practical, aimed at making disciples rethink their certitudes through a kind of negative pedagogy. There is no deconstruction of Sufi practices; we have seen how the ʿAlāwiyya requires a degree of discipline of its members, in observance of religious norms, in regularly performing rituals, and in social engagement. For example, *bayʿa*, the initiatic pact, is not easily obtained. Consequently, despite the brotherhood's universalist openness, becoming an ʿAlāwī disciple requires a degree of work, in contrast to a kind of customised Sufism influenced by New Age culture. Finally, calling everything into question in this total, disruptive way is not an absolute novelty, as it is part of the history of Sufism.

But while there is some degree of continuity in this discontinuity, the brotherhood's humanism is nonetheless characterised by novel elements, and chief among them, the cultural and epistemological hybridity. Secondly, there is a redefinition between certain principles/norms, such as apostasy, tolerance with regard to homosexuality, marriage between Muslims and non-Muslims, the relationship with nature, reform in the area of women's inheritance and accepting women imamas. Finally, there is the creation of new organisational forms, as we saw with the post-confraternity-ism discussed in this chapter.

These changes, 'based in tradition' according to Bentounes and blameworthy innovations according to his detractors, have led to tensions inside and outside the brotherhood. Some disciples have broken ties with it, and some Muslims (Sufi and non-Sufi) and even some researchers[127] believe that

[127] Haenni, 'Le centenaire de la confrérie Allaouia'.

Bentounes has betrayed Islamic tradition and embraced a postmodern view of religion. To what extent is the 'Alāwī revolution–revivification the fruit of the mystical dimension specific to Sufism? Or is it instead due to European secularisation or acculturation? I do not think a univocal response is possible. A simple antinomy would not be satisfying.

5

NAQSHBANDIYYA ḤAQQĀNIYYA

Entering the Brotherhood: Between Performance and Ritual

My first encounter with this brotherhood took place in January 2013 in Pavia, a city not far from Milan. I attended a three-day Sufi seminar and met Sheikh Hassan Dyck, the *khalīfa* (representative) of the European Naqshbandiyya Ḥaqqāniyya and a talented musician. He inaugurated the seminar by offering a concert open to all. The concert took place in an ARCI[1] cultural space in the centre of Pavia. Outside the concert venue were people with no apparent interest in Islam, complaining about having to remove their shoes. They were there for the 'Love Caravan', the Sufi musical show put on by Sheikh Hassan and his musicians. The cost of admission was €10, the price of buying an ARCI card, with a 'suggested donation' of €5 for the concert. Inside the concert venue were around fifty people, including some thirty disciples.

Before the concert begins, Sheikh Hassan introduces us to Sufism and the Naqshbandiyya. Of German origin, he speaks in English for the seminar, with the Italian *khalīfa*, Iqbal, providing simultaneous translation into Italian. This introduction is not a teaching in the classical sense of the term. It oscillates in tone between seriousness and humour; we are thus very far from the ʿAlāwī or

[1] Italian cultural association, linked to leftist associations.

Būdshīshī *mudhakara*. The key words are love, beauty and peace, with minimal references to Islam. In addition, Sheikh Hassan highlights the proximity between Islam and Christianity as well as the importance of women.

Sheikh Hassan is a consummate showman; charming and likeable, he knows how to hold the audience's attention and make everyone laugh. The Naqshbandiyya is presented as 'one big crazy family'. Even the explanation of *dhikr* becomes humorous. He explains the divine name *Ḥaq* (the True) by imitating an owl's call. Speaking of *ḥaiyy* (the Living), he laughs and says, '*Ḥaiyy* makes me high!'

Once the introduction is over, the music begins. Sheikh Hassan plays an electric cello, accompanied by a baby grand piano as well as a traditional instrument resembling the viola d'amore. The style is hard to categorise, with strains of classical music (Hassan trained at the Berlin Academy of Music), jazz (especially with the piano), New Age music (ethereal ambiances), blues (Hassan sings a poem by Rūmī using the pentatonic scale) and, at its peak intensity, this multifaceted Sufi music becomes rock. Sheikh Hassan indeed tells us that 'Rūmī is rock!' During this musical–religious show, a whirling dervish, wearing the traditional garb of the Mevleviyya brotherhood, performs the famous 'whirling dance'.

The music transforms into *dhikr* that is very easy to follow, without the polyrhythms, multiple voices or ecstatic states described in the previous chapters. It consists exclusively of a single, lilting voice singing softly. From *dhikr* we move on to *ḥaḍra* which, as we saw with the 'Alāwiyya and the Būdshīshiyya, lies somewhere between ecstatic expression and rite. Hassan's *ḥaḍra* resembles a form of collective dance. Younger people in the audience smile and hold hands, everyone participates, and even the non-believers are invited to dance. It is no accident, then, that Hassan will say with a laugh, during the seminar to follow, 'Come on everybody, let's dance the disco-*ḥaḍra*!'

The show is a success; when this 'disco-*ḥaḍra*' ends, everyone cheers and claps. However, as we will see below, the evening's structure as performance and entertainment is not due to the Naqshbandiyya's relationship with the outside world (the concert took place in a public venue); it is reproduced in Sufi seminars for Naqshbandi disciples.

Once the concert ends, I introduce myself to the Italian *khalīfa* and the disciples. The first thing that strikes me is their age; most of the disciples are between twenty-five and thirty years old. The second thing I notice are their clothes: nearly all of them wear Turkish-style traditional clothing. As for their reaction to me, they seem upset. That is, when I explain my research and why I am there, the disciples are none too enthusiastic and immediately start asking me questions. 'You're here to study us, aren't you?' demands Chadli, a young Italian man of around twenty-eight years old, who continues to interrogate me: 'Do you believe in God? What do you think of the theory of evolution? And Islam?' When I explain my 'curious agnosticism', he says, 'Those who are neutral are the first to go down when the two sides confront each other', referring to the combat between the forces of good and evil when the world ends. A young female disciple joins the discussion and predicts my conversion to Islam: 'It's only a matter of time!' she says. But their initial reaction does not amount to a refusal, and I am allowed to stay.

After the concert, we leave for the 'Mystical Rose Oasis', a beautiful building in the Pavian countryside run by the Catholic Church and used as housing for interfaith events. The following morning, over breakfast, I get to know the disciples, whose heterogeneity is striking. At my table I meet Amin, who seems very serious and respectful of Islamic and Sufi practices; a young Gurdjieffian who has not yet converted but is interested in Sufi techniques; Haifa, a 'spiritual seeker' who is unsure she believes in God; and Said, aged thirty-five, an extreme-right intellectual who speaks of conspiracy theories. Their different spiritual quests make up a mishmash of desires and needs.

While describing and understanding the Būdshīshiyya brotherhood required me to highlight the richness and intensity of its rituals, and while capturing the 'Alāwiyya meant underscoring its intellectual complexity, with the Naqshbandiyya it is a matter of revealing both the heterogeneity and the coherence of the various forms it can take. And this brotherhood does take on completely different forms according to the geographic and cultural context.

By way of illustration, the effect of my interviews and the requests I made to the Naqshbandi *khalīfat* are particularly revealing. In both France and Italy, many disciples thanked me; my presence and my approach threw some light on the Naqshbandi nebula for them. As a sociologist, I was able to ask questions the disciples could not. Before we enter the *zāwiya*s to meet the disciples, we will start by situating this brotherhood, as we did for the others, in its context and history.

Sheikh Nāzim and the Naqshbandiyya Ḥaqqāniyya

Sheikh Nāzim ʿAdil al-Qubrusī (1922–2014) was born in Larnaca, Cyprus. According to the hagiography, Sheikh Nāzim was Sharifian and a descendant of both ʿAbd al-Qādir al-Jīlānī and Jalāl al-Dīn Rūmī,[2] two of the greatest Sufi masters in history. In 1940, he moved to Istanbul to study chemical engineering[3] and, in 1945, was initiated into the Naqshbandiyya brotherhood in Damascus by the master Abdullah al-Daghestani (1891–1973), who asked him to spread knowledge of Sufism in Western countries. According to other hagiographical sources, the Prophet Muhammad himself asked Nāzim to disseminate Islam in Europe.[4] To carry out his mission, Sheikh Nāzim founded a new branch of the Naqshbandiyya, the 'Ḥaqqāniyya', in 1973.[5]

At the end of the 1970s, Sheikh Nāzim began his journey in England, attracting numerous disciples of various ethnicities who went on to organise several independent groups.[6] The English brotherhood had various temporary locales before a large donation from the Sultan of Brunei enabled the disciples to buy the priory of Saint Ann's Church in Tottenham.[7] In the 1980s, Sheikh Nāzim continued his visits abroad, travelling to the United States, France, Switzerland and Germany. During this time, his collected discourses were published in the book *Mercy Oceans*[8] (republished several times). Currently, most of his disciples are European or American, but he also has followers in Turkey and Indonesia, and to a lesser extent in the Arabic-speaking world.[9]

Although it is difficult to give a reliable count of Naqshbandi disciples, based on my ethnographical fieldwork (in Italy, France, Cyprus and Belgium) and on the academic literature, this brotherhood is probably the most widespread in

2 Kabbani, *Classical Islam and the Naqshbandi Sufi Tradition*; Kabbani, *The Naqshbandi Sufi Tradition Guidebook of Daily Practices and Devotions*.

3 Draper, 'Towards a Postmodern Sufism'.

4 Milani and Possamai, 'Sufism, Spirituality and Consumerism'.

5 Kabbani, *Classical Islam and the Naqshbandi Sufi Tradition*.

6 Sedgwick, 'The Islamization of Western Sufism after the Early New Age'.

7 Nielsen et al., 'Transnational Sufism'.

8 Haqqani, *Mercy Oceans' Divine Sources*.

9 Habibis, 'A Comparative Study of the Workings of a Branch of Naqshbandi Sufi Order in Lebanon and in the UK'; Nielsen et al., 'Transnational Sufism'.

Western Europe and the United States. And there is no doubt that the Naqshbandiyya Ḥaqqāniyya has the most significant Internet presence.[10]

At the time of this writing, the brotherhood has around thirty websites and as many Facebook pages. To quantify the Naqshbandi discourse, on the website *Saltanat.org* alone, we find 2,308 discourses and videos.[11] As one example among the dozens of Naqshbandi websites, the American site *Naqshbandi.org* provides complete instructions for prayers with audio files; online *tawi'z*, a protective talisman; *dhikr*, both written and recorded; but above all, the possibility to make the *bay'a* (initiatic pact) by carrying out the rite and the repetitions at home. Another American site, *Eshaykh.com*, makes it possible for disciples, or clients, to ask questions and request a dream interpretation.

The global success of the Naqshbandiyya of Sheikh Nāzim is due to several factors: (1) his charisma, which has attracted disciples of diverse backgrounds; (2) a flexible message that encompasses universal openness and mercifulness as well as a decidedly conservative discourse; (3) exposure to New Age culture; and, above all, (4) a very malleable organisational and doctrinal structure, managed by his *khalīfa*s who, more than simple *muqaddam*s, are true spiritual and local leaders: Sheikh Hisham Kabbani in the United States, Sheikh Hassan Dyck in Europe, Sheikh Burhanuddin Herrmann in Spain, Italy and South America, and Sheikh Ahmad Dede in Holland.

The brotherhood's complexity, heterogeneity and contradictions are embodied by the magnetic pole that was and is Sheikh Nāzim: 'the *tariqa* only fully exists where Shaykh Nazim is', according to Jørgen Nielsen.[12] The brotherhood's heart stopped in April 2014, when Sheikh Nāzim died at the age of ninety-two. Before his death, he officially named his son Mehmet as the forty-first spiritual guide of the Naqshbandiyya Ḥaqqāniyya. However, this succession was not really accepted by all the *khalīfa*s. Of course, to my knowledge they have not publicly questioned the authority of Sheikh Mehmet, instead setting the matter aside and continuing to highlight that the true spiritual source is Sheikh Nāzim. Thus, in the United States, Hisham Kabbani seems to be considered the new sheikh of the Naqshbandiyya, whereas in Italy, Sheikh Burhanuddin speaks of Mehmet as a brother. There is yet another layer of

[10] Stjernholm, 'Sufi Politics in Britain'; Piraino, 'Between Real and Virtual Communities'.

[11] Consulted on 21 July 2021.

[12] Nielsen et al., 'Transnational Sufism', 113.

complexity to Sheikh Nāzim's complicated succession: many disciples considered Nāzim to be the last spiritual leader before the end of the world.

Sheikh Nāzim's Charisma and His *Khalīfa*s

Religious charisma is understood sociologically to stem from the qualities of a religious leader and from the narratives and actions of his or her disciples, who play a significant role in building up this charisma. In the Naqshbandi case, we will therefore discuss both the personal charisma of Sheikh Nāzim, who was magnetic and won over thousands, and the monumental construction and celebration around the charisma of masters.

All Naqshbandi disciples I met during my research provided a similar description of Sheikh Nāzim: 'as strong as a lion', with deep green eyes, a long white beard, a large turban and a loose-fitting coat. The disciples describe incredible power emanating from Nāzim's physical and spiritual presence, provoking admiration and beatitude. This power and energy remained palpable even when Nāzim was confined to a wheelchair. His spiritual energy was such that even 'those who visited Sheikh Nāzim came back transfigured, more beautiful . . .', according to Paul, a French disciple.

> When I entered his home, time stood still, I felt unbridled joy. He laughed, I laughed. (Baya, aged forty-five, Italian disciple)

> Sheikh Nāzim is a mountain of light and love. (Skander, aged fifty, Canadian *khalīfa*)

> Sheikh Nāzim is a being of light. (Iqbal, aged fifty, Italian *khalīfa*)

The accounts of Sheikh Nāzim's charisma are legion, many inspired by miracle narratives. They tell how Sheikh Nāzim was gifted with ubiquity as well as clairvoyance and could influence nature. For example, Khaldoun, one of the Parisian *muqaddam*s, told me how Sheikh Nāzim saved sailors who, caught in a storm on the Mediterranean, had prayed to the *quṭb* (the saint, the spiritual pole). Sheikh Nāzim supposedly intervened, given that he was 'the *quṭb* of the *quṭb*s' (Khaldoun). During our interview, Khaldoun said, 'I saw so many miracles [brought about by Sheikh Nāzim] that I wrote a book.'[13] As for the

[13] Unfortunately, I was unable to verify this information.

Milanese disciple, Khadija, she recounted how, in 2010, Sheikh Nāzim saved Chilean miners trapped underground. According to this account, he economically supported all the miners' families, who then converted to Islam.

The spiritual power of Sheikh Nāzim and his prodigious miracles have surpassed the borders of the Naqshbandiyya and Sufism. Even non-Sufi Muslims have tried to contact Sheikh Nāzim to obtain a miracle. When I visited Cyprus, I met Bakir, a young Montenegrin suffering from multiple sclerosis and confined to a wheelchair at age thirty-five, with little hope of a cure. Since Bakir had worked in Italy as a carpenter, my Italian nationality once again helped me break the ice. His idol was Silvio Berlusconi, because of his money and his women. He admitted to me that he had not really been a good Muslim, but now religion gave him hope. Bakir has been awaiting a manifestation of grace ever since his family convinced him to meet Sheikh Nāzim.

In addition to these major miracles, I collected several anecdotes around an assortment of small daily miracles. For example, Skander, the Canadian *khalīfa* of Tunisian origin, told me that during his first meeting with Sheikh Nāzim in London, he had a beard and long hair which made him look South American. Sheikh Nāzim, without knowing anything about Skander, welcomed him and asked him directly in Arabic, 'How are things in Montréal?!', guessing his origins and the city where he was living. I heard another, more amusing story from an Italian disciple who, intimidated by the master's gaze in a photo on the wall, covered it with a sheet when making love to his wife. A little while later, when the couple visited Cyprus, Sheikh Nāzim told them the sheet was useless; he could see everything.

Miracles and extraordinary events are part of the history of Sufism. Nevertheless, unlike the Būdshīshīs and the 'Alāwīs, who consider these phenomena private affairs that are potentially dangerous and should not be revealed, the Naqshbandis showcase and openly celebrate miracles along with the charisma of the masters.

While we have seen the refusal and deconstruction of charisma by Sheikh Khaled Bentounes of the 'Alāwiyya, the process we see in the Naqshbandi case is entirely the inverse. The charismatic image of Sheikh Nāzim is bolstered and exalted in all written and non-written discourses of the brotherhood, such that we can refer to 'online charisma'.[14]

[14] Piraino, 'Between Real and Virtual Communities'; Schmidt, 'Sufi Charisma on Internet'.

> He wears the Cloak of the Light of the Divine Presence. He is unique in his time. He is the orchid planted in the earth of Divine Love. He is the Sun for all the universes. He is known as the Saint of the Two Wings: the external knowledge and the internal knowledge. He is a Miracle of Allah's Miracles, walking on the earth and soaring in the Heavens . . .[15]

The construction of charisma is not only based on discourse. Take, for example, all the non-formalised rituals of deference with regard to the sheikh. When I visited Cyprus in April 2013, at the mother-*zāwiya* in Lefke, I had the opportunity to observe how the disciples interacted with their master. Except for family members and a handful of other disciples, the Naqshbandis who had come from all over the world only had one time when they could meet Sheikh Nāzim. Each day, at around 4.30 p.m., the sheikh left the *zāwiya* and got into a car that took him on his various errands (at the time, he was ninety-one years old and confined to a wheelchair). All the disciples, around 100 of them, were waiting outside the *zāwiya* along the narrow adjacent road. When Sheikh Nāzim emerged, they all began to sing, gesturing towards the master and trying to catch his eye. 'This moment makes the trip worth it!' said Khaldoun. Many of the disciples immortalised the scene in photos or videos. The entire ritual lasted only a few minutes, but recurred every day, and also when the master returned to the *zāwiya*.

Some disciples, in their ardent desire to meet the sheikh, were not satisfied by the brief moments I have just described, leading to a cadre of 'sacred taxi drivers' who offered to take passengers and follow Sheikh Nāzim during his drive, of course for a fee. Khaldoun, the French *muqaddam*, hailed one of these taxis and invited me to follow the sheikh's car, which stopped twice: in front of the cemetery where Nāzim's wife is buried, and by the seaside. It goes without saying that our taxi was one of many. Our driver, like the others, did his best to get ahead and as close as possible to the sheikh's car. From their taxis, everyone tried to catch the sheikh's eye in the rearview mirror. Some disciples got out when the sheikh's car stopped to greet the master and take photos. As for Khaldoun, he advised us to remain in the car and leave the sheikh in peace. In effect, Nāzim seemed to have little respite owing to his success and the love of his disciples.

[15] Kabbani, *Classical Islam and the Naqshbandi Sufi Tradition*, 460.

Many Naqshbandi disciples converted to Islam because of Sheikh Nāzim's charisma. What is more, some of them openly said that if Sheikh Nāzim had been of another religion, they, too, would belong to that religion. In other words, Nāzim's magnetic charisma is more important than Sufism and Islam for some disciples. Sheikh Burhanuddin, one of the protagonists of the Italian Naqshbandiyya, described his meeting with Sheikh Nāzim this way:

> When I met *Mauwlana*, my beloved master, I instantly fell in love. I did not expect to be overcome by a Muslim, and to be frank, it was not exactly religious faith I was seeking. On the contrary, this was the last thing I could have imagined! But he stole my heart. From that moment on, I started to imitate him, to take on his appearance, because the lover wants to perfectly imitate his beloved, to totally resemble the one he loves. Had he dressed like a Pharaoh, or with feathers in his hat, it would not have made any difference to me. Even if he had worn a bikini . . . I would have thought: 'That's some kind of method!' but I would have followed him without any doubt.[16]

In this brotherhood, charisma is not only associated with the figure of the sheikh; his *khalīfa*s may also be gifted with a degree of magnetism. We will see in the following sections that Sheikh Burhanuddin is considered to possess strong charisma and even supernatural powers. One of his disciples told me he did not want to meet Sheikh Nāzim because the energy that emanated from Burhanuddin was already so powerful that he did not dare to imagine Nāzim's power. Another example comes from Sheikh Hisham Kabbani, who celebrates his spiritual power by recounting his five years of spiritual *khalwa*, during which he ate only seven olives and two small pieces of bread a day and succeeded, he says, in speaking directly to God.[17]

Before we conclude this section on Naqshbandi charisma, here is the account of Sheikh Mehmet's visit to Paris in March 2013, when his father was still alive. I consider his visit to be a perfect example of the construction of charisma in this brotherhood. Unlike his father, Mehmet does not possess any 'natural' charisma; he often looks at the ground, his voice is weak, he rarely smiles and his shoulders are slightly hunched. When he went onstage at the theatre to speak to the disciples, he did not even look them in the eye, and

[16] Herrmann, *Il derviscio metropolitano*, 53.

[17] Kabbani, *Classical Islam and the Naqshbandi Sufi Tradition*, 249.

one of the Parisian *muqaddams* held up a microphone as he spoke. As to the content of his discourse, Sheikh Mehmet did not elicit any enthusiasm from the disciples. His position was very conservative and related mainly to the Ottoman Empire – very far from the concerns of the Parisian disciples. Some disciples admitted to me they were disappointed by his discourse, while others spoke of the symbolic level, incomprehensible to non-believers.

That said, the brotherhood did everything it could in terms of constructing charisma, to make Sheikh Mehmet extraordinary. He was the centre of attention, the only person seated, on a large red divan placed on a red rug at the front of the room. Next to him on a small table were biscuits, coffee and tea. Everyone had their eyes riveted to him, should he ask for or need the slightest thing. And as soon as Sheikh Mehmet approached, everyone lowered their eyes and kissed his hand.

A Malleable Message

The Naqshbandi discourse oscillates between a message of universal love that surpasses all ethnic, cultural and religious boundaries, and a message of Islamic–Naqshbandi supremacy which, as we will see, is characterised by a degree of anti-modernism and by millenarianism. The balance between these two poles changes according to individual inclinations as well as the geographic and cultural context.

Rabbānī: *Sheikh Nāzim's Universalism*

The Naqshbandi universal message of love spread by Sheikh Nāzim overcomes all barriers, and Sufism becomes the quest for eternity and universal love. Here is Nāzim's discourse in Glastonbury before an audience of young English 'spiritual seekers':[18]

> Oh youngsters, you are like my grandsons and granddaughters. Ask to be for eternity. Make your efforts and aim for eternity, you should attain endless happiness, endless enjoyments. Don't say, I am Christian, I am Protestant, I am Catholic, I am Muslim, I am Buddhist. No, this is not important. Are you asking for eternity or not? Do you think that you would like to be for eternity?[19]

[18] Draper, 'From Celts to Kaaba'.

[19] Draper, 'Towards a Postmodern Sufism', 199.

In a similar way, Sheikh Nāzim astonished his disciples in 2010, declaring:

> If anyone asks you what your way is, say, 'I am trying to be *Rabbānī*' or 'I am *Rabbānī*' [a man of the Lord]. Finished! *Lā 'ilāha 'illā-llāh*. This is a bombardment of the fortress of *Shayṭān*. Finished! Do not say, 'I am Christian', 'I am Jewish', 'I am Maronite', 'I am Orthodox', 'I am Catholic', I am Protestant', 'I am Shiite', 'I am this, I am that.' No! And no more '*taṣawwuf*'. That name was never heard coming from the *ṣaḥābah* [companions of the Prophet Muhammad]. 'Who are you?' You must say, 'I am a Muslim *Rabbānī*.' Finished! No longer Naqshbandi, no longer *taṣawwuf*. Now the Salafis will be happy![20]

Divine love thus plays a central role in the Naqshbandi discourse. All Nāzim's discourses on love have been collected in the book *Amore*,[21] published in Italian. The chapter titles are reflective of the content: 'Your Love/The Love of Those Who Love You/The Love of Actions That Lead Me to Your Love/Infinite Love/Love Oceans/My Love for You/Hearts in Love/ . . .' We are far from the metaphysics and intellectualism we have seen up till now. The language is simple, as are the topics discussed:

> When this beautiful, young, rich, intelligent, amiable and friendly person becomes bad, old, poor and a complainer, will you still love them?[22]

> Kindness comes from love. The more you use love in your life, the more kindness you will have in your life. If you do not use it, your life will be hard and bitter . . . He who does not love is like dry wood.[23]

> What characterises souls is love. Souls live in love oceans.[24]

A good example of Nāzim's universalist appeal, which surpasses religious differences, was provided by the Italian *khalīfa*, Iqbal, who told me about a spiritual meeting that especially touched him. In the early 1990s in Switzerland,

[20] Sufi Center, 2011, 'Shaykh Nazim – There is no Sufi, only Rabbani! Be Rabbani!' *Vimeo* [video], 17 August 2022. Available at <https://vimeo.com/17486759> (last accessed 9 November 2023).

[21] Haqqani, *Amore*.

[22] Haqqani, *Amore*, 29.

[23] Haqqani, *Amore*, 47.

[24] Haqqani, *Amore*, 63.

Sheikh Nāzim was visiting a group of Hindus, who were European converts. The atmosphere was fraught because their guru had died the previous day. Sheikh Nāzim stupefied the Hindu disciples by saying he could see and speak with their deceased master and, moreover, he asked Nāzim to take care of them. Sheikh Nāzim then asked the disciples to pray with him in the Islamic way, as their guru wished them to.

This interaction can be interpreted as proof of an interreligious meta-dimension, in which spiritual masters discuss and recognise the plurality of religious forms. That said, others might interpret this interaction as a demonstration of spiritual force. According to the disciples' account at least, Nāzim recognised the value of Hinduism, but he then led these Hindus to convert to Islam. In this way, Naqshbandi universalism is unique. On one hand, it recognises a primordial universal dimension (love, eternity, and so on) and thus the validity of all religions, while on the other, it establishes Islamic and Naqshbandi supremacy over other religions and brotherhoods.

Openness to New Age Discourse

Converts in most European brotherhoods influence them by contributing their religious and cultural experiences. In these brotherhoods, then, we would be likely to observe the impact of disciples with a background in, say, Guénonian traditionalism or New Age culture. This is one of the forms of cultural hybridisation that Sufism is undergoing in Europe. However, another form of hybridisation exists, in which the brotherhood is not only 'passive' but proposes a form of 'conscious and aesthetic' hybridisation[25] by appropriating exogenous doctrines. This process is illustrated by the appropriation of the enneagram, created by the esotericist Gurdjieff and his disciples.[26]

While the process of 'Sufi-isation' of the enneagram started in Gurdjieffian milieus with Bennett and Shah, who were seeking the sources of Gurdjieff's teachings,[27] it was the Naqshbandiyya Ḥaqqāniyya that formalised its relationship with Gurdjieff.[28] According to Kabbani, the Armenian esotericist seeker

[25] Bakhtin, *The Dialogic Imagination*; Werbner, 'The Limits of Cultural Hybridity'.

[26] Ouspensky, *In Search of the Miraculous Fragments of an Unknown Teaching*.

[27] Cusack, 'The Enneagram'; Sedgwick, 'Sufism and the Enneagram'.

[28] Kabbani, *Classical Islam and the Naqshbandi Sufi Tradition*; Kabbani and Nasr, *The Naqshbandi Sufi Way*.

was a 'true saint' who had met Sheikh Abdellah al-Daghestani (Nāzim's master) in Damascus, where the master had revealed to him the nine-point doctrine, or enneagram. The Naqshbandiyya thus came to possess knowledge of the enneagram and welcomed Gurdjieffian disciples, orphaned by the death of their spiritual master.[29]

From that point onward, the various Naqshbandi *zāwiya*s (in Italy, France, the United States, and so on) organised seminars on the 'Naqshbandi enneagram'. The total absence of the enneagram in the history of the Naqshbandiyya, and more generally in the history of Sufism, might suggest that Kabbani and the Naqshbandiyya strategically appropriated Gurdjieff's legacy and his enneagram to attract potential disciples, but there is no proof of this.

We will see that the openness to New Age discourse cannot be reduced to the appropriation of doctrines and practices, such as the enneagram; it is, instead, a true reformulation concerning the conceptualisation of sacred knowledge. It also reveals the bricolage of doctrines and rituals, the criticism of institutional religions, the empirical and customised approach to religion, and the limited collective engagement, favouring the organisation of small groups (cf. Chapter 2 on the idea of the New Age as a discourse).

Islamic, Sufi and Naqshbandi Supremacy

Sheikh Nāzim's teachings form part of Sufi and Islamic tradition in that they transmit Islamic doctrines, affirm the importance of respecting Islamic norms, and underscore on the primacy of Islam, as the most recent revelation, over other religious paths.

> Now the most excellent and complete purification is possible only in Islam. A Christian or a Jew may ask, 'Why?' We answer that this is so because Christians and Jews have neglected and virtually lost their codes of law in which were contained commands and prohibitions.[30]

The superiority of Nāzim's Naqshbandiyya does not only concern other religions; it also reigns over all other forms of Islam and Sufism. Sheikh

[29] Nielsen, et al., 'Transnational Sufism'.

[30] Haqqani, *Mercy Oceans' Divine Sources*, 206.

Nāzim is undeniably *quṭb*: the 'Sultan of the saints'. As Khaldoun, the Parisian *muqaddam*, tells us, the Naqshbandiyya is a 'superior brotherhood', 'the Rolls Royce of the *ṭuruq*'. Its superiority is guaranteed by the presence of al-Khiḍr[31] and Abu Bakr[32] in the *silsila*, or spiritual genealogy.[33]

Khaldoun told me that all the French researchers and teachers who took an interest in the Naqshbandiyya became disciples of Sheikh Nāzim. According to information gleaned in the *zāwiya*s, the brotherhood also includes several famous disciples such as King Charles III, the singer Cat Stevens (also known as Yusuf Islam), the boxer Muhammad Ali, Turkish president Recep Tayyip Erdoğan, Susilo Bambang Yudhoyono (former president of Indonesia) and the writer Frank Herbert. Khaldoun also affirmed that the Naqshbandiyya is the source of Shaolin Kung Fu. These surprising and sometimes exaggerated claims make it difficult to distinguish true from false. Proof exists in some cases, such as the recording of the boxer Muhammad Ali being initiated,[34] but it is mostly a matter of whether or not you trust the sheikh.

The discourses within the French and Italian Naqshbandiyya affirm that 'the Naqshbandiyya is the only brotherhood keeping up with the times.' It is also said that Sheikh Khaled Bentounes of the 'Alāwiyya recognised Naqshbandi superiority and made the *bay'a* with Sheikh Nāzim. The Būdshīshiyya is 'too political' and the Tījāniyya too influenced by Senegalese culture, making the Naqshbandiyya Ḥaqqāniyya the only real living brotherhood. This stance is the exact opposite of the post-confraternity-ism of the 'Alāwiyya, and the Naqshbandiyya's symbolic fight for religious authority in the Sufi field leaves little room for dialogue.

31 Al-Khiḍr, a complex, enigmatic figure in the Qur'an (18: 60–82), is very important in Sufi literature, possessing hidden religious knowledge.

32 Most brotherhoods start their *silsila* with Ali (after the Prophet Muhammad) whereas the Naqshbandiyya claims to be the only brotherhood linked to Muhammad's prominent companion, Abu Bakr. In reality, there are other brotherhoods, such as the Bektāshiyya, that include Abu Bakr in their *silsila*, cf. Trimingham, *The Sufi Orders in Islam*.

33 Haqqani, *Mercy Oceans' Divine Sources*.

34 'Muhammad Ali Recites Naqshbandi Bay'ah in 2001', 17 August 2022, *Facebook* [video]. Available at <https://www.facebook.com/MawlanaShaykh/videos/276844913498673/> (last accessed 9 November 2023).

Nevertheless, in 2018, a new actor entered the French Naqshbandiyya scene: Abdelhafid Benchouk, founder of the Maison Soufie.[35] Influenced by the religionism of Massignon, Corbin and de Vitray-Meyerovitch and by Guénonian esotericism, Benchouk has developed a way of thinking comparable to the Islamic humanism described in the ʿAlāwiyya and the Būdshīshiyya. He is also involved in several cultural activities and in interfaith dialogue. Benchouk has thus focused on Sheikh Nāzim's '*rabbānī*' message, leaving Naqshbandi anti-modernism, anti-intellectualism and superiority in the background. Unfortunately, when I conducted my fieldwork, Benchouk's activities were still embryonic, so I preferred to follow other Naqshbandi *zāwiya*s.

These various 'Naqshbandi souls' can co-exist but also oppose one another. The experience I believe best illustrates this tension is the pilgrimage to the tomb of Saint Barnabas in Cyprus, which I was able to make in 2013.

In the early morning, I climb into a disciple's taxi, along with other French disciples, to travel to the sacred sites in Cyprus recommended by Sheikh Nāzim. The driver, Leith, is a cheerful young Palestinian who sings throughout the trip, lightening the mood and putting us at ease. When we bring up the tense Palestinian situation, his attitude is merciful, without the slightest trace of resentment. During the ride, he prefers to sing rather than talk politics, laying aside the Palestinian issue by saying, 'There's a lot of suffering in the world.' Leith shows us a small church on the mountainside where Nāzim went when he was younger. As a result, this church is considered a particularly sacred place, with a great deal of *baraka*.

During our pilgrimage to various sacred sites in Cyprus, we meet Tarek, another disciple/ad hoc taxi driver for pilgrims. Tarek, of Belgian origin and around fifty years old, has lived in Lefke for thirty years and is an experienced 'sacred' taxi driver. Leith, still very young and lacking Tarek's confidence on the road, asks us to share the trip with Tarek and his 'clients/disciples'.

While the young Palestinian, Leith, is a good example of the universalist and merciful thinking of the Naqshbandiyya, Tarek, with his arrogance and pride, exemplifies the brotherhood's sense of supremacy. During our visit to the city of Famagusta, Tarek passionately recounts the war against Venice,

[35] The website of the association Maison Soufie (literally, Sufi House) is available at <http://www.lamaisonsoufie.fr/> (last accessed 9 November 2023).

the 'Christian enemy', as if the siege of Famagusta by the Turks in 1571 had taken place yesterday. When Tarek realised I was a Venetian myself, he seemed slightly embarrassed and fell silent. For Tarek, who makes liberal use of such dichotomous pairs as friend/enemy and believer/non-believer, the pilgrimage to Saint Barnabas's tomb is not an homage to a Christian saint:

> Sheikh Barnabas held in his heart the true gospel, in which he announced the coming of the Prophet Muhammad. But the Church destroyed this gospel because it would have meant the end of the institution.

Tarek was referring to the Gospel of Barnabas,[36] which prefigured the coming of the Prophet Muhammad. Today historians agree that it dates from the sixteenth century; for this reason, it cannot be compared to the other gospels. While Tarek considered Barnabas as proof of Islam's superiority compared to Christianity, Leith was more interested in the saint and devotional practice. Like Muhyiddin (Būdshīshī disciple, cf. Chapter 3) and Abdel Rahman ('Alāwī disciple, cf. Chapter 4), Leith believed in the unicity of God and the unicity of sainthood. The Islamic practice of these three disciples did not prevent them from recognising the value of other religions. For Leith, Saint Barnabas was first and foremost a saint of God and of human beings, before being a Christian saint.

When I say I want to visit the church near Saint Barnabas's tomb, Tarek's reaction is harsh. He explains to me that 'they [Christians] hate us', and that Christians had even punctured the tyres of his car. When I tell him the church is too beautiful to miss, he responds that he is not interested and will not wait for me. At that point, I lose my cool, send Tarek packing, and go to visit this beautiful church anyway. To use a more elegant and sociological expression, one could say I set up an ethnomethodological approach, in defiance of the ritual rules of the frame.[37]

Leith, who does not share Tarek's attitude, waits for me and says, 'You were right to visit the church. Tarek's been here [in Lefke] for thirty years, but often that doesn't mean anything.' When it comes time to get back in the taxi, the disciples Juliette and Haroun admit that in their opinion, the Gospel of

[36] Cirillo, *Évangile de Barnabé*.

[37] Garfinkel, *Studies in Ethnomethodology*.

Barnabas is probably a historical invention. The following day, other French disciples go on the same sacred tour. This time, Khaldoun, the Parisian *muqaddam* of Syrian origin, goes along. He will visit the Church of Saint Barnabas and will even be invited by the bishop to participate in a collective lunch.

Naqshbandi Conservatism, Anti-modernism and Millenarianism

Anti-intellectualism

> [T]hese philosophers are full of many contradictions even within themselves; their philosophy is without basis, and I don't even call it 'knowledge'. Some no-mind people are now speaking of 'Islamic Philosophy,' and that sort of talk is sufficient for us to confirm their lack of understanding of Islam: Islam is based on the firmest base of reality, and that is a base upon which one may build, while those philosophical systems are based on nothing but thin air. In Islam there is reality, not philosophy.[38]

The books of Sheikh Nāzim and the brotherhood's local leaders foreground the importance of the heart, love and the emotions, rather than discursive rationality. Religion and rationality are viewed as totally separate dimensions. Būdshīshī and 'Alāwī thought around sacred epistemology, at the intersection of religious sciences, human sciences and hard sciences, is unimaginable in the Naqshbandiyya. We can even speak of a form of anti-intellectualism, favouring the pre-eminence of the emotional religious experience.

This anti-intellectualism is connected to anti-scientific and anti-technological sentiment – in other words, anti-modernism. One of the most important theological and moral topics in this brotherhood is the return to nature, leaving cities, concrete, medicine, technology, and so forth behind, in search of a 'more natural' and healthier life.

> Unbelievers have been given 'Satanic Wisdom' which enables them to invent and develop so many things – they have wonderful imagination. If not for the unbelievers, we might be living in caves yet, in huts or tents: no skyscrapers, airplanes, gigantic ocean Cruisers, tape recorders, computers, central heating, no electricity – none of these discoveries and inventions. But they have been given a Satanic Wisdom, and every day you see them coming up with a new device.[39]

[38] Haqqani, *Mercy Oceans' Divine Sources*, 112.

[39] Haqqani, *Mercy Oceans' Divine Sources*, 161.

The opposition to science targets evolutionary theories that go against religious creationism. As Sheikh Hassan explained with sarcasm, 'Only Darwin came from monkeys.' This anti-scientism also extends to scientific medicine since, according to Sheikh Nāzim's teachings, medication is entirely useless, surgery dangerous, and painkillers a way of escaping from life. Only faith is truly curative:

> When we understand this, treatment is easy for believers. For unbelievers the cure is very difficult. The souls help the believers to be cured, but unbelievers have souls that are against themselves and these will never support them.[40]

> One day, a young lady came to Sheikh Nazim who had been diagnosed as having a cancer in her thyroid. The doctors wanted to start operating, but she did not want any knife to cut into her throat. Sheikh Nazim told her to start drinking onion-juice every morning before taking anything else and then to wait for an hour. After repeating the 40-day treatment, she was completed cured.[41]

Anti-modernism: Nostalgia for the Monarchy and the Sultanate

Naqshbandi anti-modernism also applies to the political sphere. More specifically, the republican and democratic system is openly described by Sheikh Nāzim as satanic. He has gone so far as to coin the term 'dirt-o-cracy'. According to the sheikh, the only system that guarantees human values is the monarchy in Europe and the sultanate in Islamic countries. The only constitution for Muslims is sharia. Several disciples, especially in Italy, are sympathisers of the monarchist party, whereas German disciples of Turkish origin participate in the politico-cultural organisation the 'Young Ottomans'.

> Democracy! What is democracy? It is the feces of shaytan! It is to make these mindless people eat the filth it excretes. They say, 'Democracy is the best.' No way! Who says this is kafir. *Allāh* sent a constitution, He sent Sharia.[42]

It should be noted that, for many disciples and sheikhs, secular and democratic values have brought new freedom (as we saw for Khaled Bentounes after he

[40] Haqqani, *Natural Medicines*, 23.

[41] Haqqani, *Natural Medicines*, 12.

[42] The document can be consulted online: Cheikh Nazim, 'The Shar'iah & the Constitution', 3 July 2013. Available at <http://saltanat-transcriptions.s3.amazonaws.com/english/2013-07-03_en_SeriatVeAnayasa.pdf> (last accessed 9 November 2023).

fled from Algeria), whereas Sheikh Nāzim's experience has been completely different. His hagiography tells us that he was arrested for preaching Islam in the anti-religious, anti-Sufi Turkey of the 1950s. Moreover, to this day, the Lefke *zāwiya* in Cyprus seems to be in captivity. Many residents in Lefke do not like the Naqshbandi disciples, and the local disciples advise visitors to eat only in 'friendly' restaurants – that is, run by other disciples.

The moral conservatism also applies to sexuality and is even more stringent with regard to women. A particularly illuminating example is a short book Nāzim wrote about Princess Diana.[43] The princess is accused of abandoning her royal family, living with a man outside of marriage, drinking alcohol and leaving her body uncovered, all sins that purportedly led to her premature death. According to Sheikh Nāzim, women have a specific role to play in Islamic society:

> Now in our time, women are making themselves up, going out in the streets, everywhere . . . Our Grandsheikh says: Allah is not going to ask them anything about their doings. He is going to ask their husbands, fathers and brothers. Allah is commanding the family to be in the hands of the man. He must keep that position. Man has more power than women; he is supporting them. A quarrel between ladies is not on the same level as a quarrel between men. How can a lady be as a man? They are created as women. We are not equal.[44]

Naqshbandi anti-modern thought in its diverse moral, political and anti-scientific manifestations is not widespread in all *zāwiya*s. For example, it is nearly non-existent in France. On the other hand, it seems more common among converts from the Italian counter-culture, whether on the left or the right. In addition, it should not be interpreted literally, since Naqshbandi anti-modernism often seems more rhetorical and/or symbolic. For example, the anti-technology attitude runs up against the massive online presence, with websites where it is possible to pray, converse, even convert and be initiated.[45] The view of democracy as 'satanic' also loses its impact when we consider that in the United States, Sheikh Nāzim had, and Sheikh Kabbani has, good relations with American

[43] Haqqani, *Princess Diana's Death*.

[44] Haqqani, *Mercy Oceans (Book Two)*, 47.

[45] Piraino, 'Between Real and Virtual Communities'.

public institutions, and both justified the actions of George W. Bush and Tony Blair, the West's 'War on Terror'[46] and the 'exportation of democracy'.[47]

The disciples with whom I broached this theologico-political topic explained to me that the teachings are symbolic. I learned from Ahmed, an engineering professor at MIT whom I met in Cyprus, that Sheikh Nāzim, similar to Plato in *The Republic*, described a model based on religious knowledge (philosophical knowledge in the case of Plato). But, as Ahmed pointed out, Islamic theocracy, like the Platonic Republic, is an ideal model. Ultimately, in terms of systems, contemporary democracy is, its human limitations notwithstanding, the best of the worst. By contrast, others such as Tarek, mentioned above, prefer a literal interpretation of Nāzim, speak of political plans, and militate for the restoration of the monarchy and the sultanate. As in the case of the tension between universalist and particularist mindsets, what counts is the interpretation of each individual disciple.

We will not go into the political and institutional ramifications in Northern Cyprus, under Turkish control, but it is not impossible that nationalism and neo-Ottomanism influence the discourses and motives of the Sufis living there.

Naqshbandi Eschatology

The final aspect we need to examine to complete the Naqshbandi mosaic is the question of eschatology: the end of the world. As with other Naqshbandi themes, there is no consensus on this subject. Everyone explained the end of the world to me in their own way. Khaldoun, the Parisian *muqaddam*, told me that, according to the calculations of one of his friends, the world would end in '2380 or thereabouts'. Abdelhafid Benchouk, another Parisian *muqaddam*, told me we would be waiting '100 years at best'. Iqbal, the Italian *khalīfa*, admitted that he had thought the ultimate date to be 2011, and that numerous disciples had left the cities for rural areas, taking copious reserves of food. On the contrary, some disciples get annoyed when they hear of people 'fleeing to the countryside'. They criticise their brothers who, as they see it, take the

46 Dickson, 'An American Sufism'.

47 'Shaykh Muhammad Nazim al-Haqqani Obituary', *The Telegraph*, 12 May 2014. Available at <https://www.telegraph.co.uk/news/obituaries/10825296/Shaykh-Muhammad-Nazim-al-Haqqani-obituary.html> (last accessed 9 November 2023).

end of the world too literally, whereas it is a question of symbolic purification. Guénonian disciples reiterate the position of the French thinker, that it is not the end of *the* world, but of *a* world. Finally, a number of disciples, such as Haroun, do not really know what to think: 'There are many things I don't understand, like the end of the world.'

Despite this heterogeneity, we can try to recreate, based on the discourses of Sheikh Nāzim, an 'official' version of the Naqshbandi end of the world. Sheikh Nāzim reaffirmed several times that *Dajjāl*, the Antichrist (literally, the deceiver), and Mahdī, the one who would fight the Antichrist, were already among us. These eschatological figures are in direct contact with Naqshbandi sheikhs.[48] Seven European nations will become Muslim, guided by their converted kings. 'The biggest war' will then take place, a terrible, worldwide war killing millions. The forces of good and evil will confront each other in the final combat.

> For non-Muslims, it will be enough to believe in the existence of Allah in order to gain that protection; for Muslims, however, at least one prostration a day is the condition. All atheists will perish.[49]

The countdown is based on the Gregorian rather than the Islamic calendar, with the final days predicted for '1987, 1989, 1991, 1993, and 2000'.[50] The date in 2000 was one of the most significant given its link with the 'millennium bug', leading us back to anti-modern and anti-technological rhetoric. There have been other 'final dates': 1984 and 2011, according to Iqbal, the Italian *khalīfa*.

Of course, each time the world did not end, some were disappointed and abandoned the brotherhood, especially after 2000, according to Mustafa Draper.[51] Others opted for a symbolic interpretation, while still others prayed for the end of the world to take place soon. In Cyprus, I heard the following on several occasions: 'I hope this will be the year it happens.'

[48] Damrel, 'Aspects of the Naqshbandi-Haqqani Order in North America'; Conner, 'From Amuq to Glastonbury'.

[49] Haqqani, *Mercy Oceans' Divine Sources*, 195.

[50] Damrel, 'Aspects of the Naqshbandi-Haqqani Order in North America', 123.

[51] Draper, 'Towards a Postmodern Sufism'.

Beyond the various possible eschatological forms and the diverse interpretations, the Naqshbandi end of the world constitutes the theological core of this brotherhood – the *deus ex machina* that justifies everything. The celebration of Sheikh Nāzim's extraordinary charisma and the charisma of his representatives is intimately linked to the fact that Nāzim was supposedly the last saint before the end of the world. Western decadence (democratic, scientific and technological) and that of the East (wars, radicalism) are signs of the end time.

The end of the world justifies all strategies for saving as many souls as possible. In other words, in a lost, secularised world dominated by the forces of evil and facing its imminent demise, converting non-believers, even if they practise Sufi Islam 'part-time' or in a 'fragmented' way, is already a good outcome. This has led Iqbal, the Italian *khalīfa*, to state: '*Rasūl Allāh*[52] said that whoever said "*lā 'ilāha 'illā-llāh*" one time would go to heaven. That's our mission: to bring the words *'illā Allāh* into people's hearts.' To put it another way, this eschatology justifies malleability and porosity, both in the religious message and the organisational structures.

Among the Disciples: Parisian Brotherhood

The Naqshbandiyya in the Paris region is made up of three *zāwiya*s and has around 100 assiduous disciples and up to 300 who participate in major events. Sheikh Nāzim visited Paris for the first time in 1990, which marked the beginning of regular visits in the four years that followed. The first disciples met in various homes until 1996, when the first *zāwiya* was organised by the French Sheikh Philippe de Vos. Khaldoun, from Syria, then founded his *zāwiya* in the fifteenth arrondissement of Paris, and the Franco-Algerian Abdelhafid Benchouk did the same in Saint-Ouen in 2007. Through funding from the Naqshbandi brothers, Benchouk also owns a *zāwiya* in the countryside, inaugurated in 2013 and used for important celebrations or for summer vacations and retreats.

Between February and September 2013, I concentrated my ethnographical fieldwork on Khaldoun's *zāwiya* after being introduced to the Parisian *muqaddam* by an Italian disciple I had met in Pavia. I also frequented the

[52] One of the names of the Prophet Muhammad is 'the Messenger'.

others on several occasions, to obtain a general sense of the various situations. It should be noted that the French Naqshbandiyya, like the Būdshīshiyya and the 'Alāwiyya, is rapidly expanding; all the *zāwiya*s are looking for larger buildings in which to set up their headquarters.

The socio-biographical characteristics of the Parisian Naqshbandi disciples are similar in the three *zāwiya*s. There is considerable ethnic heterogeneity, including Maghrebis, Arabs, Europeans, South Americans, and even one female Chinese disciple. In terms of the ratio of women to men, it is balanced. The most interesting characteristic is the average age, much lower than in the other brotherhoods I studied. This is undoubtedly due to the more simple, appealing and direct language used by Sheikh Nāzim and his *khalīfa*s. Additionally, while disciples can maintain contact with the Būdshīshiyya and the 'Alāwiyya through books and events, in the Naqshbandi, the most powerful vehicles are the music of Sheikh Hassan and a massive digital presence.

Sheikh Nāzim liked to create a jovial atmosphere and his leaders do as well. The teachings are often accompanied with jokes and the examples are taken from daily life. I heard numerous examples of what might be called 'humorous pedagogy'. The masters use modern metaphors; for instance, to explain *baraka* – spiritual energy and the relationship between master and disciple – references to Wi-Fi and walkie-talkies are common. Such simplicity does not only concern language; the theological discourses and the rituals are also basic. There are no 'Alāwī subtleties, no symbolic discourses, no metaphysical paradoxes. The Naqshbandi theological discourse is simple and clear: there can be no doubt as to the dichotomous opposition between right and wrong, good and evil.

Rituals in the Zāwiya

Khaldoun, a Syrian of around sixty years old, is no exception when it comes to Naqshbandi happiness and kindness. His laughter is contagious. Every time I entered his *zāwiya*, he welcomed me warmly, saying, '*Magnifico fratello italiano*! How are you?' And he always had me sit next to him. During my eight months of fieldwork, Khaldoun was perennially available and friendly, blessing me and my thesis several times. Our relationship was so positive that he even invited me to join him and his disciples in Cyprus in April 2013.

The spiritual meeting is organised on Thursday evening, as in all other Naqshbandi *zāwiya*s. Khaldoun's *zāwiya* is small but well organised. To the right of the entrance is a closet for shoes, and the main room has rugs on the floor along with cushions and little mattresses, used as sofas. There is also a little bookshelf and a photo of Sheikh Nāzim. In winter, electric heating keeps the room warm. Two modest rooms flank the main room: a tiny kitchen and a bathroom. Compared to the Būdshīshiyya *zāwiya*s, this *zāwiya* obviously has limited financial resources, which in no way prevents it from being comfortable and inviting.

At 8 p.m., disciples begin to trickle in. There are no set hours; disciples come and go as they please. Khaldoun then starts the teaching component, which is neither a real class as in the Būdshīshiyya, nor a *mudhakara* as in the ʿAlāwiyya. Khaldoun generally does not prepare a structured discourse. He instead proceeds in the form of questions and answers or explains a verse from the Qurʾan or a *ḥadīth*, depending on whatever inspires him in the moment. The disciples have no formal obligation to listen; they can do so or not as they please. One disciple admitted that she always came at 9 p.m. to avoid Khaldoun's discourse.

In this little *zāwiya* which can hold up to forty people, the separation of men and women is symbolic, with the formation of separate subgroups. As for the disciples' attire, it is highly varied; some young people wear traditional dress (djellaba or Turkish clothing), but mostly the apparel is relaxed. The only distinctive sign that marks the entry into the sacred space is the little cap for men (suggested) and the headscarf for women (required). Only Khaldoun and the other *muqaddam*s wear the 'sacred uniform': the Naqshbandi turban and a Turkish shirt and vest.

At around 9 p.m., depending on the times for prayer, *dhikr* begins. Everyone comes together to form concentric circles. In the centre are placed a candle and several bottles of water, opened up to let *baraka* in. These bottles will be filled with *dhikr*, or 'dhikrised'. Later, the disciples will drink the *dhikr* water, said to have beneficial powers for both the body and the soul.

Khaldoun initiates *dhikr*, which he will guide for around an hour. As in the other brotherhoods I studied, *dhikr* consists of a set of divine names, parts of the Qurʾan, prayers and *shahāda* – the profession of faith. Many disciples described Naqshbandi *dhikr* as mild and low key. Manil, a forty-year-old Franco-Algerian disciple who used to frequent the Parisian Būdshīshiyya, admitted to me that Būdshīshī rituals were too intense and too fraught, whereas he found the relaxed atmosphere he was looking for with the Naqshbandiyya.

The Naqshbandi practice of *dhikr* is not only shorter (around an hour compared to two hours with the 'Alāwīs and four hours with the Būdshīshīs); it is also simpler. The melodies and rhythms are more basic and easier to remember. *Dhikr* is less psalmodised and more of a song. The pace of the rhythmical breathing or, in other words, the ecstatic tension, is much less intense than in the other brotherhoods. In eight months, I never heard the ecstatic expression known as *ḥāl*.

With the other brotherhoods, I used the image of a conductor to describe the role of the *muqaddam* as he sets the tempo of *dhikr*, without changing the musical notes. In the Naqshbandiyya, however, this image is misleading. The *muqaddam* does not execute the *dhikr*; rather, he interprets it. Hence, changing *zāwiya*s means hearing different *dhikr*s. For example, Abdelhafid Benchouk in Saint-Ouen, uses a small drum, lengthens *dhikr* and adds songs, making it much more musical. In the *dhikr* of Benchouk, we perceive his Algerian roots, the result resembling the 'Alāwī and Būdshīshī forms. In the Italian Naqshbandiyya/nebula, we will see that the desire for a sophisticated atmosphere pushes local leaders to add sound effects.

The importance of the *muqaddam* or *khalīfa* in leading and interpreting *dhikr* is part of his role as 'spiritual entrepreneur', a role that, unlike what is expected of *muqaddam*s in other orders, entails a degree of independence from the brotherhood. The shift from execution to interpretation of the Naqshbandi *dhikr* becomes even more evident in the absence of the *muqaddam*. On the rare occasions when the *muqaddam* was not there, I observed that the disciples participated less, and very few of them were capable of guiding the *dhikr*. I remember one evening in particular, when Khaldoun was slightly ill. Every time he left to use the restroom, the *dhikr* lost its force, becoming an indiscriminate murmur; no one seemed have it memorised. This could not have happened in the other brotherhoods I studied because most disciples knew *dhikr* by heart, even though the expressions were much more complex.

Once *dhikr* ends, the round of salutations begins. Men and women form separate circles and the expression '*Salām 'alaykum*' is repeated, accompanied by three kisses on the shoulders, or a simple kiss on the cheek of the other sisters and brothers. The salutations are part of the ritual and, as elsewhere, are not highly formalised. During them, we feel moments of joy and camaraderie, and it is possible to ask, 'How are you?' In fact, many disciples took this opportunity to enquire how my research was going.

After the salutations, the disciples once again form a circle, but this time remain standing. Khaldoun guides *du'ā,* an invocation/supplication of God lasting around three minutes. With each phrase of the invocation, the disciples respond with '*Amīn*'. Khaldoun's requests concern peace, health, mercy, love, heaven, and so on. The only memorable phrase is: 'Let *Allāh* bless France, let him allow us to practise our religion in the best way possible', which is pronounced every Thursday (we will see the meaning of this phrase below).

Around 10 p.m., we prepare a meal. Unlike in the Būdshīshiyya where all duties are assigned, in Khaldoun's Naqshbandiyya, the disciples do not have any obligations. Everyone brings something to eat and drink, and everyone helps prepare the dinner, without any difference between the genders. Food is served on paper plates and the ambiance is relaxed and lively. Khaldoun is always the last to be served, a sign of his humility. As he often says, 'I am here to serve.' During the meal, Khaldoun continues with his teachings in an informal way. Once again, he is not teaching a lesson, so everyone is free to listen or talk with their neighbour. When dinner ends, the spiritual meeting is over. Near the exit is a small box for donations to cover the expenses of the *zāwiya*.

The meetings in other *zāwiya*s take place in a similar manner. Philippe de Vos organises spiritual meetings in his home, but these evening events do not occur on a regular basis. As for the *zāwiya* of Abdelhafid Benchouk in Saint-Ouen, it is larger and better organised. Also, separation according to gender is much more pronounced; women keep to a part of the room isolated by a curtain, and they are always in charge of preparing the meals. Relative to the ritual of *dhikr* taken globally in its various forms, the French Naqshbandiyya practises a simple, minimalist form. It does not include *samā'* or *ḥaḍra*. Concerning *ḥaḍra*, both Khaldoun and de Vos expressed a degree of mistrust: '[*Ḥaḍra* is] for Europeans, they need a little more animation . . . I don't need it,' Khaldoun told me. Some disciples even see *ḥaḍra* as something outside the brotherhood, used only to draw in young people.

Khaldoun's Teachings and French Naqshbandi Themes

Khaldoun explains to us that a brotherhood is a school 'like Oxford or Cambridge'. According to him, the Naqshbandiyya is the best school, and when he proclaims its majesty and superiority, he adds with a laugh, 'I have many strengths, but modesty isn't one of them!' Nonetheless, Khaldoun is, in fact, very serious. In his discourse, the supremacy of Islam and the Naqshbandiyya is recurrent. According to him, there is a 'hierarchy among religions' and 'Islam is the only self-regenerating one', positions that sometimes make more universalist disciples roll their eyes. In addition, Khaldoun often underscores that the Naqshbandiyya is a strictly Islamic brotherhood and 'not a sect':

> We are not dervishes, we are not eccentrics, we are not bizarre; on the contrary, we are in the world, we might be physicians, millionaires or ministers. A good Naqshbandi is a good servant of God.

In his teachings, Khaldoun refers to the Qur'an, the *ḥadīth* and the lessons of Naqshbandi masters. He examines the central doctrines, such as fighting the ego and developing subtle knowledge. The influence of New Age discourse does not seem to affect the doctrinal dimension. Even so, Khaldoun has assimilated certain elements of New Age language.

> Only Sheikh Nāzim can open the love chakra.

> Being a saint means vibrating in unison with the universe . . . You won't find these things in a book.

Khaldoun emphasises the importance of serving the Other: 'There are several paths [towards God]; mine is to serve the Other.' He explains this from a theological viewpoint using an upside-down pyramid: Sheikh Nāzim is at the bottom and carries the weight of all his disciples. From a social viewpoint, this concept of 'service to the Other' means helping those in distress. Several times, I saw Khaldoun give food to people lacking resources and invite them into the *zāwiya*. 'We are not a charity organisation,' he stated, 'but the door is always open.'

Another key issue is 'self-discipline'. Khaldoun constantly reiterates that there are no obligations or rules, but that disciples themselves must take responsibility and find their place. Paul, not mincing his words, remarked that 'the brotherhood does not solve your problems; it leaves you to deal with your own shit! It's up to you to engage.' Self-discipline is one of the causes for the Naqshbandis' success, in that those who hesitate, who do not want to commit themselves totally, can still participate in the brotherhood. For example, Paul liked defining himself as a 'Sufi tourist', even after six years of frequenting the brotherhood every week. He explained to me the particularity of the Naqshbandiyya in these terms:

> Have you ever seen how monks interact? All calm and nice, speaking quietly. Everybody seems to be equal. Whereas when you enter the Naqshbandiyya, you see that everybody is different, they keep their personalities and their own abilities. They haven't taken the cloth!

In other words, pressure from the *muqaddam* and from peers is minimal. A simple example is that if a Būdshīshī or 'Alāwī disciple was found to be drinking alcohol, the other disciples would probably speak with them to find out what was going on. In the Aḥmadiyya Idrīsiyya Shādhiliyya, the disciple would risk being expelled. By contrast, in the Naqshbandiyya this behaviour would not be penalised, in that the participation in weekly ritual activities does not require the disciples to behave in a specific manner.

According to Khaldoun, we can experience the results of our journey towards spiritual purification on a daily basis. He told me that purifying the soul also means learning to navigate this world, then shared his personal experience: for more than a year, he has not encountered any rude behaviour. Purifying the soul amounts to harmonising with the world. Intimately linked to this process of harmonisation is the conception of saintliness, which is not seen as distant and inaccessible, but on the contrary, is open to all. Everyone can be a saint, even myself, Khaldoun told me.

> Francesco, it will be difficult for you to surpass the example of Fatima, our Italian sister. She's fantastic. But don't worry, you're on the right path, too. It will only take a little longer.

Khaldoun often used the term 'saint' for his disciples, referring to 'Saint Paul', 'Saint Fatima', 'Saint Bilal' and, sometimes, I myself became 'Saint Francesco'. Of course, there is a fair degree of irony in these names, but as Khaldoun put it: 'Sufis are serious even when they're joking.' Between irony and doctrine, Khaldoun explained that saintliness not only concerns the heavenly realm, because it is also here, among us, within our reach.

> [The Naqshbandiyya] is a machine for producing saintliness, a lot of young people achieve it. This is an efficient machine. (Khaldoun)

Criticising Salafism, Wahhabism and the Muslim Brotherhood is one subject all the disciples can agree on. This is a major Naqshbandi topos, particularly relevant in the United States and the United Kingdom.[53] It concerns all Muslims and comes down to a sort of self-censure. Sheikh Mehmet explained to his disciples that what prevents the Islamisation of Europe is the negative behaviour of Muslims.

Concerning the relationship between sharia and *fiqh*, Khaldoun always uses the metaphor of a 'good recipe'. Being a good Muslim and following sharia means making the best possible dish with the ingredients on hand. There is no single recipe that is perfect and equitable for all times and situations.

I have already presented the two facets of the Naqshbandiyya in describing my pilgrimage to Saint Barnabas's tomb: Khaldoun's improvised interfaith dialogue and Tarek's mistrust verging on disdain. Also, during the fieldwork in Lefke, I witnessed a similar opposition when it came to sharia–*fiqh*.

I am sitting in a café with some French Naqshbandi brothers. At the next table is a woman by herself who looks sad. Khaldoun and the other disciples try to speak with her and gradually she opens up. Her name is Carmen, she is Spanish and around thirty-five years old. Her husband is an IT technician who has been out of work for several years, as the economic crisis has been especially devastating in their city. Carmen is sad because the Naqshbandi sisters told her she should give up her work as a university researcher since, in Islam, men should work and women should stay at home with their children. So, their economic hardship is compounded by a religious issue. Khaldoun listens carefully to Carmen's story, then explains to her with kindness and joy that she can work without any qualms, without going against any religious prohibitions. On the contrary, Khaldoun tells her that if she can make a career in the university world – without renouncing her religion or her family – doing so is a divine blessing. Khaldoun's legitimacy convinces Carmen, who ends up very happy, feeling she has struck a balance.

Khaldoun has devoted many of his discourses to women's importance, their sacredness and also their rights. In his *zāwiya*, women are very involved in the discussions and are free to ask any questions they wish. Plus, all disciples participate equally in the kitchen and in serving meals. This way of seeing the

[53] Stjernholm, 'Lovers of Muhammad'; Dickson, 'An American Sufism'.

question of women is shared by most Parisian disciples. Haroun, an African man born into a Muslim family, asked this question:

> We often forget that Aïcha was the main juridical reference for the Prophet's companions. How many Muslims would accept a woman in charge of Islamic law?

Concerning politics, Khaldoun never talked about the monarchy during my eight months of fieldwork. On the contrary, when I asked him what he thought of secularism and democracy, he responded this way:

> As a Muslim and a human being, I recognise that my rights [here] are superior to my rights in Arab and Islamic countries. And I am much freer. I have 90 per cent of everything I want. Even though I'm missing 10 per cent, it's not worth ruining that 90 per cent. We should instead try to improve the situation from inside the system.

Like other disciples we have heard from, Khaldoun clearly stated the need to differentiate 'secularism' from 'secular fundamentalism'. He considers Muslims who want an application of sharia–*fiqh* in European countries as simply 'out of touch'. Khaldoun's view on sharia and politics is not very different from that of the other brotherhoods I have studied. Khaldoun advocates a humanist discourse, in that his Sufism, like that of Bentounes, seeks to engage with modernity. Khaldoun is not alone in this view; the Franco-Algerian *muqaddam* Benchouk concurs. Incidentally, it was not by chance that our paths crossed at the Congrès International Féminin – Parole aux femmes, organised by the 'Alāwiyya in Oran in 2014.

By contrast, the third *muqaddam*, Philippe de Vos, a French convert, takes pride in his noble origins and condemns secularism, democracy and the French Republic, considering them all satanic. According to this *muqaddam*, in the eschatological process, the monarchy will be re-established throughout Europe. Deeply wedded to his opinions, De Vos cannot tolerate anyone in the brotherhood having a different view than his own. For him, anyone who supports an alternative does so only because they fear police surveillance which, de Vos claims, is ubiquitous. This reveals the opposition between two conceptions of contemporary Sufism. On the one hand we have Khaldoun and Benchouk, for whom Sufism is the application of universal Islam, capable of playing a mediating role in the daily lives of disciples and even in the political sphere – or, in Khaldoun's words, 'making the best possible dish with the ingredients on hand'. Philippe de Vos, on the contrary, is seeking a traditional Islam that is monolithic, pure and impermeable to historical change. In this opposition, what was Sheikh Nāzim's role? As we have already seen, Sheikh Nāzim provided arguments to support both opposing sides, in that he oscillated between a universal discourse and a discourse around identity, favouring a loose, porous structure that can adapt to various demands.

Structure and Activities: Case of the 'Khaldounians'

Accessing the Būdshīshiyya or the 'Alāwiyya is possible in specific situations ('open house events,' lectures, and so on). However, to convert to Islam and adhere to these brotherhoods, a training period is necessary, during which the future disciple must reflect on their spiritual path. By contrast, in the Naqshbandiyya Ḥaqqāniyya case, access is direct. It is possible to enter French Naqshbandi *zāwiya*s whenever you wish, without making an appointment; the door is always open. It is also possible to attend Naqshbandi seminars and retreats; the only requirement is to pay a fee. Access is neither limited nor directly or indirectly controlled.

The freedom of local leaders implies various approaches to proselytism. For certain leaders 'in a hurry' with regard to the imminent end of the world, the conversion of new disciples to Islam means saving their souls. Shaping potential converts by making them think and deepen their knowledge is thus a risk that some local leaders are not willing to take in such a catastrophic situation. However, these 'precipitous' conversions, which often lead to 'precipitous apostasy', create a nebula of sympathisers at the edges of the Naqshbandiyya Ḥaqqāniyya, who never really commit to Islam and Sufi practices.

In the seminar-concerts of Sheikh Hassan in Italy that we will present below, I witnessed several instantaneous conversions, where the individual did not even know how to pronounce *shahāda*, or thought it was possible to be a Sufi without being a Muslim. In France, Khaldoun said that Philippe de Vos, the other Parisian *muqaddam*, had converted 9,000 people, 'even though de Vos claims that number to be 12,000'.

All this makes it very easy to become a Naqshbandi. I personally experienced intense proselytism during my fieldwork, whereby many Naqshbandis pushed me to convert to Islam and adhere to the Naqshbandiyya. For example, during the spiritual meeting with Sheikh Mehmet in Paris in 2013, an old disciple took me by the hand and led me to the sheikh, saying, 'Go ahead, do it! Now's the time!', creating an awkward situation with the sheikh, one I was unsure how to get out of.

Numerous disciples told me that the only way I could really understand Sufism was by converting. Others claimed it was just a matter of time. But curiosity reigned. Benchouk questioned me on the reasons preventing my conversion; as for Khaldoun, he was much more courteous and did not ask me to convert, saying only, 'If you want to do it, I won't tell anyone. That way, you can protect your academic career.' Another time, Khaldoun told me with a laugh, 'We'll spoil you until you convert!'

The example of Paul is edifying. Paul, a fifty-year-old French man, had been interested in Gurdjieff and Castaneda and, by chance, attended a Naqshbandi spiritual meeting in Paris. At the end of the evening, Skander, a Canadian *muqaddam* who was visiting, asked him if he was Muslim. When Paul replied he was not, Skander made him repeat the *shahāda*, without explaining its purpose or meaning. Once he had pronounced the profession of faith, Skander told him with a laugh that he had become a Muslim, leaving Paul speechless. We are faced here with a curious form of conversion that seems like a joke. Despite this strange episode, which Paul did not really appreciate, he began to frequent the *zāwiya*, without considering himself profoundly committed to this spiritual path; rather, he described himself as a 'Sufi tourist'.

Khaldoun told me he did not agree with the principle of the precipitous conversions that occurred during the seminars of Sheikh Hassan, for example:

> I generally prefer that young people take their time. I'm not in a hurry. I say, 'It's a lifelong relationship.' So, if you wait a month or six months, to be sure, it's better. I'll start talking to you if you hold out for a year. (Khaldoun)

While we have seen that the Naqshbandiyya Ḥaqqāniyya has opened up to New Age discourses to convert spiritual seekers, in the Parisian *zāwiya*s of Khaldoun and Benchouk this openness is less visible, as confirmed by the positive relations between the *muqaddam*s and the mosques in Paris. In particular, for several years Khaldoun was one of the teachers for new converts in the main Paris mosque.

The nebula of spiritual seekers is less visible, but still present, formed by people like Paul who consider themselves 'tourists', meaning they do not want much involvement with Islamic life. This little nebula owes its existence to the fluid structure and the primacy of self-discipline over discipline, leaving disciples with a great deal of freedom.

By contrast, the nebula is becoming bigger than the brotherhood in Italy. What are the causes of this difference? What are the ingredients that keep the brotherhood united? First of all, the *muqaddam* has enormous influence over life in the *zāwiya*. In the particular case of Khaldoun, he is a very pragmatic Syrian Muslim who does not like ecstatic rituals, metaphysical reflection or exogenous influences from European esotericism and/or New Age culture. Hence, he has thus set up his *zāwiya* as a simple, down-to-earth place. Secondly, the French disciples who grew up in Islam unwittingly provide a sort of structure for the brotherhood, which limits the New Age tendencies of the Naqshbandiyya as well as its ultraconservatism. Similarly, those born into Islam who gravitate towards Sufism do not seem interested in using it as an instrument for contention around identity politics. If they were looking for a protest movement strongly opposed to French society, then they would have chosen other religious groups.

During the trip to Cyprus, I called the Parisian disciples 'Khaldounians', as a joke, as if they formed another brotherhood. It was only later that I realised the sociological truth of this name. More specifically, there are several ways in which the 'Khaldounians' differ from other Naqshbandi disciples: the pilgrimage to the tomb of Saint Barnabas, the advice given to the Spanish woman concerning sharia, the discussions around the end of the world, and so on. The 'Khaldounians', with their openness to alterity, seem much closer to Būdshīshī and 'Alāwī disciples than the Italian converts or European converts living in Cyprus.

The *zāwiya*s of Khaldoun and Benchouk organise Arabic classes as well as classes on the Qur'an. Benchouk also organises spiritual retreats at the *zāwiya* in the countryside. In addition, they participate in activities around interreligious and intra-religious dialogue. The 'extra-ritual' activities are not structured according to a common action plan, as in the Būdshīshiyya and the 'Alāwiyya, but are rather initiatives stemming from the *muqaddam*'s wishes.

We have seen, from various perspectives, the fundamental importance of the *muqaddam* in this brotherhood (rituals, teachings, activities). Both

Khaldoun and Benchouk are considered 'fathers' who can be trusted in any problematic situation. Khaldoun and Benchouk are responsible economically, legally and organisationally for the operation of their *zāwiyas*. Of course, the disciples make donations and help with the work in the *zāwiya*, but the *muqaddams* are ultimately the ones responsible. In some cases, this independence and responsibility transform the role of the *muqaddam*, who becomes a sort of 'spiritual entrepreneur', as we will see below.

Enneagram of Philippe de Vos: Shedding Light on Nebulosity

Philippe de Vos is a French man born in 1948. He identifies as one of the Parisian *muqaddams* and as the first French Naqshbandi, but he is, above all, someone out of the ordinary. He is particularly cultivated, speaking Arabic and English and having written several books on Sufism.[54] He also studied under the Guénonian Michel Valsan (as his disciple) and Henry Corbin (as a student at the Sorbonne). In this same figure, we find the various elements described in Chapter 2: Guénonian esotericism, religionism and, as we will also see, some elements of New Age discourse.

After the death of Valsan in 1974, de Vos started his long journey through the Sufi brotherhoods; he frequented the 'Alāwiyya and the Būdshīshiyya and knew their masters. That said, his former disciples consider him problematic because, as one 'Alāwī disciple put it, 'He considers himself a sheikh, and didn't accept being a *faqīr* like the others.' De Vos was also unable to accept the rigid 'Alāwī and Būdshīshī structures and hierarchies.

Nonetheless, according to de Vos, Sheikh Hamza of the Būdshīshiyya recognised his spiritual power. He told me that, during a spiritual meeting in the 1980s, Sheikh Hamza stood to greet him and told him he would do important things in the future. At the end of the 1980s, he moved to the Naqshbandiyya Ḥaqqāniyya, which is not surprising; de Vos found in this brotherhood not only a charismatic master, Sheikh Nāzim, but also an order loose and porous enough for him to continue his spiritual quest without too many constraints or limitations.

De Vos pushes 'Naqshbandi supremacy', as seen with other the *muqaddams*, to its paroxysm. The Naqshbandiyya is not simply the best brotherhood;

[54] de Vos, *Sheikh nazim la preuve de la générosité*; de Vos, *Genèse de la sagesse soufie*.

it seems to be the only one. De Vos explained to me that the ʿAlāwiyya is too invested on the social level and that Bentounes is 'counter-initiatic' – that is, in Guénonian language, he represents an empty, dangerous spirituality. As for the Būdshīshiyya, it is too closely tied to the Moroccan government, and de Vos also revealed to me that he had encountered forms of idolatry in this brotherhood: 'I heard the phrase "*Allāh* Hamza".' He added that Pallavicini (Aḥmadiyya Idrīsiyya Shādhiliyya) is 'too Guénonian' and does not know Islam in depth. Finally, de Vos does not have much esteem for his Naqshbandi peers: 'Sheikh Hassan is more a singer than a Sufi sheikh', and the others lack the authority that de Vos claims as his own.

De Vos also claims he had a special relationship with Sheikh Nāzim, which allowed him to come by esoteric knowledge reserved for a spiritual elite. He offers different rituals than those celebrated in other Naqshbandi *zāwiya*s, including *al-laṭāʾif*, a silent *dhikr* that is part of the history of the Naqshbandiyya but seems to have been forgotten in the Ḥaqqāniyya branch. This *dhikr* focuses on the 'subtle centres of the body' which are physical as well as metaphysical points. De Vos explains that the *laṭāʾif* are like chakras in yoga, only they predate 'the oldest of the chakras'.

De Vos has more than one string to his bow, since Sheikh Nāzim passed on to him knowledge of the enneagram which, alongside *al-laṭāʾif*, is the basis for 'real spiritual cleansing' and 'at the root of all religious practices'. De Vos claims that these special rituals (enneagram and *al-laṭāʾif*) are not supererogatory, but rather central, and that they must be practised by all Sufi disciples. This shows, according to him, 'that Sufism has lost its esotericism'. Lastly, he shared with me his experiences of exorcising *jinn*, or demons, which he views with mercifulness: 'I prefer to convert rather than to kill them.'

In 2013, I participated in a seminar on the enneagram.[55] This geometric, pedagogical figure was revealed to the general public by Gurdjieff and, especially, by his student Ouspensky.[56] It is an esoteric instrument aimed at developing inner consciousness and well-being and was developed by Gurdjieffians as well as in the field of psychology.[57] In 1995, as we have seen, Sheikh Kabbani

[55] de Vos, *L'ennéagramme*.

[56] Ouspensky, *In Search of the Miraculous Fragments of an Unknown Teaching*.

[57] Sedgwick, 'Sufism and the Enneagram'; Cusack, 'The Enneagram'.

attributed the origins of the enneagram to the Naqshbandiyya. This led to a number of Naqshbandi seminars on this instrument, even though some disciples are doubtful as to its affiliation.

Classes on the enneagram, organised in de Vos's home, last two days. The fee is €150, including meals. Responding to my initial hesitation, de Vos only charged me €100. His spiritual enterprises also include visits to the Maghreb, at a price of €750, not including travel costs. In addition, he has plans for the future, such as setting up summer spiritual courses that will probably take place in the countryside. As for the enneagram, de Vos affirms that 'it works for everybody.' He has even taught it in Moroccan businesses which increased their profits as a result. The enneagram is not limited to a certain faith; de Vos has organised courses for Christians, citing the Bible instead of the Qur'an, but with identical results. 'The greatest satisfaction I had with atheists,' he explained, 'was when they came back and told me, "Yes, this works!"'

At the course I attended were seven participants: two Naqshbandis, two disciples from other brotherhoods, and non-Muslims. During the explanations, de Vos showcased his culture by citing Jung, Nietzsche, Sartre, Saint Francis and, of course, traditional Islamic–Sufi figures. He explained that the enneagram is a geometrical form with nine points that represent archetypes – the characters of human beings. Archetypes are neither negative nor positive but may become negative/positive according to behaviour. The first phase is determining our archetype. We then work on ourselves through the practice of a specific *dhikr*. For example, I was 'diagnosed' as the seventh archetype, which de Vos calls the 'epicurean': the archetype of vital energy, joy and art. This archetype can veer into a superficial life of carnal pleasure or, on the contrary, into a joyful and enthusiastic saintliness, like that of Saint Francis, explained de Vos.

To understand our archetypes, de Vos asked us to talk about our desires, fears and hopes. To make this easier, he had us lie down on rugs and turned on some ambient electronic music. He then said, 'Imagine yourself when you were young', to help us 'find [our] true nature'. After the 'diagnosis' came the 'treatment', which in this case was a special *dhikr* given to us by de Vos. The divine name I was to repeat was *ḥaiyy* (the Living), which would help me harmonise my life with my archetype and manifest its positive aspects. In addition, de Vos explained to me that if I wanted to convert to Islam, 'Abd al-Ḥaiyy would be my ideal first name since it represents my archetype.

The label of *muqaddam* is too restrictive for de Vos. He is a true spiritual seeker, or, as he prefers, a 'metaphysical seeker'. From a sociological point of view, de Vos is a 'spiritual entrepreneur'. His fee-based seminars are open to Muslims and non-Muslims, he promotes his activities on his website, and he faces off with the internal and external 'competition', disagreeing with his 'competitors' (cf. other brotherhoods and other *muqaddams*).

In de Vos's group, it remains possible to discern an Islamic brotherhood (with its doctrines and rituals), but the nebulosity is thickening. This entails the addition of other vocabularies to Islamic–Sufi language, the creation of new rituals (enneagram, meditation, ambient music), and the repurposing of other rituals (*al-laṭā'if*). De Vos is the exception in the French Naqshbandiyya, and most of his disciples are part of the *zāwiyas* of Khaldoun and Benchouk. Nevertheless, he remains significant in that he illustrates the process of reformulating Sufism, which then opens beyond the Islamic framework and is exposed to New Age discourses and practices.

Among the Italian Disciples

> We have a very great sheikh, a very great sheikh who chose to open the door to everyone. You can enter as a Christian, Jew, Salafi, whatever the hell you want! A thief, a murderer, a pig, a whore, and he will never close the door! (Khadija)

While in France, the 'Sufi tourist' and the 'spiritual entrepreneurs' are the exception, in Italy the brotherhood is becoming the exception. Whereas Iqbal (Italian *khalīfa*) and other disciples have devoted their lives to an austere and even conservative Islam, this brotherhood seems overtaken by a nebula, especially during community rituals.

From a doctrinal viewpoint, the Italian Naqshbandi nebulosity owes its development to strong eschatological pressure, leading to intense proselytism. This tendency leads to rapid conversions, without real concern for training the disciples or for the consequences.

> If you see a person falling into the crater of a volcano, you don't ask him if he has understood the difference between *fanā'* and *baqā*.[58] You take his hand and pull him out. If we're at the end time and can save a life, it's good to do so quickly . . . If in your heart you have repeated '*lā 'ilāha 'illā-llāh*', the angels

[58] In Sufi vocabulary, the former is eliminating the ego, the latter the return to the world.

> will be with you, they will protect you, and you will be inspired; then maybe in ten years you'll change your life. (Iqbal)

The Italian *khalīfa* is aware of the Naqshbandi nebulosity and is none too happy about it, but the eschatological pressure predominates: 'There are people who go to church on Sunday, there are people who believe in reiki and wizards . . . So what?' (Iqbal). His idea is that gradually, the disciples will come to understand.

As for the history of the Italian Naqshbandiyya, the first problem is the absence of a *zāwiya*, that is a national reference point. Iqbal justifies this absence by the simple fact that Sheikh Nāzim did not ask the Italians to establish a *zāwiya*. When I mention that in Paris there are three of them, Iqbal, a little irritated, replies, 'Because there are those who want to be sheikhs!' So, it comes down to the voluntary, almost entrepreneurial dimension of the local leaders' role. In the other brotherhoods, it is not a question of wanting this role; if there are disciples, there is a *muqaddam* and thus a *zāwiya*.

The first meetings of the Italian Naqshbandis were organised in the early 1990s by the German sheikh Burhanuddin Herrmann in collaboration with Iqbal, who translated from English to Italian. At the end of the 1990s and the beginning of the 2000s, many Italian disciples kept their distance from the German master for doctrinal and organisational reasons. Burhanuddin was accused of not respecting Islamic orthodoxy and of 'eccentric behaviour', according to Iqbal, who then started organising seminars with another German master: Sheikh Hassan. Starting in the 2000s, two Italian Naqshbandi groups formed, that of Sheikh Burhanuddin and that of Sheikh Hassan, groups that sometimes communicated and sometimes opposed each other.

The Italian Naqshbandi seminars, organised every second, third and fourth of the month, are not an extraordinary event, nor a special celebration as in France, but they are nonetheless the heart of the brotherhood. By contrast, the weekly rituals we saw in all the other brotherhoods (including the French Naqshbandiyya) seem secondary. For example, the Milanese Naqshbandis, around fifteen disciples, only meet irregularly, and when I frequented them, I never saw more than four people. The situation is similar in Venice and Turin. In addition to the question of quantity is that of 'quality'. During the meetings I attended, *dhikr* was reduced to twenty minutes, while socialising took up most of the evening. This impression was confirmed by one of the

Naqshbandi disciples, Alessia, who had been involved in other *zāwiyas* in Europe and complained that in Italy, 'We talk about the shoes we just bought, or that so-and-so is separating from her husband.' During our interview, Iqbal, the Italian *khalīfa*, assured me that this was a bad example and that, in fact, there were other, better organised groups. But I never came across them.

Sheikh Burhanuddin Herrmann: Spiritual Trainer

When I participated in Sheikh Burhanuddin's seminar in December 2013, I was about to complete my fieldwork. I had spoken to hundreds of disciples, travelled to Morocco, Cyprus, Turkey, and met Sheikh Hamza, Sheikh Bentounes, Sheikh Nāzim, Sheikh Pallavicini and Sheikh Inançer Efendi. In sum, I had acquired a degree of self-confidence and felt at ease among Sufi disciples. I thus had no way of anticipating the strange welcome Burhanuddin had in store for me.

In the prayer room, we start with the round of salutations and presentations. As usual, I explain my reason for being there and my research and ask the sheikh for permission to continue with the seminar, mentioning that I went to Cyprus and met Sheikh Nāzim. Sheikh Burhanuddin is a tall, handsome man who has a long white beard and wears the Turkish coat and turban. He eyes me over silently, then asks me my religion. No sooner have I responded than he starts attacking me: 'You're a thief! A spy! You're here to steal information!' When he accuses me of being a journalist, I respond by explaining the enormous difference between journalism and sociology. He seems to have calmed done but continues to interrogate me: 'Do you have a girlfriend? Are you married? Do you want to have children?' I explain to him that I have a girlfriend, that I would like to get married and have children, but that for the moment I lack the necessary stability to do so. Sheikh Burhanuddin caresses his long beard and says to me, 'That's not *adab* [proper conduct]', before attacking me again:

> You journalists, you come here and pretend to be upstanding to everybody! Like you're more important. You're lucky to have met two lions [Sheikhs Nāzim and Hamza] when they'd grown gentler with age. If you had spoken to them twenty years ago, they'd have eaten you alive! You'd have been terrified! Do you think you can go into the den of a lion to interview him? To ask him what?

During nearly two years of fieldwork, I can safely say that the disciples have been very friendly and available. I am thus a little shocked by Burhanuddin's welcome. I respond that I do not want to bother anyone and that, if he wishes, I will be happy to leave the seminar. He signals for me to stay, asking me enigmatically, 'What sign are you?' I answer, 'Capricorn.' Thus begins my seminar with the Italian Naqshbandis. Martino, the disciple next to me, says in a low voice, 'Bravo! You held your ground!' Then he adds, 'Don't worry. It's normal. He does that with everyone.'

Later, the disciples tell me that the verbal attack is a technique Sheikh Burhanuddin uses with newcomers. The goal is to assail the ego and shake up the emotions. Many people are reduced to tears, while others leave in a huff. Iqbal tells me that Burhanuddin used to be even more virulent: 'Now he's gentler. [I remember that] in this seminar, he wanted to convert everyone! He didn't leave them alone until they had recited the *shahāda*.'

Sheikh Burhanuddin was born in 1962[59] in Freiburg, Germany. At the age of twenty-one, he became a disciple of the Burhāniyya brotherhood, which he left after only six months when his master died. Not long after, he met Sheikh Nāzim and, at his request, began to travel throughout the world preaching the 'good news'. According to Haifa, one of his female disciples, the spiritual capacities of Sheikh Burhanuddin are also due to his experience in India with Osho when he was a young man.

Sheikh Burhanuddin has been organising Naqshbandi Sufi seminars for twenty years and has authored three books based on his discourses.[60] Burhanuddin, who is described in his autobiography as a 'loving man',[61] is considered a highly charismatic person. Matteo told me that he had helped him escape from an esoteric sect and black magic: 'I was lost and desperate.' Some disciples told me that Burhanuddin was capable of miracles, while others feared his powerful charisma.

> Burhanuddin was my first encounter with Sufism in Italy. I love him, but I had to get away from him. He has an ego and is incredibly magnetic, which sometimes . . . He knows how to manipulate your mind. So you have to be careful. He does not act in bad faith, in good faith, it's not for me to say. (Haifa, female Italian disciple)

[59] During the 2013 interview, he told me he was fifty-one years old.

[60] Herrmann, *Il cammello sul tetto*; Herrmann, *Il derviscio metropolitano*; Herrmann, *Il sufismo*.

[61] Herrmann, *Il derviscio metropolitano*, 9.

Burhanuddin's charisma is built up around his personality, enveloping it. He eats and sleeps alone on the second floor (we are on the ground floor) and if we want to talk to him, we have to sign up on a list. In the prayer room the sheikh is the last one to enter; a young disciple stationed outside the room warns the others when Burhanuddin is approaching, so they can be standing in silence when he comes in. 'He's the sultan here,' Irene explains to me. She owns the building and serves as Burhanuddin's assistant, translating between English and Italian.

The seminars are organised in the 'Rabbani House', a beautiful residence in the Umbrian countryside, the ground floor of which consists of a kitchen, a bathroom and the prayer room (which sometimes serves as a dormitory for the men). On the second floor are photos of Sheikh Nāzim and Sheikh Burhanuddin, the women's bedroom, and that of the sheikh.

The cost is €160 for three days, from Friday afternoon to Sunday morning. Concerning the fee, Burhanuddin has said he has the authorisation of Sheikh Nāzim, as Iqbal tells it. In reality, the question of fees has elicited a lot of criticism in the brotherhood. Irene, the assistant, explains to me that they also accept disciples with financial problems, and that disciples who cannot pay must work in the house. In this seminar, there are fifteen women and twenty-five men, all Italian. Their ages range from twenty-five to fifty-five. In terms of socio-economic level, there are as many people from the upper-middle class (architects, physicians, teachers, and so on) as there are working-class people (factory workers, servers, and so on).

Scattered Religious Knowledge

We can grasp the influence of New Age discourse on Burhanuddin's teachings in the conceptualisation of a scattered religious truth, which has spread beyond Islamic borders and has even informed secular phenomena, such as psychology and quantum mechanics. Burhanuddin describes his method this way:

> This system is a mix of ancient spiritual knowledge with the techniques of modern psychology. The psychological work shows the behaviour of the ego at all levels: intellectual, emotional and physical; whereas the spiritual work entails a superior form of knowledge that enables us to break free of our prison.[62]

[62] The website of the association Crescita personale is available at <https://www.spiritual.it/it/corsi-e-appuntamenti/il-sistema-uwaysi-seminario-sufi-con-sheikh-burhanuddin-herrmann,5,126581> (last accessed 9 November 2023).

> If you ask me what Sufism is, after twenty-five years on this path, I would not be able to explain it to you, because it has no form. In reality, it now belongs within Islam and uses Islamic rituals, but in the past it could have used other instruments, other vehicles. It is not set in stone.[63]

> Everybody can respond to the call. It is so simple that it goes beyond every kind of belief. We have received a truth (*ḥaqīqa*) which is beyond forms, beyond norms, beyond every name.[64]

This universalist conceptualisation implies a concentration on love, happiness, peace and self-realisation, rather than Islamic narratives. Sufism's goal then becomes 'perfect happiness, destined to last eternally; you will live in joy, in love'.[65] It is not surprising that Sheikh Burhanuddin has participated in events around interfaith dialogue with Salvatore Brizzi, a protagonist in the Italian New Age scene.[66]

And yet, on other occasions, Sheikh Burhanuddin has asserted the superiority of Islam as the most recent revelation, focusing on the Prophet Muhammad, the seal of prophethood, and the Qur'an, the only revealed text that can be considered authentic.[67] Furthermore, he is ironic about the fuzziness of the New Age sphere and the mushrooming of spiritual masters:

> Today people are engaged in all kinds of classes: family constellations and the enneagram are in vogue; then there is reiki, a timeless classic; foot reflexology, a little out of fashion; shiatsu, always on the cutting edge; and yoga, which is not that popular because it requires hard work. And there are people who speak with dolphins, with guiding spirits, who work with crystals, who know everything about cosmology, numerology, Kabbala, ying-yang and feng shui.[68]

This ambivalence, and sometimes the tension between universalism and Islamic particularism, are also evident among Burhanuddin's disciples. Some consider Islam to be the best option, while others prefer to attend several different religious groups at the same time. Yassin, who teaches martial arts, considers

[63] Herrmann, *Il derviscio metropolitano*, 315.
[64] Herrmann, *Il derviscio metropolitano*, 32.
[65] Herrmann, *Il derviscio metropolitano*, 29.
[66] Brizzi, *Risveglio*; Brizzi et al., *Risveglio Metropolitano*.
[67] Herrmann, *Il derviscio metropolitano*, 48, 82, 131.
[68] Herrmann, *Il derviscio metropolitano*, 27.

Sufism to be 'beyond religion', whereas Giovanni practises Sufism and Christianity at the same time, attending both Sunday mass and Sufi events because, in the end, 'the message is the same.' Haifa's case is illuminating as regards how religious truth is conceived and experienced. Haifa is a single independent 'businesswoman'. She focuses on the spiritual experience rather than doctrines, going so far as to question the concepts of God and religion:

> I've never referred to God, I've never been a Christian in my life, I've never been a believer. And even today when I hear the name 'God', if it brings me down in that moment, I eliminate it. I don't feel guilty anymore, because I'm on this level that's not really high, not really low, I don't want to assign an adjective to myself, but each of us grows [spiritually]. Dreams guide me a lot . . . and these are the things that brought me to Sufism.

Customised Sufism

In Burhanuddin's seminars, the accent is on the disciples, on their needs and necessities. The stated goals are to achieve happiness, share emotions, rediscover the 'magic of existence', rather than learning a religious truth and traditional religious practices. The Naqshbandiyya Ḥaqqāniyya becomes empirical and pragmatic; this is a Sufism that 'works' in daily life.

> Be more beautiful, more intelligent and more in love. (field notes)

> The only way out of tragedy is comedy. Laugh, and the world laughs with you. Cry, and you cry alone.[69]

> Which party you want to adhere to: that of depressed individualists and complainers or that of people who are joyful?[70]

This leads many disciples to create a customised Sufism. They seem to practise Sufism part-time or even occasionally, to 'charge their batteries' (Martino) or 'find a little time for [themselves]' (Daniela). The therapeutic aspect which, I should note, has always existed in Islam and Sufism, becomes the centrepiece. Doriana, for instance, is a woman of around fifty years old who fell in love

[69] Herrmann, *Il derviscio metropolitano*, 81.

[70] Herrmann, *Il derviscio metropolitano*, 12.

with Sheikh Burhanuddin. She told me he was the homeopathy that enabled her to quit drinking and eating pork, so it was very easy to become a Muslim. She prays two times a day and practises *dhikr* while commuting to work. She also told me that Sheikh Nāzim helped her stop smoking and freed her from her fear of dogs.

The therapeutic dimension is closely tied to the separation between private life and life in this group, which would be unimaginable in any other brotherhood. Matteo tells us, 'Who you are outside this room doesn't matter here. Take Rafik, a tattoo artist who is tattooed from head to toe.' Rafik is not alone; there is also a bartender who works in a club, and a belly dancer. In some cases, those who attend the seminars are not even Muslim, like Gianfranco, a follower of Gurdjieff who practises 'Naqshbandi Sufi rituals' in light of the 'proven connections' between Sufism and Gurdjieff.

At the seminar's core is sharing emotions and discussing daily life – that is, it is oriented towards 'this world here'.[71] Sheikh Burhanuddin advised one disciple not to content himself with his life, suggesting he leave his job and open a business. In the case of a couple, he recommended they have children, and when the woman said their situation was not a choice, Sheikh Burhanuddin suggested artificial insemination. Matteo, a thirty-year-old Italian, was told to remove his earring. And a female disciple was told she should wear the headscarf. 'The hijab shows the essence . . . And you are much more beautiful when you wear it!' 'Sometimes, this feels like group therapy,' Daniela told me. Sheikh Burhanuddin's group is thus an 'emotional community', to use the category of Champion and Hervieu-Léger,[72] based on Weber.[73]

Despite openness to New Age discourses, Sheikh Burhanuddin is able to win over disciples from Guénonian milieus, generally hostile to any form of New Age culture. As Khadija said:

> I forced myself not to follow my romantic, sentimental side. Guénon forced me to be more rational, to study, to delve, to intellectually understand the connections. So everything that was easy and emotional for me was New Age.

[71] Hervieu-Léger, 'Le partage du croire religieux dans des sociétés d'individus'.

[72] Champion and Hervieu-Léger, *De l'émotion en religion*.

[73] Weber, *Economy and Society*.

In spite of this, Burhanuddin helped her get out of the intellectual frame by appealing to her deep emotions: 'I realised how much I had repressed my desire for God.'

Sometimes the best sociological intuitions come from the protagonists themselves. This is exactly the case of Diego, aged thirty, who spoke of Sheikh Burhanuddin as his 'spiritual trainer'. 'Everyone comes here with their problems,' he explained. Diego's pertinent definition of a spiritual trainer reveals that at the centre of these seminars are the lives, emotions and daily problems of the disciples. Burhanuddin helps them find courage, peace, stability and love. The Islamic message seems entirely secondary. In effect, Diego admitted to me that his religious practice could be reduced to weekly *dhikr* and the seminars in question. So, in Burhanuddin's *zāwiya*, the following affirmation of Hervieu-Léger is borne out: 'The more the act of believing individualises, the more it homogenises.'[74] In other words, Sufism's complexity and richness seem here to be reduced to the therapeutic.

Bricolage of Doctrines and Rituals

If truth is everywhere, then we understand why Burhanuddin can use various metaphors, narratives and doctrines, taking them from various religious contexts. It follows that when Sheikh Burhanuddin teaches his disciples, he draws not only on Sufism and Islam, but also on Buddhism, Christianity, Taoism, the I Ching, Gurdjieff, psychology and psychoanalysis, along with quantum mysticism. He speaks of elves, extra-terrestrials, vibrations, Earth Mother, and when his disciples ask him who the enemies of faith are, he answers, 'Big corporations like Monsanto. These organisations are only interested in power and money.' Finally, Sheikh Burhanuddin uses the tales of Mulla Nasreddin as Sufi teachings, drawing on another protagonist of New Age Sufism: Idries Shah.[75]

Burhanuddin's bricolage includes the doctrine of reincarnation, generally regarded as heterodox according to Sunni Islam and one of the issues that drove Sheikh Burhanuddin to differentiate himself from other Naqshbandi groups. During our interview, he told me he does not profess the doctrine of reincarnation, but that he questions its negation. He also suggested that,

[74] Hervieu-Léger, *La religion en miettes ou La question des sectes*, 31.

[75] Sedgwick, *Western Sufism*.

according to his personal experience, there were multiple synchronic and diachronic dimensions, leaving the door open to multiple interpretations of his beliefs on reincarnation. On the other hand, in his book, he admits that:

> The science of reincarnation belongs to a kind of hidden knowledge. Officially, then, I have to say that reincarnation does not exist. But off the record, I would have to look you in the eye and say it is a reality.[76]

The process of bricolage manifests itself not only in the creation of new discourses or rituals; we also see this process in the reification of Islamic contents. Diego, for example, told me that Burhanuddin had advised him 'not to read the Qur'an on his own'. Furthermore, the moral, ethical and political aspects of the Qur'an are entirely emptied out. What remains is the possibility of an extra-sensory journey. Chiheb, who became a Naqshbandi disciple several years ago, explained to me:

> The Qur'an, with its fourteen dimensions, is not a book, but a *Stargate*,[77] allowing multidimensional journeys for those who know how to use it. The meanings and contents are relative. That's why it makes no sense to read it in Italian. What are important are the frequencies that occur when you read it in Arabic.

Concerning rituals, *dhikr* is practised on Saturday evenings. In Paris, we observed that the *khalīfa* influences the form of *dhikr*, and we find the same situation in Italy. Despite the limited number of disciples (around fifty), Burhanuddin uses a microphone, adding sound effects, such as reverb and echo, to create an evocative atmosphere. In this modified *dhikr*, the disciples' voices are drowned out; we hear only the voice of the charismatic leader.

Burhanuddin also practises special rituals, given to him by Sheikh Nāzim in person or through dreams. Among these 'special' purification techniques are the drum, the mirror exercise and breath control. I was not able to directly observe the mirror exercise, but the disciples explained that it was performed in pairs; each person speaks to the other about themselves, once again leading us into the emotional realm. As for the breathing exercise, it is a form of *dhikr*

[76] Herrmann, *Il derviscio metropolitano*, 150.

[77] *Stargate* is a science-fiction film (1994).

that starts with expiration, breathing with the belly and making 'the sound of a punctured bike tyre', as the sheikh explains. He has all the disciples try it, often with amusing results.

The most important exercise during the seminar appears to be playing the drum. Burhanuddin even advises us on the brand to buy, which is relatively expensive at around €150 to €170. I ask Martino if he plans to buy one, to which he answers, 'Let's see how long this drum thing lasts. The sheikh has a lot of ideas and not every idea has a future.' The practice of the drum is obviously based on rhythm: 'The rhythm is fundamental: everything is rhythm, everything is frequency. Keeping the rhythm is keeping to the path' (Burhanuddin). We are to hold the drum 'in the direction of the heart'. On the first day, we learn simple rhythmical forms. The second day, we add *dhikr* and some gentle dance movements.

Some Naqshbandi disciples do not care for Sheikh Burhanuddin with his exogenous doctrines and practices; others do not even recognise him as Naqshbandi. Regardless, the end justifies the means, and the end goal is proselytism, in light of the imminent end of the world. Much of the criticism directed at Burhanuddin ends with statements such as: 'In any case, he converts a lot of young people' or 'He's an attack dog' (Khadija) and, finally, 'He throws them into it [Islam].' Or, as Iqbal, the Italian *khalīfa*, says, 'Burhanuddin is the door. He makes them return [to Islam] his way.'

On Stage with Sheikh Hassan: 'Sufi Show'

> Peter Hassan Dyck is . . . an excellent storyteller who invites the audience on a voyage in a magical world of stories and tales of Sufi mysticism. His virtuosity with various musical instruments reveals to us the beauty and magic of the Orient.[78]

Sheikh Hassan, born in Berlin in 1946, studied at the Berlin Academy of Music and went on to play with the well-known sitar player Ustada Vilayat Khan (1928–2004). In 1975, he converted to Islam/Sufism and joined the group of Omar Ali Shah, the brother of the famous Idries Shah who contributed to disseminating (and de-Islamising) Sufism in Europe.[79] In 1979, he joined the Naqshbandiyya Ḥaqqāniyya.

[78] The website of the Italian Naqshbandiyya is available at <www.sufi.it> (last accessed 9 November 2023).

[79] Sedgwick, *Western Sufism*.

Sheikh Hassan is the most eminent Naqshbandi public figure in Europe. This talented musician has travelled across the continent with his Sufi group Muhabbat Caravan (Caravan of Love). His concerts go beyond the brotherhood's borders and are open to the general public.

When I meet Sheikh Hassan, he is around sixty years old, of average height with a long white beard. A large white turban covers his bald head. He wears Turkish-style clothing, with a long coat and a walking stick. When he moved to Italy in the 2000s, his mission was to bring the Italian Naqshbandiyya brotherhood back into the fold following Burhanuddin's 'deviations'. Iqbal told me that Hassan did not know how to organise seminars, as he was first and foremost a musician and a great artist.

The 'performance spirituality'[80] described in the case of Sheikh Burhanuddin is supplemented in the case of Sheikh Hassan by a sort of 'stage show spirituality'. The format of the stage show is more than just one of the forms for promoting the Naqshbandi path; it is also a sacred ritual that shapes this brotherhood's structure in Italy. These words of Hassan are illuminating: 'What is important for me is to attain the Divine Presence together with the audience.'[81]

The 'Caravan of Love' seminars are organised every three months. I personally participated in seminars in 2010 (Rimini),[82] 2013 (Pavia) and 2014 (Rimini). I also saw Hassan onstage for the *Mawlid* organised by the 'Alāwiyya in Brussels in 2013 (cf. Chapter 4). The seminars generally take place in hotels and last three days, from Friday afternoon to Sunday morning. The seminar fee covers management costs, with the voluntary donations going to Hassan and his 'caravan' of musicians. Unlike Burhanuddin's events, then, these seminars do not officially have a fee. In addition, one of the evenings of the seminar is open to all so that those who do not wish to attend the whole seminar can attend the concert.

Concerning socio-biographical characteristics, the Italian Naqshbandiyya, like its French counterpart, differs from the other brotherhoods I studied by

[80] Hervieu-Léger, *La religion en miettes ou La question des sectes*, 102.

[81] The website of the Italian Naqshbandiyya is available at <www.sufi.it> (last accessed 9 November 2023).

[82] This fieldwork was carried out before my doctorate, as part of the research for my Master's thesis. Cf. Piraino, 'Entrare nel sé divino'.

the more marked presence of young people and by a level of education that is generally inferior. This can be linked to a religious message centred on music and emotions, and to the anti-intellectual approach, which attracts neither those enamoured of European esotericism nor seekers hoping to find themselves in Sufi metaphysics.

Between Ritual and Stage Show

The seminar takes place entirely in the hotel's large conference room. Rugs have been laid over the floor, and a few images of Sheikh Nāzim and some calligraphies adorn the walls. Sheikh Hassan is seated on cushions on a small stage, where he plays and gives his teachings. The arrangement of the space highlights the master's fundamental importance as the centre of attention.

During the evening event open to all, the theatricality is all the more pronounced. Among the audience are people who know nothing about Sufism and who kiss their partner or eat as if they were at a movie theatre. Many people take photos or make video recordings, commenting on the performance.

To the canonical rituals of Sufism (*dhikr*, *ḥaḍra* and *samāʿ*), Sheikh Hassan adds a kind of '*dhikr-samāʿ*-concert', making his music the core of his seminars. He plays the cello and/or the Indian harmonium and, depending on the musicians, who change from one seminar to the next, we can hear *ṭabla* (Indian percussion), *rabāb* (Afghani lute), the didgeridoo (wind instrument from Aboriginal Australia), the frame drum, and so on. The melodies have Arab–Islamic roots, but the influences of Indian music, classical music and blues-rock are clearly discernible. Sheikh Hassan sings and gets the audience to sing in response, just like a rock star. '[*Dhikr* is] an Arabic mantra. It's very simple. I speak and you repeat – just like in grade school!' The disciples and the audience clap their hands in time with the rhythm and applaud at the end of each piece. The words of these sacred 'songs' come from Sufi poetry (Ḥāfiẓ and Jalāl al-Dīn Rūmī, in particular), or are simply sung forms of *dhikr*. The structures of the pieces are open to improvisation and follow wherever the enthusiasm leads.

This ritual/concert is not limited to the evening event open to all; it occurs on a smaller scale (without all the musicians) every day of the seminar. Before or after his teachings and the Naqshbandiyya *dhikr*, Sheikh Hassan plays the *dhikr-samāʿ*-concert, which resembles a pop-rock concert more than 'classical' *dhikr*. As for *dhikr*, it is not subject to any major variations. Sheikh Hassan speaks through a microphone, but unlike Burhanuddin, we can hear the disciples' voices and no sound effects are used.

In Hassan's seminars, another form of *dhikr* is carried out, one that is recited as the disciples sit in a circle, with a giant prayer string comprising a thousand beads and measuring several metres in length. This string is worked around clockwise, bead by bead, hand over hand. Those who cannot find a place in the circle form a second circle around the first. In keeping with Naqshbandi tradition, this *dhikr* is silent.

The *ḥaḍra* of the Italian Naqshbandiyya takes place in two separate circles formed by women and men, in the same room. Still hand in hand,[83] we inhale, raising our hands up, and exhale, lowering our torsos and arms towards the ground. This movement is repeated with increasing intensity. At a moment of climax, someone detaches from this human chain and goes inside the circle, inciting the others to do the same. Towards the end, when the rhythm reaches its peak, the circle breaks and everyone begins to jump, with the right forearm and index finger pointing upwards towards God. The ritual ends with applause.

I have attended and participated in several Naqshbandi *ḥaḍra*s (in Brussels, Pavia, Rimini, Paris and Lefke). Some were 'lighter' (those open to the public), while others were more intense (as in Lefke). All these *ḥaḍra*s helped me understand this to be a structured ritual, a sacred dance, a moment of joy and sharing.

There are significant differences compared to ʿAlawī and Būdshīshī *ḥaḍra*s, which can be described as rituals that oscillate between codification and the improvisation of ecstasy. They are considered so powerful as to be dangerous and are carefully controlled. In addition, the energy released during ʿAlawī and Būdshīshī *ḥaḍra*s shows on the disciples' faces; the tension, joy and effervescence of the ritual are apparent. Conversely, during the Naqshbandi *ḥaḍra*, the ecstatic, even dangerous element of the divine presence seems less pronounced; the disciples smile, jovial and joyous.[84]

83 In the Cyprus *zāwiya*, the disciples do not hold hands but rather place their closed fists near their chest.

84 This does not mean that Naqshbandi disciples do not attain ecstasy; my analysis concerns the ritual as such.

In Sheikh Hassan's seminars, the structure of the rituals is not immutable. Sometimes there are recitations of the Qur'an in Arabic; sometimes there are poetry readings. The openness of the Naqshbandiyya and the theatricality create a relaxed atmosphere which at times is marked by a degree of disorder and confusion. The disciples and audience members come and go as they please, and cell phones ring during the rituals and teachings. There is no real *adab* as to how disciples are supposed to conduct themselves during rituals.

Teachings Centred on Emotion: Anti-intellectualism

The content of the teachings focuses on 'unlimited and unconditional love' and the importance of fighting our ego. Sheikh Hassan encourages disciples not to fear, to accept life and its sorrows. The Islamic dimension of his teachings is not diminished by the theatricality; Hassan often cites the Qur'an and the *ḥadīth*s.

Similar to Burhanuddin's teachings, the message is very simple and linear and aimed at emotional rather than intellectual resonance. The ascetic dimension, understood as intensive and trying rituals and/or as purification of the body through a specific lifestyle (fasting, pilgrimages, long spiritual retreats), is only present in the Italian Naqshbandiyya in the form of narratives. Asceticism is only experienced through anecdotes, Sufi stories or the biographies of sheikhs living at some distant time in the past. As we have seen, asceticism is not required of the disciples; rather, it is recounted to them.

During the Sufi seminars, Sheikh Hassan delivers his teachings once or twice a day, here again on a small stage, sitting on cushions and assisted by Iqbal, who translates from English to Italian. Sheikh Hassan is a consummate showman, even when he is not on stage. His teachings are always studded with jokes and songs, and the audience and disciples adore him and pay careful attention to his words. For example, when he explains the importance of detaching from the material goods of this life, he says, 'Leave the pasta alone', because on the path of purification there is 'eternal pasta, endless spaghetti, ahhh! *Allāh Akbar! Māshā' Allāh*!' He then mimics the act of eating with gusto. Of course, in Italy, jokes about spaghetti are to be expected.

Hassan also likes to play with words and melodies. On one occasion, he improvised a sort of rap, where the donkey represented the ego.

> Do I ride on my donkey? Or is he riding on me? Do I ride on my donkey? Or is he riding on me? Is there a light at the end or not? Do I ride on my donkey? Or is he riding on me? The ego-donkey plays dirty tricks! And sometimes it kicks!

The theatricalisation of Sufism is easy to perceive in nearly all the rituals and teachings. One example I witnessed involved a conversion. First, the disciple-to-be approached the little stage, then Sheikh Hassan, still holding the microphone, asked him, 'Do you believe in God? Do you believe in the Prophet Muhammad?' The disciple-to-be responded that he did. Sheikh Hassan continued: 'Now follow me and repeat this beautiful declaration.' Hassan then said the profession of faith word for word[85] and the disciple repeated after him. Everyone started to repeat the words, but Hassan asked them to be quiet: 'Just him! You're the witnesses!' Hassan had the new disciple repeat the *shahāda* one more time, adding other words to embellish it, for example the name '*habību*', or the beloved, with regard to the Prophet. He never missed a chance to joke around, and when he said '*habību*', he briefly brought in the pop song 'Barbara Ann' by the Beach Boys, playing on the alliteration of the words. Once the *shahāda* of the new Muslim was finished, Hassan had all the participants repeat it.

Sheikh Hassan did not lose his sense of humour even when talking about the failed millenarianism of Sheikh Nāzim. During the public interview he granted me, he explained this eschatological question with a great deal of irony, making all the disciples laugh.

> Already in 1979 [Sheikh Nāzim used to say], 'We are in the last two years.' In 1981 we said to him, '*Mawlana*! [mimicking surprise and laughing]. What is happening? I told a lot of people, I told my mother, my father, my relatives, my friends . . . and now they're angry with me!' The next time he said five years. Then ten years, then he said it would be the year 2000. We're still eating the beans set aside for the year 2000! Sometimes we go to the basement looking for the lentils of the year 2000!

[85] *Shahāda*: '*Ashadu 'an lā 'ilāha illā Allāh – wa ashadu 'anna Muḥammadan rasūl Allāh*'; this translates as: 'I bear witness that there is no deity but God, and I bear witness that Muhammad is the Messenger of God.'

One of the most important narratives relates to abandoning reason in favour of emotion and religious experience, together with abandoning the pretension of understanding everything, instead placing one's trust in the sheikh.

> I'm not here to exercise my rational mind. The more I think, the less I advance. (Baya, aged forty-five, female Italian lawyer)

> As soon as I started doing *dhikr*, I could no longer finish a book. (Alessia, aged thirty-seven, Italian woman)

> There's no point in studying. Everything depends on the heart, in an invisible way, through *Mauwlana* [Nāzim]. (Khadija, aged sixty, Italian woman)

> Everything is expressed through music, poetry, directly in our unconsciousness . . . *Mauwlana*, he does everything. (Roberto, aged forty, Italian man)

Abandoning reason for the mysteries of religion can transform into a form of anti-intellectualism, which we have already seen in some of Sheikh Nāzim's discourses. Discursive knowledge not only becomes empty; it can even be considered dangerous. We are at the other end of the spectrum from the Islamic humanism described in previous chapters, where we saw conceptualisations of a hybrid epistemology between religion and the natural and human sciences. For example, when one of the disciples realised I was being paid by the Italian government to conduct this research, he angrily told me, 'I'm a farmer and with my taxes I pay you to ask questions!' Another disciple, Fahd, one of the first Italian Naqshbandi disciples, questioned me on the usefulness of my work. I explained to him the advantages of having other perspectives on European Islam, which people often talk about without knowing very much. Fahd was not convinced and explained to me that my research was useless: 'You're repairing the taps on the Titanic as it's sinking!' he exclaimed, referring to the imminent end of the world. 'Do you think you can save the Titanic by blowing up balloons?' Not satisfied with my answer, he then asked, 'How much does your research cost?' I explained that I earned €1,000 per month for three years, and that my travel costs for the fieldwork was covered. He made some calculations and said, 'Total cost of €40,000! Do you have any idea what I could do in Timbuktu with €40,000?'

Stringent but Optional Discipline

Sheikh Hassan often reiterates that the disciple must follow instructions without question. In the Naqshbandi rhetoric, the sheikh has a fundamental role; the disciple is in his hands, totally passive. As Khadija, a sixty-year-old woman from Milan, put it: 'The sheikh uses you. You're like a pawn in his hands.'

> Grandsheikh says: 'For a murid to rebel, either openly or secretly, against his Sheikh is as terrible as someone cursing the Prophets; it is abominable to think bad thoughts about one's own guide.[86]

Sheikh Nāzim explained very clearly that the sheikh must be consulted for marriages, divorces, and long trips.[87] Disciples must never say 'no' or ask 'why?' They must first believe, then understand later. Furthermore, Nāzim could also impose initiatic tests. Iqbal told me that one disciple had to eat using only a spoon for a year, while another had to speak about himself only in the third person for a year. Still another had to do *adhān* (the call to prayer) every hour throughout Ramadan, never sleeping for more than fifty minutes at a time. Many disciples also told me about marriages that the sheikh had arranged.

This rhetoric concerning discipline and unfailing obedience towards one's master runs counter to the stories of several disciples about their customised Sufism, shaped by individual desires and needs. As we have seen over the course of this chapter, the presence of completely different narratives, even narratives that are openly in opposition to each other, is not new in the Naqshbandiyya Ḥaqqāniyya. It is perhaps for this reason that Sheikh Hassan ironically described the Naqshbandiyya as the 'Chief Mental House' [mental hospital].

Fleeing Society: End of the World

In most of the narratives of conversion and/or adhesion to Islam and/or Sufism in the brotherhoods I studied, life with Sufism is better and more harmonious; everything becomes easier on a daily basis, with work and family. But many Italian Naqshbandi disciples have a radically opposed experience.

[86] Haqqani, *Mercy Oceans' Divine Sources*, 84.
[87] Haqqani, *Mercy Oceans' Divine Sources*, 51.

Adhering to Sufism has been a very difficult ordeal for them, creating conflict with their family and friends, and many have even lost their jobs.

Whereas in the Būdshīshiyya brotherhood, disciples are urged to focus on their studies and work to improve their quality of life, in the Italian Naqshbandiyya, many disciples seem lost, hoping for a manifestation of divine will in their lives. Some disciples live hand to mouth, from making jewellery, perfumes, clothing or artwork such as paintings, sculptures and Arabic calligraphies. Others have returned to the earth, still others work in the 'well-being' sector, as masseuses, yoga teachers, martial arts instructors, and so on.

For several ʿAlāwī, Būdshīshī and French Naqshbandiyya disciples, the discovery of Sufism has led to an engagement in society (with cultural and charitable activities and activities related to promoting Sufism and interfaith dialogue). But in the Italian Naqshbandiyya, we see a disengagement from society, a turning inward. Adopting the eschatology-focused mindset, nearly absent in France but very pronounced in Italy, several Italian disciples have a despairing view of the future. The corrupt world is near its end. All activities not related to prayer are useless. Likewise, before his death, Sheikh Nāzim advised abandoning cities, returning to farming and raising livestock. Pedagogical and charity activities are mere buoys for saving the Titanic, as Fahd would say.

The break with society also concerns the Italian Islamic community, which is often regarded with mistrust and sometimes disdain. In Chapter 2, we saw that the elements that make up New Age discourse include criticism of institutional religions and a limited engagement in collective practices. Take the example of Khadija, who explains her mistrust of Islam in Milan:

> I never go to the mosque, absolutely not! Absolutely not! Especially in Milan! . . . I'm resistant, the whole thing is so complicated . . . These people, they perform rites, but their rites have lost their meaning, like Catholics who go to the church to say their little prayers. I'm interested in the mystical side of religion. All these discussions on sharia . . . Enough already! It's *shayṭān* this, *shayṭān* that. That's exactly what it's like in Islam. That's the tragedy of Islam. All these claims of having the right interpretation. One intellectual says one thing, another says something else. What the hell do I care? I'm fine on my own.

Other Social Forms: Continuities and Discontinuities

While the openness to New Age discourse challenges certain organisational aspects of Sufism, this does not imply an absence of social forms. That is, openness to New Age discourse does not mean the atomisation of social ties, as certain sociologists have argued (cf. Chapter 2), but rather a reformulation. We have already demonstrated that Naqshbandi *khalīfa*s are not simply local leaders who govern the brotherhood in the local context. They are, instead, spiritual entrepreneurs who set out to create new communities, investing their time and their money. Moreover, these *khalīfa*s are often highly charismatic; some have even allegedly performed miracles.

Naqshbandi *khalīfa*s, especially in Italy, become interpreters of doctrines and rituals, whereby they create new rituals. This freedom of expression among local leaders implies a degree of dependence on the part of disciples, because without the *khalīfa* in charge, the community would be lost.

This reformulation of the role of the *khalīfa*s is not the only change; we find another form of socialisation among the disciples. In the Italian Naqshbandiyya Ḥaqqāniyya, we can speak of a 'socialisation by bricolage', influenced by New Age discourse, which focuses on the relationships between disciples, rather on than Sufism or Islam. Alessia, an Italian Naqshbandi disciple who frequented the Parisian Būdshīshiyya, provides a perfect explanation of the difference between the two brotherhoods:

> In the Būdshīshiyya, the people you do *dhikr* with don't have to be your friends. I remember asking [the other Būdshīshī disciples], 'Do you want to do something together?' And the *muqaddima* said to me, 'We don't come here because we're a group of friends, or because we don't know what to do with ourselves at home, or to socialise . . . We're here to practice our *dhikr*, to sing and recite the Qur'an.

'Socialisation by bricolage' seems to produce a weaker sense *communitas*, in terms of commitment to the path. What we might call 'do-it-yourself tourists' do not want too much of a commitment (economically and in the rituals, rules and collective activities). 'DIY socialisation' leaves more time for personal relationships, such as friendships and romantic partnerships.

The importance of emotional and personal relationships shows that the 'validation of the act of believing' is neither solitary nor atomised. As Hervieu-Léger showed, among the signs of changes in religious modernity is the shift from a 'communitarian validation' to a 'mutual validation' of the act of believing.[88] In our case, it is more of an oscillation than a shift, between 'a communitarian validation of the act of believing' by the brotherhood and a 'mutual validation of the act of believing' by the nebula of spiritual seekers.

Another sign of discontinuity in the Sufi organisational structures can be seen in the sale of objects (perfume, jewellery, books, calligraphies) organised by disciples during the seminars. While we find small-scale markets in all the Sufi brotherhoods I studied that finance shared activities, in the Italian Naqshbandiyya the sale of objects is individual and a source of income for the disciples.

Several researchers have highlighted resonances between New Age discourse and popular religion,[89] which my research on contemporary Sufism confirms. These resonances can be witnessed in the spread of protective amulets, rituals to cure disease and exorcisms, especially among disciples influenced by New Age discourse. Among the Naqshbandi disciples, I also observed the use of *tawi'z*, protective amulets against *shayṭān* and the evil eye (sold in Italy and Cyprus), the exorcism of *jinns* (cf. Philippe de Vos in Paris) and the practice of alternative medicine. This type of medicine draws on traditional Islamic medicine, called 'prophetic medicine', but also on the teachings of Nāzim[90] and the beliefs of disciples concerning homeopathy and naturopathy. Sometimes, these different elements are so intertwined that it is difficult to understand the origin of certain beliefs. For instance, in Sheikh Nāzim's book *Natural Medicine*, the master advises prayer and onion juice for overcoming cancer and advises against surgery. Cancer is also at the centre of conspiracy theories in some Naqshbandi seminars and is supposedly fabricated by 'Big Pharma'. Other disciples hold a more balanced view; they use natural remedies but also scientific medicine as needed. Once again, the variety of approaches is striking.

We also see how stereotypes are reversed. On one hand, Moroccan disciples who emigrated to Italy with a low level of education consult physicians when

[88] Hervieu-Léger, 'Le partage du croire religieux dans des sociétés d'individus'.

[89] Sutcliffe, *Children of the New Age*; Hervieu-Léger, *La religion en miettes ou La question des sectes*; Prandi, *La Religione popolare fra tradizione e modernità*.

[90] Haqqani, *Natural Medicines*.

they get sick and trust scientific medicine. On the other hand, some Italian Naqshbandi disciples, cultivated converts, prefer to turn to Naqshbandi medicine – at least at the level of discourse.

Among the new Naqshbandi social forms, a phenomenon has emerged that we might call 'Sufi mimicry', whereby the new disciple, who has just converted and now adheres to the brotherhood, is encouraged to imitate behaviours and appearances. The importance of appearances in the Italian Naqshbandiyya is primarily evident in the salutations. During the seminars, everybody repeats *Salām ʿalaykum* several times a day, with a certain insistence. The disciples also repeat the expressions *Māshā'Allāh*, *Inshallāh*, *al-Ḥamdulillāh* and *Astaghfir-ullāh*[91] much more often than all the other Muslims of Arab origin whom I encountered in my research. The disciples are encouraged to repeat these expressions, considered beneficial for purifying the soul.

The mimicry of the disciples also concerns Turkish-style Sufi clothing, considered fundamental in this brotherhood. The disciples are encouraged to wear this traditional attire: 'It's sunna,' says the *khalīfa* Iqbal. This 'sunna' comprises black leather babouches, the Turkish vest, the Turkish shirt and the turban; as for the coat and the walking stick, they are optional. Around the *zāwiya* of Lekfe are several shops which sell these items; one in particular sells the brand *Naqshbandi Store Factory*.

The importance of appearance is not limited to clothing; other accessories are also recommended, like *miswāk* (*Salvadora persica*), a stick that serves as a natural toothbrush which, according to the *ḥadīth*, was used by the Prophet Muhammad. Some disciples also apply kohl around their eyes which, in other times and places, served to protect against sand in the desert. Here, however, it is mostly aesthetic.

The new organisational and social forms, and the creation of small groups that often oppose each other, stoke internal and external conflict. I have already recounted the strange manner in which Sheikh Burhanuddin welcomed me. Speaking generally, I was both very well accepted in the Naqshbandiyya and essentially not accepted. Some disciples were helpful and kind, apologising in advance for the behaviour of other brothers. On the contrary, some disciples

[91] Respectively: 'what God has willed', 'God willing', 'by the grace of God' and 'I ask for forgiveness from God.'

objected to my presence and tried to provoke me. This oscillation, which we find at many other levels (relationship with religious, political or eschatological alterity), is perhaps one of the defining characteristics of the Naqshbandis.

A series of internal tensions, which I personally experienced during my public interview with Sheikh Hassan during a seminar, gives rise to this oscillation. Some disciples explicitly asked me to pose certain questions to challenge Sheikh Hassan and his entourage. Ali, one of the disciples displeased with the current governance, told me after the interview, 'You were our Trojan horse! I tried to ask the same questions last year, but I didn't get any answers. You did it!'

In Italy, the situation is even more fraught; during my fieldwork, the Guénonians were about to leave the brotherhood, exasperated by what they deemed its 'excessive' openness. Sheikh Burhanuddin is, in effect, only recognised by a minority of Hassan's disciples. All this tension between local leaders goes beyond the physiological tension that can occur in religious movements. The result is a lack of authority and an absence of central structure. The loose organisation and the strong proselytism have indeed facilitated the broad dissemination of the Naqshbandiyya, but at a cost: fragmentation and tension between the various groups.

Islamic or New Age Conservatism?

Based on the books and discourses of Sheikh Nāzim, a rather conservative view emerges, firstly at the political level, where the sultanate (the Ottoman Empire, in particular) and the monarchy are reference points. It is also apparent at the moral level, concerning how the relationship between sharia and *fiqh* is interpreted. I did not observe this conservative view in the Parisian *zāwiya* of Khaldoun, who seems inclined to Islamic humanism, but it is a mindset clearly present in the Italian Naqshbandiyya.

Italian Naqshbandi conservatism is characterised by its criticism of democracy and secularism which are considered the manifestation of evil in the world. As opposed to the French disciples, many Italian disciples stress that Nāzim's discourses must not be understood symbolically, but in very concrete terms. 'With democracy, Satan is making history and I believe it,' Iqbal said. It goes without saying that this conservatism does not apply to all disciples, but it does apply to most of them. Those who do not share this perspective simply ignore the matter.

As for Naqshbandi political views in Italy, they are rife with conspiracy theories and counter-culture. In Italian seminars, we run into every stripe of conspiracy. By way of example, Americans and/or Israelis supposedly organised the 11 September 2001 attacks, the Bavarian Illuminati and/or Freemasons control the world, political authorities control the weather with chemtrails, there is a gay lobby that wants to homosexualize the world, and so forth.

Sheikhs Hassan and Burhanuddin explained that the sultanate and the monarchy were the only political systems to guarantee peace and prosperity. More specifically, they told me that under the Ottoman Empire, lasting peace reigned for seven centuries. And even if the king was a bad king, he would always be better than a politician in today's world. There are many monarchist disciples who hope for the return of the king of Italy and the sultanate, to put an end to wars and divisions. Hence, Naqshbandi political conservatism tends to be rhetorical. Disciples need only wait until the end of the world to see the restoration of traditional authorities.

> A sultan could and would want to harmonise the Muslim world. No one could prevent him from doing so . . . A sultan has absolute authority, just as the Pope has absolute authority . . . Only a sultan could invoke jihad. (Sheikh Burhanuddin, field notes)

Monarchism and 'sultanism' do not entail political activism, at least not in Italy, since disciples are not called on to change society, and political engagement is not encouraged. Rather, the radical political change Nāzim predicted, which would lead to wars, but also to the return of the sultanate and the monarchy, is only understandable in the frame of Naqshbandi eschatology.

This rhetorical dimension also concerns the relationship with sharia–*fiqh*. While several disciples espouse a rigid, conservative view of sharia, this position remains merely a declaration. As we have seen, the Italian Naqshbandiyya leaves disciples total freedom in interpreting the norms, rituals, and even the doctrines of Sufism and Islam.

Once again, the stereotypes are reversed; the previous chapters described Sufi disciples who preach a universal, liberal Islam but engage in a disciplined Islam and Sufism (both in individual and collective life), whereas here we encounter highly particularist and conservative discourses, which nonetheless often correspond to flexible religious practice.

'At the Centre of the World' in Lefke

In April 2013, when I arrive in Lefke, Northern Cyprus, in the Naqshbandi *dargā* (*zāwiya*), the temperatures are mild and spring is in bloom. The *dargā* is tiny, especially when you consider the enormous presence of this brotherhood in the public sphere. The furnishings, mostly wooden, are spare, and there are only a few pieces of Arabic calligraphy on the walls.

The beauty of the *dargā* is apparent in the architecture and perceptible in the fragrances. In the main room with all the windows open, we can smell the scent of orange trees and jasmine, which comes and goes with the breeze. The *dargā* is surrounded by these essences, leading Juliette, a thirty-year-old French disciple, to muse, 'I feel like a pot of tea.'

The entire first day and night I spend in the mosque, sleeping on the floor and helping the disciples with daily tasks (cleaning and gardening). The next day, needing a place where I could take notes, I decide not to go to the mosque and head for the only hotel in Lefke, which caters almost exclusively to the disciples of Sheikh Nāzim. The brotherhood's activities in the city extend to providing food and shelter to those facing psychological and/or economic difficulties.

For the disciples, the *dargā* is a fabulous place, steeped in *baraka* and miracles. They believe the food there benefits them in both body and soul. Alessia, an Italian disciple allergic to gluten, tells me she can enjoy the bread of the *dargā* without any adverse effects. Haifa, using the esoteric language of the psychoanalyst Carl Gustav Jung, tells me she came to Sufism thanks to a series of 'synchronicities' – that is, simultaneous events that have no cause-and-effect relationship but reveal metaphysical meaning. These synchronicities are even more present in Lefke, where, as Alessia puts it, 'I think of something and ten minutes later it happens. Contentment for ten days, as if I were on drugs.'

In spite of this, some disciples from the New Age milieu like Haifa have a negative experience in Lefke. Haifa felt disappointed and almost tricked by Sheikh Burhanuddin, who had presented a very universal Sufism, without stringent rules, something that, it turned out, only existed in his seminars. Unlike what she was used to, in Lefke, Haifa found strict segregation by gender and discourses that were often conservative.

In Lefke, disciples can find intense experiences of *communitas*[92] by sharing the activities of daily life, or by simply chatting with people they wish to get to know in the village or the *dargā*. In other words, they have the possibility to decide on their pace and engagement, and which practices to carry out. This freedom in practice would be nearly impossible in the other brotherhoods I studied, in which group travels and activities are highly structured. This case illustrates the oscillation between the sacred idea of *ziyāra*, or pilgrimage/pious visits, and the more profane idea of tourism.[93]

Disciple-drivers organise pilgrimage/visits around Lefke. Among the recommended sites are: (1) Hala Sultan Tekke or the Umm Haram Mosque, where the tomb of Prophet Muhammad's wet nurse is located; (2) the tomb of Mustafa Ahi, considered to have miraculous effects, especially for fertility; (3) the tomb of Canbulat, commander of the Ottoman Empire during the 1571 siege of Famagousta, the last stronghold in Venetian Cyprus; (4) the tomb of Kutup Osman, founder of the Khalveti Fazlullah Effendi order; (5) the tomb of Saint Barnabas; (6) Omer Turbesi, the seven tombs of combatants and martyrs killed during the Arab siege of Cyprus in 647; and (7) the tomb of Hajja Amina Nāzim, wife of Sheikh Nāzim.

Once again, these pilgrimages can be interpreted in various ways; some disciples underscore the audacity of the Ottoman and Islamic forces in opposition to Christian Europe, while others prefer to accentuate ecumenical values. Sheikh Nāzim was known for his interest in Christian sacred sites; we have already mentioned the little church he visited regularly and Saint Barnabas's tomb. Likewise, in 2013, Sheikh Nāzim asked his Italian disciples to visit the tomb of Saint Francis of Assisi and, in April of the same year, around thirty Italian disciples went to Assisi with Sheikh Hassan. This religious visit was repeated in 2017 under Sheikh Mehmet.

All the complexity described up till now can be found in the little ecosystem of Lefke. There I met a Turk by the name of Bayram, a salesman in a clothing shop. He had studied philosophy at Oxford, and I enjoyed the stimulating discussions we had. There was also Leith, the Palestinian driver, a man of

[92] Turner, *Dramas, Fields, and Metaphors*, 1974.

[93] Coleman and Eade, *Reframing Pilgrimage*; Boissevain and Isnart, 'Tourisme, patrimoine et religions en Méditerranée'; Piraino, 'Pilgrimages in Western European Sufism'.

few words but always joyful. And we cannot forget the Belgian Tarek, always unpleasant and austere, or Farouk, the American caught up in his countless conspiracy theories and his quantum mysticism.

The *dargā* can also be a dangerous place, where tension rises to the surface. The disciples told me about quarrels, fights, even violence. Khaldoun, the Parisian *muqaddam*, warned me:

> There are young brothers who will be unpleasant or rude, who will bother you or try to make things difficult. Don't worry, the *zāwiya* serves to soften the forms we take. We're like precious stones in the rough. We all have our sharp edges, which become instruments for mutually improving ourselves.

This tension is understandable when we realise the high number of converts and initiates targeted by the brotherhood; inevitably, there are considerable differences between disciples. Even in Lefke, in the geographic heart of the Naqshbandiyya Ḥaqqāniyya, the oscillation between the brotherhood and the nebula described throughout this chapter is palpable.

Beyond Sheikh Nāzim

The death of Sheikh Nāzim in 2014 shattered the Naqshbandiyya, as many disciples considered him to be the last Sufi sheikh before the end times. Several competing groups took shape and, suffice to say, there was no consensus about who the legitimate successor was. European disciples recognised Sheikh Mehmet (Nāzim's son), whereas American disciples were loyal to Sheikh Kabbani.

Sheikh Nāzim's death also led to a polarisation between the two Ḥaqqāni souls: the small, orthodox, austere nucleus and the nebula with its New Age discourse. For example, Sheikh Burhanuddin continued to develop his group and his seminars independently of the mother-*zāwiya* in Cyprus, considering Sheikh Mehmet as more a peer than his new sheikh. Symmetrically, Sheikh Mehmet tried to reduce New Age heterodoxy by reforming the Naqshbandiyya Ḥaqqāniyya, focusing on Islamic orthodoxy and claiming the supremacy of Islam vis-à-vis other religions.

The narrative of the supposed spiritual crisis of Pope Benedict XVI, recounted by Sheikh Mehmet in Paris in 2013, is edifying. Mehmet presented the 'real' reasons why Pope Benedict left the pontificate, noting that in 2010, during a visit to Cyprus, Pope Benedict met Sheikh Nāzim. It was not an officially organised meeting, just a brief salutation, but according to Sheikh Mehmet, the few words exchanged were enough to set off a spiritual crisis that pushed the Pope, a few years later, to abandon his functions as the guide of the Catholic Church. For Sheikh Mehmet it was 'Sheikh Nāzim's most important miracle, because he wanted to demolish the *kuffār*, the infidels'.

There is, however, another spiritual element that holds the brotherhood and its nebula together: the concept of authenticity. In reality, some 'DIY spiritual seekers' from the New Age milieu, even if they do not want to follow the Sufi path, want the brotherhood to be Islamic – 'authentic' – and do not want a de-Islamised brotherhood. When I asked Paul, who had defined himself as a 'Sufi tourist', why he did not join Sufi Order International, where his universalism would be considered 'normal', he explained that it was a matter of *silsila* – that is, esoteric transmission, which guarantees authenticity and the quality of the Sufi message.

Conclusions

The Naqshbandiyya Ḥaqqāniyya founded by Sheikh Nāzim is part of the Sufi–Islamic tradition, reproducing the fundamental elements: a charismatic master considered a living saint by his disciples and the bearer of sacred knowledge, who enables a superior vision of reality. Sheikh Nāzim disseminated a ductile, at times contradictory message, promoting both conservative discourses on morals and politics that highlight the differences between religions, and discourses focused on universal love that go beyond ethnic and religious borders.

Over the years, the Naqshbandiyya Ḥaqqāniyya has facilitated the entry of disciples from the New Age milieu, first by appropriating Gurdjieff's legacy, then by allowing these new disciples a large degree of interpretive freedom concerning Islamic–Sufi norms and doctrines. The focus is on self-discipline rather than discipline. In this way, the Naqshbandiyya Ḥaqqāniyya has attracted disciples sharing an austere, orthodox, and even conservative view, as well as 'New Agers' who have the advantage of frequenting an 'authentic' Sufi brotherhood without all the obligations of other orders. The idea of a 'Sufism for all', described in the chapters on the 'Alāwiyya and the Būdshīshiyya, is here taken to an extreme.

This total openness, justified by the imminent end of the world, implies considerable heterogeneity. In some *zāwiya*s, like that of Khaldoun in Paris, we encounter a sober Sufism open to alterity and not very different from the other Parisian brotherhoods I have studied. In other contexts, such as Sheikh Burhanuddin's seminars in Italy, we encounter customised Sufism, based on bricolage and aimed at meeting the desires and needs of disciples. While this heterogeneity is made possible by the ductility of Nāzim's message, it takes shape through local leaders, who play the role of 'spiritual entrepreneurs', fashioning the local Naqshbandiyya Ḥaqqāniyya in their own image.

In Chapter 2, I argued that New Age discourse cannot be reduced to a series of doctrines. Nor is it synonymous with the concept of a spiritual supermarket; all European religious phenomena are framed by capitalism which, as a result, cannot be considered a criterion for understanding New Age discourse. Furthermore, if we consider the presence of so-called New Age doctrines among the narratives of European Sufi disciples as a criterion, then all Sufi brotherhoods have to be labelled as New Age. Reworking the ideas of Sutcliffe,[94] I have presented another conceptualisation of the New Age phenomenon, as a religious discourse (cf. Chapter 2), which can help us understand how the Naqshbandiyya Ḥaqqāniyya has been influenced by this discourse. It can be understood to concern scattered, sacralised knowledge dispersed between all religious phenomena and beyond, including in psychology, psychoanalysis and quantum physics. This conceptualisation of religious truth enables and facilitates a bricolage inspired by various religious, epistemological and cultural phenomena, a bricolage that includes not only doctrines, but also rituals and practices.

Today, this scattered sacred knowledge has become legible to spiritual seekers, thanks to a new cosmic consciousness – the New Age consciousness – that applies to all humanity. Consequently, New Age consciousness makes a claim on universalism, for it is a collective development of human potential. These elements imply a criticism of institutional religions that questions and contests the borders of religious identities, doctrines and dogmas.

Unlike esoteric discourse, New Age discourse is not absolute or hidden, reserved for an initiated elite; rather, it is 'close to hand' – everyone can grasp and embody it. This implies that the dialectic of secrecy is not central to New Age discourse, wherein knowledge is horizontal/egalitarian in practice. The

[94] Sutcliffe, *Children of the New Age*.

focus turns from collective salvation to an individual quest. All these elements contribute to the composition of organisational structures; New Age discourse results in small groups with a vague commitment, where seekers can participate in various religious movements, deciding for themselves on their level of engagement.

We can grasp the influence of New Age discourse on the Naqshbandiyya Ḥaqqāniyya based on a conceptualisation of sacred knowledge that favours both the bricolage of doctrines and rituals (the Qur'an as *Stargate*, the enneagram, the mirror exercise, the Sufi concert) and the formation of small groups, where the disciple has total freedom concerning commitment to and application of the rituals and norms. The influence of New Age discourse also concerns deconstructing Sufi structures and creating new organisational and social forms, such as the *muqaddam* as spiritual entrepreneur and fee-based Sufi seminars instead of weekly meetings.

Finally, New Age discourse reveals yet another form of universalism. Throughout this book, I have presented several forms of Islamic universalism: that of Muhyiddin (the Moroccan Būdshīshī who made a pilgrimage to the tomb of Saint Emilianus), that of Abdel Rahman (the Moroccan 'Alāwī who made the pilgrimage to Santiago de Compostela) and that of Leith (the Palestinian Naqshbandi who invited us to visit Saint Barnabas's tomb). In this chapter another form of universalism has emerged. Alix Philippon would probably call it 'unidiversalism' – that is, a conception of religious truth centred on the spiritual seekers' needs and desires, a DIY universalism. In the next chapter, with the Aḥmadiyya Idrīsiyya Shādhiliyya brotherhood, we will see a third form of universalism, centred on neither mystical experience nor New Age discourse, but on Guénonian thought: Guénonian–Traditionalist universalism.

6

AḤMADIYYA IDRĪSIYYA SHĀDHILIYYA

At the French National Assembly: First Meeting with the Disciples of Pallavicini

The first meeting with the Aḥmadiyya Idrīsiyya Shādhiliyya brotherhood (referred to as AIS below) did not take place in a *zāwiya* or at a seminar, but rather in one of the core institutions of the French government: the National Assembly. The occasion was a conference on ethics and interculturality, Éthique et Interculturalité, organised on 8 February 2013, by the Institut des Hautes Études Islamique (IHEI; Institute of Advanced Islamic Studies). The French AIS disciples run IHEI, which is headed by Yahya Pallavicini, the AIS sheikh, formerly with his father, ʿAbd al-Wāḥid Pallavicini.

After passing through security, I see Sheikh ʿAbd al-Wāḥid and his son, Yahya Pallavicini, in the entry hall. ʿAbd al-Wāḥid greets me warmly, mistaking me for a priest who is to participate in the conference. Once we clear up who I am, I explain to him why I am there and what my research focuses on. Pallavicini then greets me a second time, just as warmly, and immediately presents me to his disciples, promising that I will have full access to the brotherhood for my work.

Within a few minutes, I meet several disciples: Abdel, one of the members of IHEI, the institute that organised the event; Aya, affiliated with the Interreligious Studies Academy; Fatih, part of Coreis (Comunità Religiosa Islamica Italiana; Italian Islamic Religious Community); and Naim, an employee at

Halal Italia, which manages halal certification for Italian food products. All these organisations, run by AIS disciples, are but a few examples of how this brotherhood has branched out. But I will only learn that later.

Everyone seems happy to talk to me. Within a few minutes, I have a handful of business cards, and we are already discussing collaborations with my university to organise cultural events. The disciples are well dressed, probably especially so since we are at the Palais Bourbon, where the French National Assembly meets. Cultivated, cordial and available, the disciples are at the same time distant and cold, almost haughty. That day and in the coming months, all of them, even the youngest, will call me 'Mr or Dr Piraino', what you would say to a doctor or professor to maintain a certain distance. I feel like I am dealing with entrepreneurs or diplomats.

The importance of the occasion is not only reflected by the prestigious location; the eminence of the participants is striking as well. In attendance are the Vice-President of the French Senate, Bariza Khiari (see Chapter 3), the Italian politician Franco Frattini, the Paris rabbi Alain Goldmann, representatives from UNESCO and ICESCO (Islamic World Educational, Scientific and Cultural Organisation) as well as other high-profile political figures.

The conference addresses Islam in contemporary societies, specifically the relations between religions and with public institutions. The Guénonian influence could not be clearer. Guiderdoni, the French *khalīfa* of AIS, speaks of the 'metaphysical meaning of Unity' and Yahya Pallavicini of the 'primordiality of the sacred'. As for 'Abd al-Wāḥid Pallavicini, he is quick to point out that the event is a 'dialogue between orthodoxies', having nothing in common with New Age sentimentalism, the sworn enemy of Guénonian esotericism.

The conference centres on a critique of Islamic radicalism that explores possible solutions to keep this phenomenon in check. Other themes are addressed, such as the risk of an anti-religious European society, incapable of appreciating and using the resources that religions – Islam, in this case – provide access to. Guiderdoni points out that the context is 'Islam of France', putting emphasis on the article 'of'. This leads us into a religious and political discourse resembling Būdshīshī and 'Alāwī discourses (Chapters 3 and 4), even though, as we will see, the form of engagement is not the same. Here it may be defined as 'metapolitical'.[1]

[1] Bisson, *René Guénon*.

During the lunch break, we go to a restaurant not far from the Palais Bourbon. Once inside, it is difficult to make out what anyone is saying, people are rushing about, and the disciples all want to make sure everything goes smoothly. So begins a game of 'musical chairs'. No one dares to sit down until it becomes clear where their desired interlocutor will sit. After a few minutes, I drop out of the game and sit down at an empty table. Once again, luck is on my side; 'Abd al-Wāḥid Pallavicini sits down opposite me.

Before we begin to eat, Pallavicini asks me to say an 'Our Father'. Embarrassed, I reply that I am not Christian, even though I was brought up in the faith. He makes another attempt, thinking I must be Muslim: 'Perhaps a *fātiḥa*, then?'[2] When I explain my 'curious agnosticism', he seems a little disappointed. Fortunately, the French publisher of Pallavicini's book *L'Islam intérieur*,[3] seated at our table, comes to my rescue. Whether Catholic or not, he at least knows 'Our Father' by heart.

I spend a moment talking with Naim (Halal Italia). We realise we are the same age and that we studied at the same university, University of Ca' Foscari, Venice. I admit to Naim that Frattini's hypocrisy bothered me. The Italian politician separated the politics one espouses from the politics one puts into practice. Naim reassures me, telling me that Frattini is one of the leading figures in the PDL (Popolo della libertà, the centre-right alliance party led by Berlusconi). Speaking with evident political savvy, he explains that Italian politicians on the right (despite strong Islamophobia) are more reliable than their irreligious counterparts on the left. He also notes that Islamophobia on the right is more of an instrument for creating consensus rather than a real ideological position. Then he gives me an example, telling me that Matteo Salvini, a politician of the Italian Lega Nord Party known for his Islamophobia, complimented AIS disciples off-camera after a talk show: 'If there were more people like you among us,' he said, 'our country would be better off.' In this chapter, we will see that AIS has excellent relations with the right and the extreme-right.

Once lunch is over, I have a conversation with Fatih, who shows me another side of the brotherhood. Fatih is an 'iron' Guénonian, with a Traditionalist vision and a severe attitude towards the entire world. When I tell him about my

[2] *Fātiḥa* is the first sura of the Qur'an, often used for invocations.

[3] Pallavicini, *L'islam intérieur*.

research, he explains that I cannot really address Sufism because the Būdshīshiyya has become 'a religion of the state' and the Naqshbandis are 'hippies'. Fatih is obsessed by the New Age phenomenon and by all non-traditional religious forms: 'An atheist is better than someone who thinks they're spiritual.' He is critical not only of the other brotherhoods, but also of the Catholic Church, not least for switching from Latin to Italian to celebrate mass, a change he attributes to 'the little demons of counter-initiation who think they know what is best for the people'. According to Fatih, 'It is only the spiritual elite, the master, who has this knowledge.'

Pallavicini's AIS is probably the last brotherhood inspired by Guénonianism that, unlike other Guénonian brotherhoods, has seen growth both demographically and in terms of its political clout. As I will show in this chapter, the influence of the esoteric discourse on AIS is clear. It is a discourse rooted in sacred, absolute and hidden knowledge reserved for a spiritual elite, which shapes its organisational structures into what sociologists call a sectarian movement. [4]

History of the European Aḥmadiyya Idrīsiyya Shādhiliyya

'Abd al-Wāḥid Pallavicini, born in 1926, came from 'a noble family dedicated to the faith' (Yahya Pallavicini, field notes). As Mohammed, one of his disciples, put it, 'The sheikh is a prince.' In his youth, he took part in World War II as a monarchist resistance fighter.

> It's a matter of 'monism' which led me from Monarchy to Monotheism, always in observance of the hierarchical order between the two principles explained in *Autorité spirituelle et pouvoir temporel* [in translation: *Spiritual Authority and Temporal Power*], an important work by René Guénon.[5]

Pallavicini converted on 7 January 1951, the year his spiritual master, Guénon ('Abd al-Wāḥid Yaḥyā), died. He took Guénon's first Muslim given name: "Abd al-Wāḥid'. Pallavicini, by the intermediary of Julius Evola and Titus Burckhardt, joined the Swiss 'Alāwiyya brotherhood led by Frithjof Schuon. Due to doctrinal and personal differences, Pallavicini left Schuon's group and went to Asia in search of a spiritual guide. In 1971, while working in Singapore

[4] As we will see over the course of this chapter, 'sectarian' is intended in its sociological meaning, in reference to Max Weber's category, and carries no pejorative value.

[5] Nesti, 'Da partigiano monarchico durante la Resistenza all'opzione monoteista islamica', 95.

as a pianist, he joined the Aḥmadiyya Idrīsiyya Shādhiliyya brotherhood of ʿAbd al-Rashīd ibn Muḥammad Saīd.[6]

In 1980, Pallavicini returned to Milan and wrote the book *In Memoriam René Guénon*,[7] which established his reputation and garnered his first disciples, particularly in France. With the *ijāza* – the authorisation of the Singapore master – Pallavicini founded his independent branch of AIS. His disciples describe his powerful, magnetic charisma, attributed to most of the Sufi masters described in this book and manifest in both his physical body and his forceful intellect. In the words of Amina:

> Sheikh ʿAbd al-Wāḥid really had to ram his way through a very closed society. His taurine character was providential, and his authority, even his physical form, fostered his saintliness. He sacrificed everything.

Shortly thereafter, he founded the Centre d'Études Métaphysiques (Centre for Metaphysical Studies) which brought together many Italian Guénonians hailing from Catholic Traditionalism. For example, Jebril, one of the pillars of the brotherhood, told me about studying philosophy in Milan in the 1980s and his participation in Catholic Traditionalism within Alleanza Cattolica. As for Fatih, he explained how he frequented the Church of Saint-Ambroise where the mass was celebrated in Latin.

> At the time, there was the Centre d'Études Métaphysiques. We met twice a week. It was a place to engage in mental gymnastics and meet interesting people. (Boubaker)

Guénonians of any religious background could participate in the centre; its objectives were strictly intellectual, involving lectures and journals that took as their model *Études traditionnelles*, edited by Guénon. Gradually, the members of the centre converted to Islam and joined the brotherhood. The brotherhood eventually absorbed the centre, which ceased to exist.

In the 1980s and at the beginning of the 1990s, the brotherhood was characterised by tense relations with Italian society and Italian Muslims. Massimo Campanini and Stefano Allievi, Italian university professors, told me in interviews how at that time, it was impossible to give a lecture on Islam without

[6] Sedgwick, *Against the Modern World*.

[7] Pallavicini, *In Memoriam René Guénon*.

Pallavicini's disciples interrupting with Guénonian arguments. AIS's hostility was directed at both academia and the Muslim world. Pallavicini's staunch adherence to Guénon, and the absence of Qur'anic references in his discourses, created a divide between him and the new Muslim community in Italy.[8]

Metapolitical Turning Point

> We realised that a time would come where we would have to go out into the world and show our Islamicness. Because Sheikh 'Abd al-Wāḥid Yaḥyā, René Guénon, was Muslim, he chose to go and live in Cairo. There is a reason for this, isn't there? Because there, he could feel the Islamic *umma*, a rich soil in which to cultivate his ideas, his faith. (Boubaker)

AIS thus reached an important turning point. The intellectual debates, centred on metaphysics, gave way to political action, grounded in interreligious relations. In 1993, Pallavicini founded Associazione Internazionale per l'Informazione sull'Islam (International Association for Information on Islam), which in 1997 became Coreis Comunità religiosa italiana (Italian Islamic Community), whose acronym 'Coreis' calls to mind 'Quraysh', the tribe of the Prophet Muhammad.

Over the past twenty years, Coreis has made an important impact in many ways. Currently an indispensable partner of Italian institutions, it has relations with the Ministry of Education (training project for Catholic religion teachers in secondary schools), with the Ministry of Development and Health (promotion of halal foods) and with the Ministry of the Interior (national security). In addition, Coreis organises hundreds of interreligious and cultural lectures and events, both nationally and internationally. In describing them, David Bisson speaks of 'spiritual entryism' and 'ecumenism from above'.[9]

Despite its high profile and its political strength, Coreis has no more than 100 disciples. In addition, it adopted a very aggressive political policy in its early days regarding other Italian Muslim organisations. In 2005, 'Abd al-Wāḥid declared that he was the only possible choice:

> We should not look for the Islamic interlocutor for our country . . . among recent immigrants, who still suffer from significant ethical and political influences, and

[8] Sedgwick, *Against the Modern World*.

[9] Bisson, 'Soufisme et tradition', 40.

> whose representatives want to bring to Italy this revolution they were unable to wage in their home countries.[10]

Pallavicini's lack of interest in issues related to social marginalisation, citizenship and all the problems around immigration has widened the gap between AIS and other Muslim communities. This political elitism also has a metaphysical underpinning; we will see that AIS presents itself as the spiritual elite in Europe described (and hoped for) by Guénon.[11] This spiritual elite, which should slow the eschatological process due to Western decadence, is also a political elite, guiding not only initiates, but all Europeans:

> This work is the living demonstration that the intellectual elite has taken root in the West and works to thwart the hardened anti-spiritual forces.[12]

Future of AIS between the Elite and the *Umma*

In 2017, Sheikh ʿAbd al-Wāḥid Pallavicini died in Milan at the age of ninety-two. The Italian Aḥmadiyya Idrīsiyya Shādhiliyya is today experiencing a second turning point, attributable to the emergence of two pivotal figures: Sheikh Yahya Sergio (Pallavicini's son) and Bruno Guiderdoni, the *khalīfa* in France. Sheikh Yahya Pallavicini was born in 1965 and spent his youth between Switzerland, Japan (his mother's native country) and Italy, where he completed his studies. Unlike his father, Yahya speaks Arabic fluently and is well versed in Islamic theology, which he studied at the Pontifical Institute for Arabic and Islamic Studies and at Sapienza University in Rome with the famous professor Alessandro Bausani. Then he went to Syria and Egypt to perfect his knowledge of Islam. The University of Al-Azhar and ICESCO recognised Coreis thanks to Pallavicini's language skills in Arabic and his knowledge of Islamic theology. Moreover, Pallavicini is a member of the mosque in Rome and has put in place a dialogue with other Italian Islamic communities.

As for Bruno Guiderdoni, he is a French astrophysicist who, from 1993 to 1999, produced a television programme in France called '*Connaître l'islam*' (Understanding Islam). He is currently one of the most important Muslim

[10] Pallavicini, 'Lettere al Corriere', *Corriere della Sera*, 10 August 2005.

[11] Guénon, *Orient et Occident*.

[12] Pallavicini, *A Sufi Master's Message*, 17.

scientists working on the dialogue between Islam and science.[13] Guiderdoni and Y. Pallavicini, to the extent that they are no longer solely committed to conforming to Guénonian thought, have shown openness regarding other Muslim communities which, in France and Italy, recognise them as important interlocutors. Hence the brotherhood is opening to what is at play in the modern world, in both the political and scientific spheres. The principles of secularism and democracy,[14] as well as theistic evolutionism,[15] have thus entered the brotherhood.

> Sheikh Yahya became involved at a later point, at a time when this openness had already been initiated by Sheikh ʿAbd al-Wāḥid and there was more of a need for diplomacy and the ability to forge relationships. (Amina)

Other disciples view this change with a degree of mistrust. One of them acknowledged to me in 2013 that Sheikh ʿAbd al-Wāḥid feared that his disciples would not follow his son Yahya because he was not Guénonian enough. This is confirmed by Sheikh ʿAbd al-Wāḥid's own words, since he repeatedly told his disciples concerning his son Yahya, 'If you don't understand Arabic, call him master, our master, rather than sheikh.'

The openness of AIS also explains my extraordinary participation in its activities; I am the first non-disciple to frequent the weekly meetings and the annual spiritual retreat. 'The hawks have flown away,' Sheikh Yahya told me, which is to say that those with a more rigid, more sectarian vision, and who would not have approved of my participation, had already left the brotherhood.

During the spiritual retreat of the Italian AIS organised every year, in a tiny mountain village of the Aosta Valley, between France and Italy, Sheikh ʿAbd al-Wāḥid explained to me the changes they were going through and the function of my participation. We were eating breakfast at the hotel. Despite his eighty-seven years, Sheikh ʿAbd al-Wāḥid was still full of energy. His movements were

[13] Guiderdoni, *Science et religion en islam*; Piraino, 'Bruno Guiderdoni – Among Sufism, Traditionalism and Science'; Bigliardi, 'The Contemporary Debate on the Harmony between Islam and Science'.

[14] Pallavicini, *L'islâm in Europa*.

[15] Guiderdoni, *Science et religion en islam*.

gentle, his words conciliatory. He was kind and wanted my presence among them to be comfortable and pleasant.

The sheikh began his discourse by highlighting the most important themes: Primordial Tradition, eschatology, the spiritual elite, interreligious dialogue and fidelity to Guénon's work.

> The eschatological time we are living in . . . calls for a mission, a purpose that we did not want or ask for, but that we find ourselves carrying out. Not only through communication with the Church and between Muslims, but also in a higher dimension. We are here together to bear witness to the Primordial Tradition, which can be expressed as Guénon aptly did through one of its configurations, which for us is Islam, although it cannot be reduced to this configuration.

Following this introduction, the sheikh explained to me that the brotherhood was going through a period of adaptation that justified my presence.

> I am wondering if we should focus on the horizontal dimension after focusing for so many years on the metaphysical dimension. I am wondering if perhaps, due to my own fault, it is time for a new approach . . . That's why I'm asking you to help us translate our esoteric language into a lower, sociological language, so we can improve our horizontal communication . . . God has sent us a sociologist!

This role of translator I was given underscores the brotherhood's willingness to communicate and interact with the academic world. One might call this an 'openness with reservations', due to – but not exclusively – the need to enlarge and consolidate the brotherhood's political–public activities. This 'openness with reservations' is something I personally experienced during the ethnographic fieldwork when I was called upon by the disciples to speak of religion. They were not seeking at that point a confrontational dialogue, but rather to foreground the superiority of metaphysics over sociology, often using the word 'sociology' to mean basic, simple, material and superficial. This 'openness with reservations' is reflected in the paradox of a religious movement that claims to be the spiritual elite destined to save the West, without being elitist. We must bear in mind this paradox if we want to understand this brotherhood.

Esoteric Discourse

'Esotericisation' and 'Guénonisation' of Sufism

> The sheikh [ʿAbd al-Wāḥid] is pure metaphysics. He has continued the work of René Guénon . . . As a master, he is a decidedly universal, and the relationship with the disciple is never direct. The sheikh addresses us in formal language . . . The teaching is always eminently elevated, eminently principial; he is not interested in personal matters. He goes beyond the Islamic form, all while being a strong and undoubtedly deep interpreter. But he translates everything into metaphysical terms. (Mohammed)

'Are you familiar with Guénon?' That was the first question that everyone asked me during the spiritual retreat, my first contact with AIS. While the ʿAlāwīs and Būdshīshīs were not interested in my religious background, and while the Naqshbandis wanted to convert me, the AIS disciples wanted to 'Guénonise' me; in other words, they wanted to convince me that Guénonian arguments were well founded. The utmost importance of Guénon was present in all the narratives of the disciples I met:

> The only thing we have acknowledged to be true is René Guénon, so let's find him. I googled 'René Guénon Milan' and found the manifesto of the Centre d'Études Métaphysiques. God has called us here! (Dayla)

> Guénon has been imprinted on me for the rest of my life. (Boubaker)

> I was really struck by Guénon. He overwhelmed me, even threw me off balance. He upended all my ways of seeing the world. When I realised that reading Guénon put the whole world into a new perspective, the ground beneath my feet fell away . . . I was on a quest that I also experienced physically . . . from Guénon's first book . . . I read all his books in around a week, eating nothing, holing up inside my house, reading all day long. I didn't want to see anyone. (Mohammed)

In the Italian AIS, there is a sort of 'Guénonisation' of history. In relation to Guénon's explanation, Fatih told me that real Hindus do not believe in the reincarnation of souls.[16] Concerning Christian monasticism, Boubaker told

[16] Guénon, *L'erreur spirite.*

me about the concept of initiatic transmission (the esoteric secret passed down from master to master), which was exemplified by both Saint Frances and Master Eckhart, guardians of esoteric knowledge that had been passed down since the foundation of their monastic orders and continued with their spread.

Guénon's central role is evident in Pallavicini's book *Interior Islam*, where Guénon is cited sixty-six times, versus twenty-eight citations of the Prophet Muhammad. This 'Guénonisation' of Islam is also evident when Yahya Pallavicini pushes back against the Qur'anic translation, transforming '*dīn al-qaiyyama*' (Q.98: 5), an expression generally translated as 'correct or right religion', into 'Primordial Tradition'.[17] Linear Islamic eschatology predicting the end of the world, for example, is reshaped to fit the Guénonian doctrine of cosmic cycles.[18] Dayla told me that Islamic eschatology is the exoteric teaching, whereas the doctrine of cosmic cycles is the esoteric teaching.

Other words of the sheikhs reveal the Western esoteric imprint. The disciples are often called the 'initiates', the sheikhs the 'masters' and the brotherhood the 'contemplative order'. During a lesson at the University of Padua, Yahya Pallavicini started by saying '*bismi-llāhi al-raḥmāni al-raḥīmi*, in the name of God the merciful, in transcendence and in immanence', rather than the classical formula, 'the merciful and clement', thereby communicating to the public the intellectual and metaphysical dimension of his message.

Guénon's legacy may even become a limitation, weighing down AIS's expression of Sufism. This was evident when a disciple, commenting on an article written in the name of the brotherhood, exclaimed, 'Finally we've written a text that is fully Islamic, without Guénonian citations!'

As for Sheikh Yahya, Guénonian thought remains, but only as a backdrop to his discourses, since he has interiorised its metaphysical language. In the works of Sheikh Yahya Pallavicini,[19] Guénon is therefore no longer the first reference and there are considerably more references to the Qur'an and classical Sufi

[17] Pallavicini, *L'islâm in Europa*, 97.

[18] I should note that in the Ismaili (Shiite) doctrine, there is an elaborate cyclic cosmology that may be seen to resemble the interpretations of Guénon and Pallavicini. On the other hand, Guénon wrote his eschatological theories before exploring Islamic doctrines, given that, as far as I know, Pallavicini only referred to Sunni Islamic theology and Guénonian thought.

[19] Pallavicini, *L' islâm in Europa*; Pallavicini, *Dentro la moschea*.

scholars, such as Aḥmad ibn Idrīs, alGhazālī, and Ibn 'Arabī. This highlights the progressive Islamisation and the new openness of the brotherhood.

Metaphysics: Absolute Knowledge

In nearly all his discourses, written or otherwise, Sheikh 'Abd al-Wāḥid asserted that his mission was to bear witness to a metaphysical message, the 'Primordial Tradition', which is the metahistorical essence of religion and can be seen in all religious forms. Yet the Primordial Tradition cannot be experienced in its essence, only through the forms it has taken over the centuries. Pallavicini thus expresses the 'Primordial Tradition' through the form of Islam–Sufism.

Drawing on the works of Guénon, 'Abd al-Wāḥid Pallavicini and his disciples have created a metaphysical language, fundamental in the construction of their own religious orthodoxy. In Pallavicini's discourses, 'tradition', 'metaphysics' and 'esotericism' have meanings that overlap and are often interchangeable. All take on a transcendental dimension which, at the same time, goes beyond exoteric religious forms.

It is clear that AIS's metaphysics have nothing to do with the philosophy of Descartes, Hegel or Heidegger, or with Catholic or Protestant theologies, and not even with Islamic theologians, who are rarely cited. There is only Guénon, whose work, according to Pallavicini, 'represents a veritable intellectual miracle, making up for six centuries without any metaphysical perspective in the West, since the dissolution of the Order of the Temple in 1313'.[20] As one disciple put it:

> Metaphysics is beyond philosophy. Metaphysics is even beyond theology. In our interreligious meetings, we see that the true possibility of interaction between religions lies in metaphysics, because theologies must be different by definition.[21]

This metaphysical knowledge, the root of all specific religious knowledge, be it philosophical or theological, concerns all religions, in both their exoteric and esoteric dimensions.

[20] Pallavicini, *L'islam intérieur*, 147–8.

[21] Nesti, 'Da partigiano monarchico durante la Resistenza all'opzione monoteista islamica', 98.

The exoteric dimension implies the negation of any sort of exoteric exclusivism, given that all orthodox religions participate in the same essence. But this also implies that all forms of religious innovation depart from the Primordial Tradition. This is the case in Protestantism, which represents the innovation of defying the traditional authority of the Catholic Church and promoting individualism. But this is especially the case in new religious movements, alternative spiritualities, and psychological and psychoanalytical interpretations, which are not only considered as innovations, but also as 'counter-initiatic', the work of the anti-Christ,[22] for they embody a parody of religion.

From an exoteric point of view, and I wish to stress this point, Islam, Christianity and Orthodox Judaism are equivalent. To Catholic candidates who wish to convert to Islam, Pallavicini suggested that they first return to Catholicism to rediscover and re-engage with this traditional exoteric frame of reference. Returning to Christian rituals meant reconciling with religious life; converting to Islam did not mean rejecting Christianity. Take the example of Kabir, one of the early French converts. He recounted his first encounter with Pallavicini and his 'momentary return to Christianity'. Like almost all the other AIS disciples, Kabir's interest in Islam was based on Guénon's work. When he met Pallavicini for the first time, the Milanese sheikh asked him if he was Catholic. 'Yes, I'm Catholic, but not anymore,' answered Kabir.

> 'No, no! You are Catholic, it's Sunday, you should reach out to God. We're going to mass!' [said 'Abd al-Wāḥid Pallavicini]. I was stunned to hear a Muslim say, 'We're going to mass.' I tried to say yes, I'll go back, but not right away . . . 'Absolutely not! We'll both go,' [said 'Abd al-Wāḥid Pallavicini]. He would go to mass with us, to help us return to the traditional frame of reference . . . The sheikh said to me, 'Take time to think it over. For the moment you're Catholic. You're a believer once again. Keep going, reflect, and we'll see.' (Kabir)

Metaphysical knowledge also relates to the esoteric dimension of religions. While all orthodox religions participate in the Primordial Tradition, not all of them have the same esoteric value. The most significant example is that of the Catholic Church, which lost the transmission of esoteric knowledge when the Order of the Temple was eliminated at the beginning of the fourteenth

[22] Pallavicini, *In Memoriam René Guénon*, 17.

century.[23] This means that Catholics have access to salvation, but they cannot be initiated into esoteric/metaphysical knowledge.

Furthermore, according to Pallavicini, traditional and orthodox behaviours also concern everyday life; the 'Tradition' is the set of doctrines, values, rituals, religious norms, behaviours and institutions that make up religious faith. 'Traditional' becomes the antithesis of modern. For example, peasants leading a simple life become 'the defenders of tradition' (Leila). Any social innovation is anti-traditional; hence feminism and LGBTQ rights are anti-traditional and the expression of Western corruption.

This, however, has not led AIS to literalism or formalism. There are some aspects of tradition that must be respected in their form and others that must be respected in their spirit. It is difficult to clearly distinguish between the traditional and the anti-traditional, the orthodox and the non-orthodox as described by Pallavicini and his disciples. These categories are not clearly defined in AIS and may seem rather discretionary. According to Pallavicini's disciples, these differences cannot be apprehended by sociological analysis alone; an esoteric/metaphysical perspective is more effective. They thus seem to be malleable instruments in the hands of AIS, which legitimises its own existence and de-legitimises that of competitor groups.

The criticism of modernity justified by the loss of esoteric knowledge and, concomitantly, the restoration of lost metaphysical knowledge resonates with the definition of Wouter Hanegraaff, who sees esotericism as 'rejected knowledge'.[24] AIS asserts its right to re-appropriate lost metaphysical knowledge, by inverting the stigmatisation – rejecting the rejection of this knowledge by modernity. Metaphysical knowledge is thus a more elevated perspective, 'absolute knowledge' to use the category of von Stuckrad,[25] reserved for a small elite capable of understanding religious changes over the course of history. This enables evaluating the 'quality' of other religions, in their exoteric and esoteric dimensions, as one of the disciples, Jasmine, explains:

> From an initiatic point of view, you must look at things from a higher standpoint. From a detached perspective, you must see the world as a sacred theatre,

[23] Guénon, *Autorité spirituelle et pouvoir temporel*.

[24] Hanegraaff, *Esotericism and the Academy*.

[25] Von Stuckrad, *Locations of Knowledge in Medieval and Early Modern Europe*.

where everyone serves *Allāh*. We can only accomplish the action of a spiritual elite, which Guénon spoke of, if our perspective is pure. If, that is, we succeed in seeing metaphysically, in the sense of seeing all perspectives, in order to see things from above, with the same view God has.

Control over the Esoteric Field

To possess absolute metaphysical knowledge, making it possible to grasp the changes in religious phenomena over the centuries, also implies understanding and evaluating other esoteric movements in contemporary Europe.

According to AIS disciples, esoteric movements are the most vulnerable to the forces of evil: '*Corruptio optimi pessima*,' explained Jebril, citing Saint Gregory the Great. As this expression suggests, corruption of what is best is the most horrible, and switching from initiation to counter-initiation is not rare by any means.

Using sociological terms, one could say that AIS controls the European esoteric field to establish its religious authority. For example, during the spiritual retreat, much time was spent debating works by Schuonians, Guénonian Freemasons, Guénonian Catholics, and so forth. I was particularly struck by the arguments of Nabil, a young French disciple who vehemently attacked Akbarians, Sufi disciples who follow the teaching of Ibn 'Arabī.

> [They go] not only against the work of René Guénon; they make an anti-Christic attack against *taṣawwuf*, against the Primordial Tradition itself.

The Akbarians in question are deemed guilty of considering Guénon's thinking to be propaedeutic to the true metaphysics of Ibn 'Arabī. Challenging Guénon's centrality, even without denying his value, is enough to be labelled as 'satanic'. Pallavicini did not invent the merciless criticism between Guénonian groups, since they are part of the history of Traditionalism.[26]

It goes without saying that control over the esoteric field also concerns the other Sufi brotherhoods in Europe. During the spiritual retreat, in a collective meeting, the Italian disciple Mansour wanted to go through all the brotherhoods I was studying to affirm AIS's superiority. His conclusions were

[26] Sedgwick, *Against the Modern World*; Laurant, *René Guénon*.

as follows, starting with the Jerrahiyya-Khalwatiyya of Gabriele Mandel.[27] Mandel's Sufism, 'psychoanalytical with a smattering of phenomenology', is the apotheosis of counter-initiation. The 'Alāwiyya of Bentounes is guilty of being progressive, even 'socialist', enough to be labelled anti-traditional. The Naqshbandiyya of Nazim goes against the principles of Islamic–Sufi orthodoxy with its openness.

This symbolic–metaphysical battle for control of the esoteric field is even more flagrant when Mansour turns to the Būdshīshiyya of Sheikh Hamza, a brotherhood that could be considered as orthodox, even conservative in some contexts. Nonetheless, Mansour found a way to brand the Būdshīshiyya as anti-traditional: 'I take the liberty of saying what the masters can't. It's an esoteric syncretism.' According to Mansour, Sheikh Hamza mixed the teachings of the Qādiriyya and the Shādhiliyya, in addition to 'lacking clarity concerning *ijāza* (authorisation to communicate the path). When I asked whether they had evidence to challenge Hamza's authorisation, Jebril replied that 'some information is much more internal than external.' Yahya Pallavicini entered the discussion at that point – 'We do not understand why he applied a new name [Būdshīshiyya Qādiriyya instead of Qādiriyya]' – adding that the question was of no interest to him.

Another piece of 'evidence' concerning the corruption of the other Sufi brotherhoods I was studying involved my participation in their rituals. According to Fatih, I had taken a serious risk; 'practising without understanding could lead you to the bowels of hell . . . That's an example of the corruption of Sufism.' Mansour concluded that it would have been preferable to compare AIS with Asian or African brotherhoods that have maintained their traditional behaviour. But what exactly is 'traditional' behaviour? There are some aspects of tradition that must be respected in their form and others that must be respected in their spirit. Ultimately, the sheikhs determine what is 'traditional'. This was confirmed to me by the disciples themselves. Fouad affirmed that 'tradition is embodied by the master', who is even 'the voice of God'.

[27] At the beginning of my doctoral research, I had included this brotherhood but later abandoned the study due to the small number of disciples. For more information on this brotherhood, see Piraino, 'The Sufi Shaykh and His Patients'.

Eschatology and the Spiritual Elite

The eschatological question is exceedingly complex, with overlap between Guénonian eschatology and Islamic eschatology. The former is based on the doctrine of cosmic cycles, according to which we are at the end of the 'iron cycle'. It will soon cede to another cycle, another world.[28] On the other hand is Islamic eschatology, linear rather than cyclical, which foresees a terrible war pitting the forces of Mahdī and Jesus Christ against the Antichrist. This war will be followed by a period of peace before the universal judgement.

Knowing how these eschatologies interrelate remains a mystery, even a taboo. When I asked the disciples to explain this theological knot to me, none were able to give me a coherent answer (except for Amina, who distinguishes between the eschatologies by seeing them as the exoteric and esoteric forms of a teaching). The question seemed taboo for the sheikhs as well; 'Abd al-Wāḥid referred me to Sheikh Yahya, who told me with a laugh, 'I wish I could say the same thing he did!' He immediately grew serious again and explained:

> In linearity the path takes on a graduality, and in assuming a graduality, a circularity can also be assumed . . .To think that at the end of the world, everything ends, is indicative of incredible intellectual myopia, in my opinion. Because the mystery remains, and it cannot be denied that there will be another cycle.

This response is not a clarification, but Yahya highlights the fact that no one knows how or when the eschatology will take shape. Beyond these problematic overlaps, there are also certitudes, such as 'the eschatological acceleration of time'[29] – that is, the awareness that the final moment is approaching. This is increasingly clear to AIS disciples. Secondly, there is a need to resist this eschatological pressure. AIS presents itself as the ultimate bastion against modernisation, the only religious movement capable of accomplishing the Guénonian prophecy, according to which a spiritual elite saves the West from its corruption.[30]

[28] Guénon, *Orient et Occident*.

[29] Another Guénonian expression, cf. Guénon, *Le roi du monde*.

[30] Guénon (1924) foresaw other possible scenarios: (1) the collapse of the West into barbarity and (2) the assimilation of the West by Eastern civilisations through the use of force.

'Abd al-Wāḥid Pallavicini repeated several times, 'Perdition be gone from this place!' and emphasised that in the West, the esoteric dimension could only be found with him and his disciples. Other religions can only offer an exoteric form capable of saving souls, but incapable of metaphysical–esoteric realisation. 'Abd al-Wāḥid incited and provoked his disciples by saying, 'If you are not up to the task, go back to Christianity – then at least you'll be saved!'

From a practical standpoint, the spiritual elite's reorientation of the West consists in a 'testimony of faith' with respect to the Primordial Tradition, a sort of metaphysical pedagogy directed towards society. It also entails building relations and alliances against heterodoxies, New Age, relativism, religious fundamentalism and positivism. For these disciples, all these phenomena are born of modernity.

Up to this point, I have shown how AIS builds on itself by controlling the metaphysical–esoteric field, and more specifically by establishing a moral supremacy that legitimises the self-coronation of its spiritual elite. But there is nonetheless a counter-discourse within AIS that highlights the perils of elitism. 'Who are we? A sect that believes that our master alone possesses the truth?' asked 'Abd al-Wāḥid of his disciples. Sheikh Yahya condemns esoteric exclusivism, which he calls infantile, and he responds this way to the question of the spiritual elite:

> [The elite] cannot themselves affirm that they are elite. We were not founded as an elite. A debate on this matter is taken up cyclically but has not arrived at any verdict. We must focus on doing, not imagining. (Sheikh Yahya, interview conducted in 2014)

> As for us, we are not immune either. We're constantly at risk, as you heard several times in the mosque. We're always on the razor's edge. It's easy to become ideologues of ourselves . . . *Corruptio optimi pessima*. (Jebril)

During the interview with Sheikh Yahya and Jebril, one of the pillars of the brotherhood, this non-elitist narrative predominated. Sheikh Yahya does not approve of the anti-traditional or counter-initiatic condemnation of other religious organisations, telling me that his disciples had made the wrong interpretation. However, it seems more likely to me that this oscillation is part of AIS rather than a misinterpretation by the disciples.

These two opposing narratives are two sides of the same coin and represent the paradox of a religious movement that claims to be a non-elitist elite. In my opinion, this explains why Jebril described his brotherhood as being 'always on the razor's edge'. Ryad explained that being an elite does not mean being superior to anyone and is a heavy burden. As for Morad, he pointed out that there could be other spiritual elites:

> We are not the only ones. God can create a better community. God can create a better community than ours . . . If we don't carry out our tasks, God will find another community. (Morad)

AIS presents itself as one of the rare religious groups that still observes metaphysical orthodoxy. In keeping with Guénon's work, Pallavicini describes a feeling of encirclement and solitude in the quest for esoteric knowledge in contemporary society;[31] the spiritual crisis of the modern individual has become 'the most denied of conspiracies'.[32]

Metapolitics of a Spiritual Elite

Metaphysical Conservatism and Liberal Practice

AIS's political and moral vision is conservative, explaining the brotherhood's positive relations with politicians on the right[33] and with Catholic conservatism, which criticises the relativism of the social sciences and all forms of progressive theology. From a political point of view, the golden age is associated with the monarchy and the sultanate, but unlike the Naqshbandiyya, AIS is not calling for a return to this age. Democratic and secular values are not viewed as positive and even less as Islamic. More specifically, democracy is considered simply as the 'best of the bad':

> I believe that democracy is among the grandest illusions that have been foisted on the people. I'm also convinced that no other system can work any better. (Sheikh Yahya, interview conducted in 2014)

31 Guénon, *Le règne de la quantité et les signes du temps*.

32 Pallavicini, *In Memoriam René Guénon*, 14.

33 We have seen Frattini at the French National Assembly in Paris and spoken of Borghezio and Salvini, but there are other examples, such as the relationship with Rocco Buttiglione, who wrote the introduction of one of Sheikh Yahya's books.

On some occasions, Sheikh Yahya has spoken positively of the so-called values of Western societies, leaving Guénonian anti-modernism in the background. For example, in response to the terrorist attack against the satirical magazine *Charlie Hebdo* in 2015, he described freedom of opinion as 'one of the most important conquests of contemporary Western civilisation'.[34]

From a moral point of view, AIS tends to be conservative. Homosexuality is considered an imbalance and prevents access to the brotherhood. This moral conservatism also concerns the question of gender which is, of course, broken down to the metaphysical level. Women have an attitude, an inclination that is potentially dangerous, that of the 'matriarchy'. Women may only request initiation through their husbands, such that unmarried women are not admitted. While the theme of matriarchy often figures in community discussions, it is difficult to understand what it refers to.

Amel, a French female disciple, explained to me that the matriarchy is the feminine emotional propensity 'that tends to take over'. Leila, a young Italian disciple, affirmed that 'women must not assert themselves against their husbands.'

> Matriarchy is this rebellious feminine tendency that is very widespread today . . . You see it in contemporary feminism . . . You also see it in the relationships between couples where the wife commands the husband. But the husbands themselves . . . how many times have the sheikhs reproached men for not being virile enough, for not finding this ontology of the universal man? (Amel)

This theory of matriarchy has practical consequences. Women prepare food for the community meetings and do not speak unless they are called upon. However, beyond the community, the consequences of the matriarchy are not visible. AIS women participate actively in the brotherhood's activities, and some take on important roles.

Regarding Islamic law, AIS has adopted a rather liberal attitude because the rhetoric of matriarchy does not affect the liberty of female AIS members. For example, they do not wear headscarves in daily life and are totally free to go wherever they wish. Finally, Dayla stressed that this is a metaphysical question;

[34] Paolo Salvatore Orrù, 'Yahya Pallavicini: "*Fra terroristi e iman ignoranti, siamo di fronte alla volgarizzazione della religione islamica*"', *Tiscalinews.it*, 15 January 2015. Available at <https://notizie.tiscali.it/feeds/Yahya-Pallavicini-Fra-terroristi-e-iman-ignoranti-siamo-di-fronte-alla-volgarizzazione-della-religione-islamica/> (last accessed 14 November 2023).

respecting the husband's role cannot be associated with household tasks, which are evenly divided between men and women.

In addition, AIS is very liberal concerning non-halal meat and non-Islamic financing. During our interview, Sheikh Yahya Pallavicini explained to me that the doors of *ijtihād* have never been closed to Sufis, and that he is not in favour of officially reforming Islamic *fiqh*, as this would create more problems than it solves. While the rhetorical dimension is decidedly conservative, due to millenarianism, the dimension of the practical application of *fiqh* is ultimately quite liberal.

Between Metapolitics and Realpolitik: Meta-realpolitik?

When I participated in the 2013 spiritual retreat, David Bisson's book *René Guénon: une politique de l'esprit*[35] had just been published. The response of the disciples was very positive, hence their attempt to appropriate the concept of 'metapolitics' used by this author. Joseph de Maistre was the first to use the term 'metapolitics', but it was with the 'new right' of Alain de Benoist that this concept became central in anti-modernist thought.[36] By redeveloping and upending the thinking of Antonio Gramsci, metapolitics aims to influence culture and society without, strictly speaking, the intention of overtaking government powers.

Pallavicini's metapolitics only make sense if we look at history through a Guénonian lens – that is, if we understand history not as a succession of social facts, but as a sacred history, a hieratic history. According to this sacred history, the order of metaphysical truth in the West was destroyed with the dissolution of the Order of the Temple in 1313.

This hieratic–historical order cannot be re-established with the same political and social forms because 'sacred history does not repeat itself' (Guiderdoni, field notes). This means that all calls for a return to a monarchy or sultanate are nothing more than infantile pretensions. Thus, the world cannot be improved through society, the population or political institutions; the only way to do so is by correcting the metaphysical imbalance and restoring metaphysical truth. This cosmic order can be rebalanced through the action of a spiritual elite as described above.

[35] Bisson, *René Guénon*.

[36] Lecœur, *Dictionnaire de l'extrême droite*.

Once the genealogy of metapolitics is brought up to date, it becomes clear that the target is not the Islamic and/or Western population; rather, the power to rectify the metaphysical order lies with the political and religious elites. This is the 'ecumenism from above' that Bisson described.[37] Here we find ourselves in a position exactly opposite to that of the 'Alāwiyya and the Būdshīshiyya, whose attitude towards society is pedagogical.

An example will elucidate the differences between the political forms within Sufism that we have examined so far. During a discussion with Sheikh Yahya on the 'Alāwī and Būdshīshī presence in the Paris suburbs, as an alternative to the Islamist and Salafist model, he stated, 'That's not our task. They'll win! [the Islamists]. You have to remember that we are in eschatological times.' Yahya's apocalyptic vision of Sufism is the same as that influenced by the New Age discourse of the Naqshbandiyya, illustrated by Fahd's comment (Chapter 5) that engagement with social issues affecting the population is a waste of time ('like fixing the taps in the Titanic while it sinks'). The imminent end drains all social activity of its meaning.

The second goal of Pallavicinian metapolitics is to build alliances against the forces of evil. In this context, metaphysical rigor gives way to a more pragmatic attitude; metapolitics cede to realpolitik. Through Coreis, AIS organises meetings with almost everyone. During these meetings, the Pallavicini masters may find themselves sitting next to the Nazi–Maoist Claudio Mutti[38] or Alfonso Arbib,[39] a Milanese rabbi. They may rub shoulders with Mario Borghezio,[40] the racist and Islamophobic politician of the Lega Nord who defined the Pallavicini group as an 'enlightened minority, compared to the politicised and fundamentalist majority'. Or they may find themselves next to the king of Morocco, Muḥammad VI.[41]

[37] Bisson, 'Soufisme et tradition', 40.

[38] This meeting took place at the conference Against the Post-modern World, organised in Moscow in 2011.

[39] This meeting took place in 2015 at the Ambrosiana Library.

[40] This discussion took place at the book fair in Turin in 2008. Cravero, 'Librolandia, dialogo tra Borghezio e l'imam', *Repubblica Torino*, 10 May 2008. Available at <https://torino.repubblica.it/dettaglio/librolandia-dialogo-tra-borghezio-e-limam/1456991> (last accessed 14 November 2023).

[41] During Ramadam, see the IHEI website, available at <https://www.ihei-asso.org/> (last accessed 16 November 2023).

In the spirit of realpolitik, AIS-Coreis has created stable links with the Catholic Church, Italian and French public institutions, Freemasonry, Saudi Arabia[42] and other brotherhoods, such as the Senegalese Tījāniyya in Italy. The discourses of the sheikhs vary significantly according to the context. Yahya Pallavicini embodies both the system and the anti-system. Even if he maintains that 'we are practical, but for what lies beyond', AIS seems resolutely practical for this world as well, as we will see regarding its activities.

These metapolitics perfectly correspond to the analysis of Hugh Urban on elitist sectarian esoteric movements, made up of disciples from the higher classes 'who do not wish to over-throw the existing religious and political structures, but rather, either to reinforce them or else to bend and reshape them to suit their own private interests'.[43]

Activities: Teach or Inspire?

We can grasp the pre-eminence of the social activities over religious practices upon entering Pallavicini's building. The interior design and the high-tech computers and printers are impressive, whereas the condition of the mosque-*zāwiya*, unfurnished and unheated, is fair at best. AIS's activities carried out in these offices concern culture, dialogue with institutions and interreligious dialogue.

These activities could not exist without the commercial enterprises that create resources and, in turn, support Pallavicinian metapolitics. The three companies – a real estate agency, a graphic design firm and Halal Italia, which oversees the halal label for the export and import of food products – are made up exclusively of disciples.

In addition to these economic resources, masters and disciples make donations, but this money is not sufficient to provide for the hundreds of events organised by Pallavicini's brotherhood. Jebril, one of those responsible for the path, explains it this way:

> The leap we have to make now is from self-sufficiency to more external financing. Because going forward, our internal activities can no longer support our external activities. To give you some idea, we spend more than €200,000 per year on them. This means that our budget is approaching that of an institution.

[42] During a meeting with Halal Italia.

[43] Urban, 'Elitism and Esotericism', 3.

Cultural Activities

Most of AIS's activities in France are focused on culture. Through IHEI (Institute of Advanced Islamic Studies), AIS organises events in the Paris and Lyon mosques. As noted above, the *khalīfa* Bruno Guiderdoni is particularly active in the media, addressing in particular the relations between Islam and science.

Concerning the Italian AIS, the disciples created the Accademia di Studi Interreligosi, modelling itself on academic groups, even though the metaphysical–Guénonian influence is unmistakable. There is also a musical ensemble, the Sukun Ensemble, made up exclusively of disciples and which plays during events organised by Coreis. For these various manifestations, AIS uses the intellectual language of lectures and books, or it uses a simpler, more direct language suitable for other contexts, such as the EXPO de Milan in 2015.

A good example of AIS cultural activities are the lectures organised at a library, Biblioteca Ambrosiana de Milan, where between the end of 2014 and the beginning of 2015, Sheikh Yahya and his disciples were invited speak about the Christian theologian Jean de Salisbury, the Muslim philosopher Averroes and the Sufi master Ibn ʿArabī.[44]

Except for the French AIS, which maintains close ties with the Muslim community, AIS's activities are, overall, intended for Italians and Europeans whose social, cultural and economic levels are quite high. These cultural activities belong to the metapolitical sphere which is aimed at influencing society – particularly its elites – through witnessing and affirmation of the Primordial Tradition.

AIS and the Interreligious Monologue

The activities devoted to interreligious dialogue are the most significant, particularly with the Jewish and Catholic communities. There is always a good reason to organise an interreligious meeting, even around a football match.[45] Coreis's interreligious meetings, despite the organisation's very limited number of members, have national and international reach. Coreis has organised events at the French National Assembly and the Chigi Palace (headquarters

[44] The website of the Ambrosiana Library is available at <http://www.ambrosiana.eu/cms/letture_nuovi_classici-2319.html> (last accessed 14 November 2023).

[45] In 2014, a match between young Muslims, Jews and Christians was organised.

of the Italian government), bringing together the most important religious authorities in Europe.

No meeting takes place without debates on the unity of religions, without the condemnation of relativism–atheism or syncretism, without the refusal of violence, and so on. 'The only true interreligious dialogue is the monologue, where the only voice is that of God' (W. Pallavicini, field notes), a voice, one could say, that closely resembles that of Guénon.

The concrete, daily challenges posed by contemporary society are completely absent from this highly theoretical dialogue. What is sharia? How should it be approached? And apostasy? The role of women? The Palestinian question? All these 'hot button' issues are only rarely addressed and are not deemed worthy of being considered alongside metaphysical questions.

Unsurprisingly, then, despite the professionalism of the disciples in meticulously organising events, and despite the presence of prestigious figures, sometimes these meetings only attract a small number of people. This was the case for the lecture 'Il tempio d'Abramo', organised in Milan in January 2014, with the participation of the American consul Kyle Scott, the New York rabbi Marc Schneier, and the president of the province of Milan, Guido Podestà, along with other notable figures. 'Despite a full-page announcement in the *Corriere*[46] and more than a thousand emails sent out', as Jebril had told me, the public was not there, the room was almost empty.

As for the dialogue's content, we have seen that the esoteric discourse – absolute metaphysical knowledge – enables AIS to take advantage of the conformity with the esoteric and exoteric orthodoxy of other religious movements. This explains the tension within the brotherhood, between a dialogue aimed at inspiring and one that aims to teach. Sheikh ʿAbd al-Wāḥid warned his disciples: 'It would be presumptuous to try to teach metaphysics to the Church; our task is instead to guide and inspire.' Boubaker, one of the protagonists of the interreligious dialogue with the Catholic Church, also gives voice to this ambiguity:

> We have to help our [Catholic] brothers to recognise Christ when he returns, but more importantly, to distinguish Christ from the anti-Christ . . . In other words, we should try to elevate the West and this Church, helping it realise we are at the end, and if we don't rectify ourselves, we will all die.

[46] *Corriere della Sera* is one of the most important daily newspapers in Italy.

The tension between educating and inspiring is even more evident with regard to Bose, the monastic community founded by Enzo Bianchi in 1965, which in the spirit of ecumenism, brings together orthodox Christians, Protestants, and Catholics. This ecumenical approach has led Bose to question some traditional Catholic forms, which alarms AIS. That being said, realpolitik wins out over metaphysics.

> It's true that Bose has veered off course, but it's what we have for the moment. These are the anchor points for pursuing a traditional initiative. They're all we have. We'll work with what we have. (Boubaker)

Talal was more realistic than Boubaker, noting, 'I have to say, if we are collaborating [with them], things must not be so serious.'

AIS finds itself in an uncomfortable position, almost a paradox; it wants to have an interreligious dialogue with (ultra-)conservative Catholics who are challenging some dimensions of the reformism of the Second Vatican Council. But these Catholics have no interest in dialoguing with Muslims. Inversely, the Catholics who are interested in dialoguing with Muslims, such as the Camaldolese monks, the Bose community and Pope Frances, are not only opening themselves to Islam, but more generally to the contemporary world (moving in the same direction as the social sciences and softening their stance on homosexuals, divorce, and so on). These progressive and ecumenical positions are considered problematic for metaphysical orthodoxy which does not accept any social change. For instance, while for AIS, the 'ideal pope' is the theologian Ratzinger, dialogue has only been possible with Pope Frances, deemed 'minimally traditional'.

Coreis: 'A Head without a Body'

The Italian Muslim community is much younger than the French Muslim community. The process of immigration from majority Islamic countries to Italy began in the 1990s. While the 'fourth generation'[47] is sometimes referred to in France, the term 'second generation' is of recent coinage in Italy.[48]

[47] I am aware that the expression 'N generation' is problematic in that it reduces the descendants of immigrants to their origins. However, in this context, my only aim is to underscore the temporality implicit in the migratory process.

[48] Frisina, *Giovani Musulmani d'Italia*.

It is only in the past few years that the young Italian Islamic community has seen the emergence of its intellectuals, artists and politicians. In the 1990s and 2000s, most discourses around Islam focused on the 'Islamic peril' as described by Oriana Fallaci.[49] In addition to this configuration of discourses on Islam, there were right-leaning extremists who had converted to Islam[50] and a degree of anarchy in the political and media representation of Italian Muslims.

The most striking example is Adel Smith, the self-proclaimed representative of Italian Muslims. He shocked Italian public opinion with his radicalism, but his stance was, in fact, nothing more than the creation of bad journalism aiming for cheap sensationalism.[51] The political difficulties have taken place in a legal vacuum; now as in the past, the second religion in terms of members in Italy – Islam – has not been recognised by the Italian government in the way the Catholic Church and thirteen other religious organisations have.[52]

In this complex situation, AIS-Coreis has filled the political and intellectual void of Italian Islam by becoming the indispensable reference for Italian institutions. It has done so by proposing the first Intesa project, a legal agreement with the Italian government pursuant to Article 8 of the Italian Constitution,[53] and by opposing an ever-growing Islamophobia.

Coreis is 'a head without a body'. That is, it has fewer than 100 members, also AIS disciples. Nonetheless, it claims to represent the 1.5 million Italian Muslims. Even though Coreis claims it has 5,000 members,[54] this number, intended to justify its role, is not real:

> It may be that these 5,000 people [who belong to] Islamic centres are not linked to other organisations and are not part of UCOII[55] . . . But we have ongoing collaborations [with these Islamic centres]. They are not part of the Coreis Islamic Centre but are people with whom we have collaborated. (Leila)

[49] Fallaci, *La rabbia e l'orgoglio*.

[50] Allievi, *I nuovi musulmani*; Guolo, *Xenofobi e Xenofili*.

[51] Guolo, *Xenofobi e Xenofili*.

[52] Ferrari, *La libertà religiosa in Italia*.

[53] Bombardieri, *Moschee d'Italia*.

[54] Pallavicini, *Dentro la moschea*, 57.

[55] Unione delle comunità e organizzazioni islamiche in Italia, the most widespread Italian Muslim association in the country, often compared to UOIF in France.

While part of the gap between Coreis and the Islamic community is related to the political–intellectual void mentioned above, this cannot be the sole explanation. This distance is also due to the spirit of elitism, which we have seen multiple times. Coreis collaborates with other Muslims and organises interreligious meetings, yet the decision-making power always stays within the AIS frame of reference. This elitism manifests itself in the narrative of 'Italian specificity', which I often encountered in the AIS mosque-*zāwiya* and which reveals Coreis's ambition to represent 'Italian Muslims'.

For example, Alessia, an Italian Naqshbandi disciple, returned to her native city, Milan, after having lived in Paris for several years. Searching for a mosque where she could pray, she discovered Coreis and contacted them by email. Alessia was received in Coreis's offices, where the members of Coreis, polite but cold, asked her numerous questions. 'It felt like a job interview,' she said. When she told them she was married to an Algerian, one of the disciples made a face and launched into 'Italian specificity'. Later, Alessia tried several times to contact Coreis, to no avail – which begs the question: what exactly is Italian specificity? Here is what Boubaker had to say:

> This is not an Islamic centre like any other. There is a vocation, that of assuming a function that may not necessarily be understood by other Islamic centres. What sets us apart is our specificity: we are converts, but Italian nonetheless.

This Italian specificity may take on a patently paternalistic tone regarding immigrant Muslims, at which point it becomes Orientalist:

> We try to create this intra-religious dialogue so that our brothers understand that Islam isn't just about eating couscous or kebabs in the mosque. It's also making the effort to read the sacred texts, interpret them, write, and participate in the cultural, religious and public debate . . . They [Muslim immigrants] exist only as a problem for the government. Right now, citizens are justified in fearing immigration, in fearing Islam. (Boubaker)

This gap grows even wider with Coreis's lack of interest in questions involving social marginalisation, citizenship and immigration. And it grows bewildering when Coreis fans the fire of the 'Islamic peril'. In Yahya Pallavicini's book,[56]

[56] Pallavicini, *Dentro la moschea*.

the danger of fundamentalism is described as imminent. This danger is seen as justifying Coreis's political role in the eyes of the community and Italian institutions. 'Abd al-Wāḥid Pallavicini made this comment on the situation during an AIS meeting: 'All stereotypes that Europeans [have] of Muslims are true. Muslims are dangerous! What is there beyond us?'

This political strategy is not new in the world of contemporary Sufism. The Naqshbandi sheikh Hisham Kabbani in the United States shocked Americans when he said that 80 per cent of mosques were managed by fundamentalists. By contrast, Kabbani declared himself as the representative of true Islam and the only possible choice.[57]

Coreis tends to be accommodating with regard to Italian political institutions. For example, AIS does not get involved in mosque construction licences, a very sensitive issue in Italian politics, as there are several local laws that prohibit building new mosques. In 2020, there were ten official mosques for 1.5 million Muslims, the other establishments having been deemed non-authorised prayer centres. On the other hand, in the debate on the project to build a large mosque in Milan, Coreis unambiguously opposed it.[58]

Another example of the conciliatory approach to Italian institutions is the case of Consulta per l'Islam, instituted in 2010 by the Minister of the Interior Roberto Maroni, a member of the Berlusconi administration. Several famous Islamophobes participated in this commission, such as Carlo Pannella and Andrea Morigi, whereas very few Muslims took part. Among the latter, Mario Scialoja, a former Italian ambassador appointed by the minister, left the Consulta, calling it 'a mockery for the Italian Islamic community'. Paolo Branca, an eminent Catholic Islamologist, also heaped on criticism.[59] As for Coreis, it expressed satisfaction with the Consulta.

[57] Dickson, 'An American Sufism'.

[58] Leone Grotti, 'Noi musulmani di Milano non vogliamo la Grande moschea e il Caim non ci rappresenta,' *Tempi.it*, 22 February 2012. Available at <https://www.tempi.it/noi-musulmani-di-milano-non-vogliamo-la-grande-moschea-e-il-caim-non-ci-rappresenta/> (last accessed 14 November 2023).

[59] Karima Moual, 'Perde pezzi il comitato per l'Islam di Maroni', *Ilsole24ore.it*, 27 April 2010. Available at <https://st.ilsole24ore.com/art/SoleOnLine4/Editrice/IlSole24Ore/2010/04/27/Italia/15_A.shtml?uuid=068fd826-51c0-11df-92be-7a8b1f1c5244&DocRulesView=Libero> (last accessed 14 November 2023).

Rituals: Verbalisation and Intellectualisation of Sufism

The individual *dhikr* of AIS disciples lasts around an hour and is carried out in either the morning (*fajr* prayer) or the afternoon (*maghreb* prayer), but it can be reduced to fifteen minutes for work reasons. *Dhikr* can be carried out individually or exclusively with the masters but cannot be practised with other disciples in the absence of the masters. In the Būdshīshiyya, since any time is propitious to practise *dhikr*, even while driving a car, disciples enjoy considerable freedom of expression. By contrast, in AIS, *dhikr*, like all the rituals, is exactingly codified and regulated.

Every week, AIS disciples gather at the Milan mosque-*zāwiya* for the Friday prayer. Depending on the availability of the disciples, between twenty and forty people participate. At the heart of the meeting is *khuṭba*, the imam's discourse in Italian, including a short formulation in Arabic. The imam changes every week and even the youngest disciples are called on to play this role. Guiding the prayers and delivering the sacred discourse are seen as a rite of passage for Pallavicini's disciples.

Usually, the imam introduces themselves with a short, written discourse, takes the cane hanging on the wall, and enters into the main discourse with a wealth of Qur'anic, Sufi and Guénonian citations. The discourse is solemn and precise, leaving no room for improvisation or error. Most imams provide the bibliographic reference when they cite a book. The tension that such a responsibility creates can be read on the faces of every imam, especially the youngest. *Khuṭba* is followed by a metaphysical discussion and a recap of the brotherhood's activities, lasting two to four hours. The intellectual and discursive dimension obviously predominates, a point we will return to.

Every month, a meeting is organised that brings together all Italian and French disciples. It starts on Saturday night with the community dinner and *dhikr* and ends Sunday afternoon. AIS's third and final gathering is a spiritual retreat each year that lasts around nine days and takes place in the Alps between France and Italy. The masters allowed me to frequent the weekly meetings and participate in the annual spiritual retreat, but I was not allowed to participate in the monthly meetings during which the community *dhikr* is practised.

The community *dhikr*, which I attended during the spiritual retreat, is 'protected' by the disciples and considered a deeply personal moment. While the Būdshīshī and 'Alāwī disciples never miss an opportunity for prayer to benefit from the *baraka* of *dhikr*, this moment is profoundly private and hidden in AIS.

The disciples form a circle which is then adjusted by Sheikh Yahya. He changes their positions according to criteria I do not understand. Women and non-initiates (sons and daughters of the disciples) remain outside the circle. Sheikh Yahya guides *dhikr* with a large *tasbīh* (string of prayer beads). The *dhikr* becomes increasingly intense. The disciples rock their heads and, in the most intense moments, their torsos in time with the recited *dhikr*.

In this brotherhood, the bodily and emotional dimensions of the rituals seem secondary to the intellectual and discursive dimension, and all rituals are performed solemnly, even rigidly. Enthusiasm, joy and spontaneity are frowned upon. Even at the end of the prayer or at the end of *dhikr*, when the disciples shake hands and address each other with salutations, the words, formulaic, are repeated mechanically. When I participated in the annual spiritual retreat, during the metaphysical debate, two people were moved by their emotions and briefly wept. Sheikh Yahya made sure to note afterwards that their behaviour was 'out of the ordinary', as if emotion itself were problematic.

The criticism of psychologism and 'religious sentimentalism',[60] considered in opposition to metaphysical comprehension, may explain the need to control one's emotions. This need can be understood to stem from internal psychological pressure – a kind of 'metaphysical performance anxiety'. The initiates are controlled and pushed by the masters and the other disciples to choose the most correct words, practices and actions. Everything becomes an occasion to prove oneself.

> For us everything is an initiatic test! Even talking with you . . . We're careful to do the right thing which makes our behaviour a little unnatural at times, but we want to be sure we don't make a mistake. We try to go beyond the sentimental, which is a really base aspect of the human condition. (Amina)

Each action, however small, must be linked to metaphysical principles, as in the case of salutations. For example, the disciples address each other with the formulaic Arabo-Islamic greeting, '*Salām 'alaykum*'. Here again, I chose

[60] Guénon, *Le règne de la quantité et les signes du temps*.

to adapt my behaviour to the situation and used the salutations dictated by the context. I also said, '*Salām 'alaykum*', but the disciples systematically answered me with the standard Italian greeting, '*Buongiorno*'; it was not possible for them to address me, a non-Muslim, with Islamic salutations.

The most important feature of the European Aḥmadiyya Idrīsiyya Shādhiliyya brotherhood is undoubtedly the intellectualisation and verbalisation of Sufism in all its forms. Talking, debating, discussing – around metaphysics, metapolitics, the brotherhood's role, the necessary strategies, the rituals – is the most important ritual. This is also emphasised by the choice of clothing, since 'traditional' clothing is used for both the rituals (*dhikr*, prayer) and the metaphysical discussions.

Discussions take up most of the time devoted to rituals. For example, over the nine days of the spiritual retreat, there was only one community *dhikr*, whereas debates took up the rest of the time. On some occasions, the discourses became almost academic. For example, one disciple described the various etymologies of the word 'Sufism'. During the discussions, something akin to a review of the academic and esoteric literature on Sufism and Guénon was conducted. The books were then read and commented on, whether with criticism or praise. The literature review shows the extent to which the heart of the Centre d'Études Métaphysiques is still beating.

The intellectualisation and verbalisation of Sufism are apparent from the moment one enters the brotherhood. The disciple candidate must read Guénon's *Aperçus sur l'initiation*[61] (in translation: *Perspectives on Initiation*) as well as the texts of the founding master, Aḥmad ibn Idrīs. The masters then discuss this material with the candidate to check that they have intellectually and spiritually assimilated the metaphysical and Sufi principles.

Intellectual and spiritual verification through discussion is the main instrument the masters use to determine the spiritual state of the disciples. During community meetings, the disciples are invited to speak, make comments and reflect. These discussion-rituals can be highly erudite and complex, but they can also become repetitive, notably during Friday prayers. Sometimes disciples cannot find a way to express their ideas and end up beating around the bush. On two occasions, I listened to discourses so nonsensical that one of the older

[61] Guénon, *Aperçus sur l'initiation*.

disciples had to say, 'Stop! That's enough!' Amina, an Italian disciple, told me during our interview that she sometimes gets bored during community meetings and wishes she could 'bring an hourglass' to limit those disciples who like to talk too much.

> I think it doesn't occur to us . . . It's happened to me, too . . . I realised that I had repeated the same concept maybe a hundred times . . . Unfortunately, when you are invited to speak, you can't be excused. Obviously, nobody is going to kill you, but the principle is basically that you should facilitate the circulation of a blessing, of *baraka*. When you are invited to speak, the Master wants to test you. It's to check your inner state. So, if you don't say anything . . . it's worse. Because we should always have this connection with the principle. (Amina)

The importance of the intellectual dimension in European Sufism has been highlighted regarding the academic influence – that is, the religionism of Corbin, Massignon and de Vitray-Meyerovitch. And we have seen that in the ʿAlāwiyya and the Būdshīshiyya, major debates exist around the relationship between principles, norms, politics and even epistemology. However, these debates do not seem to touch on the experiential dimension of Sufi practices, whereas in the Aḥmadiyya Idrīsiyya Shādhiliyya, discursive reason seems to be the main means of moving along the spiritual and esoteric path. Disciples delve into all questions, concept by concept, word by word. Language is always carefully weighed, leaving no place for the ambiguity of silence or poetic language. Nothing is left to the ineffable. This rationalisation of the spiritual quest brings to mind Julius Evola's criticism of Guénon, described as the 'Descartes of esotericism'[62] in light of his mission to systematically and rigorously understand the esoteric.

We have seen in the other brotherhoods that *dhikr*, like ecstatic rituals in general, is the heart of the group and what holds it together – a remedy for any problem, to the point of creating dependence. Hence the need to master and control it. We have also seen in the studies of the other Sufi orders that the ecstatic rituals produce '*communitas*' by revitalising social ties, values and practices. In AIS, by contrast, the central ritual is metaphysical discussion, in which the ecstatic dimension with its liberties of emotional and cognitive

[62] Evola, *Il cammino del Cinabro*, 48.

expression is reduced to a minimum. There seems to remain no trace of *communitas*, which is to say the possibility to reproduce the religious discourses and practices but also call them into question.

Sectarian Organisational Structures: Tensions, Solidity and Homogeneity

At the socio-biographical level, AIS is particularly homogeneous. The Italian disciples have a middle-class or upper-class background. Most have university degrees and all of them are highly cultivated with a firm grasp of the philosophical–metaphysical language used in the brotherhood.

While the Italian Naqshbandiyya can at times be represented as a nebula, AIS is a compact body: solid, homogeneous and opaque. All the activities are organised and carried out by AIS disciples, and all of them are interconnected. The social homogeneity is mirrored by the brotherhood's solidity, visible in both its discourses and its metapolitical and economic activities. This is apparent in its contact with the outer world and in its narratives. Even so, as in all the other brotherhoods I have studied, the shift between the 'stage' (official narratives and behaviours) and the 'backstage' (informal narratives and behaviours) is visible in certain places and at certain times.

Once again, cigarettes offered a useful perspective. In most Sufi brotherhoods (except for those in Turkey), smoking cigarettes is seen in a negative light, but some disciples smoke without being noticed. Since I smoked at the time of my field research, I was able to go 'backstage' with the smokers, where it was easier to talk. In AIS, however, I never had backstage access; interacting with me, even 'off-stage', was always an initiatic test, as explained by Amina. While I discovered through the interviews that some disciples smoked, they could not smoke in front of me. According to Goffman's categories, AIS aims at 'maintaining expressive control' – that is, strictly controlling the impressions it gives to others.[63]

The brotherhood's solidity derives from particularly tense relations with the rest of society, which is characterised by corruption and decadence and where an imminent eschatology and satanic counter-initiation is playing out. However, strong internal tension is also present. Good behaviours are exalted

[63] Goffman, *The Presentation of Self in Everyday Life*.

and bad behaviours excoriated. The brothers publicly scrutinise and criticise each other. During the community discussion-rituals, the attitudes, behaviours, and even the private lives of the disciples, are examined by all. The good disciple must live according to esoteric principles, organising their entire existence around the brotherhood. This is at the opposite end of the spectrum from customised Sufism which is influenced by the New Age discourse and where the practices and rituals are tailor-made.

Marriage is a good example of this firm control and internal tension. The disciple cannot marry whomever they wish. The disciple's husband/wife must share the brotherhood's metaphysical vision (although they may have a different religious background) as well as its political and economic engagement. I met two disciples who divorced because of pressure from the brotherhood. Abdel explained to me that there are rules to follow, and a disciple's actions must be consistent with the brotherhood. 'You can't marry a psychoanalyst', since psychoanalysts are representatives of the counter-initiation.[64] One disciple, Hussein, did not want to leave his wife and thus had to leave AIS. Anything that threatens the brotherhood's solidity, including husbands and wives, is ostracised.

The control and the tension within the brotherhood is especially apparent in the disciples' engagement in metapolitical activities, and/or in their economic support of these activities. For this reason, I often heard criticism of Fouad, who was essentially interested in *dhikr* and did not want to commit economically or politically. After a few months, the brotherhood took its distance from him.

The activities AIS organises serve not only to disseminate the brotherhood or certain values; they are, in fact, initiatic tests for the disciples. Engagement in the brotherhood thus requires engagement in one of AIS's organisations.

This metapolitical engagement cannot be reduced to the 'quantitative' economic dimension – the masters demand total commitment. A relevant example is 'the question of the roof'. During the winter of 2014, the roof of the Milan mosque-*zāwiya* needed significant repair. The masters not only

[64] In the Guénonian frame of reference, psychoanalysis represents the parody of tradition – that is, the counter-initiation, or even the devil.

asked the disciples for donations; they also asked them to convince their families to give money. The situation was particularly complex for those whose family members felt their conversion was a form of betrayal.

> If you are unable to explain to your family your religious path, then you have failed! . . . I don't want you to participate with your money, which you can use to support the activities of Coreis and the masters. (Y. Pallavicini, field notes, 2014)

Unsurprisingly, one of the most important subjects during the meetings is obedience. This entails 'freeing oneself from the choice of choosing' (Yasser). To embody the spiritual elite, the disciples are asked to make every effort, in the rituals but especially in the brotherhood's political, cultural and economic activities.

The effort to embody this spiritual elite involves fighting against 'the adversary' – that is, *shayṭān* – who 'works in subtle ways' and who, in the 'accelerations of eschatology', attacks 'the men of God' in particular ('Abd al-Wāḥid Pallavicini, field notes). Disobedience vis-à-vis the masters, lack of participation in the activities and various improper behaviours may be interpreted as forms of attack by *shayṭān*, who may also take on a physical form.

The tense atmosphere within AIS is not solely the result of concrete problems (marriage or economic and social engagement). It is, in fact, this brotherhood's modus operandi. The internal and external tensions together make up a whole. For example, Mansour was criticised publicly for having lost the interreligious football match and for having scolded a team member. Fatih was criticised publicly for using his smartphone too much. The criticisms during the community discussion-rituals feed this tension and can be severe:

> You don't know what it means to have a master. (W. Pallavicini, field notes)

> You don't know what *Allāh Akbar* means. (W. Pallavicini, field notes)

> You don't know what prayer is. (Y. Pallavicini, field notes)

> You've already made the pilgrimage to Mecca, but you behave as if you hadn't. You are not worthy of this spiritual state. (Y. Pallavicini, field notes)

> It isn't possible to talk to walls . . . You are free to live like walls if you wish, but walls don't know how to live, how to love. (Y. Pallavicini, field notes)

The separation of AIS from the Italian Islamic community and, in general, the internal and external tension can be understood through the example of the mosque-*zāwiya* in Milan. It has been presented to the media as the second official mosque after the mosque in Rome,[65] but in reality, only AIS disciples have the right to use it; others must be invited.

During my field studies in Milan, I met several Muslims who had heard about this mosque but were never able to enter it. They were on the outside of the invisible wall Coreis-AIS had put up, a barrier that remains impervious to the requests of Milanese Muslims looking for a place of prayer. During my five months of field research, the only time I saw non-AIS Muslims was the Friday following my explicit question about who could or could not frequent the mosque. When I openly asked Sheikh Yahya about this contradiction during our interview, he told me that the mosque would be opened 'when the time [was] right'. Boubaker, one of the disciples who have been with the brotherhood the longest, explained it to me this way:

> The first reason [for the closure of the mosque] is that we don't have the authorisation to open it to the public. We don't meet the safety requirements because there are no fire extinguishers. Secondly, this is something we have chosen. We don't want it to become a mosque . . . It's unpleasant to speak of a private mosque or one that operates by invitation, as you said. We say that it is still a *zāwiya* rather than a mosque.

Finally, it is important to nuance and underscore that the sectarian structure of AIS is definitely not as strong among the French disciples. During my field research, I was struck by the near absence of the elitist mindset and the tension I had observed among the Italian disciples. There are multiple reasons for this difference between the French and the Italians. First, the participation of the French AIS in local mosques (notably in Paris and Lyon) probably made it possible to overcome certain Orientalist stereotypes. In addition, the distance from Milan and the weekly meetings have clearly influenced the structure of the French AIS. Finally, the role of the French AIS, through the Institut des Hautes Études Islamiques, is primarily pedagogical. That is, the French AIS

[65] Pallavicini, *A Sufi Master's Message*, 9; Pallavicini, *Dentro la moschea*, 67.

is not subject to the political and identity tensions of the representation of Muslims in Italy.

This situation makes it possible for us to describe AIS through the sociological ideal type of the sect, especially in the Italian context. It consists of a voluntary group that is coherent and strives to be homogeneous.[66] It has an aristocratic attitude,[67] and relations with the rest of society are particularly tense.[68] Lastly, AIS represents for its disciples the main source of identity around which they think about the world and lead their lives.[69] The characteristics of the sect ideal type are closely tied to the esoteric discourse, which conceptualises an absolute knowledge that is hidden and elitist. This favours homogeneity and solidity and justifies the sense of encirclement and the aristocratic attitude towards a decadent world.

From Sect to Brotherhood: a Change in Progress

As I have shown several times, AIS has been undergoing an important shift in recent years, progressively opening itself to other communities and other sources of knowledge. We could talk about a form of 'de-esotericisation',[70] understood as the process of broadening the Guénonian contours. The metaphysical 'absolute knowledge' is slowly opening itself to other forms of knowledge that draw on Sufi and Islamic sources, for example, but also on the human and natural sciences. Plus, the sectarian dimensions described above, such as the tense relations with the rest of society, are slowly diminishing. This progressive opening started with ʿAbd al-Wāḥid Pallavicini, but Sheikh Yahya and Bruno Guiderdoni, the *khalīfa* in France, have continued to develop it.

Several times, AIS disciples stressed the extraordinary importance of my presence – as a researcher – among them, which would have been inconceivable just a few years earlier. According to the interpretations of Guénon, the social and human sciences that examine religious phenomena are an instrument in

66 Troeltsch, *Die Soziallehren der christlichen Kirchen und Gruppen*.

67 Weber, *Sociologie des religions*.

68 Stark and Bainbridge, 'Of Churches, Sects, and Cults'.

69 Simmel, *Die Religion*; Wilson, *The Social Dimensions of Sectarianism*.

70 Piraino, 'Esotericisation and De-Esotericisation of Sufism'.

the war against the spirit of tradition.[71] In this regard, Sheikh Yahya explained that AIS is made up of 'hawks and doves'. The former would prefer to adhere to the Guénonian esoteric message and engage in intellectual debates (vertical dimension), whereas the latter would prefer an opening to the outside world to accomplish/embody the esoteric message through activities in society, such as interreligious and intra-religious dialogue (horizontal dimension).

This opening concerns not only the social sciences and communication with a broader swathe of the public, but also the natural sciences. For Guiderdoni, the dialogue between science and religion is now not only possible but also fruitful, serving a particular purpose:

> To deepen the mystery of God, to intensify it through this dialogue between science and religion. For me, the goal of this dialogue is to augment our astonishment before God. That's the spiritual goal. (Guiderdoni)

Guiderdoni is not interested in building a new theoretical system for describing the relationship between science and religion.[72] On the contrary, he is trying to develop a discussion within the Islamic scientific community whereby various perspectives can be presented that can transcend both scientific and religious simplifications. The book *Science et Islam*, which he edited in 2012, is a perfect example of various Islamic voices on the subject of the natural sciences.[73] This approach differs substantially from the 'absolute knowledge' approach described above and resembles the Islamic humanism described in earlier chapters.

The 'de-esotericisation' of AIS also implies a sort of 'Islamisation', taking Islam and Sufism beyond the Guénonian frame of reference. Unlike his father, Sheikh Yahya, and also Bruno Guiderdoni, are very familiar with Arab and Islamic doctrines. Guénon's thought remains present, but in the background, no longer the primary reference. The Qur'an along with classical Sufi scholars, such as Aḥmad ibn Idrīs, al-Ghazālī and Ibn 'Arabī, are cited more often. In this regard, Sheikh Yahya told me during our interview, 'We must free ourselves from the presumption of continuing with a Guénonian checklist.'

[71] Guénon, *Symboles fondamentaux de la science sacrée*, 5.

[72] Bigliardi, 'The Contemporary Debate on the Harmony between Islam and Science'; Piraino, 'Bruno Guiderdoni – Among Sufism, Traditionalism and Science'.

[73] Guiderdoni, *Science et religion en islam*.

Now that this progressive opening is underway, AIS's manner of approaching modernity is evolving, focused on rebuilding, restoring and resisting modernity, rather than opposing it. Yahya Pallavicini and Guiderdoni prefer to define themselves as 'ante-modern' or 'post-postmodern' rather than 'anti-modern'.

> Guénon had to confront modernity, a modernity that was arrogant, colonial and positivist. It had colonised all of reality and excluded from reality what wasn't under its control. We are in a different situation, where ideological modernity has declined and where we converse with postmodernity, which is more open to an exchange . . . We are, instead, ante [modern] – that is, we are trying to find the great metaphysical synthesis: the Primordial Tradition, which existed in the Christian and Muslim world of the Middle Ages, in the works of al-Ghazālī, Ibn Sīnā, Ibn Rushd and Ibn 'Arabī. But at the same time, the world in which we live is no longer the world of Aristotelian physics and Ptolemaic cosmology. And we have to live in today's world, to attempt a rectification using elements of current science. Absolutely! . . . Postmodern deconstruction exists, and we are involved in a post-postmodern or ante-modern reconstruction. (Guiderdoni, interview conducted in 2013)

This process of opening, of de-esotericisation and Islamisation, also concerns the social dimension. Yahya Pallavicini is a member of the mosque in Rome and has initiated a dialogue with other Italian Islamic communities, alienated during the 1990s and the 2000s.[74] Guiderdoni is not only a recognised scientist; he is also engaged in disseminating Islam to a non-Muslim public. For these activities, he has received the title of Knight of the French National Order of Merit.[75] This is an indication that AIS disciples and spokespeople are becoming more and more involved in social and cultural activities, not only in the name of the Aḥmadiyya Idrīsiyya Shādhiliyya, but also generally, in the name of the Islamic community. This process is not homogeneous, and some AIS disciples admitted to me that they prefer to concentrate on the metaphysical debate. The tension between the elitism of the 'hawks' and the openness of the 'doves' is far from resolved.

[74] Sedgwick, *Against the Modern World*.

[75] The IHEI website is available at <https://www.ihei-asso.org/> (last accessed 14 November 2023).

Conclusion

Throughout this book, we have seen the impact of Guénonian thought on European Sufism. Some disciples have adopted anti-modernism, others the universalist narrative of the Primordial Tradition, and still others the eschatological dimension. Guénonian discourses can thus be understood through divergent interpretations, in all milieus: esoteric, New Age and 'orthodox' Sunni Muslim circles.[76]

In the case of AIS, the legacy of Guénon goes deeper. 'Abd al-Wāḥid Pallavicini represented the last Guénonian Sufism – that is, a Sufism built entirely around the esoteric discourse of the French thinker. We have seen that this esoteric discourse rests on the conceptualisation of an absolute and hidden knowledge limited to a spiritual elite, which creates strong internal and external tension and imposes a sectarian structure.

The influence of this esoteric discourse on Sufism has also led to its intellectualisation and verbalisation. The metaphysical discussion has become the main ritual of this brotherhood, to the detriment of ecstatic practices which are reduced to a minimum. In addition, its elitism implies a kind of (meta) politics that does not seek to call power structures into question, but rather to mould and adapt them to its purposes. Despite a limited number of disciples and significant distance from other Islamic communities, this strong transcendental mission has enabled AIS to become known in Italian institutions as the main reference for Italian Islam.

With its new leaders, Yahya Pallavicini and Bruno Guiderdoni, AIS is going through a significant change, a sort of 'de-esotericisation'. It is relativising absolute knowledge as other forms of knowledge (Islamic, human sciences, natural sciences) are allowed in, and it is tempering the sectarian dimensions through dialogue with other religious communities. Yet the paradoxical tension of an elite striving to be non-elitist is far from resolved.

[76] Piraino, 'L'héritage de René Guénon dans le soufisme du XXIe siècle en France et en Italie'.

CONCLUSIONS

Renewal of Contemporary Sufism

The brotherhood-based Sufism described in this book is undergoing growth, expansion and renewal, led by charismatic masters who go beyond the original cultural–geographical framework to attract new disciples. All brotherhoods we have seen are in the process of expanding their prayer centres to accommodate new disciples. In addition, these brotherhoods are engaged in a number of social, cultural and political activities.

One of the common traits of these brotherhoods (except for AIS) is that they promote a 'Sufism for all' which, as we have seen, does not denote a Sufism without Islam or without religious norms, but rather a Sufism more focused on welcoming newcomers and embracing otherness and less focused on asceticism and the spiritual elite. This 'Sufism for all' in the 'Alāwiyya, Būdshīshiyya and Naqshbandiyya brotherhoods is promoted as true Islam – its essence – as well as an Islam capable of facing the challenges of modernity. What is the extent of this revivification? Is it a significant change like the one that occurred in the eighteenth–nineteenth centuries? Will Sheikhs Khaled Bentounes, Nāzim 'Adil and Hamza al-Būdshīshī have the same historical resonance as Ahmadou Bamba, Aḥmad ibn Idrīs and Aḥmad al-Tijānī? It is probably too soon to say.

At the beginning of this book, I proposed that Sufism can be understood as a dialogue between *scientia experimentalis* – direct, unstable, creative knowledge of God – and *sacra doctrina* – a *doxa* with its moral, doctrinal and social structures. This dialogical definition of Sufism has been developed throughout the foregoing chapters. We have seen that Sufi *scientia experimentalis* translates into experiential, bodily knowledge that produces dreams, visions and ecstasy, guiding the quest of many Sufi disciples in contemporary Europe. This knowledge, this direct contact with the sacred fosters and justifies a regeneration–revivification of the religious message and acts as a creative force in the cultural, artistic, political and philosophical realms. This has led to the multiplication of new forms, such as Sufi rap, epistemological hybridity, and also political and social engagement in some brotherhoods. That said, European Sufism is also *sacra doctrina*, reproducing Islamic and Sufi doctrines, morality, structures and exegesis. As we have seen, all brotherhoods interpret the relationship between sharia and *fiqh* in their own way. Religious norms can be interpreted differently, but they remain a central part of the Sufi path.

Hybridisations of Sufism: Between New Age Discourses and Esoteric Discourses

I began this book by highlighting the fact that recognising a process of Sufi hybridisation in Europe can only be a starting point; otherwise, we run the risk of a tautological conclusion. We thus need to understand the modes of this process. Which hybridisation are we talking about? The most evident hybridisation processes are the interactions between esoteric discourse and New Age discourse. The former is characterised by absolute, hidden and elitist knowledge that implies sectarian organisational structures. As for the latter, it is characterised by scattered, horizontal knowledge focused on disciples' needs and desires. Such knowledge implies minimum commitment and fluid organisational structures.

We have seen that the two discourses – New Age and esoteric – also have common points; both open the door to discussion around institutional religions by promoting new religious authorities capable of grasping sacred knowledge. In addition, these two discourses conceptualise various relationships with religious otherness that step away from dominant Islamo-Sufi interpretations. As for AIS's system of thought, it is centred on Guénon's concept of 'Primordial Tradition', which implies that all orthodox religious forms participate in the same truth. However, this universalism is at times exclusivist, creating new esoteric boundaries between religions. We have also seen the bricolage of some Naqshbandi masters and disciples in Italy, who use non-Islamic and non-religious discourses to teach and learn Sufi practice.

From these interactions, new configurations for imagining and experiencing Sufism have emerged: (1) new rituals (like the enneagram, the Naqshbandi mirror exercise, the *dhikr*-concert and AIS discussion-rituals); (2) new organisational structures (incorporating the Naqshbandi 'spiritual trainer' and AIS sectarian dimensions); and (3) new doctrines (Naqshbandi doctrinal bricolage and AIS Guénonian metaphysics).

Significant resonances between Sufism, on one hand, and New Age and esoteric discourses, on the other, have made these hybridisations possible. In this way, these disciples have not invented their Sufism *ex nihilo*; rather, they have found Sufi forms that resonate with their discourses. This means that AIS elitism and Naqshbandi bricolage are not absolute novelties in the history of Sufism. Finally, in this book we have witnessed the progressive Islamisation of New Age and esoteric discourses and practices. Both Sheikh Mehmet (Naqshbandiyya) and Sheikh Yahya (AIS) are putting the accent on the Islamic–Sufi tradition to minimise exogenous influences. This progressive Islamisation is also not new in the contemporary Sufi landscape.[1]

Hybridisations of Sufism: A Humanist and Islamic Discourse

The process of hybridisation is not always as manifest and spectacular as in AIS and the Italian Naqshbandiyya Ḥaqqāniyya. In some cases, it is harder to understand the origin of an idea or practice, especially with regard to transnational movements involving thousands of disciples of various classes, regions and cultures.

We have seen that some elements of Guénonian esotericism are also present in the Būdshīshiyya and the ʿAlāwiyya. However, other movements have shaped European Sufism such as 'Religionism' – that is, the practice of a syncretic epistemology that brings together subtle sacred experiences and scientific methodologies. We have met the pioneers of this approach – Louis

1 Sedgwick, 'The Islamization of Western Sufism after the Early New Age'; Philippon, 'De l'occidentalisation du soufisme à la réislamisation du New Age?'.

Massignon, Henry Corbin and Eva de Vitray-Meyerovitch (the latter converted to Islam–Sufism) – but this approach is also present in the discourses of this book's protagonists, including Khaled Bentounes, Faouzi Skali, Moulay Mounir al-Būdshīshī, Éric Geoffroy and Bruno Guiderdoni. It thus comes as no surprise that Edgar Morin, the agnostic French philosopher of Jewish origin, is often invited to Sufi cultural events organised by the ʿAlāwiyya and the Būdshīshiyya. Likewise, philosophers and scientists working on complex systems, such as Ilya Prigogine (1917–2003) and Alfred North Whitehead (1861–1947), are often cited.

This pluralism and hybridity also concern political thought. For example, in the ʿAlāwī cultural foundation Adlania, two political reference points for the 'culture of peace' are Emir Abdelkader (1808–83), a Sufi hero of the Algerian resistance against French colonialism, and Nelson Mandela (1918–2013), an anti-apartheid activist and South African Head of State. This epistemological hybridity and this political pluralism play a role in founding a discourse around human beings. Along these lines, I consider certain social and political activities of the ʿAlāwiyya and the Būdshīshiyya to qualify as an Islamic humanist discourse.[2]

The category of humanism is particularly problematic due to the plurality of its meanings, sometimes overlapping, sometimes in stark contrast.[3] For example, humanism is often described as a secular phenomenon,[4] while what is considered its founding text, Pico della Mirandola's *Oratio de Hominis Dignitate*,[5] is steeped in Neoplatonism, Christian esotericism and Kabbala. To complicate matters further, humanism has a political connotation; in fact, it has been used both to legitimise European colonialism and neo-colonialism and to challenge them.[6]

All these elements discourage the use of humanism as an analytical category, overcharged as it is with competing and contradictory meanings and uses. Be that as it may, I consider the category of 'Islamic humanism' to be a useful tool in describing the Sufi ʿAlāwiyya and Būdshīshiyya brotherhoods,

[2] Parts of this section have been published in Piraino, 'Islamic Humanism'.

[3] Reichmuth et al., *Humanism and Muslim Culture*, 17.

[4] Copson, 'What Is Humanism?'.

[5] Pico della Mirandola, *Oration on the Dignity of Man*.

[6] Alessandrini, 'Humanism in Question'.

or at least some trends within them. To begin with, several Sufis use it, making it an emic category. Secondly, it will allow us to distinguish among different kinds of universalist discourses: New Age and Traditionalist.

We can describe the different meanings and uses of humanism using three broad categories. Humanism has been understood: (1) as an educational and institutional approach to learning, (2) as a secular human-centred approach to life and meaning and (3) as a universalist discourse – *Weltanschauung* – focused on the cosmogonic role of the human being. As we will see, these abstractions can also be found in the Islamic context.

The first approach regards humanism as an educational and institutional method of learning, related to literary arts, which developed in Europe starting in the Italian Renaissance.[7] The humanist institution comprised a corpus of professionals in the field of *studia humanitatis* who studied poetry, philology, moral philosophy and rhetoric. This perspective, described by Paul Oskar Kristeller, is reflected in George Makdisi's analysis within the Islamic frame.[8]

The second approach regards humanism as 'a non-religious, human-centred approach to life and meaning'.[9] Andrew Copson describes humanism not only as a secular phenomenon, but also as anti-religious.[10] Other elements are the scientific method as well as compassion and the pursuit of happiness.[11] In the Islamic frame, there is no anti-religious conceptualisation of humanism, but there are several formulations which emphasise its secular dimension. In effect, as Shahab Ahmed has masterfully argued, there has been a sort of secularisation of humanism in the Islamic context.[12] For example, Lenn Goodman has argued that the Islamic humanism of the Middle Ages was 'another Islam, tolerant, pluralistic, cosmopolitan without triumphalism, and spiritual without repression'.[13] In short, humanist Islam was a way of accommodating the secular. A similar pattern of reasoning may also be found in Ira Lapidus[14] and Hamid

7 Kristeller, *Renaissance Thought and Its Sources*.

8 Makdisi, *Rise of Humanism in Classical Islam and the Christian West*.

9 Copson, 'What Is Humanism?', 4.

10 Copson, 'What Is Humanism?', 3.

11 Copson, 'What Is Humanism?', 8, 15.

12 Ahmed, *What Is Islam?*, 197–221.

13 Goodman, *Islamic Humanism*, 23.

14 Lapidus, *A History of Islamic Societies*, 13.

Dabashi.[15] The Algerian scholar Mohammed Arkoun (1928–2010) helped polarise this topic further. He portrayed a golden age of Islamic humanism in the tenth century in Iran, Iraq and Spain. This Islamic humanism was characterised by pluralistic knowledge and aesthetics, which were challenged by the 'Sunni politics of orthodox-isation' that the Ottoman Empire promoted, and later by the emergence of Islamic nationalism and populism in contemporary societies. According to Arkoun, orthodoxy and humanism are the two poles of Islamic thought.[16]

The third conceptualisation of humanism focuses on the relationships between God, nature and the human being.[17] I consider this approach to be the most relevant here and, in particular, I will employ Eugenio Garin's definition of humanism. The main elements of the humanism Garin describes in the Christian Neo-Platonic Renaissance are: (1) the anthropo-cosmic role of the human being; (2) a universalist truth, which goes beyond religious and cultural differences, but is embedded in a specific religion; (3) a pluralistic epistemology; and (4) a sense of responsibility towards society.

According to Garin, humanism was a reaction to the intellectual calcifications of Scholasticism, a way of rediscovering an intellectual and spiritual quest along with creativity. Hence, philology was not only a method of finding the correct meaning of words, but also an instrument to probe the deeper meaning of reality. This intellectual, spiritual and moral change was possible only through rethinking the role of the human being. Rather than adopting a human-centric perspective, following on from Pico's and Ficino's works, Garin describes the cosmic dimension of the human being as 'a knot of everything' tying together God and nature, microcosm and macrocosm.[18]

In Pico's *De Homini Dignitate*, the nature of the human being is described as a miracle and a marvel. God created the human being so that someone 'might comprehend the meaning of so vast an achievement' and 'might be moved with love at its beauty and smitten with awe at its grandeur'.[19] Furthermore, Pico

[15] Dabashi, *Being a Muslim in the World*, 13.

[16] Arkoun, *Humanisme et islam*, 26, 21.

[17] Schöller, 'Zum Begriff Des "islamischen Humanismus"'; Reichmuth, 'Humanism in Islam between Mysticism and Literature'; Garin, *L'umanesimo italiano*.

[18] Garin, *L'umanesimo italiano*, 74, 212.

[19] Pico della Mirandola, *Oration on the Dignity of Man*, 5.

depicted the indefiniteness and possibility of the human being, who is not determined by their nature. The human being can embody all the elements of nature, but also reach for their divine embodiment. Following Pico's conceptualisations, human freedom and potential are not separate from God's law and nature. Rather, the opposite is true; humanity's indefiniteness is part of God's plan.

One of the most important elements of Pico's oration is the focus on universal truth rather than Christianity alone. This implies a universal harmony among all 'sincere thoughts'[20] and a quest for universal peace. This universal truth took on different names in the Renaissance context, such as *docta religio*, *pia philosophia*, *teologia platonica*, *prisca philosophia* and *philosophia perennis*. However, they all share the idea of a common truth beyond religious differences, and the common quest of all human beings. Universal truth does not imply, for Garin, the creation of a new religion; in fact, humanism is steeped in Christianity and 'summarises and accomplishes, for those who can understand, the whole of human knowledge'.[21]

According to Garin, the humanist's porous and never-ending quest has deep epistemological consequences. In fact, not only do philology and history become central in attempting to understand the role of the human being in the history of humankind; there is also an opening towards other philosophies and religions (Greek, Jewish, Islamic, Zoroastrian), which can contribute to understanding reality. For Garin, humanist epistemology is characterised by a pluralistic approach towards other cultures, but also towards non-discursive rationality, such as bodily senses, poetry, dreams and visions. Finally, Garin's humanism also has a political and civic dimension, implying a renewed faith in human beings and in their shared existence. Hence, the pious philosopher's quest also influences their social life.

A conceptualization similar to Garin's humanism can be found in the Islamic context in the works of Ahmed[22] and Rahimjon Abdugafurov,[23] who describe *al-insān al-kāmil* of Ibn 'Arabī and 'Abd al-Karīm al-Jīlī. The idea of a perfect human being and the knot between God and nature, capable of

[20] Garin, *L'umanesimo italiano*, 123.

[21] Garin, *L'umanesimo italiano*, 112.

[22] Ahmed, *What Is Islam?*.

[23] Abdugafurov, 'Soteriology in 'Abd al-Karīm al-Jīlī's Islamic Humanism'.

incorporating divine attributes, resonates with Pico's ideas.[24] As Ahmed masterfully argues, 'The concept of *al-insān al-kāmil* makes the cosmos in terms of man, and makes man in terms of the cosmos.' This shatters the dichotomy of theocentric versus anthropocentric, creating 'a simultaneously and inter-prismically anthropocosmic/cosmoanthropic imagination and reality'.[25]

Abdugafurov adds other elements to the concept of Islamic humanism, showing how al-Jīlī adopted a pluralistic approach to knowledge and truth. Furthermore, he describes how al-Jīlī promoted 'human equality, freedom, human potential and acceptance of non-Muslims'.[26] A pluralistic approach to truth is not the only characteristic common to Garin's and Abdugafurov's humanism; another is that humanism is embedded in a specific religion. Just as Pico's humanism is steeped in Christianity, al-Jīlī's humanism 'is tightly knitted to the Prophet Muhammad' and stems from the Qur'an.[27]

We can grasp the dimensions of Garin's humanism in the ideas and practices of the 'Alāwiyya and Būdshīshiyya brotherhoods in the European context. For Būdshīshīs and 'Alāwīs, this 'humanist engagement' is not contrary to orthodoxy. Their humanist discourse is not a forgotten golden past, as Arkoun[28] argues, but rather the expression of Islamic tradition. At times, this implies a re-imagination of history to promote these universalist ideals, as we have seen. Likewise, we have seen that this humanist discourse thrives on narratives concerning ecology, human rights, the importance of women, democracy and, especially, natural and human sciences. Moreover, this humanism is influenced by the daily lives of European masters and disciples.

Islamic Humanism: Another Reformist Project?

Readers who are familiar with the history of Islamic reformism, especially in the work of Muḥammad 'Abduh (1849–1905), Maḥmūd Muḥammad Ṭāhā (1909–85) and Naṣr Ḥāmid Abū Zayd (1943–2010), will undoubtedly

[24] Badawi, 'L'Humanisme dans la pensée arabe'; Abdugafurov, 'Soteriology in 'Abd al-Karīm al-Jīlī's Islamic Humanism'.

[25] Ahmed, *What Is Islam?*, 223.

[26] Abdugafurov, 'Soteriology in 'Abd al-Karīm al-Jīlī's Islamic Humanism', 115.

[27] Abdugafurov, 'Soteriology in 'Abd al-Karīm al-Jīlī's Islamic Humanism', 119.

[28] Arkoun, *Humanisme et islam*.

notice the continuity between the humanist discourse presented here and the Islamic reformism of the aforementioned authors. I am referring to epistemological hybridity, which merges social sciences, Qur'anic exegesis, universalist discourse on religious truth and gender equality. ʿAbduh, in particular, developed the idea of a 'Muslim humanism' characterised by a sense of social responsibility and a rationalist, historical approach to religion. According to ʿAbduh, humanism was able to challenge the rigidity of Islamic traditional forms, playing a role in reforming religious teaching.[29]

Despite these common threads, there are also some discontinuities, especially as regards the conceptualisation of rationality. We have seen that the humanist discourse of the ʿAlāwiyya and the Būdshīshiyya emphasises the equilibrium between rationality and intuition, between rationalist analysis and metaphysics. But the most significant difference concerns the idea of reform. In effect, these Sufis are not proposing a reform of Islam, which would remain within the framework of exterior forms, leaving the core untouched.[30] According to Geoffroy, Muslims do not need a reformation; they need to focus on the interior and spiritual dimension of Islam, implying a 'revolution of meaning'.[31] Hence, these Sufis do not challenge the Islamic 'tradition' and Maliki *fiqh* in which they are embedded, but they do reformulate some aspects, emphasising spiritual comprehension, freedom and responsibility, without questioning the whole structure of tradition and *fiqh*.

One could argue that this approach is reformist in its essence – another reformist strategy – even if it does not call for reform. That said, the absence of a clear, coherent reformist programme suggests something different: an approach that encourages pluralistic discussion instead of monistic understanding. The former is part of Islamic history, since in Islam, 'the ethics of disagreement' (*l'éthique du désaccord*) has flourished.[32] Again, the vagueness, porosity and ambiguity of the humanist discourse represent both a strength and a weakness. There is no normative programme to follow, creating competing views, but at the same time this opens the door to debate.

[29] Vatikiotis, 'Muḥammad ʿAbduh and the Quest for a Muslim Humanism'.

[30] Geoffroy, *L'islam sera spirituel ou ne sera plus*, 87.

[31] Geoffroy, *L'islam sera spirituel ou ne sera plus*, 85.

[32] Geoffroy, *L'islam sera spirituel ou ne sera plus*, 54.

A Universalist Discourse Among Others

This Islamic humanism highlights the diffuse European ethnocentric prejudice that exists among researchers and others and that holds that all forms of universalism are European. On the contrary, universalist narratives are not a novelty in the history of Islam. Thus, the discourses of Bentounes and Skali are neither the first nor the last Islamic attempt to think about otherness.

Consequently, it is possible to say that the universalist discourse, be it esoteric, New Age, humanist, democratic or socialist, is only one way to think about and approach otherness, in the name of a political and/or religious project. That said, each universalist discourse also excludes some subjects, thereby constructing another alterity. In this way, each universalist discourse sets limits.

In like manner, we have seen that Guénonian universalism works towards interfaith dialogue with Christians and Jews but erects in parallel new walls against religious 'innovations'. Similarly, we have seen that New Age universalism, which conceptualises a scattered truth in all phenomena, at times entails a turning inward and a lack of interest in otherness, or a laying claim to a superior vision, due to the imminent end of the world. Even Islamic humanism, as described in the French Alāwiyya, the Būdshīshiyya and the Naqshbandiyya, at times excludes some, namely Islamists and Salafists, who are accused of both betraying Islamic tradition and being incapable of facing the challenges of modernity. We have thus arrived at another of this book's knots: the relationship between Sufism and politics in Europe.

Relationship Between Sufism and Politics in Europe

Western and non-Western government institutions are seeking out 'good Muslims' – sometimes Sufis – as opposed to 'Bad Muslims' – often Islamists – to govern the Islamic religious field.[33] As a result, Sufi masters and disciples are called upon to play a role in the public sphere, thereby benefiting from new legitimisation.

Based on my research and the academic literature, it is possible to develop four ideal types of relationships between Sufism and politics: (1) disinterest, (2) control, (3) influence and (4) reconciliation with modernity. The first of

[33] Safi, 'Good Sufi, Bad Muslims'; Philippon, '"Bons Soufis" et "mauvais Islamistes"'.

these denotes the absence of engagement and the lack of interest in politics and society in favour of turning inward. This is the case of the Italian Naqshbandiyya, characterised by communitarian fragmentation, condemnation of a corrupt society, and the fear of/desire for the end of the world. All forms of social engagement are stigmatised and considered pointless.

The second ideal type is the 'domination of modernity', a category borrowed from Paul Heck.[34] The typical example is al-'Adl wa al-Iḥsān movement (Justice and Spirituality), founded by the ex-Būdshīshī *muqaddam* 'Abd al-Salām Yāssīn. This movement is superposed on Islamist groups through opposition to traditional power structures (the king of Morocco) and the principles of secularism and democracy. It also calls for *fiqh*–sharia to be implemented within the Moroccan government. Crossover between Sufism and Islamism is not rare (cf. examples in Indonesia,[35] Egypt[36] and Syria[37]).

The third ideal type is 'the influence on modernity' or 'metapolitics'. Its representatives are Sheikh Hisham Kabbani of the Naqshbandiyya in the United States[38] and Sheikh Yahya Pallavicini of AIS in Italy. Pallavicini and Kabbani share a conservative vision from both a political and a moral standpoint. Democratic values are not considered positive, and even less so Islamic, but instead are the consequences of the progressive advent of the eschatological moment. These sheikhs have presented themselves as representatives of Muslims in their respective countries, at times adopting aggressive attitudes to discredit other Muslim actors. These Sufis aim to guide and influence, even subtly, Italian or American politics, without seeking to dominate modernity, in their opinion a futile fight. As I see it, this engagement can be called 'metapolitical', as it underscores the attempt by the spiritual elite to inspire and/or influence religious and political elites.

The last ideal type is what Heck calls 'reconciliation with modernity',[39] which in this book relates especially to the cases of the 'Alāwiyya and the

[34] Heck, 'The Politics of Sufism', 28.

[35] Howell, 'Sufism and the Indonesian Islamic Revival'.

[36] Luizard, 'Le rôle des confréries soufies dans le système politique égyptien'.

[37] Weismann, *Taste of Modernity*.

[38] Dickson, 'An American Sufism'.

[39] Heck, 'The Politics of Sufism', 28.

Būdshīshiyya; I also use the term 'Islamic humanism'. To a lesser degree, we can see it in the French Naqshbandiyya and in AIS, headed by Yahya Pallavicini and Bruno Guiderdoni. I will dedicate the next section to discussing the political implications of Islamic humanism as a form of reconciliation with modernity.

Islamic Humanism and its Cultural Politics

Unlike 'religious humanism' as described by Azhar Ibrahim,[40] which is characterised by self-referentiality and is mostly an academic phenomenon, Islamic humanism moves towards, or tries to move towards a broader public. As I have explained, this Islamic humanism aims to impact European and North African societies.

From another perspective, this engagement cannot be described as 'Islamist' in the sense that this qualifier implies a strategy generally focused on influence and conquest in legislative activities and by government powers.[41] Rather, it entails a discourse around politics and religion, moral performance[42] or daily politics.[43] In this regard, I consider the category 'post-Islamism' used by Asef Bayat to be more relevant:

> [P]ost-Islamism is neither anti-Islamic nor un-Islamic or secular. Rather it represents an endeavour to fuse religiosity and rights, faith and freedom, Islam and liberty. It is an attempt to turn the underlying principles of Islamism on its head by emphasising rights instead of duties, plurality in place of a singular authoritative voice.[44]

Even if the post-Islamism category may be problematic in other contexts,[45] I consider it particularly effective in this frame, as it describes political engagement as cultural expression and as cultural resistance in everyday life. This religious, cultural and political engagement is implemented through various

40 Ibrahim, 'Contemporary Islamic Thought', 288.

41 Mandaville, *Islam and Politics*.

42 Pinto, 'Mystical Metaphors'.

43 Soares and Osella, 'Islam, Politics, Anthropology', 2.

44 Bayat, *Islam and Democracy*, 19.

45 Cavatorta and Merone, 'Post-Islamism, Ideological Evolution and "La *Tunisianité*"'; Mandaville, *Islam and Politics*, 369–99; Vicini, 'Post-Islamism or Veering Toward Political Modernity?'.

political strategies of negotiation, collaboration and/or co-optation by nation-state powers.

In addition, I consider the 'Islamic humanism' category to be more relevant than the 'progressive' category used by Omid Safi,[46] which criticises power and contradicts the strategies of collaboration with, and/or co-optation by nation-state powers. This is even more true if we use the frame of progressive Islam developed by Farid Esack,[47] who considers anti-imperialism and liberation theology as a basis for progressive Islamic engagement.

Using Saba Mahmood's categories, we can ask whether this type of Islamic humanism is the result of a subjectivity that conforms with the liberal political normativity.[48] Is it an expression of 'secular normativity'?[49] Is it a 'secular religion'? We could add: is it 'secular Sufism'?

The possibility of secular Sufism of course depends on the definition of 'secular'. If we define the privatisation of religion as 'secular', we can affirm that this is not the case, given the participation of these Sufis in North African and European public contexts. Furthermore, Mahmood proposes other criteria for identifying a secular Islam that conforms to American political imperialism, based on a RAND Corporation report.[50] Mahmood asserts that the central issue is not activism for or against certain policies, but rather hermeneutics, insofar as the secular–liberal Muslim understands the Qur'an as a historically determined form of literature without ethical or political value.

The 'secular Muslim' described by Mahmood cannot contradict reason and science. According to these 'secular Muslims', the rigorous practice of rituals, liturgies and norms is considered to result from a 'distorted relationship with religious truth'.[51] Likewise, women who wear headscarves for doctrinal and ethical reasons are deemed victims of a false consciousness.

These criteria cannot be applied to the Sufis described in this book. For them, the Qur'an is the word of God and the Prophet Muhammad the supreme example of piety. Moreover, while we have seen that the discussion between

[46] Safi, *Progressive Muslims*.

[47] Esack, 'Progressive Islam – A Rose by Any Name?', 80.

[48] Mahmood, 'Secularism, Hermeneutics, and Empire', 327.

[49] Mahmood, 'Secularism, Hermeneutics, and Empire', 327.

[50] Benard, *Civil, Democratic Islam*.

[51] Mahmood, 'Secularism, Hermeneutics, and Empire', 342.

sharia and *fiqh* is open and lively, no Sufi described in this frame would call for an Islam without sharia. Finally, religious rituals and norms are considered by these Sufis as crucial for the path of purifying the soul.

It is now clear that secular Islam, as defined by Mahmood, cannot be identified with the Islamic humanism of the ʿAlāwiyya and the Būdshīshiyya. However, grey areas persist, where the border between secular and religious narratives is blurred. For example, we have seen how Sufi intellectuals use social and human sciences in dialogue with Islamic and Sufi hermeneutics: 'The Qur'an is both imminent and transcendent,' Éric Geoffroy explains.[52] It then becomes fundamental to note that the antinomies described by Mahmood – Islam/modernity, norm/freedom, tradition/reform, religious/secular – are not employed by these Sufis because they maintain that *tertium datur est*.

Finally, following on from Mahmood, we could also ask whether this Islamic humanism is the result of politics sponsored by the United States, Europe and North African countries to create a tolerant, moderate and inoffensive Islam. Are the adepts of this Sufism their 'natural allies'?[53] Or is this an 'abstract utopia' incapable of mitigating 'the failures of social and economic government policies' and endemic European racism, as asserted by Jeanette Jouili[54] with regard to the Sufi rapper Abd Al Malik?

The conciliatory approach of the ʿAlāwiyya and the Būdshīshiyya, quietist political positions, concentration on universal values such as love, tolerance, religious pluralism, environmental consciousness and the common good – all these elements that avoid direct confrontation can be read as pious wishes and/or an ineffective political strategy. On the other hand, they can be read as forms of pragmatism, as asserted by Andrea Brigaglia.[55]

Beyond these various possible readings, considering this contemporary Sufism as a false consciousness, an abstract utopia, and a natural ally of secular–liberal imperialism, masking racial and religious discrimination (in Europe) and social injustice (in North Africa),[56] could lead to a sociological or anthropological

[52] Geoffroy, *L'islam sera spirituel ou ne sera plus*, 126.

[53] Mahmood, 'Secularism, Hermeneutics, and Empire', 329.

[54] Jouili, 'Rapping the Republic', 74.

[55] Brigaglia, 'Eurapia: Rap, Sufism and the Arab Qaṣīda in Europe', 109.

[56] Jouili, 'Rapping the Republic', 74.

determinism that focuses on geopolitical tensions but discredits the initiatives of social actors.

Keeping to the field of Marxist theories, other categories might be more effective, like the hegemonic and anti-hegemonic discourses of Antonio Gramsci,[57] which pervade both hegemonic and subordinate classes. As for the condition of subordination, it is not limited to economics or politics, but also concerns gender, ethnicity, culture and religion.[58]

In a complex, globalised world, it is difficult to grasp what is hegemonic and what is counter-hegemonic. Each phenomenon must be considered in its context; generalisation is extremely difficult. In this book I showed that Sufism participates in hegemonic discourses when it is co-opted by the powers of nation states and invalidates protests against social injustice, reducing them to a problem of extremism (cf. Khiari on the February 20 Movement in Morocco). On the other hand, promoting gender equality in Algeria could be read as an anti-hegemonic discourse, opposed to a patriarchal society that is characterised by violence and discrimination (cf. the ʿAlāwiyya in Algeria). Similarly, political engagement in the fight against Islamophobia in Europe could be understood as anti-hegemonic, as could Muslim promotion of citizenship in the Parisian suburbs, where disillusionment with French political institutions is growing (cf. Muslim scouts).

What I wish to highlight here is that these Sufis are at the crux of social tensions concerning religion, secularism, ethnicity and social justice, and that they use and personify both hegemonic and counter-hegemonic discourses. This cannot be reduced to narratives of the 'good Sufi' or the 'domesticated Sufi'. We need a more nuanced perspective, capable of encompassing both religious and secular narratives, and hegemonic and anti-hegemonic discourses.

A Few Comments on the Socio-anthropology of Religions

With this book, I hope to have contributed to clearing the fog that often envelops Sufism and, more generally, phenomena defined as spiritual, mystical and/or esoteric. Beyond the objective of understanding and recognising

57 Buttigieg, 'Subaltern Social Groups in Antonio Gramsci's Prison Notebooks'; Gramsci, *Quaderni del carcere*.

58 Green and Ives, 'Subalternity and Language'.

the various New Age and esoteric discourses, I have tried to help renew the socio-anthropological study of mysticism.

I have shown that mysticism – *scientia experimentalis* – is one of the component dimensions of religious phenomena that focuses on experiential contact with the divine, enables a subtle reading of sacred texts, and implies a degree of linguistic and epistemological porosity. This dimension is expressed through charismatic figures capable of revivifying the religious message. In this frame, the religious norm is not replaced by anomie; on the contrary, *scientia experimentalis* is the *fons et origo* of norms. This dimension cannot exist without *sacra doctrina* – or *doxa* – that is, discursive knowledge that enables linguistic and epistemological stability and reproduces religious authorities, institutions and norms.

The sociology of religions has often focused on *sacra doctrina*, neglecting *scientia experimentalis* because the latter is less visible and harder to study.[59] As Linda Woodhead has argued, this imbalance has often led sociologists to conceptualise a 'real' organised, structured religion as opposed to other forms defined as 'blurry', 'individualistic', 'eclectic' and even 'narcissistic'.[60]

I should add that a socio-anthropology centred exclusively on *sacra doctrina* is not capable of grasping the creative, experiential, and individual dimension and the incessant dynamism of religious phenomena, considering any change as the fruit of exogenous influence (that of other cultural forms: the religious marketplace, post-modernity, and so on). Furthermore, we have seen how Religionist interpretations in the history of religions have reversed this perspective by formalising the mystical dimension as 'true religion'. I consider these two 'analytical imbalances' to be obstacles/prejudices in the study of religious phenomena, and I hope that with this book I have contributed to a more balanced discussion.

Concerning the socio-anthropological field of Islam, throughout the foregoing I have tried to apply two approaches often considered to oppose each other – that is, Talal Asad's approach to 'discursive tradition',[61] focused on sacred texts and religious power and authority, and Samuli Schielke's approach

[59] Luckmann, *The Invisible Religion*.

[60] Woodhead, 'Five Concepts of Religion', 122.

[61] Anjum, 'Islam as a Discursive Tradition'.

to daily practices,[62] as well as Gabriele Marranci's approach to emotions[63] and Amira Mittermaier's approach on dreams and visions.[64]

To combine these two seemingly irreconcilable analyses of Islam, I used Shahab Ahmed's masterpiece, *What is Islam?* Ahmed gives us novel hermeneutic keys for interpreting the history of Islam. Unfortunately, he died prematurely and there has not been an adequate response to his work. I have taken the liberty of developing his categories and making them operational in the socio-anthropology of Islam. We can conceptualise Islam as three symbiotic dimensions: the Text, the Context, and the Pre-Text. The 'Text' concerns the Qur'an and the *ḥadīth* – that is, the discursive production around the sacred texts of Islam in relation to the authorities who interpret them. The 'Context' concerns the cultural, social and religious influences that affect Islam and Muslims. Studying Islam also implies studying other religious and cultural phenomena that contribute to shaping it. Finally, the 'Pre-Text' concerns philosophical reason, emotions, values and practices, which possess a universal value that is difficult to attribute to one religious phenomenon rather than another. Studying Islam, like studying any other religion, also means studying human beings in their universality.

In this book, I have shown how Sufis in Europe (re)produce discursive knowledge around the Islamic tradition, focusing on sacred texts and religious norms and claiming spiritual and epistemological authority (the 'Text'). I have also shown the 'Context' – that is, the importance of European cultural influences (social and human sciences), such as the influence of other religious discourses (Guénonian European esotericism and New Age).[65] Finally, in the discussion of the ecstatic experiences of Sufi disciples, we have seen the 'Pre-Text' as it relates to politics, the common good, social justice and religious pluralism. These elements surpass the borders between religions and touch on universal themes. Ahmed's three dimensions help us understand the 'coherent contradiction'[66] that is Islam.

62 Schielke, 'Second Thoughts about the Anthropology of Islam'.

63 Marranci, *The Anthropology of Islam*.

64 Mittermaier, *Dreams That Matter*.

65 In this regard, we might add other elements of the 'Context' concerning European Sufism, like the immigration process for Maghrebi and African Muslims, which has not been discussed in this book.

66 Ahmed, *What Is Islam?*, 405.

Epilogue

When we analyse Sufism, we must bear in mind that each brotherhood is a microcosm – that is, including or excluding a given brotherhood in this research would have considerably changed my analyses. That said, I have tried to describe major trends within European Sufism. I do not claim to have exhausted the subject; its protean nature makes that impossible. In addition, this book lacks key elements on the question of migration, which has nonetheless been extensively discussed elsewhere. While I focused on France and Italy, it is true that these major trends concern the whole Mediterranean region and even have a global dimension.[67] In fact, we can see the influence of the New Age discourse not only in the West, but in all majority Islamic countries, where it is more or less widespread.

The protean nature of contemporary Sufism in the European frame makes it difficult to use general categories. For example, the 'universalist' category, used by some New Age Sufis[68] as well as many researchers, may be deceptive, as it supposes a single form of universalism, whereas several forms of Islamic and non-Islamic universalism exist. In addition, I do not find the 'neo-Sufism' category used by Sedgwick[69] entirely convincing, first of all because it might lead to confusion with the 'neo-Sufism' described in the sixteenth century,[70] and secondly because in fact, the new dimension is not entirely new. In history, religious movements have appeared in which Sufi rituals and doctrines were practised without conversion to Islam. Such was the case with the movement of Abraham ibn Musa Maimonides (1186–1237),[71] son of the famous Jewish philosopher, and in some Hindu branches of the Naqshbandiyya.[72]

Moreover, we have seen that Sufism influenced by the Guénonian esoteric discourse and Sufism influenced by the New Age discourse are so different that it would be problematic to place them in one and the same category. For

[67] Piraino and Sedgwick, *Global Sufism*.

[68] Geaves, 'Sufism in the West'.

[69] Bennett, *Witness*.

[70] O'Fahey and Radtke, 'Neo-Sufism Reconsidered'.

[71] Fenton, 'Some Judaeo-Arabic Fragments by Rabbi Abrahm He-Hasīd, the Jewish Sufi'.

[72] Dahnhardt, *Change and Continuity in Indian Sufism*; Boivin, *The Hindu Sufis of South Asia*.

all these reasons, rather than speaking of universalist Sufism or of neo-Sufism, I prefer to describe the interactions between Sufism and the various discourses that exist in the European context.

In this book, I have shown that, far from representing an archaic past, Sufis play a central role in culture, art, politics and, of course, in the Islamic religion. This is not obvious in all cases, given that Sufis do not always identify as Sufis, but often as Muslims instead.

I hope I have contributed to deconstructing 'presentism' in this book, that is, the tendency to forget historic depth by considering each phenomenon as new and as the product of contemporary society. I also hope to have made the continuities and discontinuities with historical Sufism apparent, even regarding its characteristic creativity and epistemological instability.

Finally, I hope I have contributed to deconstructing some of the stereotypes about Sufism. We have seen that Sufism is not a 'light' or 'domesticated' Islam, instead requiring practices and non-negligible individual and collective discipline. Regarding the supposed necessity of reforming Islam, often discussed by politicians and journalists, particularly in France, it is important to note that, among the Sufis I met during my research, those most open to otherness and dialogue seemed to be the most assiduous and 'orthodox' practitioners, often of Maghrebi origin. This calls into question the widespread stereotype whereby intense religious–Islamic practice implies a form of fundamentalism, and inversely, moderate religious–Islamic practice implies an openness to alterity. On the contrary, anti-modernist, anti-Western and anti-democratic narratives come from New Age and esoteric milieus, made up of European converts. In other words, they come from Europe itself.

BIBLIOGRAPHY

Abd Al Malik. *Le dernier Français*. Paris: Éd. Points, 2013.

______. *L'Islam au secours de la République*. Paris: Flammarion, 2013.

______. *Place de la République: pour une spiritualité laïque*. Montpellier: Indigène éditions, 2015.

______. *Qu'Allah bénisse la France!* Paris: A. Michel, 2007.

Abdel Haleem, M. A. S., trans. *The Qur'an*. Oxford: Oxford University Press: 2010.

Abdugafurov, Rahimjon. 'Soteriology in 'Abd al-Karīm al-Jīlī's Islamic Humanism'. *Journal of Islamic and Muslim Studies* 4, no. 2 (2019): 114–21.

Abenante, Paola. 'Essentializing Difference: Text, Knowledge, and Ritual Performance in a Sufi Brotherhood in Italy'. In *Performing Religion: Actors, Contexts, and Texts. Case Studies on Islam*, edited by Ines Weinrich, 219–34. Beirut: Ergon-Verlag, 2016.

______. 'La Tariqa Burhaniyya, una via dell'Islam in Italia'. *Afriche e Orienti* 3 (2004): 163–71.

Accart, Xavier. *Guénon ou le renversement des clartés: influence d'un métaphysicien sur la vie littéraire et intellectuelle française (1920–1970)*. Milan: Arché, 2005.

Acquaviva, Sabino Samele. *L'eclissi del sacro nella civiltà industriale: dissacrazione e secolarizzazione nella società industriale e postindustriale*. Milan: Edizioni di Comunità, 1966.

Agamben, Giorgio. *Altissima Povertà. Regola e forma di vita nel monachesimo*. Vicenza: Neri Pozza, 2011.

Ahmed, Shahab. *What Is Islam? The Importance of Being Islamic*. Princeton: Princeton University Press, 2015.

Alam, Muzaffar. *Languages of Political Islam in India 1200–1800*. Chicago: University of Chicago Press, 2004.

Al-ʿAlawī, Aḥmad ibn Muṣṭafā. *L'Arbre aux secrets*. Beirut: Albouraq, 1984.

______. *Extraits du Dīwān*. Paris-Drancy: Les Amis de l'Islam, 1984.

______. *Lettre ouverte à ceux qui critiquent le soufisme*. Paris: Entrelacs, 2011.

Alessandrini, Anthony C. 'Humanism in Question: Fanon and Said'. In *A Companion to Postcolonial Studies*, edited by Henry Schwarz and Sangeeta Ray, 431–50. Malden: Wiley-Blackwell, 2000.

Allievi, Stefano. *I nuovi musulmani: i convertiti all'islam*. Roma: Edizioni Lavoro, 1999.

Anjum, Ovamir. 'Islam as a Discursive Tradition: Talal Asad and His Interlocutors'. *Comparative Studies of South Asia, Africa and the Middle East* 27, no. 3 (2007): 656–72. <https://doi.org/10.1215/1089201x-2007-041> (last accessed 15 November 2023).

Arberry, A. J. *Sufism: An Account of the Mystics of Islam*. New York: Routledge, 2008.

Arkoun, Mohammed. *Histoire de l'islam et des musulmans en France du Moyen Âge à nos jours*. Paris: Albin Michel, 2006.

______. *Humanisme et islam: combats et propositions*. Paris: Librairie philosophique J. Vrin, 2014.

Asad, Talal. 'The Concept of Cultural Translation in British Social Anthropology'. In *Writing Culture: The Poetics and Politics of Ethnography*, edited by George E. Marcus and James Clifford, 141–64. Berkeley: University of California Press, 1986.

______. *Genealogies of Religion: Discipline and Reasons of Power in Christianity and Islam*. Baltimore: Johns Hopkins University Press, 1993.

Asprem, Egil. 'Beyond the West Towards a New Comparativism in the Study of Esotericism'. *Correspondances* 2, no. 1 (2014): 3–33.

Asprem, Egil and Asbjørn Dyrendal. 'Close Companions? Esotericism and Conspiracy Theories'. In *Handbook of Conspiracy Theory and Contemporary Religion*, edited by Asbjørn Dyrendal, David G Robertson and Egil Asprem, 207–33. Leiden: Brill, 2018.

Aupers, Stef and Dick Houtman. 'Beyond the Spiritual Supermarket: The Social and Public Significance of New Age Spirituality'. *Journal of Contemporary Religion* 21, no. 2 (2006): 201–22.

Badawi, Abdurrahmân. 'L'Humanisme dans la pensée arabe'. *Studia Islamica* 6 (1956): 67–100.

Bahloul, Kahina. *Mon Islam ma liberté*. Paris: Albin Michel, 2021.

Bainbridge, William Sims and Rodney Stark. 'Client and Audience Cults in America'. *Sociological Analysis* 41, no. 3 (1980): 199–214.

Bakhtin, M. Michael. *The Dialogic Imagination: Four Essays*. Austin: University of Texas Press, 1981.

Baldini, Massimo. *Il linguaggio dei mistici*. Venice: Edizione Queriniana, 1986.

Barks, Coleman. *Rumi: The Big Red Book: The Great Masterpiece Celebrating Mystical Love and Friendship*. New York: Harper Collins, 2010.

Barone, Francesco. 'Islām in Sicilia Nel XII e XIII Secolo: Ortoprassi, Scienze Religiose e Tasawwuf'. *Incontri Mediterranei. Rivista Semestrale Di Storia e Cultura* 6, no. 2 (2003): 104–15.

Basset, Jean-Claude. 'Henry Corbin: philosophe de la religion'. *Revue de Théologie et de Philosophie* 117 (1985): 17–31. <https://doi.org/10.5169/SEALS-381282> (last accessed 15 November 2023).

Bastide, Roger. *Les amériques noires: les civilisations africaines dans le nouveau monde*. Paris: Payot, 1967.

Bava, Sophie. 'Reconversions et nouveaux mondes commerciaux des Mourides à Marseille'. *Hommes & Migrations* 1224, no. 1 (2000): 46–55.

Bayat, Asef. 'Islam and Democracy: What Is the Real Question?' *Isim Papers, Volume 8*. Amsterdam: Amsterdam University Press, 2007.

Belal, Youssef. 'Mystique et politique chez Abdessalam Yassine et ses adeptes'. *Archives de sciences sociales des religions* 135 (2006): 165–84. <https://doi.org/10.4000/assr.3790> (last accessed 15 November 2023).

Ben Driss, Karim. *Sidi Hamza al-Qâdiri Boudchich: le renouveau du soufisme (au Maroc)*. Beirut and Milan: Albouraq and Archè, 2002.

Benard, Cheryl. *Civil, Democratic Islam: Partners, Resources, and Strategies*. Santa Monica: Rand, 2004.

Bennett, John G. *Gurdjieff: A Very Great Enigma*. London: Turnstone Books, 1969.

______. *Gurdjieff: Making a New World*. New York: Harper & Row, 1973.

______. *Witness: The Autobiography of John G. Bennett*. London: Turnstone Books, 1975.

Bentounes, 'Adda. 'Editorial'. *Les Amis de L'Islam* 2 (1982): 2–14.

Bentounes, Khaled. *La fraternité en héritage: histoire d'une confrérie soufie*. Paris: Albin Michel, 2009.

______. *Le soufisme, cœur de l'Islam*. Paris: La Table ronde, 1996.

______. *Soufisme l'héritage commun: centenaire de la voie soufie 'Alâwiyya, 1909–2009*. Alger: Zaki Bouzid Editions, 2009.

______. *Thérapie de l'âme*. Paris: Albin Michel, 2011.

Berger, Peter L. *The Sacred Canopy: Elements of a Sociological Theory of Religion*. Garden City, NY: Doubleday, 1967.

Bergson, Henri. *Les deux sources de la morale et de la religion*. Paris: Flammarion, 2012.

Berque, Augustin. 'Un mystique moderniste: le Cheikh Benalioua'. *Revue Africaine* 79, no. 2 (1936): 688–776.

Bidar, Abdennour. *Comment sortir de la religion*. Paris: La Découverte, 2012.

______. *Un islam pour notre temps*. Paris: Points, 2004.

______. *Self islam: histoire d'un islam personnel*. Paris: Seuil, 2016.

Bigliardi, Stefano. 'The Contemporary Debate on the Harmony between Islam and Science: Emergence and Challenges of a New Generation'. *Social Epistemology* 28, no. 2 (2014): 167–86.

Bisson, David. *René Guénon: une politique de l'esprit*. Paris: Pierre-Guillaume de Roux, 2013.

______. 'Soufisme et tradition. L'influence de René Guénon sur l'islam soufi européen'. *Archives de Sciences Sociales des Religions* 140 (2007): 29–47.

Boissevain, Katia and Cyril Isnart. 'Tourisme, patrimoine et religions en Méditerranée. Usages culturels du religieux dans le catholicisme et l'islam contemporains (Europe Du Sud-Maghreb)'. *Mélanges de l'École Française de Rome-Italie et Méditerranée Modernes et Contemporaines* 129 (2017). <https://journals.openedition.org/mefrim/3423> (last accessed 17 November 2023).

Boivin, Michel. *The Hindu Sufis of South Asia: Partition, Shrine Culture and the Sindhis in India*. London: Bloomsbury, 2019.

Bombardieri, Maria. *Moschee d'Italia: il diritto al luogo di culto, il dibattito sociale e politico*. Bologna: EMI, 2011.

Bonaccorso, Giorgio. *La liturgia e la fede: la teologia e l'antropologia del rito*. Padua: Messaggero, 2005.

______. *Il Tempo come segno: vigilanza, testimonianza e silenzio*. Bologna: EBD, 2004.

Bouamrane, Chikh and Louis Gardet. *Panorama de la pensée islamique*. Paris: Sinbad, 1984.

Bourderionnet, Olivier. 'A "Picture-perfect" Banlieue Artist: Abd Al Malik or the Perils of a Conciliatory Rap Discourse'. *French Cultural Studies* 22, no. 2 (2011): 151–61.

Bourdieu, Pierre. *La distinction: critique sociale du jugement*. Paris: Les éditions de minuit, 1979.

Bouyer, Louis. 'Mysticism: An Essay on the History of the Word'. In *Understanding Mysticism*, edited by Richard Woods, 42–55. London: Athlone Press, 1980.

Böwering, Gerhard. 'Régles et rituels soufis'. In *Les Voies d'Allah. Les ordres mystiques dans le monde musulman des origines à aujourd'hui*, edited by Alexandre Popovic and Gilles Veinstein, 139–56. Paris: Fayard, 1996.

Böwering, Gerhard and Yousef Casewit. *A Qur'ān Commentary by Ibn Barrajān of Seville (d. 536/1141)*. Leiden: Brill, 2015.

Bram, Chen. 'Spirituality under the Shadow of the Conflict: Sufi Circles in Israel'. *Israel Studies Review* 29, no. 2 (2014): 118–39.

Brigaglia, Andrea. 'Eurapia: Rap, Sufism and the Arab Qaṣīda in Europe'. In *Global Sufism. Boundaries, Structures, and Politics*, edited by Francesco Piraino and Mark Sedgwick, 75–91. London: Hurst, 2019.

Brizzi, Salvatore. *Risveglio: con gli esercizi delle Antiche Scuole Esoteriche*. Milan: Anima, 2011.

Brizzi, Salvatore, Burhanuddin Herrmann and Fausto Taiten Guareschi. *Risveglio Metropolitano*. Rimini: GDL Edizioni, 2014.

Bruce, Steve. *God Is Dead: Secularization in the West*. Vol. 3. Oxford: Blackwell Oxford, 2002.

Bruinessen, Martin van. 'Les soufis et le pouvoir Temporel'. In *Les Voies d'Allah: Les ordres mystiques dans le monde musulman des origines aujourd'hui*, edited by Gilles Veinstein and Alexandre Popovic, 242–53. Paris: Fayard, 1996.

van Bruinessen, Martin and Julia Day Howell, eds. *Sufism and the 'Modern' in Islam*. London and New York: I. B. Tauris, 2007.

Burr, Vivien. *Social Constructionism*. London: Routledge, 2015.

Buttigieg, J. A. 'Subaltern Social Groups in Antonio Gramsci's Prison Notebooks'. In *The Political Philosophies of Antonio Gramsci and B. R. Ambedkar: Itineraries of Dalits and Subalterns*, edited by Cosimo Zene, 35–42. New York and London: Routledge, 2013.

Campbell, Colin. 'Clarifying the Cult'. *British Journal of Sociology* 28, no. 3 (1977): 375–88.

Carret, Marcel. 'Dans l'intimité du Cheikh al-Alawi'. In *Cheikh Al Alawi, Documents et témoignages*, edited by Johan Cartigny, 11–31. Paris-Drancy: Les Amis de l'Islam, 1984.

Carrette, Jeremy and Richard King. *Selling Spirituality: The Silent Takeover of Religion*. London, New York: Routledge, 2005.

Cavatorta, Francesco and Fabio Merone. 'Post-Islamism, Ideological Evolution and "La *Tunisianité*" of the Tunisian Islamist Party al-Nahda'. *Journal of Political Ideologies* 20, no. 1 (2015): 27–42. <https://doi.org/10.1080/13569317.2015.991508> (last accessed 15 November 2023).

Certeau, Michel de. *La fable mystique: XVIe-XVIIe siècle*. Paris: Gallimard, 1982.

Certeau, Michel de. *The Mystic Fable: Vol. 1: The Sixteenth and Seventeenth Centuries*, translated by Michael B. Smith. Chicago: University of Chicago Press, 1995.

Champion, Françoise. 'Les sociologues de la post-modernité religieuse et la nébuleuse mystique-ésotérique'. *Archives de Sciences Sociales des Religions* 67, no. 1 (1989): 155–69.

Champion, Françoise and Danièle Hervieu-Léger. *De l'émotion en religion: renouveaux et traditions*. Paris: Centurion, 1990.

Chih, Rachida. 'Shurafā' and Sufis: The Qādiriyya Būdshīshiyya in Contemporary Morocco'. In *Family Portraits with Saints: Hagiography, Sanctity, and Family in the Muslim World*, edited by Catherine Mayeur-Jaouen and Alexandre Papas, 198–221. Berlin: De Gruyter, 2014.

Chittick, William C. *Divine Love: Islamic Literature and the Path to God*. New Haven: Yale University Press, 2013.

______. 'Worship'. In *The Cambridge Companion to Classical Islamic Theology*, edited by Tim Winter, 218–36. Cambridge: Cambridge University Press, 2008.

Christmann, Andreas and Mary Searle-Chatterjee. 'Reclaiming Mysticism: Anti-Orientalism and the Construction of "Islamic Sufism" in Postcolonial Egypt'. In *Religion, Language, and Power*, edited by Nile Green, 67–90. New York: Routledge, 2008.

Chryssides, George D. 'Defining the New Age'. In *Handbook of New Age*, edited by James R. Lewis and Daren Kemp, 1–24. Leiden and Boston: Brill, 2007.

Cirillo, Luigi. *Évangile de Barnabé: recherches sur la composition et l'origine*. Paris: Beauchesne, 1977.

Coelho, Paulo. *L'alchimiste*. Paris: Flammarion, 2017.

______. *Veronika décide de mourir*. Paris: Flammarion, 2014.

Coleman, Simon and John Eade. *Reframing Pilgrimage: Cultures in Motion*. London and New York: Routledge, 2004.

Colli, Giorgio. *La Sapienza Greca. Dioniso, Apollo, Eleusi, Orfeo, Museo, Iperborei, Enigma*. Vol. 1. Milan: Adelphi, 1977.

Collins, Randall. *Interaction Ritual Chains*. Princeton: Princeton University Press, 2014.

Conner, Rhiannon. 'From Amuq to Glastonbury: Situating the Apocalypticism of Shaykh Nazim and the Naqshbandi-Haqqaniyya'. PhD thesis, University of Exeter, 2015.

Copson, Andrew. 'What Is Humanism?' In *The Wiley Blackwell Handbook of Humanism*, edited by Andrew Copson and A. C. Grayling, 1–33. Malden: Wiley-Blackwell, 2015.

Corbin, Henry. *Histoire de la philosophie islamique*. Paris: Gallimard, 1964.

______. *L'homme de lumière dans le soufisme iranien*. Paris: Desclée De Brouwer, 1971.

______. *L'imagination créatrice dans le soufisme d'Ibn Arabi*. Paris: Flammarion, 1977.

______. *Le paradoxe du monotheisme*. Paris: L'Herne, 1981.

Corbin, Henry and Christian Jambet. 'Post-scriptum biographique à un entretien philosophique'. In *Henry Corbin*, edited by Christian Jambet, 38–56. Paris: Herné, 1981.

Cornell, Vincent J. *Realm of the Saint: Power and Authority in Moroccan Sufism.* Austin: University of Texas Press, 1998.

di Corpo, Ulisse and Antonella Vannini. *Caritas/Migrantes: Dossier Statistico Immigrazione*. Roma: Idos, 2011.

Cottin, Sylvie. 'La Tijâniyya Lyonnaise. Une voie dans son temps'. *Archives de Sciences Sociales des Religions* 140 (2007): 69–89.

Cusack, Carole M. 'The Enneagram: G. I. Gurdjieff's Esoteric Symbol'. *Aries* 20, no. 1 (2020): 31–54. <https://doi.org/10.1163/15700593-02001002> (last accessed 15 November 2023).

Dabashi, Hamid. *Being a Muslim in the World*. New York: Palgrave Macmillan, 2013.

Dahnhardt, Thomas. *Change and Continuity in Indian Sufism*. New Delhi: DK Print World, 2002.

Damrel, David W. 'Aspects of the Naqshbandi-Haqqani Order in North America'. In *Sufism in the West*, edited by Jamal Malik and John R Hinnells, 115–26. London and New York: Routledge, 2006.

Desrues, Thierry. 'Mobilizations in a Hybrid Regime: The 20th February Movement and the Moroccan Regime'. *Current Sociology* 61, no. 4 (2013): 409–23. <https://doi.org/10.1177/0011392113479742> (last accessed 15 November 2023).

Dickson, William Rory. 'An American Sufism: The Naqshbandi-Haqqani Order as a Public Religion'. *Studies in Religion/Sciences Religieuses* 43, no. 3 (2014): 411–24.

______. *Living Sufism in North America: Between Tradition and Transformation*. Albany: State University of New York Press, 2016.

Dickson, William Rory and Merin Shobhana Xavier. 'Disordering and Reordering Sufism: North American Sufi Teachers and the Ṭarīqa Model'. In *Global Sufism. Boundaries, Structures, and Politics*, edited by Francesco Piraino and Mark Sedgwick, 137–56. London: Hurst, 2019.

Dieste, Josep Lluís Mateo. 'Sufi Sainthood, Modernity, and Reformism: Sheikh Bin 'Alīwa and the Colonial Maghreb'. In *Saints and Sanctity in Judaism, Christianity, and Islam*, edited by Alexandre Coello de la Rosa and Linda G. Jones, 242–56. London: Routledge, 2020.

Dominguez-Diaz, Marta. 'The One or the Many? Transnational Sufism and Locality in the British Būdshīshiyya'. In *Sufism in Britain*, edited by Ron Geaves and Theodore Gabriel, 111–35. London, New Delhi, New York and Sydney: Bloomsbury, 2013.

______. *Women in Sufism: Female Religiosities in a Transnational Order*. London and New York: Routledge, 2014.

Draper, Ian. 'From Celts to Kaaba: Sufism in Glastonbury'. In *Sufism in Europe and North America*, by David Westerlund, 156–68. London and New York: Routledge, 2004.

Draper, Mustafa. 'Towards a Postmodern Sufism: Eclecticism, Appropriation and Adaptation in a Naqshbandiyya and a Qadiriyya Tariqa in the UK'. PhD thesis, University of Birmingham, 2002.

Durkheim, Émile. *Les formes élémentaires de la vie religieuse: le système totémique en Australie*. Paris: Alcan, 1912.

Ebstein, Steven Michael. *Mysticism and Philosophy in al-Andalus: Ibn Masarra, Ibn al-ʿArabi and the Ismaʿili Tradition*. Leiden and Boston: Brill, 2014.

Eco, Umberto. *The Limits of Interpretation*. Bloomington: Indiana University Press, 1990.

Edwards, Gill. *Stepping into the Magic: A New Approach to Everyday Life*. London: Hachette UK, 1993.

Elahmadi, Mohsine. *Le mouvement Yasiniste*. Mohamadia: Moultaka, 2006.

Elwell-Sutton, L. P. 'Sufism and Pseudo-Sufism'. *Encounter* 5, no. 44 (1975): 9–17.

El-Zein, Amira. *Islam, Arabs, and the Intelligent World of the Jinn*. New York: Syracuse University Press, 2009.

Erdogan, Birsen. *Humanitarian Intervention and the Responsibility to Protect: Turkish Foreign Policy Discourse*. London: Palgrave, 2016.

Esack, Farid. 'Progressive Islam – A Rose by Any Name? American Soft Power in the War for the Hearts and Minds of Muslims'. *ReOrient* 4, no. 1 (2018): 78–106.

Evola, Julius. *Il Cammino del Cinabro*. Milan: Scheiwiller, 1972.

Ewing, Katherine Pratt. *Arguing Sainthood: Modernity, Psychoanalysis, and Islam*. Durham, NC: Duke University Press, 1997.

Fadil, Nadia. 'De la religion aux traditions: quelques réflexions sur l'œuvre de Talal Asad'. *Archives de Sciences Sociales des Religions* 180 (2017): 99–116. <https://doi.org/10.4000/assr.29722> (last accessed 15 November 2023).

Faivre, Antoine. *Accès de l'ésotérisme occidental*. Paris: Gallimard, 1986.

______. *L'ésotérisme*. Paris: Presses universitaires de France, 2012.

______. 'Kocku von Stuckrad et la notion d'ésoterisme'. *Aries* 6, no. 2 (2006): 205–14.

Fallaci, Oriana. *La rabbia e l'orgoglio*. Milan: Bur, 2010.

Fenn, Richard K. *Liturgies and Trials: The Secularization of Religious Language*. New York: Pilgrim Press, 1982.

Fenton, Paul. 'Some Judaeo-Arabic Fragments by Rabbi Abrahm He-Hasīd, the Jewish Sufi'. *Journal of Semitic Studies* 26, no. 1 (1981): 47–72.

Fernández-Morera, Darío. *The Myth of the Andalusian Paradise: Muslims, Christians, and Jews under Islamic Rule in Medieval Spain*. New York: Open Road Media, 2016.

Fernando, Mayanthi L. 'Reconfiguring Freedom: Muslim Piety and the Limits of Secular Law and Public Discourse in France'. *American Ethnologist* 37, no. 1 (2010): 19–35.

Ferrari, Alessandro. *La libertà religiosa in Italia: un percorso incompiuto*. Roma: Carocci, 2012.

Foucault, Michel. *Les mots et les choses. Une archéologie des sciences humaines*. Paris: Gallimard, 1966.

Frisina, Annalisa. *Giovani musulmani d'Italia*. Rome: Carocci, 2007.

Gaborieau, Marc and Nicole Grandin. 'Le renouveau confrérique'. In *Les Voies d'Allah: Les ordres mystiques dans le monde musulman des origines aujourd'hui*, edited by Alexandre Popovic and Gilles Veinstein, 66–86. Paris: Fayard, 1996.

Gaborieauu, Marc. 'Tarîqa et orthodoxie'. In *Les Voies d'Allah: Les ordres mystiques dans le monde musulman des origines aujourd'hui*, edited by Alexandre Popovic and Gilles Veinstein, 195–204. Paris: Fayard, 1996.

Garfinkel, Harold. *Studies in Ethnomethodology*. Hoboken: Prentice-Hall, 1967.

Garin, Eugenio. *L'umanesimo italiano: filosofia e vita civile nel Rinascimento*. Bari: Laterza, 2008.

Geaves, Ron. 'Sufism in the West'. In *The Cambridge Companion to Sufism*, edited by Lloyd Ridgeon, 233–56. Cambridge: Cambridge University Press, 2015.

_______. *The Sufis of Britain: An Exploration of Muslim Identity*. Cardiff: Cardiff Academic Press, 2000.

Geaves, Ron, Markus Dressler and Gritt Maria Klinkhammer, eds. *Sufis in Western Society: Global Networking and Locality*. London and New York: Routledge, 2009.

Geaves, Ron and Theodore P. C. Gabriel, eds. *Sufism in Britain*. New York: Bloomsbury Academic, 2013.

Geertz, Clifford. *Islam Observed: Religious Development in Morocco and Indonesia*. New Haven: Yale University Press, 1968.

Gellner, Ernest. *Muslim Society*. London and New York: Cambridge University Press, 1981.

Geoffroy, Éric. *Allah au féminin*. Paris: Albin Michel, 2020.

_______. *Un éblouissement sans fin : la poésie dans le soufisme*. Paris: Seuil, 2014.

_______. *L'islam sera spirituel ou ne sera plus*. Paris: Seuil, 2009.

_______. *Le soufisme voie intérieure de l'Islam*. Paris: Points, 2009.

_______. 'Les voies d'accès à la réalité dans le soufisme'. In *Science et Religion En Islam*, edited by Abd-al-Haqq Guiderdoni, 179–212. Beirut: Albouraq, 2012.

Giordan, Giuseppe. 'Spirituality: From a Religious Concept to a Sociological Theory'. In *A Sociology of Spirituality*, edited by Peter C. Jupp and Kieran Flangan, 161–80. London: Routledge, 2007.

Godwin, Joscelyn. 'Blavatsky and the First Generation of Theosophy'. In *Handbook of the Theosophical Current*, edited by Mikael Rothstein and Olav Hammer, 13–31. Leiden: Brill, 2013.

Goffman, Erving. *The Presentation of Self in Everyday Life*. Edinburgh: University of Edinburgh Press, 1956.

Goodman, Lenn E. *Islamic Humanism*. Oxford: Oxford University Press on Demand, 2003.

Gramsci, Antonio. *Quaderni del carcere*. Torino: Einaudi, 1975.

Granger, Jean. 'In Mémoriam Henry Corbin'. *Cahiers Verts* 5 (1979): 55–65.

Granholm, Kennet. 'Esoteric Currents as Discursive Complexes'. *Religion* 43, no. 1 (2013): 46–69. <https://doi.org/10.1080/0048721X.2013.742741> (last accessed 15 November 2023).

Green, Marcus E. and Peter Ives. 'Subalternity and Language: Overcoming the Fragmentation of Common Sense'. *Historical Materialism* 17, no. 1 (2009): 3–30.

Green, Nile. *Sufism: A Global History*. Malden, MA: Wiley-Blackwell, 2012.

Griffith, Sidney. 'Sharing the Faith of Abraham: The "Credo" of Louis Massignon'. *Islam and Christian–Muslim Relations* 8, no. 2 (1997): 193–210.

Gril, Denis. 'Doctrine et croyances'. In *Les Voies d'Allah: Les ordres mystiques dans le monde musulman des origines aujourd'hui*, edited by Alexandre Popovic and Gilles Veinstein, 121–38. Paris: Fayard, 1996.

______. 'Les débuts du soufisme'. In *Les Voies d'Allah: Les ordres mystiques dans le monde musulman des origines aujourd'hui*, edited by Alexandre Popovic and Gilles Veinstein, 27–43. Paris: Fayard, 1996.

Guénon, René. *Aperçus sur l'initiation*. Paris: Éditions Traditionnelles, 1946.

______. *Autorité spirituelle et pouvoir temporel*. Paris: J. Vrin, 1929.

______. *La crise du monde moderne*. Paris: Bossard, 1924.

______. *L'erreur spirite*. Paris: Éditions Traditionnelles, 1952.

______. *Initiation et réalisation spirituelle*. Paris: Éditions Traditionnelles, 1952.

______. *Introduction générale à l'étude des doctrines hindoues*. Paris: Marcel Rivière, 1921.

______. *Orient et Occident*. Paris: Payot, 1924.

______. *Le règne de la quantité et les signes du temps*. Paris: Gallimard, 1950.

______. *Le roi du monde*. Paris: Charles Bosse, 1927.

______. *Symboles fondamentaux de la science sacrée*. Paris: Gallimard, 1962.

______. *Le symbolisme de la Croix*. Paris: Éditions Véga, 1970.

Guiderdoni, Abd-al-Haqq. *Science et religion en islam: des musulmans parlent de la science contemporaine*. Beirut: Albouraq, 2012.

Guolo, Renzo. 'L'islam nascosto. Adattamento e trasformazione della religiosità nella confraternita senegalese Muride in Italia'. *Sociologia Urbana e Rurale* 64 (2001): 265–74.

______. *Xenofobi e Xenofili. Gli Italiani e l'islam*. Bari: Laterza, 2003.
Gurdjieff, Georges Ivanovitch. *Meetings with Remarkable Men*. New York: Dutton, 1974.
Habibis, Daphne. 'A Comparative Study of the Workings of a Branch of Naqshbandi Sufi Order in Lebanon and in the UK'. PhD thesis, London School of Economics and Political Science, 1985.
Hackett, Rosalind I. J. 'New Age Trends in Nigeria: Ancestral and/or Alien Religion?' In *Perspectives on the New Age*, edited by James R. Lewis and J. Gordon Melton, 215–31. New York: Suny Press, 1992.
Haenni, Patrick. 'Le centenaire de la confrérie Allaouia: un réformisme postmoderne de l'islam est-il possible?' *Religioscope Etudes et Analyses* 23 (2009): 1–13.
Haenni, Patrick and Raphael Voix. 'God by All Means ... Eclectic Faith and Sufi Resurgence among the Moroccan Bourgeoisie'. In *Sufism and the 'Modern' in Islam*, edited by Martin van Bruinessen and Julia Day Howell, 241–56. London and New York: I. B. Tauris, 2007.
Hakl, Hans Thomas. *Eranos: An Alternative Intellectual History of the Twentieth Century*. Montreal: McGill-Queen's University Press, 2012.
Halbwachs, Maurice. *La mémoire collective*. Paris: Presses universitaires de France, 1950.
Hammer, Olav. 'Deconstructing "Western Esotericism": On Wouter Hanegraaff's *Esotericism and the Academy*'. *Religion* 43, no. 2 (2013): 241–51. <https://doi.org/10.1080/0048721X.2013.767609> (last accessed 15 November 2023).
______. 'Sufism for Westerners'. In *Sufism in Europe and North America*, edited by David Westerlund, 127–43. London and New York: Routledge-Curzon, 2004.
Hanegraaff, Wouter J. *Esotericism and the Academy: Rejected Knowledge in Western Culture*. Cambridge: Cambridge University Press, 2012.
______. 'The Globalization of Esotericism'. *Correspondences* 3, no. 1 (2015): 55–91.
______. 'The New Age Movement and Western Esotericism'. In *Handbook of New Age*, edited by James R. Lewis and Daren Kemp, 25–50. Leiden and Boston: Brill, 2007.
______. *New Age Religion and Western Culture: Esotericism in the Mirror of Secular Thought*. New York: Suny Press, 1998.
______. *Western Esotericism: A Guide for the Perplexed*. London: Bloomsbury, 2013.
Haqqani, Nazim. *Amore*. Warda and Hellenthal: Zero Productions, 2005.
______. *Mercy Oceans (Book Two)*. Nicosia: Spohr Publishers, 2008.
______. *Mercy Oceans' Divine Sources: The Discourses of Our Master Sheikh Nazim al-Qubrusi (Imam ul-Haqqaniyyin)*. Konya: Sebat, 1984.

______. *Natural Medicines*. London: Zero Productions, 1995.

______. *Princess Diana's Death*. London: Zero Productions, 1997.

Hashas, Mohammed. 'Reading Abdennour Bidar: New Pathways for European Islamic Thought'. *Journal of Muslims in Europe* 2, no. 1 (2013): 45–76.

Haviland, Charles. 'The Roar of Rumi – 800 Years On'. *BBC News*, 30 September 2007. <http://news.bbc.co.uk/1/hi/world/south_asia/7016090.stm> (last accessed 15 November 2023).

Heck, Paul. 'The Politics of Sufism: Is There One?' In *Sufism Today: Heritage and Tradition in the Global Community*, edited by Leif Stenberg and Catharina Raudvere, 13–32. London: I. B. Tauris, 2009.

Heelas, Paul. *The New Age Movement: Religion, Culture and Society in the Age of Post-modernity*. Oxford: Blackwell Oxford, 1996.

Hendrick, Joshua D. *Gülen: The Ambiguous Politics of Market Islam in Turkey and the World*. New York: NYU Press, 2013.

Hermansen, Marcia. 'Hybrid Identity Formations in Muslim America'. *Muslim World* 90, no. 1 (2000): 158–98.

______. 'What's American about American Sufi Movements?'. In *Sufism in Europe and North America*, edited by David Westerlund, 40–63. London and New York: Routledge-Curzon, 2004.

Herrmann, Burhanuddin. *Il cammello sul tetto: discorsi sufi: una guida mistico-pratica alla via dei Dervisci*. Milan: Armenia, 2006.

______. *Il derviscio metropolitano: vivere oggi la tradizione Sufi*. Milan: Armenia, 2007.

______. *Il sufismo: mistica, spiritualità e pratica*. Milan: Armenia, 2010.

Hervieu-Léger, Danièle. 'Bricolage vaut-il dissémination? Quelques réflexions sur l'opérationnalité sociologique d'une métaphore problématique'. *Social Compass* 52, no. 3 (2005): 295–308.

______. 'Le partage du croire religieux dans des sociétés d'individus'. *L'Année Sociologique* 60, no. 1 (2010): 41–62.

______. *Le pèlerin et le converti: la religion en mouvement*. Paris: Flammarion, 1999.

______. *La religion en miettes ou la question des sectes*. Paris: Calmann-Lévy, 2001.

______. *La religion pour mémoire*. Paris: Cerf, 1993.

Hervieu-Léger, Danièle and Jean-Paul Willaime. *Sociologies et religion: approches classiques*. Paris: PUF, 2001.

Hessel, Stéphane and Dalaï-Lama. *Déclarons la paix! Pour un progrès de l'esprit*. Montpellier: Indigène éd., 2012.

Hillgarth, Jocelyn Nigel. *Ramon Lull and Lullism in Fourteenth-century France*. Oxford: Clarendon Press, 1971.

Hodgson, Marshall G. S. *The Venture of Islam: Conscience and History in a World Civilization*. Chicago: University of Chicago Press, 1974.

Holbraad, Martin and Morten Axel Pedersen. *The Ontological Turn: An Anthropological Exposition*. Cambridge: Cambridge University Press, 2017.

Holdo, Markus. 'Cooptation and Non-Cooptation: Elite Strategies in Response to Social Protest'. *Social Movement Studies* 18, no. 4 (2019): 444–62. <https://doi.org/10.1080/14742837.2019.1577133> (last accessed 15 November 2023).

Höllinger, Franz. 'Does the Counter-cultural Character of New Age Persist? Investigating Social and Political Attitudes of New Age Followers'. *Journal of Contemporary Religion* 19, no. 3 (2004): 289–309.

Hoover, Jon. *Ibn Taymiyya*. New York: Simon and Schuster, 2019.

Howell, Julia Day. 'Indonesia's Salafist Sufis'. *Modern Asian Studies* 44, no. 5 (2010): 1029–51. <https://doi.org/10.1017/S0026749X09990278> (last accessed 15 November 2023).

______. 'Modernity and Islamic Spirituality in Indonesia's New Sufi Networks'. In *Sufism and the 'Modern' in Islam*, 217–40. London: I. B. Tauris, 2007.

______. 'Sufism and the Indonesian Islamic Revival'. *The Journal of Asian Studies* 60, no. 3 (2001): 701–29.

Hoyt, Sarah F. 'The Etymology of Religion'. *Journal of the American Oriental Society* 32, no. 2 (1912): 126–9.

Al-Hujwīrī. *Kashf-ul-Mahjūb*. London: E. J. W. Gibb Memorial, 2014.

Hussein Mansur al-Hallaj. *Dîwân*. Paris: Seuil, 1992.

Huxley, Aldous. *The Doors of Perception*. New York: Harper & Brothers, 1954.

Ibn 'Arabī. *Les illuminations de la Mecque Futûhât al-Makkiyya*. Paris: Albin Michel, 1988.

______. *L'interprète des désirs: Turjumân al-Ashwâq*. Paris: Albin Michel, 2012.

______. *Le livre des chatons des sagesses*. Beirut: Albouraq, 1997.

Ibrahim, Azhar. 'Contemporary Islamic Thought: A Critical Perspective'. *Islam and Christian–Muslim Relations* 23, no. 3 (2012): 279–94. <https://doi.org/10.1080/09596410.2012.676781> (last accessed 15 November 2023).

Ingram, Brannon. 'René Guénon and the Traditionalist Polemic'. In *Polemical Encounters: Esoteric Discourse and Its Others*, edited by Olav Hammer and Kocku von Stuckrad, 199–226. Leiden: Brill, 2007.

Introvigne, Massimo and PierLuigi Zoccatelli. *New Agen next Age: Una Nuova Religiosità Dagli Anni'60 a Oggi*. Florence: Giunti, 1999.

Irwin, Robert. 'Global Rumi'. In *Global Sufism. Boundaries, Structures, and Politics*, edited by Francesco Piraino and Mark Sedgwick, 15–34. London: Hurst, 2019.

Jambet, Christian. 'Le soufisme entre Louis Massignon et Henry Corbin'. In *Louis Massignon et l'Iran. Travaux et mémoires de l'Institut d'études Iraniennes*, edited by Eve Piérunek and Richard Yann. Leuven and Paris: Peeters, 2000.

James, William. *The Varieties of Religious Experience: A Study in Human Nature: The Gifford Lectures on Natural Religion Delivered at Edinburgh in 1901–1902.* London: Longmans Green and Co, 1902.

Janet, Pierre. *De l'angoisse à l'extase: ètudes sur les croyances et les sentiments*. Paris: F. Alcan, 1926.

Jantzen, Grace M. *Power, Gender and Christian Mysticism*. Cambridge: Cambridge University Press, 2004.

Joassin, Thomas. 'Algerian "Traditional" Islam and Political Sufism'. In *Global Sufism. Boundaries, Structures, and Politics*, edited by Francesco Piraino and Mark Sedgwick, 209–24. London: Hurst, 2019.

Jouili, Jeanette S. 'Rapping the Republic: Utopia, Critique, and Muslim Role Models in Secular France'. *French Politics, Culture & Society* 31, no. 2 (2013): 58–80.

Jung, Carl Gustav. *Collected Works of C. G. Jung, Volume 7: Two Essays in Analytical Psychology*. Princeton: Princeton University Press, 1953.

______. *Psychologie et alchimie*. Paris: Éditions Buchet/Chastel, 1944.

______. *Psychology and Alchemy*. Princeton: Princeton University Press, 1980.

_____. *Reponse à Job*. Paris: Buchet/Chastel, 1964.

Kabbani, Muhammad Hisham. *Classical Islam and the Naqshbandi Sufi Tradition*. Fenton, MI: Islamic Supreme Council of America, 2004.

______. *The Naqshbandi Sufi Tradition Guidebook of Daily Practices and Devotions*. Washington, DC: Islamic Supreme Council of America, 2004.

Kabbani, Muhammad Hisham and Seyyed Hossein Nasr. *The Naqshbandi Sufi Way: History and Guidebook of the Saints of Golden Chain*. Chicago: Kazi, 1995.

Kahn, Joel. *Asia, Modernity and the Pursuit of the Sacred: Gnostics, Scholars, Mystics, and Reformers*. London: Palgrave, 2016.

Karamustafa, Ahmet T. *Sufism, the Formative Period*. Edinburgh: Edinburgh University Press, 2007.

Kars, Aydogan. *Unsaying God: Negative Theology in Medieval Islam*. Oxford: Oxford University Press, 2019.

Keck, Frédéric. 'Le primitif et le mystique chez Lévy-Bruhl, Bergson et Bataille'. *Methodos. Savoirs et Textes* 3 (2003): 1–17.

Kersten, Carool. *Contemporary Thought in the Muslim World: Trends, Themes, and Issues*. London: Routledge, 2019.

Khiari, Bariza. 'Le soufisme et engagement citoyen'. *Nafahat Tarik*, 12 April 2012.

______. *Le soufisme: spiritualité et citoyenneté*. Paris: Fondation pour l'innovation politique, 2015.

King, Richard. *Orientalism and Religion: Postcolonial Theory, India and 'the Mystic East'*. Abingdon and New York: Routledge, 1999.

Knysh, Alexander. 'Historiography of Sufi Studies in the West'. In *A Companion to the History of the Middle East*, edited by Youssef M Choueiri, 106–31. Malden: Blackwell, 2005.

______. *Sufism: A New History of Islamic Mysticism*. Princeton: Princeton University Press, 2017.

______. 'Sufism as an Explanatory Paradigm: The Issue of the Motivations of Sufi Resistance Movements in Western and Russian Scholarship'. *Die Welt Des Islams* 42, no. 2 (2002): 139–73.

Kristeller, Paul Oskar. *Renaissance Thought and Its Sources*. New York: Columbia University Press, 1979.

Lapidus, Ira M. *A History of Islamic Societies*. Cambridge: Cambridge University Press, 1998.

Lassen, Søren Christian. 'Strategies for Concord: The Transformation of Tariqa Burhaniya in the European Environment'. In *Sufism Today: Heritage and Tradition in the Global Community*, 198–209. London and New York: I. B. Tauris, 2009.

Laude, Patrick. *Pathways to an Inner Islam: Massignon, Corbin, Guenon, and Schuon*. Albany: State University of New York Press, 2010.

Laurant, Jean Pierre. *L'ésotérisme chrétien en France au XIXe siècle*. Lausanne: L'Age d'homme, 1993.

Laurant, Jean-Pierre. 'La "non-conversion" de René Guénon (1886–1951)'. In *De la conversion*, edited by Jean-Christophe Attias, 133–9. Paris: Cerf, 1997.

______. *René Guénon: les enjeux d'une lecture*. Paris: Dervy, 2006.

Le Pape, Loïc. 'Engagement religieux, engagements politiques. Conversions dans une confrérie musulmane'. *Archives de Sciences Sociales des Religions* 140, no. octobre-décembre (2007): 9–27.

Lecœur, Erwan, ed. *Dictionnaire de l'extrême droite*. Paris: Larousse, 2007.

Lemonnier, Marie. 'L'islam n'est pas en rupture avec le christianisme'. *L'OBS*, 17 December 2009. <https://www.nouvelobs.com/societe/contre-debat-sur-l-identite-nationale/20091217.OBS1033/l-islam-n-est-pas-en-rupture-avec-le-christianisme.html> (last accessed 15 November 2023).

Lévy-Bruhl, Lucien. *L'expérience mystique et les symboles*. Paris: F. Alcan, 1938.

Lewis, James and Daren Kemp. *Handbook of New Age*. Leiden: Brill, 2007.

Lings, Martin. *A Moslem Saint of the Twentieth Century: Shaikh Aḥmad al-ʿAlawī: His Spiritual Heritage and Legacy*. London: G. Allen & Unwin, 1961.

Lory, Pierre. 'Les ambassadeurs de l'Islam mystique'. In *L'Occident en quête de sens*, edited by Jean-Philippe de Tonnac and Catherine David. Paris: Maisonneuve et Larose, 1996.

______. 'Soufisme et Sciences Occultes'. In *Les Voies d'Allah: Les ordres mystiques dans le monde musulman des origines aujourd'hui*, edited by Alexandre Popovic and Gilles Veinstein, 185–94. Paris: Fayard, 1996.

Löwy, Michael and Erwan Dianteill. *Sociologies et religion. Approches dissidentes*. Paris: PUF, 2005.

Luckmann, Thomas. *The Invisible Religion: The Problem of Religion in Modern Society*. London: MacMillan, 1967.

Luizard, Pierre-Jean. 'Le rôle des confréries soufies dans le système politique égyptien'. *Monde Arabe: Maghreb Machrek* 131 (1991): 26–53.

Luther, Martin. *On the Babylonian Captivity of the Church*. Washington, DC: Fortress Press, 1520.

Lyon, David. *Jesus in Disneyland: Religion in Postmodern Times*. Oxford: Polity, 2000.

MacIntyre, Alasdair C. *Whose Justice? Which Rationality?* London: Duckworth, 1988.

Mahmood, Saba. 'Secularism, Hermeneutics, and Empire: The Politics of Islamic Reformation'. *Public Culture* 18, no. 2 (2006): 323–47.

Makdisi, George. *Rise of Humanism in Classical Islam and the Christian West*. Edinburgh: Edinburgh University Press, 1990.

Mandaville, Peter. *Islam and Politics*. London and New York: Routledge, 2014.

Marchi, Alessandra. 'Il sufismo in Italia: molteplici cie per civere l'Islam'. *Religioni e Società* 65 (2009): 53–60.

Marchisio, Roberto. *Sociologia delle forme religiose*. Rome: Carocci, 2000.

Marranci, Gabriele. *The Anthropology of Islam*. Oxford: Berg, 2008.

Martin, David A. 'The Denomination'. *The British Journal of Sociology* 13, no. 1 (1962): 1–14.

Mary, André. 'En finir avec le bricolage . . .?' *Archives de Sciences Sociales des Religions* 116 (2001): 27–30. <https://doi.org/10.4000/assr.494> (last accessed 15 November).

Massignon, Louis. *Sur l'Islam*. Paris: Herné, 1995.

______. *Les trois prières d'Abraham*. Paris: Cerf, 1997.

McGuire, Meredith B. *Lived Religion: Faith and Practice in Everyday Life*. Oxford and New York: Oxford University Press, 2008.

Mériboute, Zidane. *La fracture islamique: demain, le soufisme?* Paris: Fayard, 2004.

Milani, Milad and Adam Possamai. 'Sufism, Spirituality and Consumerism: The Case Study of the Nimatullahiya and Naqshbandiya Sufi Orders in Australia'. *Contemporary Islam* 10, no. 1 (2016): 67–85. <https://doi.org/10.1007/s11562-015-0335-1> (last accesed 15 November 2023).

Mittermaier, Amira. *Dreams That Matter*. Berkeley: University of California Press, 2010.

Moberg, Marcus. 'First-, Second-, and Third-level Discourse Analytic Approaches in the Study of Religion: Moving from Meta-theoretical Reflection to Implementation in Practice'. *Religion* 43, no. 1 (2013): 4–25. <https://doi.org/10.1080/0048721X.2013.742742> (last accessed 15 November 2023).

Moncelon, Jean. 'La foi de Henry Corbin: "Terre-Ange-Femme"'. *Les Cahiers d'Orient et Occident* (2004): 1–7.

______. 'Sous le signe d'Abraham: Louis Massignon, l'ami de Dieu, Khalil Allâh'. PhD thesis, Université Paris 10, 1990.

Moore, James. 'Neo-Sufism: The Case of Idries Shah'. *Journal of Contemporary Religion* 3, no. 3 (1986): 4–8.

Morin, Edgar. *La méthode*. Vol. 4. Paris: Seuil, 1991.

Mosès, Stéphane. *L'ange de l'histoire: Rosenzweig, Benjamin, Scholem*. Paris: Gallimard, 1992.

Mouna, Khalid and Abdelaziz Hlaoua. 'Du corps incarné au corps identitaire'. In *Penser le corps au Maghreb*, edited by Mona Lacheb, 21–33. Paris: Khartala, 2012.

Muedini, Fait. 'The Promotion of Sufi Sm in the Politics of Algeria and Morocco'. *Islamic Africa* 3, no. 2 (2012): 201–26.

______. *Sponsoring Sufism: How Governments Promote 'Mystical Islam' in Their Domestic and Foreign Policies*. New York: Palgrave Macmillan, 2015.

______. 'Sufism, Politics, and the Arab Spring'. *American Journal of Islamic Social Sciences* 29, no. 3 (2012): 23–41.

Nabti, Mehdi. 'Des soufis en banlieue parisienne. Mise en scène d'une spiritualité musulmane'. *Archives de Sciences Sociales des Religions* 140 (2007): 49–68.

Nesti, Arnaldo. 'Da partigiano monarchico durante la Resistenza all'opzione monoteista islamica. Un'intervista Allo Shaykh Abd al Wahid Pallavicini'. *Religioni e Società* 65 (2009): 95–108.

Nielsen, Jørgen S, Mustafa Draper and Galina Yemelianova. 'Transnational Sufism: The Haqqaniyya'. In *Sufism in the West*, edited by Jamal Malik and John R Hinnells, 103–14. London and New York: Routledge, 2006.

Nietzsche, Friedrich. *Généalogie de la morale*. Paris: Flammarion, 1877.

Nietzsche, Friedrich. *On the Genealogy of Morality*. New York: Russell & Russell, 1964.

O'Fahey, Rex S. and Bernd Radtke. 'Neo-Sufism Reconsidered'. *Der Islam: Zeitschrift für Geschichte und Kultur des Islamischen Orients* 70 (1993): 52.

Ornstein, Robert E. *The Psychology of Consciousness*. New York: Harcourt Brace, 1972.

Otto, Rudolf. *Mysticism East and West: A Comparative Analysis of the Nature of Mysticism*. New York: The Macmillan Co., 1932.

Ouspensky, Pyotr. *The Fourth Way*. New York: Knopf, 1957.

______. *In Search of the Miraculous Fragments of an Unknown Teaching*. New York: Ishi Press, 2011.

Ozment, Steven E. *Mysticism and Dissent: Religious Ideology and Social Protest in the Sixteenth Century*. New Haven: Yale University Press, 1973.

Pace, Enzo. *Raccontare Dio: la religione come comunicazione*. Bologna: Il mulino, 2008.

Palacios, Miguel Asín. *La escatología Musulmana en la Divina Comedia*. Madrid: E. Maestre, 1919.

Pallavicini, 'Abd al-Wahid. *In Memoriam René Guénon*. Milan: Archè, 1981.

______. *L'islam intérieur: message d'un maître soufi*. Paris: Bartillat, 2013.

______. *A Sufi Master's Message*. Louisville, KY: Fons Vitae, 2011.

Pallavicini, Yahya Sergio. *Dentro la moschea*. Milan: Rizzoli, 2007.

______. *L' islâm in Europa: riflessioni di un imâm italiano*. Milan: Il Saggiatore, 2004.

Palmer, Edward Henry. *Oriental Mysticism: A Treatise on Sufistic and Unitarian Theosophy of the Persians*. London: Routledge, 2013.

Pasi, Marco. 'The Problems of Rejected Knowledge: Thoughts on Wouter Hanegraaff's *Esotericism and the Academy*'. *Religion* 43, no. 2 (2013): 201–12. <https://doi.org/10.1080/0048721X.2013.767611> (last accessed 15 November 2023).

Pénicaud, Manoël. *Louis Massignon: Le 'Catholique Musulman'*. Paris: Bayard, 2019.

Penner, Hans. 'The Mystical Illusion'. In *Mysticism and Religious Traditions*, by Steven T. Katz, 109–16. Oxford: Oxford University Press, 1985.

Pétrarque, François. *Lettres familières: Tome III: Livres VIII–XI*. Paris: Les belles lettres, 1374.

Pfleiderer, Otto. *Religion and Historic Faiths*. London: Fisher Unwin, 1907.

Philippon, Alix. '"Bons Soufis" et "mauvais Islamistes". La sociologie à l'épreuve de l'idéologie'. *Social Compass* 62, no. 2 (2015): 187–98.

______. 'De l'occidentalisation du soufisme à la réislamisation du New Age? Sufi Order International et la globalisation du religieux'. *Revue des Mondes Musulmans et de la Méditerranée* 135 (2014): 209–26.

Pico della Mirandola, Giovanni. *Oration on the Dignity of Man*. Chicago: Gateway Edition, 1956.

Pinto, Paulo G. 'Mystical Metaphors: Ritual, Symbols and Self in Syrian Sufism'. *Culture and Religion* 18, no. 2 (2017): 90–109. <https://doi.org/10.1080/14755610.2017.1326957> (last accessed 15 November 2023).

Piraino, Francesco. 'Between Real and Virtual Communities: Sufism in Western Societies and the Naqshbandi Haqqani Case'. *Social Compass* 63, no. 1 (2016): 93–108.

______. 'Bruno Guiderdoni – Among Sufism, Traditionalism and Science: A Reply to Bigliardi'. *Social Epistemology* 3, no. 11 (2014): 21–4.

______. 'Entrare nel sé divino: un confronto etnografico comparato, tra mistica cristiana e mistica musulmana in Italia'. *Religioni e Società* 71, no. 71 (2011): 97–105.

______. 'Esotericisation and De-esotericisation of Sufism: The Aḥmadiyya-Idrīsiyya Shādhiliyya in Italy'. *Correspondences* 7, no. 1 (2019): 239–76.

______. 'L'héritage de René Guénon dans le soufisme du XXIe siècle en France et en Italie'. *Religiologiques* 33, no. printemps (2016): 155–80.

______. '"Islamic Humanism": Another Form of Universalism in Contemporary Sufism'. *Religion*, 53, no. 2 (2022): 246–68.

______. 'Pilgrimages in Western European Sufism'. In *Muslim Pilgrimage in Europe*, edited by Ingvild Flaskerud and Richard Natvig, 157–69. London and New York: Routledge, 2017.

______. 'Les politiques du soufisme en France: le cas de la Qādiriyya Būdshīshiyya'. *Social Compass* 66, no. 1 (2019): 134–46.

______. 'Sufi Festivals as a Social Movement: Spirituality, Aesthetics, and Politics'. *Sociologica* 15, no. 3 (2021): 145–68. <https://doi.org/10.6092/issn.1971-8853/11364> (last accessed 15 November 2023).

______. 'The Sufi Shaykh and His Patients: Merging Islam, Psychoanalysis, and Western Esotericism'. In *Esoteric Transfers and Constructions Judaism, Christianity, and Islam*, by Mark Sedgwick and Francesco Piraino, 195–218. London: Palgrave, 2021.

______. 'Sufism Meets the New Age Discourse: Part 1: A Theoretical Discussion'. *International Journal for the Study of New Religions*, 11, no. 1 (2020): 13–34.

______. 'Sufism Meets the New Age Discourse: Part 2: An Ethnographic Perspective: The Nasqhbandiyya-Haqqaniyya in Italy'. *International Journal for the Study of New Religions* 11, no. 2 (2020): 235–56.

______. 'Who Is the Infidel? Religious Boundaries and Social Change in the Shadhiliyya Darqawiyya Alawiyya'. In *Global Sufism. Boundaries, Structures, and Politics*, by Francesco Piraino and Mark Sedgwick, 75–91. London: Hurst, 2019.

Piraino, Francesco and Mark Sedgwick, eds. *Global Sufism. Boundaries, Structures, and Politics*. London: Hurst, 2019.

Piraino, Francesco and Laura Zambelli. 'Queer Muslims in South Africa: Engaging Islamic Tradition'. *Journal for Islamic Studies* 37 (2018): 120–40.

Pittman, Michael. *Classical Spirituality in Contemporary America: The Confluence and Contribution of G. I. Gurdjieff and Sufism*. London: Bloomsbury Academic, 2013.

Plato. *Phaedo*. Cambridge University Press, 1972.

Popovic, Alexandre. 'Les turuq balkaniques à l'épreuve de la modernité'. *Archives de sciences sociales des religions* 135 (2006): 141–63. <https://doi.org/10.4000/assr.3777> (last accessed 15 November 2023).

Porpora, Douglas V. 'Methodological Atheism, Methodological Agnosticism and Religious Experience'. *Journal for the Theory of Social Behaviour* 36, no. 1 (2006): 57–75.

Possamai, Adam. *In Search of New Age Spiritualities*. Aldershot: Ashgate, 2005.

Prandi, Carlo. *La religione popolare fra tradizione e modernità*. Brescia: Queriniana, 2002.

Probst-Biraben, Jean-Henry. 'La Tariqa Alawiyya'. In *Cheikh Al Alawi document et témoignages*, edited by Jihan Cartigny, 79–88. Paris-Drancy: Éditions Les Amis de l'Islam, 1984.

Quinn, Charlotte A. and Frederick Quinn. *Pride, Faith, and Fear: Islam in Sub-Saharan Africa*. Oxford and New York: Oxford University Press, 2003.

Rābiʿa al-ʿAdawiyya. *Les chants de la recluse*. Paris: Arfuyen, 1988.

Rahman, Fazlur. *Islam*. New York: Anchor Books, 1968.

Rambo, Lewis Ray. *Understanding Religious Conversion*. New Haven: Yale University Press, 1993.

Raphael, Melissa. *Rudolf Otto and the Concept of Holiness*. Oxford: Clarendon, 1997.

Reetz, Dietrich. 'Sûfî Spirituality Fires Reformist Zeal: The Tablîghî Jamâʿat in Today's India and Pakistan'. *Archives de sciences sociales des religions* 135 (2006): 33–51. <https://doi.org/10.4000/assr.3715> (last accessed 15 November 2023).

Reichmuth, Stefan. 'Humanism in Islam between Mysticism and Literature'. In *Humanism and Muslim Culture: Historical Heritage and Contemporary Challenges*, by Stefan Reichmuth, Jörn Rüsen and Aladdin Sarhan. Göttingen and Taipei: V&R Unipress and National Taiwan Press, 2012.

Reichmuth, Stefan, Jörn Rüsen and Aladdin Sarhan. *Humanism and Muslim Culture: Historical Heritage and Contemporary Challenges*. Göttingen and Taipei: V&R Unipress and National Taiwan Press, 2012.

Renan, Ernest. *Averroès et l'averroïsme*. Paris: Michel-Lévy frères, 1867.

Reynolds, Gabriel Said. *The Qur'an and Its Biblical Subtext*. Vol. 10. London: Routledge, 2010.

Ribot, Théodule. *La logique des sentiments*. Paris: F. Alcan, 1905.

Riffard, Pierre A. *Nouveau dictionnaire de l'ésotérisme*. Paris: Payot, 2008.

Rindfleish, Jennifer. 'Consuming the Self: New Age Spirituality as "Social Product" in Consumer Society'. *Consumption Markets & Culture* 8, no. 4 (2005): 343–60. <https://doi.org/10.1080/10253860500241930> (last accessed 15 November 2023).

Robbins, Joel. 'Anthropology and Theology: An Awkward Relationship?' *Anthropological Quarterly* 79, no. 2 (2006): 285–94. <https://doi.org/10.1353/anq.2006.0025> (last accessed 15 November 2023).

Rocalve, Pierre. *Louis Massignon et l'islam: place et rôle de l'islam et de l'islamologie dans la vie et l'œuvre de Louis Massignon*. Damascus: Presses de l'Ifpo, 1993.

Rocher, Lisbeth and Fatima Cherquaoui. *D'une doi l'autre: les conversions à l'islam en Occident*. Paris: Seuil, 1986.

Roy, Olivier. *Globalized Islam: The Search for a New Ummah*. New York: Columbia University Press, 2004.

Saccone, Carlo. *I Percorsi dell'Islam: dall'esilio di Ismaele alla rivolta dei nostri giorni*. Padua: Messagero, 2003.

Safi, Omid. 'Good Sufi, Bad Muslims'. *Sightings*, 27 January 2011. <https://tabsir.net/?p=1353> (last accessed 15 November 2023)

______, ed. *Progressive Muslims: On Justice, Gender and Pluralism*. Oxford: Oneworld, 2003.

______. *Radical Love: Teachings from the Islamic Mystical Tradition*. New Haven: Yale University Press, 2018.

Said, Edward. *Orientalism*. New York: Vintage Books, 1978.

Saif, Liana. 'Between Medicine and Magic: Spiritual Aetiology and Therapeutics in Medieval Islam'. In *Demons and Illness from Antiquity to the Early-modern Period*, edited by Siam Bhayro and Catherine Rider, 313–38. Leiden: Brill, 2017.

______. 'What Is Islamic Esotericism?' *Correspondences* 7, no. 1 (2019): 1–59.

Salvatore, Armando. 'Sufi Articulations of Civility, Globality, and Sovereignty'. *Journal of Religious and Political Practice* 4, no. 2 (2018): 156–74.

Schielke, Samuli. 'Second Thoughts about the Anthropology of Islam, or How to Make Sense of Grand Schemes in Everyday Life'. *Berlin: Zentrum Moderner Orient Working Papers* 2 (2010): 1–27.

Schmidt di Friedberg, Ottavia. *Islam, solidarietà e lavoro: i muridi senegalesi in Italia*. Torino: Fondazione Giovanni Agnelli, 2006.

Schmidt, Garbi. 'Sufi Charisma on Internet'. In *Sufism in Europe and North America*, edited by David Westerlund. London and New York: Routledge-Curzon, 2004.

Scholem, Gershom. *On Jews and Judaism in Crisis: Selected Essays*. Berlin: Schocken Books, 1976.

Schöller, Marco. 'Zum Begriff Des "islamischen Humanismus"'. *Zeitschrift Der Deutschen Morgenländischen Gesellschaft* 151, no. 2 (2001): 275–320.

Schuon, Frithjof. *De l'unité transcendante des religions*. Paris: Seuil, 1979.

Sedgwick, Mark. *Against the Modern World: Traditionalism and the Secret Intellectual History of the Twentieth Century*. Oxford and New York: Oxford University Press, 2004.

______. 'The Islamization of Western Sufism after the Early New Age'. In *Global Sufism. Boundaries, Structures, and Politics*, edited by Francesco Piraino and Mark Sedgwick, 35–53. London: Hurst, 2019.

______. 'The Making of a Sufi Saint of the Twentieth Century: Shaykh Ahmad al-ʿAlawî (1869–1934)'. *Journal of the History of Sufism/Tasavvuf Tarihi Araştırmaları Dergisi/Journal D'histoire Du Soufisme* 6 (2015): 225–40.

______. 'The Reception of Sufi and Neo-Sufi Literature'. In *Sufis in Western Society: Global Networking and Locality*, edited by Ron Geaves, Markus Dressler and Gritt Maria Klinkhammer, 180–97. London: Routledge, 2009.

______. 'In Search of a Counter-reformation: Anti-Sufi Stereotypes and the Budshishiyya's Response'. In *An Islamic Reformation*, edited by Michaelle Browers and Charles Kurzman, 125–46. Oxford: Lexington Books, 2004.

______. 'Sufism and the Enneagram'. In *Esoteric Transfers and Constructions Judaism, Christianity, and Islam*, edited by Mark Sedgwick and Francesco Piraino, 219–48. London: Palgrave, 2021.

______. *Western Sufism: From the Abbasids to the New Age*. New York: Oxford University Press, 2016.

Shafak, Elif. *The Bastard of Istanbul*. New York: Viking, 2007.

______. *The Forty Rules of Love*. New York: Penguin, 2011.

______. *Soufi, mon amour*. Paris: Phébus, 2010.

Shaffir, William B. 'Managing a Convincing Self-presentation: Some Personal Reflections on Entering the Field'. In *Experiencing Fieldwork: An Inside View of Qualitative Research*, edited by Robert Stebbins and William B Shaffir, 72–81. Thousand Oaks, CA: Sage, 1991.

Shah, Idries. *The Exploits of the Incomparable Mulla Nasrudin*. London: Octagon Press Ltd, 1966.

______. *Learning How to Learn: Psychology and Spirituality in the Sufi Way*. London: Octagon Press Ltd, 1978.

______. *Oriental Magic*. New York: Philosophical Library, 1957.

______. *The Sufis*. London: W. H. Allen, 1964.

______. *The Way of the Sufi*. New York: Dutton, 1968.

Shaikh, Sa'diyya. *Sufi Narratives of Intimacy: Ibn Arabi, Gender, and Sexuality*. Chapel Hill, NC: University of North Carolina Press, 2012.

Shamdasani, Sonu. *Jung and the Making of Modern Psychology: The Dream of a Science*. Cambridge: Cambridge University Press, 2003.

Shapiro, Roberta. 'Artification as Process'. *Cultural Sociology* 13, no. 3 (2019): 265–75. <https://doi.org/10.1177/1749975519854955> (last accessed 15 November 2023).

Sharify-Funk, Meena, William Rory Dickson and Merin Shobhana Xavier. *Contemporary Sufism: Piety, Politics, and Popular Culture*. Abingdon and New York: Routledge, 2018.

Shayegan, Daryush. *Henry Corbin: Penseur de l'islam Spirituel*. Paris: Albin Michel, 2011.

Shibli, Fatima El. 'Islam and the Blues'. *Souls* 9, no. 2 (2007): 162–70. <https://doi.org/10.1080/10999940701382615> (last accessed 15 November 2023).

Simmel, Georg. *Die Religion*. Frankfurt am Main: Literarische Anstalt Rütten & Loening, 1906.

______. 'The Sociology of Secrecy and of Secret Societies'. *American Journal of Sociology* 11, no. 4 (1906): 441–98.

Skali, Faouzi. *Le souvenir de l'être profond: propos sur l'enseignement du maître soufi Sidi Hamza*. Paris: Relié, 2012.

Faouzi Skali and Eva de Vitray-Meyerovitch, Eva. *Jésus dans la tradition soufie*. Paris: Albin Michel, 2013.

Sluhovsky, Moshe. *Believe Not Every Spirit: Possession, Mysticism, & Discernment in Early Modern Catholicism*. Chicago: University of Chicago Press, 2008.

Soares, Benjamin and Filippo Osella. 'Islam, Politics, Anthropology'. *Journal of the Royal Anthropological Institute* 15 (2009): 1–23.

Sorgenfrei, Simon. 'Hidden or Forbidden, Elected or Rejected: Sufism as "Islamic Esotericism"?' *Islam and Christian–Muslim Relations* 29, no. 2 (2018): 145–65. <https://doi.org/10.1080/09596410.2018.1437945> (last accessed 15 November 2023).

Spadola, Emilio. *The Calls of Islam: Sufis, Islamists, and Mass Mediation in Urban Morocco*. Bloomington: Indiana University Press, 2013.

Speziale, Fabrizio. 'Adapting Mystic Identity to Italian Mainstream Islam: The Case of a Muslim Rom Community in Florence'. *Balkanologie. Revue d'études pluridisciplinaires* 9, nos 1–2 (2005): 195–211.

Stark, Rodney and William Sims Bainbridge. 'Of Churches, Sects, and Cults: Preliminary Concepts for a Theory of Religious Movements'. *Journal for the Scientific Study of Religion* 18, no. 2 (1979): 117–31. <https://doi.org/10.2307/1385935> (last accessed 15 November 2023).

Stausberg, Michael. 'What Is *It* All about? Some Reflections on Wouter Hanegraaff's *Esotericism and the Academy*'. *Religion* 43, no. 2 (2013): 219–30. <https://doi.org/10.1080/0048721X.2013.767612> (last accessed 15 November 2023).

Stjernholm, Simon. 'Lovers of Muhammad'. PhD thesis, University of Lund, 2011.

______. 'Sufi Politics in Britain: The Sufi Muslim Council and the "Silent Majority" of Muslims'. *Journal of Islamic Law and Culture* 12, no. 3 (2010): 215–26.

Stora, Benjamin. *Ils venaient d'Algérie: l'immigration algérienne en France (1912–1992).* Paris: Fayard, 2014.

Stuckrad, Kocku von. 'Ancient Esotericism, Problematic Assumptions, and Conceptual Trouble'. *Aries* 15, no. 1 (2015): 16–20. <https://doi.org/10.1163/15700593-01501004> (last accessed 15 November 2023).

______. 'Esoteric Discourse and the European History of Religion: In Search of a New Interpretational Framework'. *Scripta Instituti Donneriani Aboensis* 20 (2008): 217–36.

______. *Locations of Knowledge in Medieval and Early Modern Europe: Esoteric Discourse and Western Identities*. Leiden: Brill, 2010.

______. 'Western Esotericism: Towards an Integrative Model of Interpretation'. *Religion* 35, no. 2 (2005): 78–97. <https://doi.org/10.1016/j.religion.2005.07.002> (last accessed 15 November 2023).

Suhrawardī. *A Sufi Rule for Novices*. Cambridge, MA: Harvard University Press, 1975.

Al-Sulamī. *Futuwah. Traité de Chevalerie Soufie*. Paris: Albin Michel, 2012.

Sutcliffe, Steven. *Children of the New Age: A History of Spiritual Practices*. London: Routledge, 2003.

Talbi, Yahya. 'Immigration et intégration de la confrérie 'Alawiya en France depuis 1920'. PhD Thesis, EHESS, 1998.

Tigra, Anass. *À la recherche de l'islam perdu*. Saint-Denis: Édilivre, 2018.

Tozy, Mohammed. *Le prince, le clerc et l'Etat: la restructuration du champ religieux au Maroc*. Paris: Seuil, 1990.

Trimingham, J. Spencer. *The Sufi Orders in Islam*. Oxford: Clarendon Press, 1971.

Troeltsch, Ernst. *Die Soziallehren der christlichen Kirchen und Gruppen*. Tübingen: J. C. B. Mohr (Paul Siebeck), 1912.

Turner, Denys. *The Darkness of God: Negativity in Christian Mysticism*. Cambridge: Cambridge University Press, 1998.

Turner, Victor. *Dramas, Fields, and Metaphors: Symbolic Action in Human Society*. Symbol, Myth, and Ritual Series. Ithaca, NY: Cornell University Press, 1974.

______. *Dramas, Fields, and Metaphors: Symbolic Action in Human Society*. Ithaca, NY: Cornell University Press, 1987.

______. *The Ritual Process: Structure and Anti-structure*. Ithaca, NY: Cornell University Press, 1977.

Tweed, Thomas A. 'On Moving Across: Translocative Religion and the Interpreter's Position'. *Journal of the American Academy of Religion* 70, no. 2 (2002): 253–77.

Urban, Hugh. 'Elitism and Esotericism: Strategies of Secrecy and Power in South Indian Tantra and French Freemasonry'. *Numen* 44, no. 1 (1997): 1–38.

______. 'The Torment of Secrecy: Ethical and Epistemological Problems in the Study of Esoteric Traditions'. *History of Religions* 37, no. 3 (1998): 209–48. <https://doi.org/10.1086/463503> (last accessed 15 November 2023).

Vâlsan, Michel. *L'Islam et la fonction de René Guénon*. Paris: Chacornac Frères, 1953.

Vatikiotis, Panayiotis J. 'Muḥammad 'Abduh and the Quest for a Muslim Humanism'. *Arabica* 4 (1957): 55–72.

Veinstein, Gilles and Nathalie Clayer. 'L'empire Ottoman'. In *Les Voies d'Allah: Les ordres mystiques dans le monde musulman des origines aujourd'hui*, edited by Gilles Veinstein and Alexandre Popovic, 322–41. Paris: Fayard, 1996.

Veinstein, Gilles and Alexandre Popovic, eds. *Les Voies d'Allah: Les ordres mystiques dans le monde musulman des origines aujourd'hui*. Paris: Fayard, 1996.

Vicini, Fabio. 'Post-Islamism or Veering Toward Political Modernity?' *Sociology of Islam* 4, no. 3 (2016): 261–79.

de Vitray-Meyerovitch, Eva. *Anthologie du soufisme*. Paris: Albin Michel, 1995.

______. *Universalité de l'Islam*. Paris: Albin Michel, 2015.

de Vitray-Meyerovitch, Eva, Rachel Cartier and Jean-Pierre Cartier. *Islam, l'autre visage*. Paris: Albin Michel, 1995.

Voas, David, and Steve Bruce. 'The Spiritual Revolution: Another False Dawn for the Sacred'. In *A Sociology of Spirituality*, edited by Peter C. Jupp, 43–61. London: Ashgate, 2007.

Voix, Raphael. 'Implantation d'une confrérie marocaine en France: mécanismes, méthodes, et acteurs'. *Ateliers d'anthropologie. Revue Éditée par le Laboratoire d'ethnologie et de sociologie comparative* 28 (2004): 1–54.

de Vos, Philippe. *L'ennéagramme: dans la pratique soufie*. Paris: L'Originel, 2005.

______. *Genèse de la sagesse soufie*. Beirut: Albouraq, 2014.

______. *Sheikh nazim la preuve de la générosité*. Avignon: Éditions du Relié, 1998.

Wach, Joachim. *Sociologie de la religion*. Paris: Payot, 1955.

Wasserstrom, Steven M. *Religion after Religion: Gershom Scholem, Mircea Eliade, and Henry Corbin at Eranos*. Princeton: Princeton University Press, 2001. <http://www.jstor.org/stable/10.2307/j.ctt7pds6> (last accessed 15 November 2023).

Weber, Max. *Economy and Society: An Outline of Interpretive Sociology*. New York: Bedminster Press, 1968.

______. *Sociologie des religions*. Paris: Gallimard, 2006.

Weismann, Itzchak. *Taste of Modernity: Sufism, Salafiyya, and Arabism in Late Ottoman Damascus*. Leiden and Boston: Brill, 2001.

Werbner, Pnina. *Pilgrims of Love: The Anthropology of a Global Sufi Cult*. Bloomington: Indiana University Press, 2003.

______. 'The Limits of Cultural Hybridity: On Ritual Monsters, Poetic Licence and Contested Postcolonial Purifications'. *Journal of the Royal Anthropological Institute* 7, no. 1 (2001): 133–52.

Werenfels, Isabelle. 'Beyond Authoritarian Upgrading: The Re-emergence of Sufi Orders in Maghrebi Politics'. *The Journal of North African Studies* 19, no. 3 (2014): 275–95.

Westerlund, David, ed. *Sufism in Europe and North America*. London and New York: Routledge-Curzon, 2004.

Willaime, Jean-Paul. *Sociologie Des Religions*. Paris: PUF, 1995.

Williams, George Huntston. *The Radical Reformation*. Philadelphia: Truman State University Press, 1992.

Wilson, Bryan R. *Contemporary Transformations of Religion*. London and New York: Oxford University Press, 1976.

______. *The Social Dimensions of Sectarianism: Sects and New Religious Movements in Contemporary Society*. Oxford: Clarendon Press, 1992.

Wilson, M. Brett. 'The Failure of Nomenclature: The Concept of "Orthodoxy" in the Study of Islam'. *Comparative Islamic Studies* 3, no. 2 (2009): 169–94. <https://doi.org/10.1558/cis.v3i2.169> (last accessed 15 November 2023).

Woodhead, Linda. 'Five Concepts of Religion'. *International Review of Sociology* 21, no. 1 (2011): 121–43. <https://doi.org/10.1080/03906701.2011.544192> (last accessed 15 November 2023).

Woodward, Mark, Muhammad Sani Umar, Inayah Rohmaniyah and Mariani Yahya. 'Salafi Violence and Sufi Tolerance? Rethinking Conventional Wisdom'. *Perspectives on Terrorism* 7, no. 6 (2013): 58–78.

York, Michael. *The Emerging Network: A Sociology of the New Age and Neo-Pagan Movements*. New York: Rowman & Littlefield, 1995.

Zarcone, Thierry. 'La Turquie républicaine'. In *Les Voies d'Allah. Les ordres mystiques dans le monde musulman des origines à aujourd'hui*, edited by Alexandre Popovic and Gilles Veinstein, 372–79. Paris: Fayard, 1996.

Zarcone, Thierry and Juliet Vale. 'Rereadings and Transformations of Sufism in the West'. *Diogène* 47, no. 187 (1999): 110–21.

Zoccatelli, PierLuigi. 'AAA. Sociologia dell'esoterismo cercasi'. *La Critica Sociologica* 151 (2004): 84–92.

INDEX

Abd Al Malik, 5, 99, 137, 144, 146–51
Abdal Hakim Murad, 47
Abdelkader, Emir, 121, 145, 202, 326
Abū Zayd, N. H., 330
'Abduh, M., 330–1
adab, 11, 41, 110, 121, 173, 254, 266
agnosticism, 12, 27, 158, 211, 218, 284, 326
Aguéli, I. 57
aḥwāl, 109, 110, 113, 120
'Aṭṭār, F., 5, 30, 41
Al-Azhar, 35, 83, 88, 118, 288
al-Baqlī, R., 31
al-Baṣrī, H., 37
al-Bisṭāmī, A. Y., 28, 39
alchemy, 57
al-Darqāwī, 165, 186n
al-Ghazālī, 33, 41, 146–7, 320, 321
al-Ḥallāj, M., 29, 32, 39, 82, 85, 86, 203, 204
al-Hujwīrī, J., 35
al-Jazūlī, M., 108
al-Junayd, A., 39
al-Kharrāz, A., 29, 39
al-Khidr, 29n, 229
al-Nawanī, 121
al-Sanūsī, M., 44
al-Sirhindī, 18n, 43
al-Sulamī, 40
al-Tijānī, A., 32, 323
al-Tirmidhī, A., 39
al-Wahhāb, A., 44
al-Ya'qūbī, M., 10n, 47
anti-modernism, 137, 225, 230, 232–4
apostasy, 199, 214, 246, 306
Arab Spring, 110, 139
asceticism, 1, 39, 39, 53, 74, 99, 100, 266, 306
atheism, 12, 306
Augustine of Hippo, 18

Bacon, R., 21
Badaliya, 84
Bahá'í, 157
baqā', 39

baraka, 841, 96, 98, 101, 116, 119, 124, 131, 178, 213, 230, 238, 239, 276, 312, 314
Barrajān, I., 29
bāṭin, 29, 34n, 53, 56
bay'a, 39, 56, 89, 103, 106, 168, 176, 214, 220, 229
Bektāchīyya, 32, 42
Bennett, A., 74–6, 227
Bible, 17–18, 77, 135, 158, 251
bid'a, 33, 44
Bouteflika, A., 201
Buddhism, Buddhist, 160, 225, 260
Būdilmiyya Habibiyya, 159
Burckhardt, Titus, 6, 1l, 285

Castaneda, Carlos, 62, 247
Cat Stevens / Yusuf Islam, 229
Catholicism, 24, 83, 135, 294
Christianity, 17, 24, 38, 42, 45, 56, 57, 69, 74, 83–5, 92, 135, 157, 159, 193, 217, 231, 258, 260, 294, 299, 329, 330
colonialism, 43, 44, 83, 96, 145, 153, 156, 158, 159, 200, 326
communitas, 24, 25, 119, 120, 271, 277, 314, 315
conspiracies, 135, 300
conspiracy theories, 135, 218, 272, 275, 278
Corbin, H., 3, 35, 49–50, 79, 80, 82, 85–92, 103, 185, 189, 230, 249, 314, 326

de Vitray-Meyerovitch, E., 49, 79, 84, 88–90, 103, 189, 196, 230, 314, 326
Deleuze, G., 147
Derrida, J., 147
Dionysius the Areopagite, 18

Eckhart, M., 11, 86, 292
EHESS, 7, 79
Einstein, A., 158, 188
Eliade, M., 3, 80
Emre, Y., 30, 41
enneagram, 75, 76, 227–8, 249, 250, 251, 257, 281, 325
EPHE, 52, 80, 84, 85, 199
Evola, J., 285, 314

fiqh, 30, 107, 126, 134–5, 142, 161, 170, 178, 192, 196–7, 199, 200, 213, 244–5, 274–5, 302, 324, 331, 333, 336
fiṭra, 55, 185
Freemason, 160, 275, 296
Freemasonry, 57, 60, 304
Fröbe-Kapyten, O., 80

Gnosticism, 12, 57, 74, 82, 85–6, 208
Guénon, R., 3, 12, 20, 49, 50, 56–63, 91–3, 103, 106, 121, 132, 134, 136–7, 156, 159, 189, 194, 204, 213–14, 227, 230, 236, 249, 250, 259, 274, 281, 283–96, 298, 300–2, 305–6, 311, 313–14, 316, 319–22, 324, 325, 332, 339–40
Gurdjieff, G. I., 49, 50, 62, 66, 73–8, 91, 92, 106, 134, 227, 247, 250, 259–60

ḥadīth, 33, 36, 48, 108, 121, 128, 133, 136, 161, 173, 181, 189, 196, 207, 213–14, 239, 242, 266, 273, 339

ḥaḍra, 10, 29, 69, 111, 115, 117, 119–20, 173, 175, 217, 241, 264–5
Ḥāfeẓ, 5
Ḥajj, 61, 277
ḥāl, 69, 109–10, 113, 240
Hamza, Y., 47
Hanbalism, 196
Hanafism, 196, 198
Hegel, F., 47, 293
Heidegger, M., 11, 86, 88, 293
Herbert, F., 229
Hinduism, 42–3, 57, 58, 85, 92, 227, 291, 340
ḥīyrat, 89
homosexuality, 192–3, 214, 301
Huxley, A., 19

Ibn ʿAjība, 121
Ibn ʿArabī, 2, 11, 28, 28–9, 33–4, 41–3, 63, 86, 88, 147, 184, 293, 296, 305, 320–1, 329
Ibn ʿAshir, 121
Ibn ʿAṭāʾ Allāh, 41, 121
ibn Idrīs, A., 44, 293, 313, 320, 323
Ibn Khaldoun, 35
Ibn Taymiyya, 42, 44
ibn Zayd, A., 38
idhn, 99, 103, 108
ijāza, 39, 121, 286, 297
ijtihād, 127, 197–8, 200, 302
ʿimāra, 69, 173–5, 177
Inayat Khan, 14, 45, 53, 66, 72, 78, 86
Inayat Khan, Z., 46
Inayat Khan, V., 50, 78
Iqbal, M., 88, 145, 189
Islamism, 4, 44, 46, 201, 210, 333–4

jamāʿ, 172–3, 175
Jamaʿat al-Tabligh, 47
Jerrahiyya-Khalwatiyya, 297
jinn, 31, 68, 250, 272
John Scotus Eriugena, 18
Judaism, 38, 57, 92, 294
Jung, C. G., 3, 19, 58, 80–1, 86, 91, 251, 276

Kabbala, 56–7, 129, 257, 326
Kali Yuga, 58, 60
karāmāt, 101, 116, 178
khalwa, 114–15, 176–8, 198, 224
khāṣṣa, 33, 40, 56
Khayyām, U., 77
Khiari, B., 88, 144–6, 151, 283, 337
King Charles III, 229
King Muḥammad VI, 138

Madaniyya, 159
Maimonides, A., 93, 192
Maimonides, M., 191
Malāmatiyya, 40
Malikism, 99, 127, 134, 138, 143–4, 170, 18, 196, 198–9, 331
Mandela, N., 326
Maridort, R., 61
Marxism, 81, 88, 161, 193, 337
Maryamiyya, 61, 159
Massignon, L., 3, 38, 49, 79–80, 82–6, 89–92, 189, 205, 230, 314, 326
Mawlid, 94, 97, 101, 111, 116–21, 167, 211–12, 263
maʿrifa, 28, 39, 55
Mevleviyya, 6, 179, 217
millenarianism, 43, 225, 232, 267, 302

miracles, 12, 18, 99, 101, 116, 122, 163, 171, 213, 221–5, 255, 271, 276
Muhammad Ali, 229
Mulla Nasreddin, 77, 260
Mulla Sadrā, 87
Muslim Brotherhood, 210, 229

nafs, 29, 108, 131, 136
neo-paganism, 65
Neoplatonism, 6, 18, 26, 34, 85, 183, 326
Nietzsche, F., 21, 251

Otto, R., 25, 80, 83
Ottoman, 35, 41, 139, 225, 233, 235, 274–5, 277, 328
Ouspensky, P., 74, 250

perennialist, 50
philosophia perennis, 58, 60, 82, 87, 329
post-Islamism, 334
Prigogine, Y., 326
Primordial Tradition, 3, 58, 59, 62, 92, 132, 213, 290, 292–4, 296, 299, 305, 321–2, 324
Prophet Muhammad, 31, 40, 56, 77, 116, 122, 124, 128, 133, 140, 212, 219, 226, 231, 257, 267, 273, 277, 287, 292, 330, 351

Qur'an, 29, 32, 36, 48, 84–5, 90, 108, 110, 115, 118, 121, 127, 133–5, 158, 160–2, 171–2, 180–3, 187, 189, 191, 194, 196, 197, 207, 211, 213–14, 239, 242, 248, 252, 257, 261, 266, 271, 281, 287, 292, 311, 320, 330–1, 335–6, 339

Rābiʿa al-ʿAdawiyya, 30, 38
reformism, 44, 110, 196, 307, 330–1
reincarnation, 65, 260–1, 291
Religionism, 49–50, 79–80, 90–1, 132, 214, 230, 249, 314, 325
Renaissance, 49, 58, 195, 327–9
Rūmī, J., 5–6, 30, 34, 41, 46, 78, 88–9, 181, 217, 219, 264
Ruqiyya, 68

St Barnabas, 230–2, 244, 248, 277, 281
St Francis, 251, 277
Salafism, 3–4, 44, 138–9, 170, 187, 201–2, 210, 226, 244, 252, 303, 332
ṣalāt, 30, 108, 112, 115, 176–7
samāʿ, 6, 98, 111, 115–20, 124, 169, 172–4, 176, 241, 264
Sartre, J., 161, 251
Scholem, G., 3, 16, 80, 82, 91
Schrödinger, E., 80
Schuon, F., 50, 61–2, 91–2, 103, 285, 296
secularism, 82, 140, 144, 146–67, 205, 245, 274, 289, 333, 336–7
Shabistarī, M., 41
Shafak, E., 5
Shāfiʿīsm, 39, 196
Shah, I., 49–50, 73–9, 92, 181, 227, 239, 260, 262
Shah, O., 262
shahāda, 239, 246–7, 255, 267
Sharia, 4, 30, 92, 106–7, 121, 125–7, 135, 142, 192, 196–7, 200, 233, 244–5, 248, 270, 274–5, 306, 324, 333, 336

Sharifian, 77, 133, 181, 219
shayṭān, 41, 181, 183, 226, 233, 270, 272, 317
silsila, 39, 56, 134, 229, 279
Sorbonne, 91, 103, 249
Spinoza, B., 147
Sufi Order International, 44–5, 66, 279
Suhrawardī, 41, 82, 86–7, 93,
Suzuki, D., 80
Swedenborg, E., 86

Ṭāhā, M., 330
tajdīd, 33
Taoism, 57, 260
Tawfīq, A., 99, 139
tawḥīd, 190
Theosophical Society, 4, 58, 65–6
tomb, 41, 116, 119, 122, 133, 159, 178, 194, 230–1, 244, 248, 277, 281
Traditionalism, 3, 8, 11, 50, 57, 61, 91, 281, 284, 327

'ulamā', 33, 47, 94–5, 118, 197–8, 200, 211
umma, 33, 72, 205, 287–8
'Umra, 178, 209

Valsan, M., 61, 63–4, 249

waḥdat al-wujūd, 28
Wahhabism, 3, 44, 48, 159, 244
waẓīfa, 110–15, 133, 135, 172
Whitehead, A., 326
wird, 107, 171–2, 176–7

Yāssīn, A., 47, 97, 333

ẓāhir, 29, 56
Zoroastrianism, 38, 85, 87

EU representative:
Easy Access System Europe
Mustamäe tee 50, 10621 Tallinn, Estonia
Gpsr.requests@easproject.com

www.ingramcontent.com/pod-product-compliance
Lightning Source LLC
Chambersburg PA
CBHW061342300426
44116CB00011B/1957
* 9 7 8 1 3 9 9 5 3 6 1 0 3 *